Lecture Notes in Computer Science 13719

More information about this series at https://link.springer.com/bookseries/558

Andrey Ronzhin · Roman Meshcheryakov ·
Zhen Xiantong (Eds.)

Interactive Collaborative Robotics

7th International Conference, ICR 2022
Fuzhou, China, December 16–18, 2022
Proceedings

Editors
Andrey Ronzhin ⓘ
St. Petersburg Federal Research Center
of the Russian Academy of Sciences
St. Petersburg, Russia

Roman Meshcheryakov ⓘ
V. A. Trapeznikov Institute of Control
Sciences of Russian Academy of Sciences
Moscow, Russia

Zhen Xiantong ⓘ
Guangdong University of Petrochemical
Technology (West Gate)
Maoming, China

ISSN 0302-9743   ISSN 1611-3349 (electronic)
Lecture Notes in Computer Science
ISBN 978-3-031-23608-2   ISBN 978-3-031-23609-9 (eBook)
https://doi.org/10.1007/978-3-031-23609-9

This Springer imprint is published by the registered company Springer Nature Switzerland AG
The registered company address is: Gewerbestrasse 11, 6330 Cham, Switzerland

Preface

The International Conference on Interactive Collaborative Robotics (ICR) was first started in 2016 and the 7th International Conference on Interactive Collaborative Robotics was held in Fuzhou, China, during December 16–18, 2022. The conference brings together experts and scholars from different fields to discuss the use and challenges of human-robot collaboration in different industries such as manufacturing, healthcare, and education. The conference focuses on foundations and means of collaborative behavior of one or more robots physically interacting with humans in operational environments configured with embedded sensor networks and cloud services under conditions of uncertainty and environmental variability.

ICR is highly recognized and supported by experts in the field internationally, therefore, this year's conference was co-hosted by Tsinghua University and the St. Petersburg Federal Research Center of the Russian Academy of Sciences, with committee chairs and members from all over the world. The Honorary Chairs of the conference were Hong Qiao, Academician of the Chinese Academy of Sciences, China, and Igor Kalyaev, Academician of the Russian Academy of Sciences, Russia.

During the conference, academicians, industry experts, and scholars from academia and business at home and abroad were invited to share their ideas and discuss cutting edge technologies, industrial products, and industry trends, making it a highly influential event in the robotics industry.

ICR 2022 was organized by Tsinghua University (Beijing, China), St. Petersburg Federal Research Center of the Russian Academy of Sciences (St. Petersburg, Russia), Fuzhou University (Fuzhou, China), and Gaitech Intelligence (Zoucheng, China), and held jointly with the 7th International Conference on Cognitive Systems and Information Processing (ICCSIP 2022). More information can be found on the conference website: https://icr2022.gaitech.net/.

This volume contains a collection of 25 papers presented at ICR 2022, which were thoroughly reviewed by members of the Program Committee consisting of more than 20 top specialists in the conference topic areas. The papers were selected from 45 submissions in an single blind peer review process, with each submission receiving at least 3 reviews. Theoretical and more general contributions were presented in oral sessions. Problem oriented sessions as well as discussions then brought together specialists in specific problem areas with the aim of exchanging knowledge and skills resulting from research projects of all kinds.

Special thanks are due to the members of the Program Committee and Organizing Committee for their tireless effort and enthusiasm during the conference organization. We express our gratitude to all participants for their valuable contribution to the successful organization of ICR 2022. We look forward to meeting you at the next International

Conference on Interactive Collaborative Robotics in 2023. More details are available at:
http://icr.nw.ru/.

November 2022
Andrey Ronzhin
Roman Meshcheryakov
Zhen Xiantong

Organization

Honorary Chairs

Igor Kalyaev — Russian Academy of Sciences, Russia
Hong Qiao — Chinese Academy of Sciences, China

General Chairs

Jenssen Chang — Gaitech Intelligence, China
Andrey Ronzhin — St. Petersburg Federal Research Center of the Russian Academy of Sciences, Russia
Fuchun Sun — Tsinghua University, China

Steering Committee

Mun Sang Kim — Gwangju Institute of Science and Technology, South Korea
Nan Ma — Beijing University of Technology, China
Roman Meshcheryakov — V.A. Trapeznikov Institute of Control Science of the Russian Academy of Sciences, Russia
Yuanchun Shi — Tsinghua University, China
Jianhua Tao — Chinese Academy of Sciences, China
Le Xie — Shanghai Jiao Tong University, China

Program Committee Chairs

Roman Meshcheryakov — V.A. Trapeznikov Institute of Control Science of the Russian Academy of Sciences, Russia
Zhen Xiantong — Guangdong University of Petrochemical Technology, China

Program Committee

Christos Antonopoulos — University of Thessaly, Greece
Yasar Ayaz — National Center of Artificial Intelligence, Pakistan
Branislav Borovac — University of Novi Sad, Serbia
Sara Chaychian — University of Hertfordshire, UK
Ivan Ermolov — Ishlinsky Institute for Problems in Mechanics of the Russian Academy of Sciences, Russia

Viktor Glazunov	Mechanical Engineering Research Institute of the Russian Academy of Sciences, Russia
Mehmet Guzey	Sivas University of Science and Technology, Turkey
Dimitrios Kalles	Hellenic Open University, Greece
Alexey Kashevnik	St. Petersburg Federal Research Center of the Russian Academy of Sciences, Russia
Anis Koubaa	Prince Sultan University, Saudi Arabia
Dongheui Lee	Institute of Robotics and Mechatronics, Germany
Huaping Liu	Tsinghua University, China
Evgeni Magid	Kazan Federal University, Russia
Ilshat Mamaev	Karlsruhe Institute of Technology, Germany
Iosif Mporas	University of Hertfordshire, UK
Xin Pan	Shanghai Jiao Tong University Press, China
Viacheslav Pshikhopov	Southern Federal University, Russia
Mirko Rakovic	University of Novi Sad, Serbia
Hooman Samani	University of Hertfordshire, UK
Yulia Sandamirskaya	Intel, Switzerland
Jesus Savage	National Autonomuous University of Mexico, Mexico
Evgeny Shandarov	Tomsk State University of Control Systems and Radioelectronics, Russia
Lev Stankevich	Peter the Great St. Petersburg Polytechnic University, Russia
Tilo Strutz	Leipzig University of Telecommunications, Germany
Sergey Yatsun	Southwest State University, Russia
Lei Zhang	Guangdong University of Petrochemical Technology, China
Qinghai Zheng	Fuzhou University, China

Organization Committee Chairs

Bin Fang	Tsinghua University, China
Anton Saveliev	St. Petersburg Federal Research Center of the Russian Academy of Sciences, Russia
Yuanlong Yu	Fuzhou University, China

Organization Committee Members

Marina Astapova	St. Petersburg Federal Research Center of the Russian Academy of Sciences, Russia
Zhejing Chen	Gaitech Intelligence, China

Contents

Gesture Control System for Desktop Robotic Arm

Yunhan Li[1]([✉]) [iD], Jingjing Lou[2] [iD], Xiyuan Wan[2] [iD], Qingdong Luo[2] [iD],
and Pengfei Zheng[2,3] [iD]

[1] Huzhou College, Huzhou 313000, Zhejiang, China
lizjuee@outlook.com
[2] Yiwu Industrial and Commercial College, Yiwu 322000, Zhejiang, China
[3] Zhejiang Provincial Key Laboratory of Third Generation Semiconductor Materials and
Devices, HC Semitek Corporation, Yiwu, Zhejiang, China

Abstract. As an important human-machine interaction method, gesture control
attracts lots of researchers' concentration in recent years. Different from other
literatures on industrial manipulator, this paper presents the possibility of using
Leap motion gesture sensor to control a desktop robotic arm's movement by means
of gestures. It describes the system framework and control algorithm of robot
control. A Leap motion senser, a desktop robotic arm and one computer are used to
construct the system. In the control flow of the system. Coordinate transformation
between the palm position detected by Leap motion gesture sensor and the tool
center point (TCP) of the desktop robotic arm is calculated using the method of
spatial mapping. The mapping data can be used to control the desktop robotic arm.
To filter the noise and smooth the gesture signal acquired by the sensor, mean filter
and Kalman filter are applied. The program for the system is developed in Python
language with Leap motion Python SDK and xArm Python SDK. The experiments
show that the system can operate stably and can control the movement of the
desktop robotic arm accurately in real time by human palm' gesture.

Keywords: Desktop robotic arm · Palm gesture · Leap motion · Gesture
control · Coordinate transformation

1 Introduction

Gesture recognition plays an important role in human-machine interaction. In the process
of human-machine interaction, the user can control or interact with the device through
gesture recognition to achieve specific tasks. As shown in Fig. 1, there are several types of
gesture recognition implementation methods. (1) Simple gesture sensors, gesture recognition sensor modules such as PAJ7620U2 are relatively inexpensive and can recognize
a certain number of gesture actions. For example, PAJ7620U2 can recognize 9 kinds of
gestures, including up, down, left, right, front, and back, but its detection area is relative
small; (2) The method based on Kinect sensor [1–5], which uses Microsoft Kinect sensor for detection, can detect human movements such as arms and expressions, and has
a large detection range, but cannot detect changes of palms and fingers; (3) The method

© The Author(s), under exclusive license to Springer Nature Switzerland AG 2022
A. Ronzhin et al. (Eds.): ICR 2022, LNCS 13719, pp. 1–11, 2022.
https://doi.org/10.1007/978-3-031-23609-9_1

of using RGB camera has the advantage that the processing of two-dimensional image information is relatively simple, but ordinary cameras are greatly affected by lighting conditions, it can only recognize limited gestures, and cannot detect motion information such as position and direction [6–10]; (4) Depth camera based method(such as Intel realsense, ZED Stereo Camera, etc.) [11–15], these methods need to fuse image information and depth information, and their accuracy depends to a certain extent on whether the fusion algorithm used is appropriate. (5) Radar method [16, 17], this type of method essentially judges the movements of the arm through the overall posture of a person, and can detect the movements at a longer distance, but it is difficult to obtain the position of the palm or fingers; (6) Method of gesture-sensing wearable devices (such as armbands or wristbands) [18–21], this contact-based methods require a specific gesture-sensing wristband (such as Myo bracelet) to be worn on a person's forearm or wrist, the gestures are judged by the EMG signals or the acceleration direction of the hand sensed by the different movements of the human hand, and the gestures that can be judged are less, and the signals of the wristband need to get in touch with the skin; (7) The method based on Leap motion gesture sensor [22–26], the advantage of this type of method is that it can identify information such as palms, fingers and finger-like tools, and the identification is accurate, but its detection range is relatively small; (8) Multi-sensor fusion method [22, 24, 27], this method use two or more sensors for detection, which can detect a larger range and obtain more detailed information, but the difficulty of fusing sensor data also increases.

(a) PAJ7620U2   (b) webcam   (c) lidar   (d) Myo

(f) Kinect   (g) realsense   (h) leap motion

Fig. 1. Common gesture recognition sensors/modules.

Prior studies on gesture control related to robotic arms are mainly about the control of industrial robotic arms and collaborative robotic arms, it is rare to use gestures to control desktop robotic arms. The main research content of this paper is to use Leap motion gesture sensor to detect the position of a single palm then use the signal to control the movements of a four-joint desktop robotic arm in cartesian coordinate system.

Subsequent sections of the paper are organized as follow:

- Section 1. System structure, including the functions and characteristics of each component of the system;
- Section 2. Control flow, describe the control process in detail;
- Section 3. Test results, test the designed system, analyze, and discuss the results in detail;

- Section 4. Conclusion, summarize the research of this paper and look ahead to the next step research work.

2 System Structure

The designed system includes a Leap motion gesture sensor, a four-joint desktop robotic arm and a PC, the composition is shown in Fig. 2.

Fig. 2. System composition.

Leap motion sensor is an optical gesture tracking module from Ultraleap, it can quickly and accurately capture the movements of hands and tools, and the data list it can track includes hands, fingers and tools with endpoints, fingers, tools, and gestures. The response time is 4ms, the typical detection distance is between 0 and 60 cm, and the typical detection range is a $140° \times 120°$ area centered on the center point of the Leap motion sensor. The plan view of detection area is shown in Fig. 3 [28].

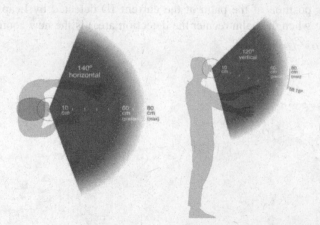

Fig. 3. Plane diagram of the detection area of Leap motion.

The controlled object of this work is a four-joint desktop robotic arm which call uArm swift pro. Its arms span is between 50 mm and 320 mm, and the accuracy is 0.2 mm The working area of it is shown in Fig. 4 [29].

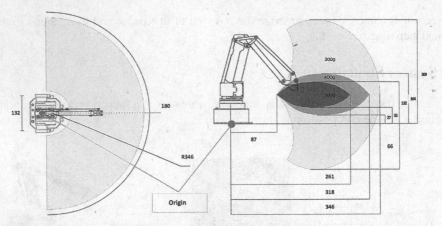

Fig. 4. Working area of uArm swift pro.

Use a computer installed with Windows 10 operating system as control center. The programming language is Python, the Python version is 3.8.6. Leap motion Python 3 compatibility package [30] and uArm Python SDK [31] need to be installed.

3   Control Flow

Use Leap motion to detect gestures, and then control the movement of uArm swift pro, which requires corresponding coordinate transformation. Set the origin of Leap motion coordinates as $O_L = [x_{LO}, y_{LO}, z_{LO}]$. Because the detection area of Leap motion is different from the working area of uArm swift pro. For better control result, assume that the center position of the palm of the current ID detected by Leap motion (the ID will change when the palm reenter the detection area) is the new coordinate origin $O'_L = [x'_{LO}, y'_{LO}, Z'_{LO}]$ (Fig. 5).

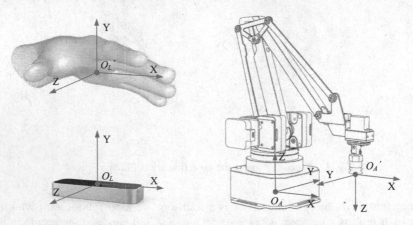

Fig. 5. Schematic diagram of the origin of coordinates.

uArm swift pro coordinate origin is $O_A = [x_{AO}, y_{AO}, z_{AO}]$, new coordinate origin is $O_A' = [x_{AO}', y_{AO}', Z_{AO}']$, where,

$$\begin{cases} x_{AO}' = (max(x_A) - min(x_A)/2) = 115.5 \\ y_{AO}' = 0 \\ z_{AO}' = max(x_A)/2 = 154.5 \end{cases} \tag{1}$$

Place Leap motion gesture sensor horizontally so that its x-axis direction is the same as that of uArm swift pro. In the form of homogeneous coordinates, the center position of the palm $P_L = [x_{LP}, y_{LP}, z_{LP}]$ based on the coordinates $O_L' = [x_{LO}', y_{LO}', Z_{LO}']$ is converted to the coordinates of the tool center point of the uArm swift pro $P_A = [x_{AP}, y_{AP}, z_{AP}]$ based on:

$$P_A = P_L T_1 T_2, \tag{2}$$

where

$$T_1 = \begin{bmatrix} -1 & 0 & 0 & 0 \\ 0 & -1 & 0 & 0 \\ 0 & 0 & -1 & 0 \\ x_{LO}' & y_{LO}' & y_{LO}' & 1 \end{bmatrix}; \tag{3}$$

$$T_2 = \begin{bmatrix} 1 & 0 & 0 & 0 \\ 0 & 1 & 0 & 0 \\ 0 & 0 & 1 & 0 \\ x_{AO}' & y_{AO}' & y_{AO}' & 1 \end{bmatrix} \tag{4}$$

So P_A can be described as:

$$P_A = \begin{bmatrix} x_{LP} & y_{LP} & z_{LP} & 1 \end{bmatrix} \begin{bmatrix} -1 & 0 & 0 & 0 \\ 0 & -1 & 0 & 0 \\ 0 & 0 & -1 & 0 \\ x_{LO}' & y_{LO}' & y_{LO}' & 1 \end{bmatrix} \begin{bmatrix} 1 & 0 & 0 & 0 \\ 0 & 1 & 0 & 0 \\ 0 & 0 & 1 & 0 \\ x_{AO}' & y_{AO}' & y_{AO}' & 1 \end{bmatrix}. \tag{5}$$

When programming, initialize the new coordinate origin of uArm swift pro first, set the desktop robot arm mode to 0 (suction cup mode), then start the Leap motion sensor.

Set a flag to obtain the palm center position O_L' detected by Leap motion at one time. When entering the loop detection state, set the palm center position obtained for the first time as O_L', and set the flag to 0 when the process is complete.

Use formula (2) to calculate P_A, then use the set position function in the uArm swift pro Python SDK to control the robotic arm to move to P_A. $P_{AC} = [x_{AC} \ y_{AC} \ z_{AC}]$ is the current position of the tool center point of the robotic arm obtained by using the get position function. The specific process:

```
Control Algorithm
Initial O'_L
swift. set_mode (0)
Thread.start()
flag←1
while True do
  if flag==1 do
    O'_L← hand.parm_position()
  flag←0
  tic← time.perf_counter()
  P_L← hand.parm_position()
  P_A←P_LT_1T_2
  swift.set_position(P_A)
  toc← time.perf_counter()
  P_AC← swift.get_position()
  delayTime← toc−tic
  error← |P_ACP_A|
end
```

4 Testing Results

4.1 Experimental Setup

The test platform is built according to the hardware structure shown in Fig. 2, and the physical hardware is shown in Fig. 6. According to the wait parameter of Ture and False in the *set_position* function of uArm swift pro respectively, experimental tests are conducted, each test is 500 times cycle, typical speed parameter is 20000 and speed factor is 0.0005(use these parameters uArm swift pro will not run too fast or too slow). The results of four of these experiments were randomly selected for analysis. The position tracking error (error) and the response delay time (delayTime) of position tracking are calculated for each cycle. The position tracking error is the spatial distance between the position point P_A calculated according to formula (2) and the actual position point acquired using P_{AC} after executing the motion command. Calculated by formula (6), and the position tracking response delay is the time difference from the beginning of acquiring the palm position to the end of the current cyclic motion command.

$$error = distance(P_{AC}, P_A) = \sqrt{(x_{AC} - x_{AP})^2 + (y_{AC} - y_{AP})^2 + (z_{AC} - z_{AP})^2}. \quad (6)$$

Fig. 6. Test platform.

4.2 Experimental Results

Table 1 records the corresponding data of the four tests. The data include the minimum error (*min_error*), maximum error (*max_error*), and average error (*avg_error*) as well as the minimum delay (*min_delay*), maximum delay (*max_delay*), and average delay (*avg_delay*) for each test. From the statistical data, when the wait parameter is False, the maximum value of the position tracking error of the four selected tests is more than 5 mm, among which three tests are more than 10 mm. The error of each test that more than 1mm is shown in Fig. 7, it is obvious that the difference between the position tracking error under the two parameters is large. When the wait parameter is True, the maximum error and average error of position tracking are small, but the average tracking response delay is about twice as when the wait parameter is False, and the robotic arm runs with a significant lag in gesture movement, its real-time performance is not ideal.

Table 1. Position tracking error and tracking response delay of 4 tests.

Times	error(mm)						delayTime(ms)					
	min_error		max_error		avg_error		min_delay		max_delay		avg_delay	
	T	F	T	F	T	F	T	F	T	F	T	F
1	0.33	0.18	21.18	26.09	0.62	1.45	90.4	59.52	383.52	184.01	159.9	77.65
2	0.3	0.29	1.0	12.95	0.63	2.25	93.89	70.71	731.96	184.79	141.96	79.49
3	0.41	0.1	1.19	6.46	0.75	1.17	73.22	60.27	763.27	202.78	161.27	77.32
4	0.31	0.14	1.16	12.43	0.57	1.27	75.79	71.58	643.85	162.68	155.31	76.86

Without filtering, the robot's motion trajectory is unsmooth, and the jitter is relatively large, so mean filter and Kalman filter are added to compare with the raw data. The mean filter method is as follows, $O'_E(j)$ represents the filtered value in j step,

$$\begin{cases} QO'_E(j) = \sum_{i=0}^{i=j} O'_E(j)(j < 10) \\ QO'_F(j) = \sum_{i=j-9}^{i=j} O'_E(j)(j \geq 10) \end{cases} \qquad (7)$$

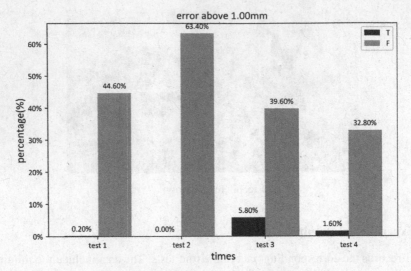

Fig. 7. Comparison of tracking error.

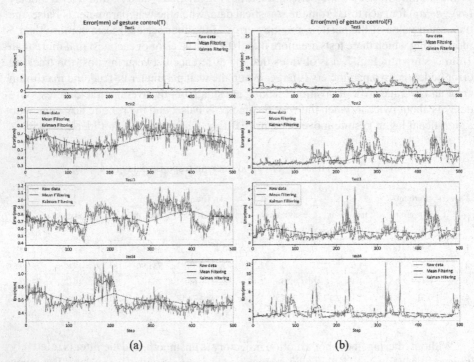

Fig. 8. Position tracking error.

Kalman filter used here is a typical three-dimensional Kalman filter. The initial estimate position is set to 0, other parameters of the filter are as follows:

$$\begin{cases} P(0) = O \\ A = H = I \end{cases}.$$ (8)

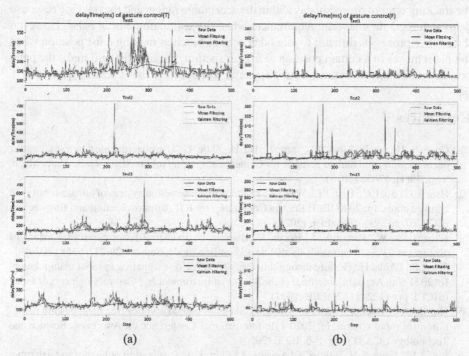

Fig. 9. Position tracking response delay.

Figure 8a shows the error when the wait parameter is Ture and Fig. 8b shows the error when the wait parameter is False. The horizontal axis of every graph is the number of steps, and the vertical axis is the error (unit mm). When the wait parameter is Ture, the position tracking error is gathered in the interval less than 1 mm, and when the wait parameter is False, the error is larger than that when the parameter is True. That is because in the True state, uArm swift pro will move to the target position before it receive a new position signal. Similarly, in the False state, uArm swift pro will move to the next target position even if it does not reach current target position when it receives the signal of Leap motion sensor. This always happen because of Leap motion sensor's update frequency (less than 20 ms) is faster than the movement of uArm swift pro.

Figure 9 show the relationship between the number of steps and the tracking response delay(ms) when the wait parameter is Ture and False. The tracking response delay is longer when the wait parameter is Ture than when the parameter is False. Because when the parameter is Ture, uArm swift pro needs to finish current movement, that takes longer time. From the curves display in different color, we can see that Kalman filter can smooth the trajectory of uArm swift pro to the greatest extent.

5 Conclusion

This paper addresses the problem of using Leap motion gesture sensor to control the movement of a desktop robotic arm (uArm swift pro), spatial mapping method is studied and used to transform the palm center position detected by the Leap motion gesture sensor into the TCP of the desktop robotic arm. Through experimental tests, it is verified that the tracking error of the method is within the acceptable range, and the tracking response delay can meet the real time requirement when the wait parameter is False. However, the control process is difficult to join other actions (such as making a fist position when the palm moves to a certain position to trigger suction, because fist will make the palm position detection inaccurate). Future research will consider this scientific question.

References

1. Chao, F., Huang, Y., Lin, C.M., Yang, L., Hu, H., Zhou, C.: Use of automatic Chinese character decomposition and human gestures for Chinese calligraphy robots. IEEE Trans. Hum. Mach. Syst. **49**(1), 47–58 (2018)
2. Hsu, R.C., Su, P.C., Hsu, J.L., Wang, C.Y.: Real-time interaction system of human-robot with hand gestures. In: 2020 IEEE Eurasia Conference on IOT, Communication and Engineering (ECICE), pp. 396–398. IEEE (2020)
3. Kaczmarek, W., Panasiuk, J., Borys, S., Banach, P.: Industrial robot control by means of gestures and voice commands in off-line and on-line mode. Sensors **20**(21), 6358 (2020)
4. Togo, S., Ukida, H.: Gesture recognition using hand region estimation in robot manipulation. In: 2021 60th Annual Conference of the Society of Instrument and Control Engineers of Japan (SICE), pp. 1122–1127. IEEE (2021)
5. Xu, J., Li, J., Zhang, S., Xie, C., Dong, J.: Skeleton guided conflict-free hand gesture recognition for robot control. In: 2020 11th International Conference on Awareness Science and Technology (iCAST), pp. 1–6. IEEE (2020)
6. Lee, J.W., Kang, S.H., Talluri, T., Angani, A., Shin, K.J.: Realization of human and fish robot interaction with artificial intelligence using hand gesture. In: 2020 IEEE 2nd International Conference on Architecture, Construction, Environment and Hydraulics (ICACEH), pp. 99–101. IEEE (2020)
7. De Melo, C.M., Rothrock, B., Gurram, P., Ulutan, O., Manjunath, B.S.: Vision-based gesture recognition in human-robot teams using synthetic data. In: 2020 IEEE/RSJ International Conference on Intelligent Robots and Systems (IROS), pp. 10278–10284. IEEE (2020)
8. Nazarova, E., et al.: CobotAR: interaction with robots using omnidirectionally projected image and DNN-based gesture recognition. In: 2021 IEEE International Conference on Systems, Man, and Cybernetics (SMC), pp. 2590–2595. IEEE (2021)
9. Nuzzi, C., Pasinetti, S., Lancini, M., Docchio, F., Sansoni, G.: Deep learning-based hand gesture recognition for collaborative robots. IEEE Instrum. Meas. Mag. **22**(2), 44–51 (2019)
10. Yahaya, S.W., Lotfi, A., Mahmud, M., Machado, P., Kubota, N.: Gesture recognition intermediary robot for abnormality detection in human activities. In: 2019 IEEE Symposium Series on Computational Intelligence (SSCI), pp. 1415–1421. IEEE (2019)
11. Chang, J.Y., Tejero-de-Pablos, A., Harada, T.: Improved optical flow for gesture-based human-robot interaction. In: 2019 International Conference on Robotics and Automation (ICRA), pp. 7983–7989. IEEE (2019)
12. Gao, Q., Chen, Y., Ju, Z., Liang, Y.: Dynamic hand gesture recognition based on 3D hand pose estimation for human-robot interaction. IEEE Sens. J. **22**(18), 17421–17430 (2022)

13. Luan, K., Matsumaru, T.: Dynamic hand gesture recognition for robot ARM teaching based on improved LRCN model. In: 2019 IEEE International Conference on Robotics and Biomimetics (ROBIO), pp. 1269–1274. IEEE (2019)
14. Moh, J.J., Kijima, T., Zhang, B., Lim, H.O.: Gesture recognition and effective interaction based dining table cleaning robot. In: 2019 7th International Conference on Robot Intelligence Technology and Applications (RiTA), pp. 72–77. IEEE (2019)
15. Zhang, J., Geng, T., Shi, H., Wang, D., Lu, J.: A gesture recognition method based on YCbCr and SURF for service robot interaction. In: 2021 6th International Conference on Robotics and Automation Engineering (ICRAE), pp. 270–274. IEEE (2021)
16. Chamorro, S., Collier, J., Grondin, F.: Neural network based lidar gesture recognition for realtime robot teleoperation. In: 2021 IEEE International Symposium on Safety, Security, and Rescue Robotics (SSRR), pp. 98–103. IEEE (2021)
17. Zhang, K., Yu, Z., Zhang, D., Wang, Z., Guo, B.: RaCon: a gesture recognition approach via Doppler radar for intelligent human-robot interaction. In: 2020 IEEE International Conference on Pervasive Computing and Communications Workshops (PerCom Workshops), pp. 1–6. IEEE (2020)
18. Anderez, D.O., Dos Santos, L.P., Lotfi, A., Yahaya, S.W.: Accelerometer-based hand gesture recognition for human-robot interaction. In: 2019 IEEE Symposium Series on Computational Intelligence (SSCI), pp. 1402–1406. IEEE (2019)
19. Chico, A., et al.: Hand gesture recognition and tracking control for a virtual UR5 robot manipulator. In: 2021 IEEE Fifth Ecuador Technical Chapters Meeting (ETCM), pp. 1–6. IEEE (2021)
20. Kaplanoglu, E., Nasab, A., Erdemir, E., Young, M., Dayton, N.: Hand gesture based motion control of collaborative robot in assembly line. In: 2021 International Conference on Engineering and Emerging Technologies (ICEET), pp. 1–4. IEEE (2021)
21. Zhao, X., Ma, Y., Huang, J., Zheng, J., Dong, Y.: An adaptive real-time gesture detection method using EMG and IMU series for robot control. In: 2021 IEEE International Conference on Unmanned Systems (ICUS), pp. 539–547. IEEE (2021)
22. Du, G., Han, R., Yao, G., Ng, W.W., Li, D.: A gesture-and speech-guided robot teleoperation method based on mobile interaction with unrestricted force feedback. IEEE/ASME Trans. Mechatron. 27(1), 360–371 (2021)
23. Forgo, Z., Hypki, A., Kuhlenkoetter, B.: Gesture based robot programming using ROS platform. In: ISR 2018; 50th International Symposium on Robotics, pp. 1–7. VDE (2018)
24. Qi, W., Ovur, S.E., Li, Z., Marzullo, A., Song, R.: Multi-sensor guided hand gesture recognition for a teleoperated robot using a recurrent neural network. IEEE Robot. Autom. Lett. 6(3), 6039–6045 (2021)
25. Sorgini, F., et al.: Tactile sensing with gesture-controlled collaborative robot. In: 2020 IEEE International Workshop on Metrology for Industry 4.0 & IoT, pp. 364–368. IEEE (2020)
26. Wu, B., Zhong, J., Yang, C.: A visual-based gesture prediction framework applied in social robots. IEEE/CAA J. Autom. Sin. 9(3), 510–519 (2021)
27. Fiorini, L., et al.: Daily gesture recognition during human-robot interaction combining vision and wearable systems. IEEE Sens. J. 21(20), 23568–23577 (2021)
28. Ultraleap. Leap motion controller datasheet. https://www.ultraleap.com/datasheets/Leap_Motion_Controller_Datasheet.pdf. Last Accessed 22 August 2022
29. UFACTORY. uArm swift pro user manual, p. 29. https://cdn.shopify.com/s/files/1/0012/6979/2886/files/uArm_Swift_Pro_User_Manual-V1.1.23.pdf?v=1615973868. Last Accessed 21 August 2022
30. Cipulot. Leap-motion-python-3. https://github.com/Cipulot/Leap-Motion-Python-3. Last Accessed 22 August 2022
31. UFACTORY. UFACTORY uArm Python SDK. https://github.com/uArm-Developer/uArm-Python-3DK. Last Accessed 22 August 2022

Supervisory System for a Collaborative Robotic Cell Based on RGBD Camera

Guo Wu[1](✉) ⓘ, Leonard Pak[2] ⓘ, Madin Shereuzhev[2] ⓘ, and Vladimir Serebrenny[1] ⓘ

[1] Bauman Moscow State Technical University, 5/1, Ul. Baumanskaya 2-Ya, 105005 Moscow, Russia
ug@student.bmstu.ru
[2] Moscow State University of Technology "STANKIN", 1, Vadkovsky Lane, 127055, Moscow 127994, Russia

Abstract. The task of supervision in a collaborative robotic system is an important issue. Supervisory system is primarily necessary for the organization of safe human-robot interaction. In this paper, another approach to the application of the similar systems is considered. Two RGBD cameras are proposed for modeling the human state and conditions and further organization of the dialogue between robots and humans. This dialog is necessary to arrange the dynamic allocation of tasks, validity of which depends on analysis of human behavior and intention. In view of that, four algorithms based on neural networks are used: for face recognition, body recognition, gestures recognition and tools recognition. The Python library "face_recognition" provided by Adam Geitgey is applied to face recognition. The OpenPose library is applicable to body and hand key points detection. Finally, the YOLOv5 model of convolutional neural network is used to train our own dataset and recognize mechanical tools. These four algorithms were verified for accuracy and real-time performance respectively, and then constituted this supervisory system. The simulation of this technological process is presented as finite state machine based on ROS2 package. In conclusion, experimental results demonstrate the effectiveness of proposed supervisory system.

Keywords: Human robot collaboration · Human robot interaction · Dynamic task allocation

1 Introduction

Since Industry 4.0 was proposed in 2013, the development of collaborative robots has become one of the trends in the field of manufacturing [1]. Therefore, human-robot collaboration (HRC) and human-robot interaction (HRI) have become popular topics among researchers in recent years. In order to achieve HRC in a collaborative robotic cell, vision-based supervisory systems are wildly used to perform many tasks including safety ensuring, speculation of human intentions and decision-making.

According to [2], three levels of visual understanding are integrated into supervisory system: object-level, human-level and environment-level. Object-level mainly refers to identification and localization [3–5] of objects such as workpieces and tools, which exist

A. Ronzhin et al. (Eds.): ICR 2022, LNCS 13719, pp. 12–24, 2022.
https://doi.org/10.1007/978-3-031-23609-9_2

in shared workspace. Human-level means recognition and prediction of human intentions including gesture and pose recognition via body [6–8] and hand [9, 10] detection. Environment-level, which is 2D or 3D representation of the environment [11], is not considered in our work. From [3–10], we can see that massive studies have used these supervisory systems, which have reached high accuracy in detection and recognition of objects and human intention, as well as achieved on-site communication and collision avoidance. Furthermore, in this paper we hope to contribute to human robot collaboration beyond previous researches by providing a new perspective: application of dynamic task allocation in specific industrial scenarios [12–14]. Therefore, task allocation is an important issue in multi-agent systems. In human-robot collaboration, what we need to consider is how to assign tasks to human and robot to minimize overall completion time and maximize efficiency.

Task allocation is usually divided into three steps. The first step is task decomposition. In some simple assembly tasks, the overall task can be directly decomposed into different subtasks [15], sub-processes [16], and sub-phases [17]. In complex assembly tasks, Hierarchical Task Networks can be used to decompose the overall task [18]. Some researchers use AND/OR graph to complete task representation of assembly plan [19].

The second step is to allocate tasks to robots and humans. It is first necessary to determine the capabilities of humans and robots, measuring the advantages of each and the types of tasks for which they are better suited [16]. Likewise, we need performance metrics such as completion time, safety, ergonomics, and accuracy to describe the property of each subtask [17]. In [15] the author defined positive and negative resources in the environment. After synthesizing these factors, result of allocation will be more feasible. In [17] they adopted decision tree, which takes various criteria as input, and outputs which tasks are suitable for humans, and which are suitable for robots. In [19] they adopted the POMDP model to plan subtasks.

The third step is dynamic allocation. After the planning in the second step, unpredictable deviations may occur in the actual situation, such as changes in human abilities, unexpected factors such as fatigue. For example, in the task of drilling and riveting aircraft bodies, it is necessary to coordinate the movements of a robot and a person in real time [20, 21] and redistribute tasks between humans and robots according to current state of the process. Therefore, adaptive planning and real-time optimization are more challenging, but [15, 16, 18] do not consider this step. Only [17] uses the average time when calculating the completion time of each operation, so the tasks are reassigned when there is a large time deviation in the actual process. However, there are other possibilities of deviation, which should be paid more attention.

The purpose of this paper is to develop a vision-based supervisory system using convolutional neural networks to ensure human-robot interaction. Figure 1 shows our general scheme of supervisory system. There are two RGBD camera sensors supervising the worker at the same time. While the robotic cell responds based on the image information from the first RGBD camera, the mobile robot responds according to the image information of the second RGBD camera. The supervisory system consists of four algorithms: 1) algorithm for face detection, 2) algorithm for body detection, 3) algorithm for hand gesture recognition, 4) algorithm for mechanical tools recognition. All these tools are presented for use in the dynamic allocation of tasks.

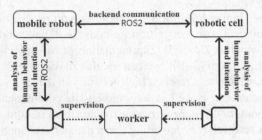

Fig. 1. Scheme of supervisory system.

2 Using Face, Body, Hand, and Gesture Recognition Systems in Collaborative Robot-Human Interaction

2.1 Face Recognition Using Python Library Provided by Adam Geitgey

The face recognition algorithm is based on the Python library "face_recognition" provided by Adam Geitgey [22]. After simplifying the image with HOG [23] algorithm, he completed face landmark estimation using OpenFace [24] provided by Brandon Amos. With 128 measurements generated by the neural network ResNet-34 [25], he used a SVM classifier to find the person's name from encoding.

This algorithm allows a dynamic adapted face learning by adding automatic face learning mode, if no matching exists. Nevertheless, we just need to confirm whether the detection result is a registered worker. Therefore, we need to upload a frontal photo of the worker before the detection starts, the supervisory system directly returns the name of a most matching person or unknown otherwise.

While Fig. 2a is the photo of the tester, which is uploaded to the folder, Fig. 2b is the result of face detection, which shows the correct name of the tester in a bounding box.

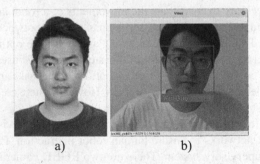

a)   b)

Fig. 2. Example of face detection: a) photo of tester; b) result of face detection.

2.2 Determination of Spatial Coordinates of Key Points of Body and Hands Using OpenPose

There are four main deep learning-based pose estimation methods: OpenPose [26], AlphaPose [27], DeepPose [28], DeeperCut [29]. Except for DeepPose, the other three are open-source algorithms. A comparative experiment has proved that DeeperCut, the improved version of DeepCut, is not as accurate as AlphaPose and OpenPose [30]. While the research team of AlphaPose focuses more on accuracy, OpenPose has the advantage of running faster, which can achieve real-time multi-person 2D pose estimation using PAFs. Although AlphaPose has made improvements in real-time running in the last year, OpenPose is still more popular among researchers. In addition, OpenPose also has excellent performance in the extraction of facial and hand key points, which provides convenience for our future work. Therefore, OpenPose is chosen to gain coordinates of key points of body and hands in our supervisory system. As mentioned in the repository of OpenPose [31], hand detector is much more accurate when body detection is enabled.

After obtaining two-dimensional coordinates of key points, it is necessary to use the aligned depth values of the depth camera channel and restore them to there-dimensional coordinates. We propose to use a pinhole camera model with internal parameters f_x, f_y, c_x, c_y corresponding to the focal length and optical center. This allows calculation of the position of the point (i, j) in the resulting image with a known position of the body $(x, y, z)^T$ using the formula (1):

$$\pi(i, j, 1) = \left(\frac{f_x x}{z} + c_x, \frac{f_y y}{z} + c_y, 1 \right).\tag{1}$$

Now it is possible to restore the three-dimensional point corresponding to pixel $(i, j)^T \in \mathfrak{R}^2$ with depth $z = I_d(i, j)$, using the formula (2):

$$p(x, y, z) = \left(\frac{(i - c_x)z}{f_x}, \frac{(j - c_y)z}{f_y}, z \right)^T.\tag{2}$$

To calculate the internal parameters f_x, f_y, c_x, c_y, the camera calibration method is used.

2.3 Hand Gesture Recognition

Understanding human intention plays a critical role in the maintenance of human-robot collaboration. Human intention is expressed through hand gestures, body poses and facial expressions, among which the most obvious way to send instructions is through hand gestures.

Hand gesture recognition includes three parts: hand localization, pose estimation and gesture recognition [32]. From 2.2 we have already obtained spatial coordinates of hand key points, just gesture recognition is needed. Connecting hand key points with lines turns into a skeleton image, which greatly simplifies the image feature. Among all the recognition methods, commonly used methods are Hidden Markov Model (HMM) [33–35], Convolutional Neural Network (CNN) [36–39], Support Vector Machine (SVM) [40], k-Nearest Neighbors (k-NN) [41], etc.

Since we only have two gestures: start and stop, it is very convenient to apply a simple algorithm to derive the gestures on top of the segmented skeleton data. The state of each finger is either bent or straight, determined by the cumulative angle of the joints. We then recognize gestures by computing the state of a set of fingers. Figure 3 shows the recognition results for both start and stop gestures, in addition key points of hands and body are drawn on the original image captured by the camera.

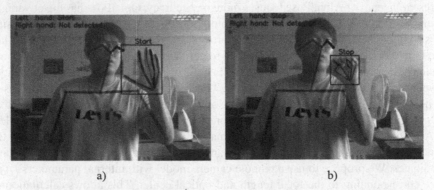

a)   b)

Fig. 3. Results of hand gesture recognition: a) hand gesture "start"; b) hand gesture "stop".

3 Mechanical Tool Recognition with YOLOv5 Neural Network

Compared to two-stage RCNN series algorithms, one-stage YOLO (You Only Look Once) series algorithms have greater advantages in running speed. We used YOLOv5 to recognize mechanical tools in worker's hands, which is the latest iteration of YOLO series of object detection algorithms.

YOLOv5 models must be trained on labelled data in order to learn classes of objects in that data. The dataset we chose is the existing mechanical tool data set on the Kaggle website [42]. In our supervisory system, we just used four categories: screwdriver, hammer, wrench, and pliers. Figure 4 shows part of our customized dataset of just four categories. Then we used platform Roboflow to label every image and automatically export the dataset in YOLOv5 format. YOLOv5 does online augmentation during training, so we just applied two preprocessing steps: auto-orient and resize.

Among five models, we selected the smallest and fastest pre-trained model YOLOv5s to start training. The biggest feature of YOLOv5 is that the size of its model is very small, among which YOLOv5s 14 MB and YOLOv5l 89 MB, while the Darknet architecture version of YOLOv4 is 244 MB in size. Then we specified batch-size 16, image size 640 and number of epochs 300.

Figure 5 shows the training results, we can see those values of loss functions drop to a low level. We used three mechanical tools to validate the accuracy of our trained model, and Fig. 6 presents returned image with bound boxes in ROS system. From left to right, the first tool is detected as a screwdriver with similarity score 0.87, the second tool is detected as pliers with similarity score 0.89, and the third tool is detected as a wrench with similarity score 0.80.

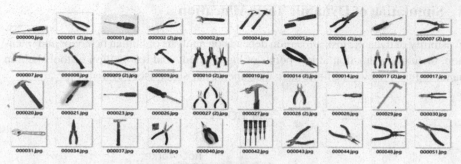

Fig. 4. Dataset of mechanical tools.

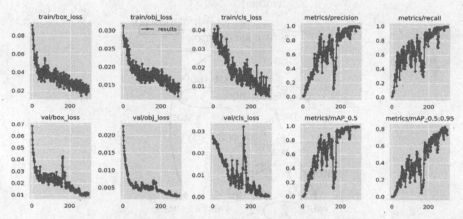

Fig. 5. Training results.

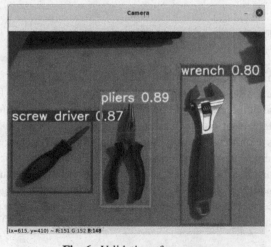

Fig. 6. Validation of accuracy.

4 Simulation of Dynamic Task Allocation

Feasibility of dynamic task allocation depends on analysis of human behavior and intention, including extraction of key points of human body and recognition of tools held in hand. Figure 7 shows the finite state machine of our supervisory system.

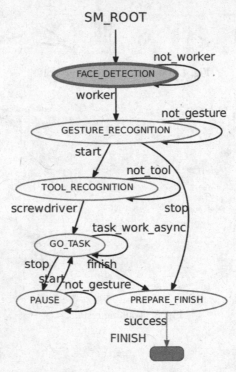

Fig. 7. Finite state machine of our supervisory system.

This state machine is based on ROS2 package SMACH. Before starting the initial state, our supervisory system waits signal of human body detection. After identification, the key points of the human body will be detected and then coordinates of these points will be passed to the robot control system. For the accuracy of motion planning of collaborative robots and the safety of human robot interaction, it is necessary to compute the position and orientation of the worker. In the initial state of the workflow, the RGBD camera detects human faces. If the detection result is a stranger, the supervisory system will prompt that this is not your workplace, please leave, and then go back the initial state. If the detected face belongs to a registered worker, the supervisory system will move to the next state (Fig. 8).

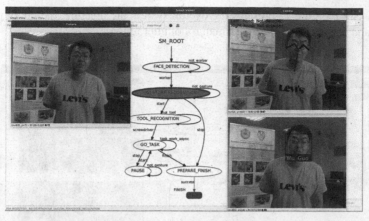

Fig. 8. State of face detection.

With the coordinates of the hand, the entire hand area is segmented so that the supervisory system can continuously detect and recognize the hand gestures of the worker, for example, stop or start (Fig. 9).

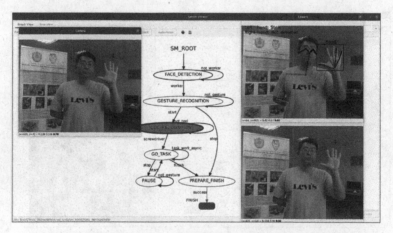

Fig. 9. State of hand gesture recognition.

Understanding the intention of the worker, the collaborative robot can either start operation or finish. Likewise, the supervisory system will recognize mechanical tools in the worker's hands. The supervisory system can not only supervise workers to focus on work without desertion, but also can decide how to help workers to complete tasks according to the tools. If the tool held by the worker is screwdriver (Fig. 10), then the robot starts working. If the tool held by the worker is not screwdriver, the robot will not start working until recognizing the screwdriver. During robot operation, the robot pauses if the worker shows a "stop" gesture (Fig. 11). All detection and recognition tasks are done by RGBD camera. The video of this is available on YouTube (https://youtu.be/

f9ToAzfWSn4). Figure 12 presents the overall system architecture, including program modules and data streams, during human robot interaction.

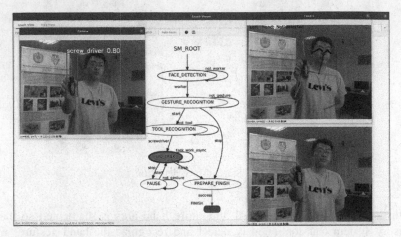

Fig. 10. State of tool recognition.

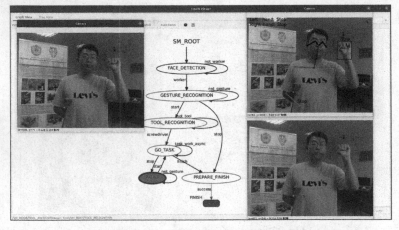

Fig. 11. State of pause when recognizing "stop".

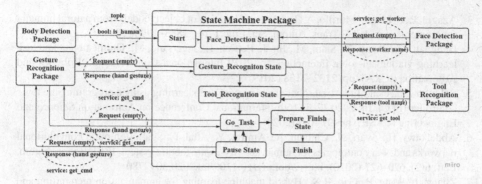

Fig. 12. The overall system architecture.

5 Conclusions

In this paper we presented four algorithms based on neural networks, specially selected for the possibility of implementing dynamic task allocation. The first algorithm of face detection is used to confirm the identity of the worker. The second algorithm of body detection is used to compute the position of worker and his hands. The third algorithm of hand gesture recognition is used to provide instructions to our supervisory system in human-robot interaction. The fourth algorithm of mechanical tool recognition allows the system to choose correct task type, for different tools are manifestations of human intentions. The simulation of the technological process is shown that a set of presented tools can participate in the supervisory system for the dynamic allocation of tasks. The use of such technologies facilitates productivity and flexibility in human-robot interaction.

Further research will be aimed at carrying out experiments of assembly task in real-world conditions in order to validate our proposed supervisory system. Another appealing direction is to integrate and recognition of other forms of human intention in our supervisory system, such as facial expressions and actions, as well as to add more complex classifications in the training set. In the future, it is necessary to move on to assessing the intentions of a person. For example, it is possible to extend face recognition with gaze direction analysis and body recognition with body direction. Then, based on the rotation of the person relative to the camera of the collaborative robot, it can be concluded whether the person intends to interact with the robot.

Acknowledgements. This research is financially supported by the Ministry of Science and Higher Education of the Russian Federation, project № FSFS-2021–0004.

References

1. Lasi, H., Fettke, P., Kemper, H.-G., Feld, T., Hoffmann, M.: Industry 4.0. Bus. Inf. Syst. Eng. **6**(4), 239–242 (2014). https://doi.org/10.1007/s12599-014-0334-4
2. Fan, J., Zheng, P., Li, S.: Vision-based holistic scene understanding towards proactive human robot collaboration. Robot. Comput. Integr. Manuf. **75**, 102304 (2022)

3. Azagra, P., Civera, J., Murillo, A.: Incremental learning of object models from natural human–robot interactions. IEEE Trans. Autom. Sci. Eng. **17**(4), 1883–1900 (2020)

4. Dehghan, M., Zhang, Z., Siam, M., Jin, J., Petrich, L., Jagersand, M.: Online object and task learning via human robot interaction. In: 2019 International Conference on Robotics and Automation (ICRA), pp. 2132–2138 (2019)

5. Solowjow, E., et al.: Industrial robot grasping with deep learning using a programmable logic controller (PLC). In: 2020 IEEE 16th International Conference on Automation Science and Engineering (CASE), pp. 97–103 (2020)

6. Abdelkawy, H., Ayari, N., Chibani, A., Amirat, Y., Attal, F.: Spatio-temporal convolutional networks and N-ary ontologies for human activity-aware robotic system. IEEE Robot. Autom. Lett. **6**(2), 620–627 (2020). https://doi.org/10.1109/lra.2020.3047780

7. Zhang, J., Wang, P., Gao, R.X.: Hybrid machine learning for human action recognition and prediction in assembly. Robot. Comput. Integr. Manuf. **72**, 102184 (2021). https://doi.org/10.1016/j.rcim.2021.102184

8. Liu, H., Wang, L.: Collision-free human-robot collaboration based on context awareness. Robot. Comput. Integr. Manuf. **67**, 101997 (2021). https://doi.org/10.1016/j.rcim.2020.101997

9. Mazhar, O., Navarro, B., Ramdani, S., Passama, R., Cherubini, A.: A real-time human-robot interaction framework with robust background invariant hand gesture detection. Robot. Comput. Integr. Manuf. **60**, 34–48 (2019). https://doi.org/10.1016/j.rcim.2019.05.008

10. Qi, W., Ovur, S.E., Li, Z., Marzullo, A., Song, R.: Multi-sensor guided hand gesture recognition for a teleoperated robot using a recurrent neural network. IEEE Robot. Autom. Lett. **6**(3), 6039–6045 (2021). https://doi.org/10.1109/LRA.2021.3089999

11. Moughlbay, A.A., Herrero, H., Pacheco, R., Outón, J.L., Sallé, D.: Reliable workspace monitoring in safe human-robot environment. In: International Joint Conference SOCO'16-CISIS'16-ICEUTE'16, pp. 256–266. Springer, Cham (2016)

12. Serebrenny, V., Lapin, D., Lapina, A.: The concept of perspective flexible manufacturing system for a collaborative technological cells (2021). https://doi.org/10.1007/978-981-15-8273-8_18

13. Serebrenniy, V., Lapin, D., Mokaeva, A.: Study of the mechanisms of perspective flexible manufacturing system for a newly forming robotic enterprise (2020). https://doi.org/10.1007/978-3-030-39216-1_39

14. Serebrenny, V., Lapin, D., Mokaeva, A.: The concept of an aircraft hull structures assembly process robotization. AIP Conf. Proc. **2171**, 170007 (2019). https://doi.org/10.1063/1.5133318

15. Tsarouchi, P., Michalos, G., Makris, S., Athanasatos, T., Dimoulas, K., Chryssolouris, G.: On a human–robot workplace design and task allocation system. Int. J. Comput. Integr. Manuf. **30**(12), 1272–1279 (2017). https://doi.org/10.1080/0951192x.2017.1307524

16. Ranz, F., Hummel, V., Sihn, W.: Capability-based task allocation in human-robot collaboration. Procedia Manuf. **9**, 182–189 (2017). https://doi.org/10.1016/j.promfg.2017.04.011

17. Antonelli, D., Bruno, G.: Dynamic distribution of assembly tasks in a collaborative work cell of humans and robots. FME Trans. **47**(4), 723–730 (2019)

18. Roncone, A., Mangin, O., Scassellati, B.: Transparent role assignment and task allocation in human robot collaboration. In: 2017 IEEE International Conference on Robotics and Automation (ICRA), pp. 1014–1021 (2017). https://doi.org/10.1109/icra.2017.7989122

19. De Mello, L.H., Sanderson, A.C.: AND/OR graph representation of assembly plans. IEEE Trans. Robot. Autom. **6**(2), 188–199 (1990). https://doi.org/10.1109/70.54734

20. Serebrenny, V., Lapin, D., Mokaeva, A., Shereuzhev, M.: Technological collaborative robotic systems. AIP Conf. Proc. **2171**, 170008 (2019). https://doi.org/10.1063/1.5133319

21. Serebrenny, V., Lapin, D., Mokaeva, A.: Selection of a rational architecture of multi-agent system for group control of robotic collaborative cell. AIP Conf. Proc. **2171**, 190004 (2019). https://doi.org/10.1063/1.5133348
22. Geitgey, A.: Face recognition. https://github.com/ageitgey/face_recognition. Last Accessed 3 June 2022
23. Dalal, N., Triggs, B.: Histograms of oriented gradients for human detection. In: 2005 IEEE Computer Society Conference on Computer Vision and Pattern Recognition (CVPR) (2005). https://doi.org/10.1109/cvpr.2005.177
24. Amos, B., Ludwiczuk, B., Satyanarayanan, M.: Openface: a general-purpose face recognition library with mobile applications. CMU Sch. Comput. Sci. **6**(2), 20 (2016)
25. He, K., Zhang, X., Ren, S., Sun, J.: Deep residual learning for image recognition. In: 2016 IEEE Conference on Computer Vision and Pattern Recognition (CVPR) (2016)
26. Zhe, C., Tomas, S., Shih-En, W., Yaser, S.: OpenPose: realtime multi-person 2D pose estimation using part affinity fields. In: Proceedings of the IEEE Conference on Computer Vision and Pattern Recognition (CVPR), pp. 7291–7299 (2017)
27. Fang, H.S., Xie, S., Tai, Y.W., Lu, C.: Rmpe: regional multi-person pose estimation. In: IEEE International Conference on Computer Vision, pp. 2334–2343 (2017)
28. Toshev, A., Christian S.: DeepPose: human pose estimation via deep neural networks. In: Proceedings of the IEEE Conference on Computer Vision and Pattern Recognition (2014)
29. Insafutdinov, E., Pishchulin, L., Andres, B., Andriluka, M., Schiele, B.: DeeperCut: a deeper, stronger, and faster multi-person pose estimation model. In: Lecture Notes in Computer Science, pp. 34–50. Springer International Publishing, Cham (2016). https://doi.org/10.1007/978-3-319-46466-4_3
30. Li, B., et al.: The overview of multi-person pose estimation method. In: Plant Long Non-Coding RNAs, pp. 600–607. Springer Singapore, Singapore (2019)
31. OpenPose. https://github.com/CMU-Perceptual-Computing-Lab/openpose. Last Accessed 3 June 2022
32. Suarez, J., Murphy, R.R.: Hand gesture recognition with depth images: a review. In: 2012 IEEE RO-MAN: The 21st IEEE International Symposium on Robot and Human Interactive Communication, pp. 411–417 (2012). https://doi.org/10.1109/ROMAN.2012.6343787
33. Yang, C., Yujeong, J., Beh, J., Han, D., Ko, H.: Gesture recognition using depth-based hand tracking for contactless controller application. In: Consumer Electronics (ICCE), pp. 297–298 (2012). https://doi.org/10.1109/ICCE.2012.6161876
34. Hassani, A.: Touch versus in-air hand gestures: evaluating the acceptance by seniors of human-robot interaction using Microsoft Kinect. M.S. In: Electrical Engineering, Mathematics and Computer Sciences, University of Twente (2011). https://doi.org/10.1007/978-3-642-25167-2_42
35. Zafrulla, Z., Brashear, H., Starner, T., Hamilton, H., Presti, P.: American sign language recognition with the Kinect. In: International Conference on Multimodal Interfaces, pp. 279–286. Alicante, Spain (2011). https://doi.org/10.1145/2070481.2070532
36. Devineau, G., Moutarde, F., Xi, W., Yang, J.: Deep learning for hand gesture recognition on skeletal data. In: 13th IEEE International Conference on Automatic Face and Gesture Recognition, pp. 106–113. Xi'an, China (2018). https://doi.org/10.1109/FG.2018.00025
37. Nyirarugira, C., Choi, H.-R., Kim, J., Hayes, M., Kim, T.: Modified levenshtein distance for real-time gesture recognition. In: 6th International Congress on Image and Signal Processing (CISP), Hangzhou, China (2013). https://doi.org/10.1109/CISP.2013.6745306
38. Saqib, S., Ditta, A., Khan, M.A., Kazmi, S.A.R., Alquhayz, H.: Intelligent dynamic gesture recognition using CNN empowered by edit distance. Comput. Mater. Cont. **66**(2), 2061–2076 (2020). https://doi.org/10.32604/cmc.2020.013903

39. Al-Hammadi, M., Muhammad, G., Abdul, W., Alsulaiman, M., Bencherif, M.A., Mekhtiche, M.A.: Hand gesture recognition for sign language using 3DCNN. IEEE Access. **8**, 79491–79509 (2020). https://doi.org/10.1109/ACCESS.2020.2990434
40. Biswas, K.K., Basu, S.K.: Gesture recognition using Microsoft Kinect. In: Automation, Robotics and Applications (ICARA), pp. 100–103 (2011). https://doi.org/10.1109/ICARA.2011.6144864
41. Malassiotis, S., Aifanti, N., Strintzis, M.G.: A gesture recognition system using 3D data. In: 3D Data Processing Visualization and Transmission, pp. 190–193 (2002). https://doi.org/10.1109/tdpvt.2002.1024061
42. Mechanical Tools Classification Dataset. https://www.kaggle.com/datasets/salmaneunus/mechanical-tools-dataset. Last Accessed 3 June 2022

Design and Implementation of an Interactive Docent Robot for Exhibitions

Yizhou Chen, Jie Li, Rongrong Ni [ID], and Xiaofeng Liu[(✉)] [ID]

College of IoT Engineering, Hohai University, 200 Jinlingbei Road, Changzhou 213100, China
xfliu@hhu.edu.cn

Abstract. Interactive docent robot is a novel and interesting service in modern exhibition hall research. However, due to the complexity of human-robot interaction, it is still a challenging to develop a tour assistant robot used in exhibition halls that can naturally interact with visitors and guide them through the exhibits. To fulfill these requirements for intelligent docent robots, this paper first analyzes the basic functions that a service robot should have, and then develops a physical anthropomorphic robotic head platform with soft skin, which can present facial motions, for presentation and interaction. The service robot completes the functions of multi-point navigation, autonomous obstacle avoidance and explanation in the local embedded device through path planning algorithm. To achieve the anthropomorphic interaction effect, an anthropomorphic robotic head for interaction is designed to realize the facial action change in the process of explanation and interaction. In addition, the functions of human-robot dialogue and facial recognition based on convolutional neural network are realized on the cloud platform. The experimental results in navigation accuracy evaluation and human-robot interaction show that the service robot designed in this paper can maintain stable motion, accurate navigation, and natural interaction.

Keywords: Docent robot · Anthropomorphic · Multi-point navigation · Cloud platform · Human-robot interaction

1 Introduction

With the development of artificial intelligence, docent robots are widely used to assist the visitors in the exhibition halls. The docent robots can provide navigation and human-robot interaction services and enrich the experience of tourists [1]. In previous studies on anthropomorphic robots, Park et al. [2] proposed that robots with anthropomorphic appearance allow humans to remember more details of interactions and can provide more engaging and credible interaction information. Thus, anthropomorphic docent robots with precise navigation and natural human-robot interaction can act as intelligent guides in the exhibition halls and provide better navigation and interaction services for visitors.

Previous researches on docent robots mainly focused on path planning and visual perception. For example, Choi et al. [3] proposed a position tracking compensation algorithm for path search of exhibition hall-guided robots. Michaud et al. [4] proposed

A. Ronzhin et al. (Eds.): ICR 2022, LNCS 13719, pp. 25–34, 2022.
https://doi.org/10.1007/978-3-031-23609-9_3

a distributed approach based on directional visual perception and inter-robot communication. These studies all provide references for the research of docent robots. However, these studies are based on the powerful computing and storage capabilities of computers. If these functions are deployed in the embedded devices of docent robots, it will cause the problems of insufficient memory and high latency.

In previous studies, many literatures have reported the research progress of navigation and interaction for docent robots. Nourbakhsh et al. [5] installed an affective mobile robot at the Carnegie Museum of Natural History. Ghosh et al. [6] described the development, test, and analysis of a museum guide robot system to manage audiences. They both have made an achievement in guidance, explanation, perception, and interaction. However, none of them have used anthropomorphized robots. Studies on human-robot interaction point out that the appearance of a robot is as important as its behavior [7], and a robot with an anthropomorphic appearance has a stronger comprehensive ability, which can shorten the distance between the robots and the tourists and realize natural human-robot interaction.

To improve upon these deficiencies, this paper designs a docent robot for exhibition halls. The overall design and hardware structure of the docent robot is shown in Fig. 1. The Raspberry Pi is used to build a grid map in indoor environment through lidar sensors and perform real-time path planning and obstacle avoidance according to the coordinates of the explanation points. In addition, to avoid the problems of high latency and insufficient memory caused by deploying the convolutional neural network on the Raspberry Pi, this paper implements the functions of human-computer dialogue and face recognition in the cloud server. Service robots can quickly retrieve, and match based on cloud knowledge base and face database, communicate naturally with tourists and welcome important guests. Finally, the anthropomorphic head allows the docent robot to increase the effectiveness of information transfer and intimacy with the visitor during navigation and interaction.

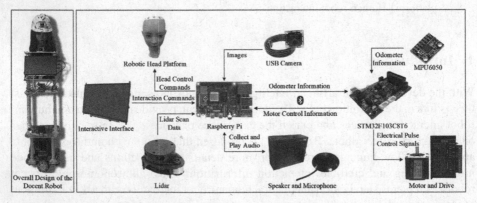

Fig. 1. Overall design and hardware structure of the docent robot.

2   Computation on the Edge

The navigation and explanation functions are deployed locally. The docent robot will build a grid map in an unknown environment and navigate using Adaptive Monte Carlo Localization (AMCL) algorithm. Global and local path planning algorithms are combined to realize autonomous obstacle avoidance. Finally, the docent robot will make a presentation after reaching the explanation points [8].

2.1   Mapping and Location

The docent robot will build a grid map in an unknown environment through the Lidar sensor. The states of each gird in the map are classified as free, occupied and unknow. We use $p(f)$ to denote the probability of Free and $p(o)$ to denote the probability of Occupied. Therefore, the state probability of each grid can be described as Eq. (1):

$$State(g|z) = log\frac{p(o|z)}{p(f|z)}, \tag{1}$$

where z is the observations of Lidar measurements. In the initial state, each grid is unknow, where $p(o) = p(f) = 0.5$, and $State(g|z) = 0$. Each time a Lidar scan is obtained, the $p(o)$ value of the grid at real obstacles in grid map will increase and $p(f)$ value will decrease. Thereupon then the state probability when the grid is occupied will increase and approach to 1, while the state probability when the grid is free tends to 0. Therefore, the probability distribution of the final grid map can be described as Eq. (2):

$$p(G|z_{1:t}) = \prod p(g_i|z_{1:t}), \tag{2}$$

where the occupancy probability of each grid is described as Eq. (3):

$$p(g_i|z_{1:t}) = 1 - \frac{1}{1 + e^{State(g_i|z_{1:t})}}. \tag{3}$$

Figure 2 a shows the result of building the map in our laboratory, which is shown on the Robot Visualization (RViz).

In this paper, the AMCL algorithm [9] is used to localize the docent robot in the grid map. The particles distributed on the map are scored according to the map data and the initial posture of the robot. The score determines the probability of the robot being in a certain area. In the next round of particle generation, higher-scoring area have more particles generated. Through continuous iterations, the particles will converge to an area that is the best point for evaluating the position and posture of the docent robot. In addition, the accuracy of the position estimation is determined by judging the aggregation degree of particles. When the estimation is accurate, the maintained particles will be decreased to reduce the computational cost of the algorithm. The positioning results are shown in Fig. 2b.

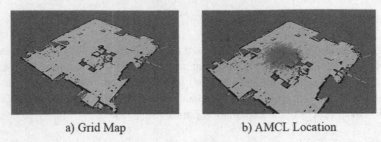

a) Grid Map   b) AMCL Location

Fig. 2. Mapping and Location Results. a) Grid map created by the docent robot. b) ACML sample distribution.

2.2 Navigation and Autonomous Obstacle Avoidance

Figure 3 is the structure of the robotic navigation system [10]. The navigation node can get the navigation target from a topic published on RViz. The AMCL node provides robot global position information by using the particle filter algorithm. The odometer information serves two purposes, one is used to select the optimal path for local path planner, and the other is to use the estimated pose information for positioning. The odometer information is obtained from the encoder motor and gyroscope on the mobile platform. The Lidar data is used to match the static map to correct the robot's position and get a more accurate position to compensate for odometer drift errors. In addition, the grid occupancy map and cost map are built according to the Lidar data. The cost map is divided into global cost map and local cost map, where global cost map is initialized via the Static Grid Map node. The local cost map includes Obstacle Map Layer and Inflation Layer. The obstacles detected by Lidar are added to Obstacle Map Layer. The Inflation Layer scales the obstacle to a user-defined expansion radius to ensure that the robot and the obstacle will not collide.

The global path planner reads the global cost map for planning based on the input start and target points. The local planner reads the local cost map and performs local planning based on the tracked global path to make it conform to the global optimal path and achieves real-time obstacle avoidance.

Fig. 3. Structure of the navigation system.

3   Computation on the Cloud

In order to reduce the power consumption of the CPU and improve the real-time path planning, we deployed the facial recognition, human-robot dialogue and voice-text conversion function in the cloud. Then the local needs to send the data to the cloud and receive the processed data from the cloud.

3.1   Human-Robot Dialogue

The docent robot supports an open and customized dialogue system. The docent robot will save the dialogue as an audio file and send the audio file to the cloud for voice-text conversion and human-robot dialogue. Questions can be quickly retrieved and matched in the knowledge base in the cloud after word separation and feature extraction. Then, a cosine similarity algorithm is used to calculate the matching scores of questions and answers. Finally, the matching scores in conjunction with the thresholds are analyzed to determine which answer is returned.

In addition, users can upload topics and corresponding responses to the cloud to customize the dialogue system and enrich the robot's knowledge base. The cloud server will segment the new topic to determine where the topic is stored in the knowledge base and create a reverse index of the topic. The classifier model is retrained to update the knowledge base in the cloud. When a similar topic is received, the system can reply by searching the knowledge base for an index that matches the topic based on the preprocessed topic. In practice, this function can allow the robot to provide customized language guidance and presentations depending on different exhibition halls.

3.2   Face Recognition

The camera embedded in the robotic head platform also enables facial recognition during the human-robot interaction, which can be used to sign in, take attendance and welcome important guests. Facial detection and recognition are realized in the cloud server. As shown in Fig. 4, we use the Multi-task Convolutional Neural Networks (MTCNN) [11] for facial detection, which combines three cascaded lightweight CNNs. Then, we use faceNet [12] for facial recognition, which is to map face images into a multi-dimensional space and represent the similarity of faces by spatial distance. The spatial distance of the same face image is small, and the spatial distance of different face images is large.

As shown in Fig. 5, we visualized the results of facial recognition. The results reflect that if the Euclidean distance between the feature vectors is lower than the threshold, the docent robot will receive the successful recognition signal and the corresponding face information. Conversely, if the Euclidean distances calculated are all higher than the threshold, the output will be set as a stranger and the docent robot will not react.

4   Experiments

To evaluate the performance of the robot, experiments for evaluating the navigation, autonomous obstacle avoidance, and human-robot interaction have been conducted in this section. During the test, a Lithium battery with 24 V and 100 Ah is used to power the robot for about 24 hours of working.

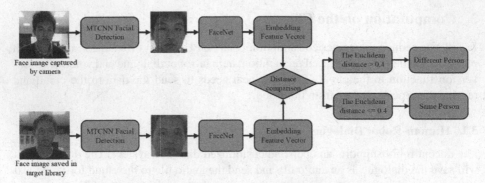

Fig. 4. The implementation process of facial recognition.

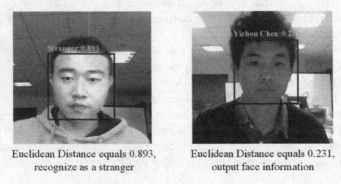

Euclidean Distance equals 0.893,   Euclidean Distance equals 0.231,
recognize as a stranger   output face information

Fig. 5. The results of facial recognition.

4.1 Evaluation of Navigation Path and Explanation Points

In order to evaluate the precision of the navigation, we recorded the coordinates of the docent robot when moving, and the position and posture data when it stops near the explanation points. Figure 6(a) shows the top view of the grid map, which is built by lidar in the experimental environment. In the grid map, the red dots are the explanation points we set, and the blue line is the moving path planned by the global path planning algorithm prior to navigation.

In terms of the precision of the navigation, the actual moving path of the docent robot was recorded in real time. Meanwhile, the path predicted by the path planning algorithm was also recorded. As shown in Fig. 6(b), we compared the similarity between the actual docent robot movement path and the predicted path with our method. The results show that the robot can move according to the path planning algorithm, which demonstrates the reliability and stability of the mobile chassis.

The position and posture data of the docent robot were recorded when it reached the explanation points. Then we compared the preset coordinates of the explanation points and the posture of robot with the actual coordinates and posture when the docent robot reached the explanation points. As shown in Fig. 6(c), P(x, y, z) represents the position, O(x, y, z, w) represents the direction. Within the tolerance, the robot can reach the explanation points and adjust the orientation accurately. Even if the position of the indoor object changes, the robot can still accurately reach the explanation points during navigation.

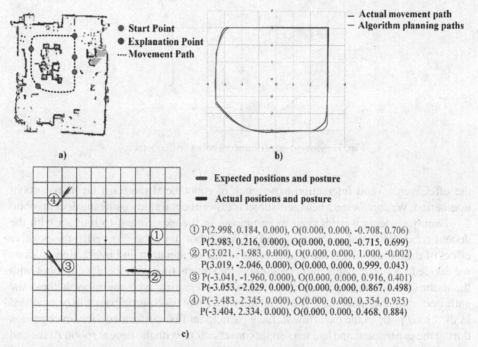

Fig. 6. Evaluation of Navigation Algorithms. a) Moving path and explanation points of the docent robot in grid map. b) Comparison of predicted path and actual path without obstacles. c) Comparison of the coordinates and posture of the docent robot.

4.2 Evaluation of Autonomous Obstacle Avoidance

In order to evaluate the obstacle avoidance function of the docent robot, obstacles were randomly placed in its path. As shown in Fig. 7, the blue dots represent the obstacles, and the red dots represent the explanation points. When the docent robot detects an obstacle within the detection range set by the local path planner, it will immediately react and replan the path to the next explanation point to bypass the obstacle. The obstacle detection range is determined by the incircle radius of the robot contour. The results reflect that our docent robot can accurately and stably avoid obstacles in its moving path when guiding the visitors.

4.3 Evaluation of Human-Robot Interaction

For the performance of human-robot interaction, the accuracy of facial recognition and the rationality of human-robot dialogue were evaluated. In addition, we also evaluated

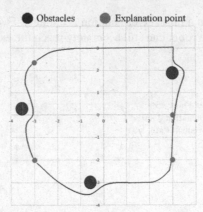

Fig. 7. Moving path of docent robot with obstacles.

the effectiveness and interaction experience of robot head platform on human-robot interaction. We conducted a between-subjects experimental study using the docent robot.

Twenty students were invited to participate in the experiment to interact with the docent robot for facial recognition and human-robot dialogue. To verify the positive effect of the anthropomorphic docent robot on the explanation and interaction process, we divided the participants into two groups, one interacting with the docent robot with the anthropomorphic appearance and the other interacting with the robot without the anthropomorphic appearance. The facial information of each participant will be recorded in the cloud prior to the experiment. Each participant first performed facial recognition during the experiment and had ten simple conversations with the docent robot. At the end of the experiment, participants were asked to fill out a questionnaire on the participants' evaluation of the intimacy and interaction experience of the docent robot.

The results of the experiments were collected for statistical and analytical purposes, where the evaluation of the rationality of human-robot dialogue was based on the logic of daily conversation. The results show that the accuracy of facial recognition is 100% and the rationality of human-robot dialogue is 90%. In addition, we also calculated the mean value and standard deviation of the evaluation scores corresponding to the participants, the results of the questionnaire are shown in Table 1. The results reflect that the scores from participants on the intimacy and interactive experience of the docent robot with an anthropomorphic appearance are higher than that without an anthropomorphic appearance, which indicates that the docent robot with anthropomorphic appearance can indeed play a positive role in human-robot interaction.

Table 1. Evaluation on the effectiveness of information transmission.

	Intimacy	Interaction Experience
Robot with anthropomorphic head	4.2 (0.60)	4.0 (0.77)
Robot without anthropomorphic head	3.3 (0.46)	3.1 (0.54)

5 Conclusion

This paper presents an interactive robot docent for exhibition, the robot can lead visitors to visit different attractions in the exhibition hall and provide human-robot interaction services. During the test, the mechanical structure of the robot is basically stable, can stably perform lidar mapping and multi-point navigation, and effectively perform autonomous obstacle avoidance during the navigation, perform vivid demonstrations at the explanation point. In terms of interaction, face recognition and human-robot dialogue were tested for interaction to verify the stability of human-robot interaction. The results show that the robot can lead visitors to the exhibition hall and provide human-robot interaction services without any malfunction. High-precision lidar can help robots navigate and avoid obstacles autonomously, and sophisticated neural networks help explain that robots interact with humans more naturally.

Further work can be focused on using a single-tube coupling system for low-power autonomous wireless charging and the design and use of robotic arms. In addition, it can further improve the problem of inaccurate repositioning of robots when the flow of people is dense.

Acknowledgments. This work was supported in part by National key R\&D program of China 2018AAA0100800, the Key Research and Development Program of Jiangsu under grants BK20192004B and BE2018004, Guangdong Forestry Science and Technology Innovation Project under grant 2020KJCX005, International Cooperation and Exchanges of Changzhou under grant CZ20200035, China Postdoctoral Science Foundation 2021M701051.

References

1. Goodrich, M.A., Schultz, A.C.: Human–robot interaction: a survey. Found. Trends Hum.-Comput. Interact. **1**(3), 203–275 (2008)
2. Kim, B.C., Kim, S.M., Moon, J.I., Kwon, J.H., Cho, I.K.: Shielding for reduction of magnetic field strength from docent robot being charged by wireless power transfer technology. In: 2015 IEEE Global Electromagnetic Compatibility Conference (GEMCCON), pp. 1–3. IEEE (2015)
3. Choi, J.H., Choi, B.J.: Design of self-localization based autonomous driving platform for an electric wheelchair. IEMEK J. Embed. Sys. Appl. **13**(3), 161–167 (2018)
4. Michaud, F., Letourneau, D., Guilbert, M., Valin, J.M.: Dynamic robot formations using directional visual perception. In: IEEE/RSJ International Conference on Intelligent Robots and Systems, vol. 3, pp. 2740–2745. IEEE (2002)
5. Nourbakhsh, I.R., Bobenage, J., Grange, S., Lutz, R., Soto, A.: An active mobile robot educator with a full-time job. Artif. Intell. **114**(1–2), 95–124 (1999)
6. Ghosh, M., Kuzuoka, H.: An ethnomethodological study of a museum guide robot's attempt at engagement and disengagement. J. Robot. **2014**, 1–20 (2014)
7. Minato, T., Shimada, M., Ishiguro, H., Itakura, S.: Development of an android robot for studying human-robot interaction. In: International Conference on Industrial, Engineering and Other Applications of Applied Intelligent Systems (2004)
8. Kaelbling, L.P., Littman, M.L., Cassandra, A.R.: Planning and acting in partially observable stochastic domains. Artif. Intell. **101**(1–2), 99–134 (1998)

9. Shi, Y., et al.: Design of a hybrid indoor location system based on multi-sensor fusion for robot navigation. Sensors **18**(10), 3581 (2018)
10. Pajaziti, A.: SLAM–map building and navigation via ROS. Int. J. Intell. Syst. Appl. Eng. **2**(4), 71–75 (2014)
11. Saxena, S., Tripathi, S., Sudarshan, T.S.B.: Deep dive into faces: pose & illumination invariant multi-face emotion recognition system. In: 2019 IEEE/RSJ International Conference on Intelligent Robots and Systems (IROS), pp. 1088–1093. IEEE (2019)
12. Schroff, F., Kalenichenko, D., Philbin, J.: Facenet: a unified embedding for face recognition and clustering. In: Proceedings of the IEEE Conference on Computer Vision and Pattern Recognition, pp. 815–823 (2015)

Attention Guided 6D Object Pose Estimation with Multi-constraints Voting Network

Guoyu Zuo[1,2(✉)], Zonghan Gu[1,2], Gao Huang[1,2], and Daoxiong Gong[1,2]

[1] Faculty of Information Technology, Beijing University of Technology, Beijing 100124, China
zuoguoyu@bjut.edu.cn
[2] Beijing Key Laboratory of Computing Intelligence and Intelligent Systems, Beijing 100124, China

Abstract. For visual-based robotic manipulation, it has always been a challenging task to perform real-time and accurate pose estimation of target objects under cluttered background, illumination variations, occlusion, and weak texture, especially under severe occlusion conditions. In recent years, the RGB-based methods based on vector field prediction are proved to be robustness on 6D object pose estimation under occlusion. At the same time, network with attention mechanism has achieved outstanding performance in 2D object detection. In this paper, we propose an attention-driven 6D pose estimation method with multi-constraints loss and pixel-wise voting. We calculate the distance weighted unit vector length and included angle length based on prediction results to regularize unit vectors prediction. Moreover, we introduce Dense Atrous Spatial Pyramid Pooling (DenseASPP) and Channel-wise Cross Attention (CCA) mechanisms into the network structure to improve the accuracy of output prediction. Experiments on LINEMOD and Occlusion LINEMOD datasets manifest that our method outperforms state-of-the-art two-stage sparse 2D keypoints prediction methods without pose refinement.

Keywords: 6D pose estimation · Attention mechanism · Multi-constraints loss · Pixel-wise Voting

1 Introduction

Efficiently and accurately estimating the 6D pose of an object relative to the camera is a key step of the high-dimensional space manipulation tasks represented by robotic arm grasping. The 6D pose refers to the $(R; T)$ transformation of the object coordinate system relative to the camera coordinate system, R and T respectively represent the rotation transformation and translation transformation between the two coordinate systems in three degrees of freedom.

The traditional hand-crafted feature matching 6D pose estimation methods realize accurate object pose estimation but decrease significantly under severe conditions such as complex background, insufficient illumination, severe occlusion, and weak texture. In response to the above problems, 6D pose estimation methods based on deep learning

A. Ronzhin et al. (Eds.): ICR 2022, LNCS 13719, pp. 35–47, 2022.
https://doi.org/10.1007/978-3-031-23609-9_4

are proposed. It is difficult to obtain the RGBD information of images and the algorithm reaches high demand for hardware. Hence, the RGB-based 6D object pose estimation methods meet the requirements of practical applications.

Among RGB-based methods, deep learning end-to-end methods take RGB images and label information as input, then directly output the 6D pose of objects. While, the algorithm is inexplicable and overfitting always occurs during the prediction process. In contrast, two-stage object pose estimation methods have stable generalization and algorithm interpretability. The first stage predicts the 2D-3D corresponding information of the target object through the deep neural network, the second stage uses the predicted information to solve the Perspective-n-Point (PnP) [1] problem to obtain the 6D pose of objects. Although two-stage methods are more affected by the occlusion of keypoints, Pixel-wise Voting Network (PVnet) [2] achieves good results in solving the occlusion problem by regressing unit vectors pointing to the sparse keypoints for each pixel in RGB images and obtaining the predicted sparse 2D keypoints through Huffman voting.

Inspired by PVnet, this paper proposes a new network architecture. We adopt Unet [3] like network backbone with two attention mechanisms to improve the accuracy of output. The Dense Atrous Spatial Pyramid Pooling (DenseASPP) [4] module is introduced after the end of the downsampling stage to effectively capture multi-scale feature information by using the densely connected dilated convolution layer. In the upsampling stage, Channel-wise Cross Attention (CCA) [5] module is added to eliminate the ambiguity of decoder features. Except for that, we add distance weighted unit vector length and included angle length loss constraints into the loss function. Specifically, for pixels far away from the keypoints, the small angle between the two direction vectors leads to a large positioning deviation, distance weighted information helps regularize predicted unit vectors and reduce voting deviation. The main work of this paper is as follows:

- We propose an occlusion robust network for 6D object pose estimation, which realizes more accurate unit vector field and segmentation predictions by introducing DenseASPP and CCA attention modules.
- We add distance weighted unit vector length loss and included angle vector length loss constraints into loss function to regularize unit vector field prediction.
- Our method is tested on public datasets and achieves the performance of state-of-the-art compared with the most advanced RGB-based sparse 2D keypoints prediction methods without pose refinement.

2 Related Work

In this section, we mainly review the RGB-based 6D object pose estimation methods of deep learning RGB-based methods. Deep learning RGB-based methods are classified into end-to-end regression methods and two-stage methods.

End-to-end regression methods. End-to-end regression methods input RGB images, train the complete network, directly output the 6D pose of the object in the form of regression or classification tasks. The 6D pose information includes translation matrix, Euler angle or quaternion. Xiang et al. [6] propose the end-to-end network PoseCNN in which a symmetric loss function is proposed and Hoffman voting that our method adopts is used to predict the center point dealing with occlusion. SSD-6d [7] and EfficientPose [8] design end-to-end architectures for 6D pose estimation by extending the 2D target detection architectures. The advantage of such methods is high efficiency, but inexplicability and the reliance on pose refinement with further computation limit the development of this kind of methods in the field of 6D pose estimation and the practical application of robot operation tasks.

Two-stage methods. The first type of two-stage methods are 2D–3D dense correspondence methods. The first stage of such methods is to predict the intermediate representation, and the second stage is to obtain the 6D pose through the depth network or the pixel by pixel RANSAC PNP [1] method. Dense Pose Object Detector (DPOD) [9] constructs a 2D–3D correspondence by predicting the UV graph as an intermediate representation, then uses the discrete classification method to obtain 6D pose results. Geometry-Guided Direct Regression Network (GDR-Net) [10] classifies the surface area of target objects into 64 discrete segments and then trains another encoding-decoding network to regress 6D pose. The 2D–3D dense correspondence prediction methods have a large demand for computational power and need a long training time for another trained network to obtain 6D pose.

In contrast, the second type of two-stage methods is 2D–3D sparse keypoints matching methods which combine the advantages of traditional methods' interpretability and deep learning methods' efficiency. Rad et al. [6] train depth network to regress 2D coordinates of the eight vertices of objects' bounding box and further calculate the 6D pose with PNP. Peng et al. [2] solve the problems of occlusion and image outliers by pixel-wise voting, while there is still much room to improve the accuracy of semantic segmentation and unit vector field prediction. HybridPose [11] predicts edge vectors and the intermediate representation corresponding to symmetry with predictions in [2] for pose refinement. The added two intermediate representations greatly increase the network parameters, and the method relies too much on the pose refinement. Our method accurately and real-time estimates the 6D pose of the occluded object without post pose refinement.

3 Proposed Approach

Our method takes RGB image as input and obtains 6D pose with two-stage keypoints prediction. Our backbone is the Unet [2] like network with DenseASPP [4] module and CCA [5] upsampling attention module. The output of our network are segmentation and unit vector field predictions. In the process of back propagation of network, in addition to two output loss, we add the distance weighted unit vector length loss and included angle vector length loss into loss function. The four loss constraints jointly guide the network to regularize unit vector prediction. Then, the position of sparse 2D keypoints is determined by Hoffman voting and we obtain 6D pose regressed by EPNP [1]. The overall structure of the method is shown in Fig. 1.

3.1 Network Architecture

The backbone of the downsampling network is a pretrained Resnet18 [12] network. The images are downsampled to the size of $\frac{H}{8} \times \frac{W}{8}$, and the subsequent downsampling layers

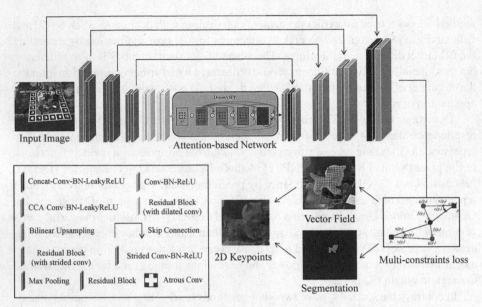

Fig. 1. Overview of our framework.

of [12] are replaced by two convolution layers with dilated convolutions for dimension raising operation. Then, the information is put into the DenseASPP module to extract multi-scale and dense features. After the regularization processing of BN layer and Relu layer, the information is unsampled to image size for three times which contain two times of CCA module and regularization combination module.

DenseASPP attention module. The DenseASPP [4] module is an optimized version of the ASPP [13] module. DenseASPP introduces different rate of atrous convolutions and connects them in the form of dense connections to extract multi-scale dense information of RGB images. We introduce the DenseASPP module containing the dilated convolutions layers of rates = $(3, 6, 12, 18, 24)$ to obtain larger receptive fields and extract denser feature information in the form of dense connections at the same time. Through ablation experiments, we confirm that the DenseASPP module we add helps improve the accuracy of 6D pose estimation.

CCA attention module. The improved network UCtransnet [5] network based on the Unet [3] structure has achieved amazing results in the field of medical image semantic segmentation. We successfully introduce Channel-wise Cross Attention (CCA) module after upsampling parts of our 6D pose network structure. CCA module is used to perform feature fusion processing based on channel attention before the concat of the information after bilinear interpolation upsampling and skip connection layer information. Because of the bad performance in narrow channels, CCA module is ultimately added to the first two of the three upsampling layers to improve the effect of 6D pose estimation.

3.2 Multi-constraints Loss Function

The design of our loss function is inspired by [2]. In terms of the outputs of our network, we still retain the two outputs of segmentation and unit vector field. The loss function of [2] is described as:

$$L = L_{seg} + L_{vf}, \tag{1}$$

where

$$L_{seg} = -\sum_{c=1}^{C} y_c \log(p_c), \tag{2}$$

$$L_{vf} = \sum_{k_i \in K} \sum_{p \in O} l_1(e_i|_x) + l_1(e_i|_y), \tag{3}$$

where the L_{seg} is the semantic segmentation loss, L_{vf} is the vector fild loss. K represents the kepoints, O is the target object region and e_i is the unit included angle vector. p_c is the predicted probability of the object category and y_c is the ground truth probability of object category.

However, the prediction of the unit vector ignores the actual distance between each pixel and the 2D keypoints. For pixel points far from 2D keypoints, a little deviation in direction leads to a large error in the intersection voting process. Therefore, we add two additional regular terms weighted according to the distance information to the loss function in our loss to regularize the unit vector field prediction. Specifically, the pixels far from keypoints are also considered with the distance information, even a small, included angle is punished. Our multi-constraints loss function is defined as:

$$L^* = L_{seg} + L_{vf} + \alpha L_{dis} + \beta L_{gra}, \tag{4}$$

where

$$L_{dis} = \sum_{k_i \in K} \sum_{p \in O} l_1(\mu \times (|u_i|_2 - |v_i|_2)), \tag{5}$$

$$L_{gra} = \sum_{k_i \in K} \sum_{p \in O} l_1(\mu \times |e_i|_2), \tag{6}$$

where α and β are balance weights of loss function. μ is the distance weight matrix, u_i is ground truth unit vector and v_i is predicted unit vector.

The regularization term L_{dis} is the distance loss between the length of the predicted unit vector and the length of the ground truth unit vector. Because of the use of distance compensation, the further calculation with distance weight is needed with smooth l_1 loss to ensure the implementation effect of Huffman voting strategy.

L_{gra} is the loss of distance weighted unit included angle vector length that directly represents the distance information. On the basis of preserving L_{vf}, we add the length of included angle vector as the regular term L_{gra} to the loss function and carry out back propagation with L_{vf}, L_{seg} and L_{dis} to guide network in training. The overall principle is shown in Fig. 2.

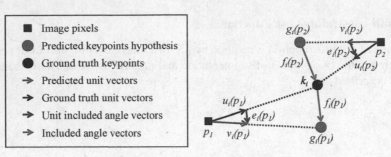

Fig. 2. Motivation of multi-constraints loss.

Huffman Voting Strategy. With the predicted semantic segmentation and the unit vectors from each pixel, we get the direction of each foreground pixel to the target keypoint. Follow [5], for the combination of two vectors of foreground pixel points, the intersection of vectors is taken as the hypothetical candidate keypoint. The specific strategy is defined as:

$$w_{k,i} = \sum_{p \in O} I \left(\frac{(g_{k,i} - p)^T}{|g_{k,i} - p|_2} v_k(p) \geq \theta \right). \tag{7}$$

4 Experiments

4.1 Datasets

We evaluate our experimental results on two benchmark datasets, LINEMOD [14] and Occlusion LINEMOD [15].

LINEMOD is the reference dataset for 6D object pose estimation. It consists of 15783 images of 13 objects. The specific objects in each RGB image are annotated with image number information, semantic segmentation coordinate information, object 3D model information and camera internal parameter information K. LINEMOD is used widely as testing dataset and training dataset for many challenging tasks including cluttered background, non-textured objects and lighting changes.

Occlusion LINEMOD is created specifically for challenging tasks that the target objects are severe occluded. It includes 1214 images of 8 objects, each of which is severely occluded. The RGB images are generated by the additional annotation of some object subsets in the LINEMOD dataset. Occlusion LINEMOD is usually used as testing dataset only to test the robustness of the model trained on LINEMOD dataset to occlusion.

4.2 Evaluation Metrics

We use the most common metrics including 2D Projection metric [17] and average 3D distance of model points (ADD) metric [14] of 6D pose estimation to evaluate the performance of our method.

2D Projection metric measures the average distance between the 2D projection points of the 3D model keypoints from the ground truth 6D pose and the 6D pose predicted by our model. We regard the predicted pose with the average distance error of the projection points less than 5 pixels as the correct pose.

ADD metric calculates the average distance of the overall 3D model point set. According to the measurement standards of most models, we consider the error distance between the predicted 6D pose and ground truth 6D pose 3D model average point set less than 10% of the model diameter as correct. For symmetric objects eggbox and glue, we use the metric ADD(−S) to evaluate the prediction of the symmetric object model and avoid the ambiguity of the model evaluation results.

4.3 Implementation Details

Preparing Training Dataset. We divide the real data in the LINEMOD [14] dataset into two parts, of which 15% is used as the training dataset to train the model, 85% is used as the testing dataset to evaluate model effect. Following [2] , we individually introduce 10 K synthetic images for each of the 13 objects in LINEMOD dataset as training data. According to the "Cut and Paste" strategy proposed by [18] , these composite images are generated by splicing the pictures in sun397 [19] dataset as the background and the objects in LINEMOD as foreground part.

Training setting. We set the initial learning rate to 0.001 and it is divided by 0.5 every 20 epochs. We set the batchsize to 32 and train 200 epochs separately for each object model with Resnet18 based network. For the regular term parameters α and β of the multi-constraints loss function, we dynamically set them to make four loss terms in the same order of magnitude. For filtering strategy, the direction parameter θ is set to 0.99. For keypoints samplings, we use the farthest point sampling method (FPS) to sample 8 keypoints on the surface of the object and regard the center point as another one. The network architecture uses pytroch version 1.9 and is trained on the GPU of RTX3090.

4.4 Comparison with State-Of-The-Art Methods

We compare our method with RGB-based state-of-the-art 6D object pose estimation methods.

Results on LINEMOD dataset. We compare our method with the RGB-based two-stage 6D pose estimation methods BB8 [6], Tekin [16], HybridPose [11], PVNet [2] and DPOD [9] in terms of 2D projection metric and ADD metric as shown in Table 1 and Table 2.

The results represent that without pose refinement, our method achieves state-of-art performance in both indicators especially in ADD metric. After introducing attention mechanisms, our method is 2.55% higher than the current best method PVnet. Especially in the small-scale objects "ape", our ADD result increases by 17.05%. The adding of multi-constraints loss further increases the average ADD result of all 13 objects to 90.83%. The results are shown in "ours with L^*".

Results on Occlusion LINEMOD dataset. We compare our method with DPOD [9], Oberweger [20], Single-Stage [21], SegDriven [22], HybridPose [11] and PVNet

Table 1. 2D Projection metric on LINEMOD

Methods	w/o refinement					w/ refinement
	BB8 [6]	Tekin [16]	PVnet [2]	Ours (with L)	Ours (with L^*)	BB8 [6]
Ape	95.3	92.10	99.23	99.14	**99.33**	96.6
Benchvise	80.0	95.06	99.81	99.71	**99.90**	90.1
Cam	80.9	93.24	99.21	99.22	**99.41**	86.0
Can	84.1	97.44	**99.90**	99.80	99.80	91.2
Cat	97.0	97.41	99.30	**99.90**	99.90	98.8
Driller	74.1	79.41	96.92	**98.51**	97.61	80.9
Duck	81.2	94.65	98.02	**98.97**	98.59	92.2
Eggbox	87.9	90.33	99.34	**99.44**	99.44	91.0
Glue	89.0	96.53	98.45	98.84	**99.32**	92.3
Holepuncher	90.5	92.86	100.0	**100.0**	100.0	95.3
Iron	78.9	82.94	99.18	99.59	**99.69**	84.8
Lamp	74.4	76.87	98.27	98.18	**99.27**	75.8
Phone	77.6	86.07	99.42	**99.62**	99.62	85.3
Average	83.9	90.37	99.00	99.30	**99.38**	89.3

Table 2. ADD metric on LINEMOD.

Methods	w/o refinement						w/ refinement		
	BB8 [6]	Tekin [16]	DPOD [9]	PVnet [2]	Ours (with L)	Ours (with L∗)	BB8 [6]	DPOD [9]	HybridPose [11]
Ape	27.9	21.62	53.28	43.62	60.67	66.19	40.4	**87.73**	63.1
Benchwise	62.0	81.80	95.34	99.90	99.71	**100.0**	91.8	98.45	99.9
Cam	40.1	36.57	90.36	86.86	91.96	92.16	55.7	**96.07**	90.4
Can	48.1	68.80	94.10	95.47	94.29	97.64	64.1	**99.71**	98.5
Cat	45.2	41.82	60.38	79.34	85.03	87.62	62.6	**94.71**	89.4
Driller	58.6	63.51	97.72	96.43	97.52	98.61	74.4	**98.80**	98.5
Duck	32.8	27.23	66.01	52.58	56.90	62.44	44.3	**86.29**	65.0
Eggbox	40.0	69.58	99.72	99.15	99.34	99.91	57.8	99.91	**100.0**
Glue	27.0	80.02	93.83	95.66	95.37	96.04	41.2	96.82	**98.8**

(*continued*)

Table 2. (*continued*)

Methods	w/o refinement						w/ refinement		
	BB8 [6]	Tekin [16]	DPOD [9]	PVnet [2]	Ours (with L)	Ours (with L *)	BB8 [6]	DPOD [9]	HybridPose [11]
Holepuncher	42.4	42.63	65.83	81.92	83.73	85.92	67.2	86.87	**89.7**
Iron	67.0	74.97	99.80	98.88	98.98	99.28	84.7	**100.0**	100.0
Lamp	39.9	71.11	88.11	99.33	99.14	**99.62**	76.5	96.84	99.5
Phone	35.2	47.74	74.24	92.41	92.03	**95.39**	54.0	94.69	94.9
Average	43.6	55.95	82.98	86.27	88.82	90.83	62.7	**95.15**	91.3

[2] on Occlusion LINEMOD dataset in terms of ADD metric. The results are shown in Table 3. The results show that our method improves the accuracy of ADD by 3.86% compared with PVnet. It confirms the validity of attention mechanisms and constraints strategy. The attention mechanisms improve the final 6D pose estimation results under severe occlusion conditions. The qualitative results are shown in Fig. 3.

Table 3. ADD metric on occlusion LINEMOD.

Methods	w/o refinement							w/ refinement	
	Oberweger [20]	SegDriven [22]	DPOD [9]	Single-Stage [21]	PVnet [2]	Ours (with L)	Ours (with L *)	DPOD [9]	HybridPose [11]
Ape	17.6	12.1		19.2	15.81	25.21	26.32		20.9
Can	53.6	39.9		65.1	63.3	67.77	69.84		75.3
Cat	3.31	8.2		18.9	16.68	22.07	22.41		24.9
Driller	62.4	45.2		69.0	65.65	64.83	69.03		70.2
Duck	19.2	17.2		25.3	25.24	28.05	31.15		27.9
Eggbox	25.9	22.1		52.0	50.17	40.43	46.21		52.4
Glue	39.6	35.8		51.4	49.62	45.96	44.19		53.8
Holepuncher	21.3	36.0		45.6	39.67	45.44	47.85		54.2
Average	30.4	27.0	32.79	43.3	40.77	42.47	44.63	47.25	47.5

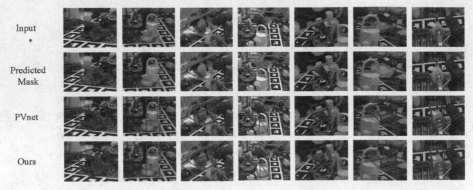

Fig. 3. Some visualization results of predicted pose and mask of our method on Occlusion LINEMOD comparing with PVnet.

4.5 Ablation Study

In order to compare the effects of different components in our proposed method, we design ablation experiments then test them on LINEMOD and Occlusion LINEMOD. The results are shown in Table 4.

Table 4. Ablation study on the combination of 2 attention modules.

Methods	LINEMOD	Occlusion LINEMOD
PVnet [2]	86.27	40.77
Ours + DenseASPP	88.01	41.96
Ours + DenseASPP + CCA	**88.82**	**42.47**

Attention mechanism ablation experiment. We design ablation experiments for the synergistic effects of different attention mechanisms. The results prove that the best effect is achieved by the simultaneous application of the two attention mechanisms.

As shown in the results in Table 4, the simultaneous application of the two attention mechanisms to our network maximize the effect of 6D object pose estimation.

The performance of the strategy acting on PVnet is shown in Table 5.

Table 5. Ablation study on multi-constraints loss function.

Methods	LINEMOD	Occlusion LINEMOD
PVnet [2]	86.27	40.77
Ours(with L)	88.82	42.47
Ours(with L + L_{gra})	89.97	44.29
Ours(with L^*)	**90.83**	**44.63**

Multi-constraints loss ablation experiment. We design ablation experiment to evaluate the impact of the multi-constraints loss function. After adding the multi-constraints loss function, the effect is significantly improved. It is verified that the multi-constraints loss function improves the accuracy of 6D pose estimation.

5   Conclusion

We propose an attention guided multi constraint 6D pose estimation network based on pixel-by-pixel voting. We introduce DenseASPP and CCA attention modules into the appropriate positions of encoding-decoding structure network to improve the accuracy of output predictions, add distance weighted unit vector length and unit included angle vector length into the loss function to regularize the unit vector field prediction. Experiments on LINEMOD and Occlusion LINEMOD show that our method has occlusion robustness and reaches higher accuracy of 6D pose estimation than the most advanced methods based on voting strategy without pose refinement.

Although our method improves the accuracy of 6D object pose estimation under occlusion and other harsh conditions, it is very dependent on the annotation information provided by the dataset, while the ground truth annotation information is difficult to obtain under many conditions and our method cannot estimate the 6D pose of category-level objects. Therefore, we will focus on exploring the performance of attention mechanisms and dense pixel voting methods in the field of pose estimation without CAD model and category-level 6D pose estimation.

Acknowledgements. Supported by Nation Natural Science Foundation of China (61873008) and Beijing Natural Science Foundation (4192010).

References

1. Lepetit, V., Moreno-Noguer, F., Fua, P.: Epnp: An accurate o (n) solution to the pnp problem. Int. J. Comput. Vision **81**(2), 155–166 (2009). https://doi.org/10.1007/s11263-008-0152-6

2. Peng, S., Liu, Y., Huang, Q., Zhou, X., Bao, H.: PVnet: pixel-wise voting network for 6dof pose estimation. In: Proceedings of the IEEE/CVF Conference on Computer Vision and Pattern Recognition, pp. 4561–4570 (2019). https://doi.org/10.48550/arXiv.1812.11788

3. Ronneberger, O., Fischer, P., Brox, T.: U-Net: convolutional networks for biomedical image segmentation. In: International Conference on Medical Image Computing and Computer-Assisted Intervention, pp. 234–241 (2015). https://doi.org/10.1007/978-3-319-24574-4_28

4. Yang, M., Yu, K., Zhang, C., Li, Z., Yang, K.: Denseaspp for semantic segmentation in street scenes. In: Proceedings of the IEEE Conference on Computer Vision and Pattern Recognition, pp. 3684–3692 (2018). https://doi.org/10.1109/CVPR.2018.00388

5. Wang, H., Cao, P., Wang, J., Zaiane, O.R.: Uctransnet: rethinking the skip connections in U-Net from a channel-wise perspective with transformer. In: Proceedings of the AAAI Conference on Artificial Intelligence, vol. 36(3), pp. 2441–2449 (2022). https://doi.org/10.48550/arXiv.2109.04335

6. Xiang, Y., Schmidt, T., Narayanan, V., Fox, D.: Posecnn: a convolutional neural network for 6D object pose estimation in cluttered scenes. arXiv preprint arXiv:1711.00199 (2017). https://doi.org/10.48550/arXiv.1711.00199

7. Kehl, W., Manhardt, F., Tombari, F., Ilic, S., Navab, N.: SSD-6D: Making RGB-based 3D detection and 6D pose estimation great again. In: Proceedings of the IEEE International Conference on Computer Vision, pp. 1521–1529 (2017). https://doi.org/10.48550/arXiv.1711.10006

8. Bukschat, Y., Vetter, M.: EfficientPose: an efficient, accurate and scalable end-to-end 6D multi object pose estimation approach. arXiv preprint arXiv:2011.04307 (2020). https://doi.org/10.48550/arXiv.2011.04307

9. Zakharov, S., Shugurov, I., Ilic, S.: DPOD: 6D pose object detector and refiner. In: Proceedings of the IEEE/CVF International Conference on Computer Vision, pp. 1941–1950 (2019). https://doi.org/10.1109/ICCV.2019.00203

10. Wang, G., Manhardt, F., Tombari, F., Ji, X.: GDR-Net: geometry-guided direct regression network for monocular 6D object pose estimation. In: Proceedings of the IEEE/CVF Conference on Computer Vision and Pattern Recognition, pp. 16611–16621 (2021). https://doi.org/10.1109/CVPR46437.2021.01634

11. Song, C., Song, J., Huang, Q.: Hybridpose: 6D object pose estimation under hybrid representations. In: Proceedings of the IEEE/CVF Conference on Computer Vision and Pattern Recognition, pp. 431–440 (2020). https://doi.org/10.1109/CVPR42600.2020.00051

12. He, K., Zhang, X., Ren, S., Sun, J.: Deep residual learning for image recognition. In: Proceedings of the IEEE Conference on Computer Vision and Pattern Recognition, pp. 770–778 (2016). https://doi.org/10.1109/CVPR.2016.90

13. Chen, L.C., Papandreou, G., Schroff, F., Adam, H.: Rethinking atrous convolution for semantic image segmentation. arXiv preprint arXiv:1706.05587 (2017). https://doi.org/10.48550/arXiv.1706.05587

14. Hinterstoisser, S., et al.: Model based training, detection and pose estimation of texture-less 3D objects in heavily cluttered scenes. In: Asian Conference on Computer Vision, pp. 548–562. Springer, Berlin, Heidelberg (2012). https://doi.org/10.1007/978-3-642-37331-2_42

15. Brachmann, E., Krull, A., Michel, F., Gumhold, S., Shotton, J., Rother, C.: Learning 6D object pose estimation using 3D object coordinates. In: European Conference on Computer Vision, pp. 536–551. Springer, Cham (2014). https://doi.org/10.1007/978-3-319-10605-2_35

16. Tekin, B., Sinha, S.N., Fua, P.: Real-time seamless single shot 6D object pose prediction. In: Proceedings of the IEEE Conference on Computer Vision and Pattern Recognition, pp. 292–301 (2018). https://doi.org/10.1109/CVPR.2018.00038

17. Brachmann, E., Michel, F., Krull, A., Yang, M.Y., Gumhold, S.: Uncertaintydriven 6D pose estimation of objects and scenes from a single RGB image. In: Proceedings of the IEEE

Conference on Computer Vision and Pattern Recognition, pp. 3364–3372 (2016). https://doi.org/10.1109/CVPR.2016.366

18. Dwibedi, D., Misra, I., Hebert, M.: Cut, paste and learn: surprisingly easy synthesis for instance detection. In: Proceedings of the IEEE International Conference on Computer Vision, pp. 1301–1310 (2017). https://doi.org/10.48550/arXiv.1708.01642

19. Xiao, J., Hays, J., Ehinger, K.A., Oliva, A., Torralba, A.: Sun database: large-scale scene recognition from abbey to zoo. In: 2010 IEEE Computer Society Conference on Computer Vision and Pattern Recognition, pp. 3485–3492. IEEE (2010). https://doi.org/10.1109/CVPR.2010.5539970

20. Oberweger, M., Rad, M., Lepetit, V.: Making deep heatmaps robust to partial occlusions for 3D object pose estimation. In: Proceedings of the European Conference on Computer Vision (ECCV), pp. 119–134 (2018). https://doi.org/10.1007/978-3-030-01267-0_8

21. Hu, Y., Fua, P., Wang, W., Salzmann, M.: Single-stage 6D object pose estimation. In: Proceedings of the IEEE/CVF Conference on Computer Vision and Pattern Recognition, pp. 2930–2939 (2020). https://doi.org/10.1109/CVPR42600.2020.00300

22. Hu, Y., Hugonot, J., Fua, P., Salzmann, M.: Segmentation-driven 6D object pose estimation. In: Proceedings of the IEEE/CVF Conference on Computer Vision and Pattern Recognition, pp. 3385–3394 (2019). https://doi.org/10.1109/CVPR.2019.00350

Design of Intra-oral Radiograph Assisted Robot Based on Face Recognition

Xiaolong Hao[1,2(✉)], Qiang Cheng[1,2], Chengru Jia[1], He Huang[1,2], Shuai Zhao[1,2], and Yi Wang[3]

[1] Institute of Advanced Manufacturing and Intelligent Technology, Beijing University of Technology, Beijing 100124, China
haoxiaolong@emails.bjut.edu.cn

[2] Beijing Key Laboratory of Advanced Manufacturing Technology, Beijing University of Technology, Beijing 100124, China

[3] Department of Stomotology, General Hospital of the PLA, Beijing, People's Republic of China
wangyi301@126.com

Abstract. To ensure the high quality and stability of oral diagnosis and treatment images. It is required that the position of the X-ray ball tube is accurate during the shooting process. The artificial difference should be eliminated. In order to avoid cross infection between doctors and patients, an overall solution of intra-oral radiograph assisted robot (IRAR) was proposed, including face recognition, camera calibration, end effector spatial positioning and robot-oral interaction. The working environment and mechanism kinematics of IRAR were analyzed. Based on the establishment of binocular vision calibration system, a face recognition algorithm aided image method was proposed. The interaction model between virtual image and robot pose was analyzed. By analyzing the function of the robot end effector, the related parameter requirements of the end effector were established. Finally, the imaging work area planning scheme of the imaging robot was obtained. Through the interaction between the robot and the oral cavity, the non-contact dental medical images were photographed and disinfected. The repeated positioning accuracy of IRAR system shall not be greater than 1 mm. The average error is 0.5 mm. The experiment proved that IRAR can finish the shooting task smoothly and accurately.

Keywords: Face recognition · Intra-oral radiograph robot · Interactive implementation · Visual positioning

1 Introduction

With the remarkable progress of robot system, medical robots have gradually become professional service robots, playing an increasingly important role in hospitals, clinics, families and other medical scenes [1]. The first medical surgical robot was produced in the 1980s [2]. Since then, medical surgical robot technology has been widely recognized. Extensive research and applications have been carried out in various fields of medicine. After entering the 21st century, medical surgical robot technology can be roughly divided

A. Ronzhin et al. (Eds.): ICR 2022, LNCS 13719, pp. 48–58, 2022.
https://doi.org/10.1007/978-3-031-23609-9_5

into four directions based on the development and application of robot technology. Medical surgical robot technology was based on industrial robot platform, special medical surgical robot technology [3], small modular medical surgical robot technology [4] and telesurgical medical robot technology [5].

But now, did not focus on the research of oral medical robot technology to assist in taking intra-oral radiograph. In order to promote the rapid development of intra-oral radiograph process with more efficient, accurate and low-cost [6, 7]. Akhoondali [8] proposed an automatic tooth segmentation method based on region growth. Keyhaninejad [9] proposed a level set model based on 3D regions to extract teeth. Keustermans [10] proposed a method of interactive segmentation of three-dimensional teeth using a graph cutting algorithm. Barone [11] proposed a new framework to simulate the three-dimensional shape information of a single tooth in a CT image. This method did not directly process the three-dimensional volume data, but outlined the two-dimensional contours of the target teeth from a set of projection images. Then he used the contour to perform 3D tooth modeling. And finally he got the tooth segmentation results. The Renaissance robot manufactured by Israel Mazor Robotics company used the intraoperative 2D image obtained by the C-arm X-ray machine to perform real-time registration with the preoperative 3D graphics, which greatly improved the accuracy [12].

However, no auxiliary oral imaging diagnosis and treatment robot has been developed to reduce medical exposure. Therefore, the design and development of intra-oral radiograph assisted robot is an important part of the research. Based on this, the robot system is designed and analyzed, which can assist the medical process, expand the ability of medical personnel, reduce unnecessary human and resource investment. It can improve the efficiency of the medical process or medical production process.

2   Design of Intra-oral Radiograph Robot System

2.1   Overall Design Scheme

The Intra-oral Radiograph Assisted Robot based on face recognition (IRAR) combined robotic technology with the expert knowledge system of oral medical treatment. It could realize the process of non-contact mechanized auxiliary function. It mainly included patient face recognition, binocular camera calibration, lesion space location and robot interaction.

The overall design of IRAR was proposed on the basis of oral medical treatment and non-contact. First, the kinematics of IRAR was analyzed with the goal of operating space accessibility and high movement flexibility. Then the calibration of the binocular camera, the face recognition of the patient and the optimization of the position of IRAR were completed. Finally, the stable interaction of the robot with the goal of stability and reducing medical exposure were realized, as shown in Fig. 1.

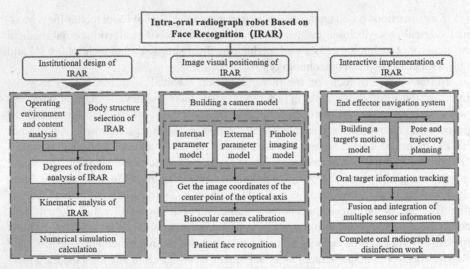

Fig. 1. IRAR overall structure composition.

2.2 Kinematics Model of IRAR

The end clamp of the mechanism has 6 degrees of freedom in space. When a certain constraint is given, the degree of freedom of the object will be reduced accordingly. But the remaining actual degrees of freedom are not completely free. In medical space motion, the maximum number of independent motions of the end manipulator is six, which are respectively rotated along three coordinate axes and about three coordinate axes.

The complete motion of the IRAR appears as an independent six-dimensional motion in space. The basic unit of this six-dimensional motion is called the standard basis of the degree of freedom of the mechanism. And it is represented by a screw as:

$$\mathcal{S}_1 = (1\,0\,0\,;0\,0\,0);\mathcal{S}_2 = (0\,1\,0\,;0\,0\,0);\mathcal{S}_3 = (0\,0\,1\,;0\,0\,0), \tag{1}$$
$$\mathcal{S}_4 = (0\,0\,0\,;1\,0\,0);\mathcal{S}_5 = (0\,0\,0\,;0\,1\,0);\mathcal{S}_6 = (0\,0\,0\,;0\,0\,1).$$

According to the definition and establishment method of the Jacobian matrix of the tandem robot, the singularity type is studied. The IRAR speed Jacobian matrix can be directly derived from the robot's screw motion Eq. [12]. The quantity is expressed as:

$$\mathcal{S}^i = \begin{pmatrix} s^i \\ r_i \times s^i + h_i s^i \end{pmatrix} (i = 1,2,\cdots,n), \tag{2}$$

where r_i is an arbitrary point on the axis of rotation, s^i is a unit vector representing the direction of the axis of rotation, and h_i is the pitch.

When using the screw of a pair of motion to characterize, only kinematic equivalent substitution is needed. For example, the cylindrical pair can be written as a combination of a rotating pair and a coaxial moving pair.

Consider the IRAR is an open-chain system consisting of 6 degrees of freedom consisting of 6 links connected in series to the base in sequence, as shown in Fig. 2.

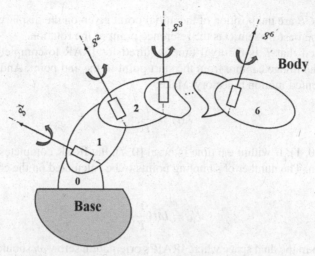

Fig. 2. Modeling of screw degrees of freedom in IRAR.

The relative motion between the 6 links can be represented by 6 angle line vectors: $\omega_1 \mathcal{S}^1, \omega_2 \mathcal{S}^2, \dots, \omega_6 \mathcal{S}^6$

For IRAR, the motion of the end manipulator can be considered as a linear combination of the spirals of each kinematic pair:

$$\vec{V}^b = \begin{bmatrix} \vec{\omega}_n \\ \vec{v}_n \end{bmatrix} = \sum_{i=1}^n \dot{\theta}_i \, \mathcal{S}^i{}_b = \left(\mathcal{S}^1{}_b \ \mathcal{S}^2{}_b \ \cdots \ \mathcal{S}^n{}_b \right) \begin{pmatrix} \dot{\theta}_1 \\ \dot{\theta}_2 \\ \cdots \\ \dot{\theta}_n \end{pmatrix} \tag{3}$$

Simplify Eq. (3) as:

$$\vec{V}^b = J^b(\theta)\dot{\theta}, \tag{4}$$

where $J^b(\theta) = [\mathcal{S}^1{}_b \ \mathcal{S}^2{}_b \ \cdots \ \mathcal{S}^n{}_b]$, $\dot{\theta} = [\dot{\theta}_1 \ \dot{\theta}_2 \ \cdots \ \dot{\theta}_n]^T$. J^b represents the Jacobian matrix of the end effector in the tool coordinate system. $\vec{V}^b$ represents the generalized space velocity of the end effector. $\dot{\theta}$ is the joint velocity. And $\mathcal{S}^i_b$ is the Plucker coordinate of the i joint in the current configuration.

2.3 Analysis of Motion Path for the IRAR

The posture of the IRAR is the position and posture of the end-sensitive camera. We can use the angular displacement vector ω to describe the orientation of robot. Let θ be the equivalent rotation angle of the Cartesian coordinate system around the instantaneous axis. κ represents the unit vector of the instantaneous axis of rotation in the base system. Angular displacement vector $\omega = \theta \cdot \kappa$.

According to the definition of the screw, it can be proved that the orientation vector of the equivalent angular displacement. Vector is the screw expressed as:

$$\omega = \omega + \lambda \vec{OA} \times \omega = \omega + \lambda \vec{OB} \times \omega, \tag{5}$$

where $\overrightarrow{OA}$ and $\overrightarrow{OB}$ are the position of the initial point given on the displacement vector. The origin of the base system O is the reference point of the rotation.

It is assumed that T is the total time required for IRAR to complete the overall movement of the image capture from the start point to the end point. And t is the time from the segmented motion trajectory. Make:

$$\lambda(t) = \frac{t}{T}, \tag{6}$$

where $\lambda(t) \in [0, 1]$. If within the time interval $[0, t]$, the IRAR completes the imaging of an oral lesion. The number of sampling points to be calculated on the entire working track:

$$N_0 = Int(\frac{t}{T}). \tag{7}$$

The point A in the dual space where IRAR's orientation screw ω_i should be assumed to move along a continuous trajectory:

$$\omega_i = f(\hat{q}) = \omega_i + \lambda S_i^0, \hat{q} = \hat{q}[\lambda(t)], \tag{8}$$

where q is a dual function of $\lambda(t)$. The orientation vector ω_i is the free vector on the instantaneous axis of rotation. Only when the position of A_i point is determined. It will be uniquely positioned on the axis. The positioning of ω_i in space can be given by the position vector r_{i_p} of A_i on the instantaneous rotation axis, $S_i^0 = r_{i_p} \times \omega_i$, then

$$\omega_i = [\omega_{x_i}, \omega_{y_i}, \omega_{z_i}] \begin{bmatrix} i \\ j \\ k \end{bmatrix} + \lambda \begin{bmatrix} i & j & k \\ x_{p_i} & y_{p_i} & z_{p_i} \\ \omega_{x_i} & \omega_{y_i} & \omega_{z_i} \end{bmatrix}, \tag{9}$$

where x_{p_i}, y_{p_i} and z_{p_i} are the coordinate vector ω_i of the imaging camera at the end of the IRAR relative to the coordinates of the P_i point on the axis relative to the base system. The above formula is the orientation rotation of robot.$\omega_{x_i}, \omega_{y_i}$ and ω_{z_i} determine the end-sensitivity of the robot. The camera's orientation track is derived from x_{p_i}, y_{p_i} and z_{p_i}

The ideal position and posture trajectory of the patient's oral lesions are set. Moreover, the posture screw of the robot in the dual space can be determined by substituting in the above formula.

3   Image Visual Positioning of IRAR

3.1   Calibration of Parameters Inside and Outside the Camera

In order to determine the correlation between the three-dimensional geometric position of a point on the patient's oral tooth surface and its corresponding point in the image. A geometric model of the camera imaging needs to be established. And the camera parameters are solved for camera calibration. Camera calibration is to eliminate distortion caused by camera lens. The parameters generated by calibration include camera internal parameters and camera external parameters. The accuracy directly affects subsequent results. In order to obtain the unique solution of the internal parameters, multiple calibration plate images are needed for joint solution [13]:

$$D(c) = \sum_{j=1}^{n}\sum\sum_{i=1}^{m} \|P_{i,j} - Q_i(p_i, c)\|^2 \to D(c)_{min}. \tag{10}$$

$P_{i,j}$ is the central coordinate in the image coordinate system. $Q_i(p_i, c)$ is the coordinate calculated by projection. The first consecutive symbol on the right side of the equation is for multiple calibration images.

The more images, the higher the accuracy. The second consecutive plus symbol is for several marks on the calibration plate, using Euclidean distance. When calculating this optimization problem, the initial values of the parameters in the camera need to be provided. The initial values are determined according to the parameters of the camera and the lens.

3.2 Binocular Vision Calibration

The calibration of IRAR binocular vision system is to obtain the pose matrix of the robot coordinate system relative to the virtual image coordinate system. It is necessary to establish the camera T, the robot base R, the end calibration plate coordinate system C, the virtual image coordinate system V and the oral calibration plate coordinate system H, as shown in Fig. 3.

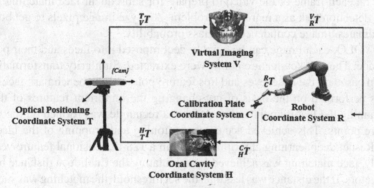

Fig. 3. IRAR system based on binocular camera calibration.

Binocular vision calibration mainly uses coordinate transformation to obtain unknown parameters. Equivalent relationship of coordinate transformation:

$$_V^R T = _C^R T \cdot _H^C T \cdot _T^H T \cdot _V^T T \tag{11}$$

Among them, $_V^R T$ described the pose relationship of the virtual image relative to the robot in the real world, which was the quantity to be determined. $_C^R T$ described the pose relationship of the robot base relative to the end calibration plate. $_H^C T$ described the pose relationship of the robot end relative to the oral calibration plate. $^H_T T$ described the pose relationship of the oral calibration plate relative to the camera, which was an external parameter of the camera. $^T_V T$ described the pose relationship of the camera relative to the virtual image coordinate system.

In order to convert the pixel coordinates of oral medical images into spatial poses, a series of coordinate transformations are required. During the calibration, the coordinate system of the calibration plate in the first calibration image has been determined as the reference coordinate system. Convert feature points in the image to points in the reference coordinate system. The relative pose of the coordinate system of the oral cavity and the reference coordinate system is determined. Use the calibration result to perform coordinate transformation. Convert the end camera pose to robot coordinates using the equivalent formula. The end pose is sent to the robot controller through Ethernet communication. When the target pose of the robot is known, the joint angles of the robot are obtained by inverse solution based on kinematics. The robot is guided to move to the target position to work.

3.3 Facial Feature Recognition

Based on the deep learning algorithm, the functions of image preprocessing, patient face detection, and patient face matching were realized.

Image preprocessing serves two purposes. On the one hand, it is to improve the quality of the encoded video. On the other hand, the influence of environmental factors can be reduced. Use the more efficient deep learning model YOLO to perform face target detection on each frame of the video to prepare for subsequent face matching. YOLO treats the detection task as a regression problem. Analyze image pixels to get bounding box coordinates, image confidence and class probability.

With YOLO, each image can be quickly decomposed into faces and their positions in the image. Then 68 key feature points were extracted. Similarity transformation was performed based on the nose, eyes and lips feature points of the benchmark face. Alignment was performed on the basis of not changing the important features of the face. After obtaining the feature points of each face, a rectangle was formed on the basis of the feature points. This achieved accurate positioning and cropping of the face. Then used the Resnet deep learning algorithm to obtain a 128-dimensional feature vector.

Finally, face matching was achieved by calculating the Euclidean distance between feature vectors. If the distance was less than the set threshold, the matching was successful for the same face. Otherwise it did not match, for different faces. After matching, the patient's medical image information was automatically imported into the navigation system, as shown in Fig. 4.

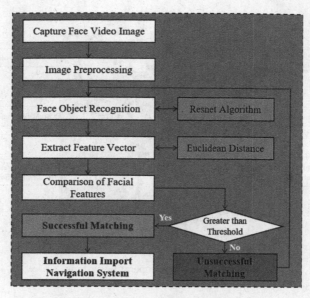

Fig. 4. Face recognition algorithm flow.

4 Interactive Implementation

Cross-infection in dental clinics is mainly related to factors such as operating standards, disinfection behavior, use of disposable instruments, and out-patient environment. The medical operation equipment and treatment materials used will contact the patient's oral saliva, blood, and mucosal tissues, etc., on a larger and more frequent basis. These body fluids contain a large number of pathogenic bacteria. There may also be pathogenic bacteria in medical personnel and various treatment devices.

4.1 Multi-sensor Information Fusion Control

IRAR aims to cross integrate robot technology and expert knowledge system of oral medicine. The process mainly includes spatial localization of oral lesions, ball tube trajectory tracking and interaction between doctors and robots. The image aided robot system is mainly composed of four parts: robot, vision system, control platform and dental X-ray machine.

The vision system mainly obtains the patients' maxillofacial spatial position. Use the calibration plate to calibrate the patient's maxillofacial region. Capture and locate the patient's maxillofacial region in real time. The maxillofacial position information is transmitted to the control terminal. The control terminal processes and displays the information are collected by the vision system. And it transmits the maxillofacial position information to the manipulator. The mechanical arm clamps the ball tube of the X-ray machine to the designated shooting position through track tracking control, as shown in Fig. 5.

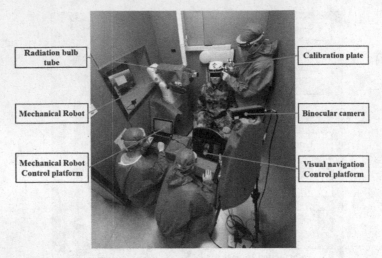

Fig. 5. IRAR control operating system.

In terms of completing the practical system of IRAR, the degree of freedom of the robot has reached 6 degrees of freedom. The task requires that the positioning error accuracy is less than or equal to 1 mm. The average error accuracy is 0.5 mm after the third-party test, meeting the project requirements.

4.2 IRAR Kinematics Experiment

Suppose that the time for IRAR to complete a routine positioning path is 120 s.
The experimental data are shown in Fig. 6.

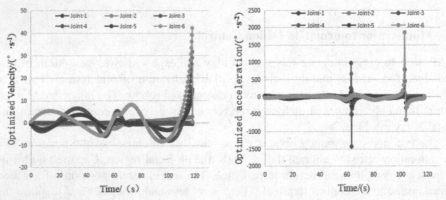

Fig. 6. The kinematics of IRAR is analyzed. The left figure shows the speed analysis of each joint. The right figure shows the acceleration analysis of each joint.

In the velocity image, the velocity of each joint is smooth and continuous. In the acceleration image, the acceleration of joints 3 and 6 has a large abrupt change, while the acceleration of other joints is relatively stable. Since joints 3 and 6 bear the main load torque, large acceleration mutation will not affect the stability of the robot. And it meets the needs of task.

5 Conclusion

In this paper, the robot innovatively integrated image recognition, camera calibration, face recognition and other technologies based on screw theory. The rapid identification, precise positioning and flexible follow-up contact of IRAR were realized. It provides a theoretical basis for the coordinated control of multi-sensor in the process of oral medical radiography. A visual and touchable motion planning system was established. The stable interaction between the robot and the oral cavity was realized. And the patient receives low radiation does to obtain accurate image. Finally, the velocity and acceleration data of the robot were analyzed to meet the needs of oral medical radiography tasks.

The IRAR requires that the positioning error accuracy is less than or equal to 1mm. The average error accuracy is 0.5 mm. It proves the engineering practical value of the related technology research in this paper.

Acknowledgement. This work was supported by the grants of the National Natural Science Foundation of China (51975012), Beijing Nova Programme Interdisciplinary Cooperation Project (Z191100001119010), China Postdoctoral Science Foundation (2021M700301) and the 23rd Spark Fund Project of BJUT (XH-2022-03-19).

References

1. Niu, G., Pan, B., Zhang, F., Feng, H., Fu, Y.: Kinematic analysis of a novel uncoupled and isotropic 2-degree-of-freedom parallel mechanism. Adv. Mech. Eng. **8**(3), 1–17 (2016). https://doi.org/10.1177/1687814016638040
2. Kwoh, Y.S., Hou, J., Jonckheere, E.A., Hayati, S.: A robot with improved absolute positioning accuracy for CT guided stereotactic brain surgery. IEEE Trans. Biomed. Eng. **35**(2), 153–160 (1988). https://doi.org/10.1109/10.1354
3. Varma, T.R.K., Eldridge, P.: Use of the NeuroMate stereotactic robot in a frameless mode for functional neurosurgery. Int. J. Med. Robotics Comput. Assist. Surg. **2**(2), 107–113 (2006). https://doi.org/10.1002/rcs.88
4. Lieberman, I.H., et al.: Bone-mounted miniature robotic guidance for pedicle screw and translaminar facet screw placement: Part I - Technical development and a test case result. Neurosurgery **59**(3), 641–650 (2006). https://doi.org/10.1227/01.NEU.0000229055.00829.5B
5. Gharagozloo, F., Margolis, M., Tempesta, B.: Robot-assisted thoracoscopic lobectomy for early-stage lung cancer. Ann. Thorac. Surg. **85**(6), 1880–1886 (2008). https://doi.org/10.1016/j.athoracsur.2008.02.085
6. Tim, J., Brägger, U.: Digital vs. conventional implant prosthetic workflows: a cost/time analysis. Clin. Oral Implants Res. **26**(12), 1430–1435 (2015). https://doi.org/10.1111/clr.12476

7. Yuzbasioglu, E., Kurt, H., Turunc, R., Bilir, H.: Comparison of digital and conventional impression techniques: evaluation of patients' perception, treatment comfort, effectiveness and clinical outcomes. BMC Oral Health **14**(1), 10 (2014). https://doi.org/10.1186/1472-6831-14-10

8. Akhoondali, H., Zoroofi, R.A., Shirani, G.: Rapid automatic segmentation and visualization of teeth in CT-scan data. J. Appl. Sci. **9**(11), 2031–2044 (2009). https://doi.org/10.3923/jas.2009.2031.2044

9. Keyhaninejad, S., Zoroofi, R.A., Setarehdan, S.K., Shirani, G.: Automated segmentation of teeth in multi-slice CT images. Int. J. Comput. Assist. Radiol. Surg. **3**(6), 339–344 (2006). https://doi.org/10.1007/s11548-008-0255-0

10. Hiramatsu, Y., Hotta, K., Imanishi, A., Matsuda, M., Terai, K.: Cell image segmentation by integrating multiple CNNs. In.: Proceedings of the IEEE Conference on Computer Vision and Pattern Recognition Workshops, vol. 93(6), pp. 2286–2292 (2018). https://doi.org/10.1109/CVPRW.2018.00296

11. Barone, S., Paoli, A., Razionale, A.V.: CT segmentation of dental shapes by anatomy-driven reformation imaging and B-spline modelling. Int. J. Numer. Method Biomed. Eng. **32**(6), 1–17 (2016). https://doi.org/10.1002/cnm.2747

12. Merlet, J.P., Clément, G., Tian, H.: Parallel mechanisms. In: Springer Handbook of Robotics. Springer, Cham (2016)

13. Soyel, H., Demirel, H.: Facial expression recognition based on discriminative scale invariant feature transform. Electron. Lett. **46**(5), 343–345 (2010). https://doi.org/10.1049/el.2010.0092

Moving⁺: Semantic Scene Classification on YOLOv5

Yue Zhang[1] , Yehui Wang[1,2] , Xin Li[1,3](✉) , and Viswanath Goud Bellam[3,4]

[1] Guangdong University of Petrochemical Technology, Maoming 525011, China
lixin@gdupt.edu.cn
[2] South China University of Technology, Guangzhou, China
[3] Gaitech Intelligence, Shanghai, China
[4] China University of Mining and Technology, Xuzhou 100083, China

Abstract. For intelligent moving agents, robots especially, it is important to be aware of the surroundings to help analyze the situation and what might happen in the future. Scene classification is a hotspot with the development of moving agent. Different from the approach directly solving the problem caused by moving platform, our approach does the classification on object detection results from YOLOv5, which is with meaningful and semantic information. Since YOLOv5 works on frames in video, with state of art detect speed and accuracy in area of object detection, it can perfectly avoid performance degradation caused by the moving platform. By further integrating with TF-IDF, five ways to train the model are obtained, the semantic representation sequence is feed into LSTM to handle the temporal relations among frames. Our dataset was consisted with three parts: moving+ dataset: taken from a mobile robot platform, extension dataset: downloaded from internet by keywords retrieval and mixed dataset: mix both of them. Experiment results on three datasets prove the effectiveness of our approach particularly in the moving+ dataset and mixed dataset, our approach shows a high recognize accuracy up to 93% and 92%.

Keywords: Moving agent · Scene classification · YOLOv5 · LSTM · TF-IDF

1 Introduction

1.1 A Subsection Sample

For an intelligent moving robot, scene information can help to analyze what the surrounding objects are and what might happen in the future. Robots can respond to the environment timely and intelligently with a fast scene recognition algorithm. An autonomous mobile robot, for example, may pass through different places on the way to its destination, so it should change its actions to accomplish tasks or adapt to the dynamically changing surroundings along the way. It can show more robustness than just remembering its schedule. Scene recognition can provide some vital information about the environment from an image or a video that helps the intelligent system to analyze the surroundings. It is also regarded as the prior knowledge for other advanced computer vision tasks such as image retrieval and object detection.

Traditional scene recognition algorithm relies on some hand-crafted vision features and has a low recognition precision and robustness. For the last few years, with the significant breakthrough of deep learning networks in the field of computer vision, researchers begin designing algorithms for the problem with deep learning network.

Object detector has made significant breakthroughs last few years like YOLO, but the accuracy of scene recognition has not been so drastically improved [1]. On the one hand, it is attributed to the semantic gap between traditional deep learning features and the meaning of the scene. On the other hand, the spatial layouts and context get more complicated in a scene recognition task, which means a higher robustness algorithm is required. Human beings can categorize the scene of an image by catching some high-level semantic information such as some discriminative objects and the high-level meaning pertaining to the scenes [2]. Object information can represent a scene regardless of the diversity of the perspective and the ray of an image and decrease the effect of spatial layout. For example, as is shown in Fig. 1, we can find tables, chairs and service windows from both perspectives and of course, the recognition result will be similar to an object-based scene recognition algorithm.

Fig. 1. Canteen from different perspectives.

We focus on the scene classification of a moving agent, in which, the platform is moving with an object in the scene may be also moving, that is the meaning of moving+ . In order to reduce the influence of moving platforms, such as camera shaking, we propose a two-stage scene recognition scheme on object detection. Besides, a video consists of a sequence of scene frames with temporal information and the capacity of handling temporal information and a fast recognition speed is required.

In this paper, we follow the two-stage idea and propose a new video-based approach for semantic scene classification on YOLOv5. Our contributions can be summarized as follows:

1. We select YOLOv5 as an object detector in the first stage, not only for its fast speed and high accuracy but also for its processing of video as frame sequence, which can

minimize the influence of camera trembling and reduce the influence caused by the variant perspectives as shown in Fig. 1.

2. Based on the object information as category likelihood, location and size of object in each frame, we add a semantic embedding layer to fuse that information into a representation vector. Additionally, TF-IDF is also considered in the semantic embedding.

3. To capture the temporal information in the video, we further adopt LSTM as the final classifier.

The pipeline of the proposed method is showed in Fig. 2.

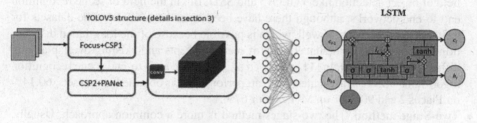

Fig. 2. Pipeline of the proposed method.

2 Related Work

Scene recognition methods can be mainly classified into two categories: hand- crafted feature methods and learning-based feature methods [3].

2.1 Hand-Crafted Method

Hand-crafted methods, inspired by prior knowledge, recognize scenes by some vision features such as SIFT points and spatial envelope attributes.

Holistic feature method: In the early 2000s, the Holistic feature method is the mainstream approach to scene recognition, which is conducted by some low-level visual features of an image. Typical holistic feature method, such as GIST [4], semantic typicality [5], CENTRIST [6], often has a fast inference speed but low accuracy. Although these features build a direct and visualized relation between image and semantic knowledge, these are not enough to generalize the whole scene and result a poor scene recognition performance.

Local feature method: To improve the recognition performance, plenty of researchers distracted their attention to local feature methods, especially after the proposal of the Bag-of-Visual-words [7] framework which was introduced to integrate a large number of local features into a fixed dimensions image representation. Local feature extraction methods include SIFT [8], HOG [9], OTC [10]. It is believed that the local features can provide more discriminative information and clues for scene recognition and are more robust than holistic features. But these kinds of features are still at a low semantic level and are hardly capable of scene recognition.

2.2 Learning-Based Feature Representation

Although hand-crafted features are proven to represent an image effectively, they are at a low semantic level [2]. The wide 'Semantic gap' between this feature and the meaning of the scenes limits their performance and robustness. A deep learning network can extract discriminative features adaptively and with the increase of the layer of the network, the semantic level increase. Two board categories are contained: end-to-end network and two-stage method.

- **End-to-End network.** An end-to-end network, which means we get the scene information from the input image directly, has been proven to be an excellent method in the field of object detection like YOLOv5 and SSD. But in the field of scene recognition end-to-end networks, although there have been some large-scale scene datasets for training, don't perform so well, which is possible because of the long-tailed distribution of scene images, the uncertainty of scene concepts and existing overlap among different categories [1]. In [11] proposed a CNN-based end- to-end scene recognition algorithm FOSNet with a state-of-the-art performance is obtained in two sets: 60.14% on Places 2 and 90.30% on MIT indoor 67%.
- **Two-Stage method.** The two-stages method is more a common approach. Usually, the two-stage method is consisted of a feature extractor and a classifier. The feature extractor is a deep learning network that needs to be trained independently and learn some features, such as spatial layout, discriminative region and object information [1]. In [12] proposed a two-stage scene recognition algorithm, which includes a encoder train by supervised contrastive learning to learning discriminative feature and a classifier using re-sampling or re-weighting, and outperforms existing methods that time.

3 Model Architecture

As shown in Fig. 2, our model consists of three board parts: a YOLOv5 model, a semantic embedding layer, and a LSTM classifier as below.

4 YOLOv5

YOLOv5 is a popular and widely used algorithm [13]. Inspired by the success of YOLOv5 [14], our model is based on YOLOv5, which can quick capture the object information based on video frame and provide robust semantic information for scene classification.

- **Backbone: Focus+CSP1.** YOLOv5 adopts focus and CSP1 to compose as backbone. In Fig. 3, it is worth to note that the focus layer can reorganize the pixel's order by slice and concatenation without any information loss. Additionally, Cross Stage Partial (CSP) is proposed to strengthen the network's ability to fuse features. Two branches of CSP structures as CSP1_x and CSP2_x are shown in Fig. 3, in which CBL means convolution, BN and Leaky RELU respectively. Compared with CSP2_x, CSP1_x adopts residual structure to increase the gradient value of back propagation between layers, which avoids the disappearance of gradient due to deepening of backbone network, i.e., the first row in Fig. 3.

- **Neck: CSP2+PANet.** Neck part in YOLOv5 adopts path aggregation network (PANet) structure based on CSP2_1, as shown in Fig. 4, which aims at boosting information flow by bottom-up path augmentation.

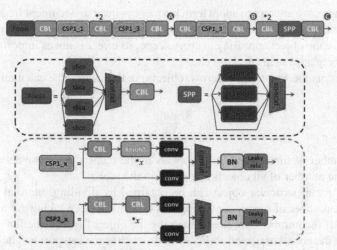

Fig. 3. The first diagrammatic sketch shows Backbone structure in YOLOv5, which is a modified FPN consisted of some CSP block, and the other shows two branch of CSP structure in YOLOv5 as CSP1_x and CSP2_x.

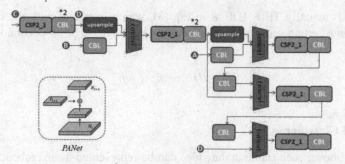

Fig. 4. Neck structure in YOLOv5 contains 3 outlets connected with up sampling for multi-scales detection with focal loss function in Head of YOLOv5.

4.1 Semantic Embedding Layer

By YOLOv5, we can extract semantic information as object category likelihood, location, and size of detected object. Since YOLOv5 works on frames in video, it can eliminate the impact of movement caused by mobile platform. However, a side shortcoming as sparse problem turns up. For instance, our object categories come from COCO dataset with 80 categories. While in one frame, only few objects can be found, and most categories are missed. This causes the sparse representation which is filled with zeros for the missing objects.

We add a semantic embedding layer to solve the sparse problem, which keeps a structure as multi-layer perceptron (MLP). It is worth to note that our MLP with smaller output than input, which also conducts a feature selection and compacts the representation tightly.

Furthermore, we attempt to adopt term frequency–inverse document frequency (TF-IDF) technique to reduce the effect noisy word, or noisy object. The key idea of TF-IDF here is that, for the object appearing in every scene, its effect is not as important as those objects that only appear in special scene.

TF represents the frequency of terms (objects) in the scene. The calculation formula of TF is:

$$tf_{ij} = \frac{n_{i,j}}{\sum_k n_{kj}},$$ (1)

$n_{i,j}$ is the number of times the object i appears in the scene d_j, and the denominator is the sum of the number of all objects appearing in the scene d_j.

The IDF for a particular object can be obtained by dividing the total number of scenes by the number of scenes containing that object, and then taking the logarithm of the quotient. If the number of scenes containing the object t is less, the IDF is larger. It indicates that the entry has a good ability to distinguish scene categories. The calculation formula of IDF is:

$$df_i = log\frac{|D|}{|\{j : t_i \in d_j\}|}.$$ (2)

TF-IDF is actually TF × IDF as in Eq. (3), which increases with the increase of proportion in a certain scene and decreases with the increase of proportion in the total scene.

$$TF - IDF = tf_{ij} \times idf_i.$$ (3)

4.2 LSTM Classifier

As analysis above, each frame in the video can be represented as an embedding vector and thus the whole video can be viewed as sequence information. By introducing input gate, i_t, forget gate f_t, output gate o_t in a cell (shown in Fig. 2), long short-term memory (LSTM) [15] provides an effective way to deal with sequence information. Through the setting of these gates, LSTM effectively solves the problem of gradient vanishing problem. This is the main reason to adopt LSTM as classifier here. The information entering into LSTM can be judged whether it is useful according to cell state, as shown below equation.

$$c_t = f_t \times c_{t-1} + i_t \times tanh(W_c \cdot [h_{t-1}, x_t] + b_c),$$ (4)

where *tanh* is activation function, and $\{W_c, b_c\}$. are parameters about cell state in LSTM. From Eq. (4), it can be seen that the information of cell state passes from previous state $t - 1$ to state t depending on forget gate f_t, input gate i_t, last cell output h_{t-1} and input x_t. The forget gate in the LSTM will refine the cell state by absorbing information from previous state c_{t-1}. By this equation, temporal information can be transmitted by c_{t-1} and h_{t-1} with the variation of t. The last frame output h_T seals all the information of preceding frames.

5 Experiments

5.1 Datasets

- **Moving+ Dataset.** The dataset is taken from a mobile robot platform (RIA E100 and RIA E100 system is based on ROS-kinetic on Ubuntu 16.04) shown in Fig. 5 with a Viper camera by us. Four scenes are collected: basketball courts (BC), campuses (CP), canteen (CT), a. laboratory (Lab). We record 68 videos, and each one length is about 30 s. The detail numbers are: 21 campus's videos, 14 laboratory's videos, 18 basketball court's videos and 15 canteen's videos. Example from each scene is listed in Fig. 6.
- **Extending Dataset.** This dataset downloads from internet by keywords retrieval. There are 56 videos, including 14 campus's videos, 9 laboratory's videos, 18 basketball court's videos and 15 canteen's videos. Since most of video from internet are recorded from static camera, pulsing our moving+ dataset, we verify our approach on the videos from dynamic and static platform.

Fig. 5. RIA E100 and Viper camera.

Fig. 6. Examples from moving+ dataset.

5.2 Implementation Details

We follow the setting in YOLOv5, which is as 640×400 pixels per frame, and the scale of the output as $3 \times 80 \times 450$. After detecting, the object confidence and the centre coordinate $\{x, y\}$ of the object provide meaningful semantic information, such as what and where it is. This information is not influenced by moving platform, which is important to our final accuracy. When more than one same object is detected, we only use the one with maximum confidence, since it is believed that the maximum one shows the more robustness than others.

5.3 Analysis and Comparisons

The experiments are conducted on moving + dataset, extending dataset and mixed dataset, which put the former two datasets together.

We firstly verify the effectiveness of YOLOv5 on moving platform. Figure 7 shows the middle object detection results on YOLOv5 for moving+ dataset. Since YOLOv5 converts video into a sequence of frame of image for detection, it can avoid the tremble impact caused by the dynamic platform. Furthermore, YOLOv5 are with quick speed and high accuracy of object detection. From Fig. 7, it can be seen that even small basketball in BC scene can be detected. It is a typical moving object taken by the moving platform.

Secondly, we prove the effectiveness of our approach on scene classification. Table 1 lists the comparison of different datasets with distinct approaches.

The output of YOLOv5 contains class information, confidence and position information of an object, which will utilized by followed semantic layer. Depending on the relationship among TF-IDF, object confidence and position information, we verify five different combination effectiveness in following experiments, which are as: A1 with (confidence information $\times$ TF-IDF) $\oplus$ position information; A2 with confidence information $\oplus$ position information $\oplus$ TF-IDF; A3 with confidence information $\oplus$ TF-IDF; A4 as confidence information $\oplus$ position information; A5 with only confidence information $\oplus$ means concatenation operation.

From the first block in Table 1, we can obtain the accuracy on moving+ dataset. By training and test on the same dataset, the performances of our approaches are about

Fig. 7. Object detection results on YOLOv5 for moving⁺ dataset.

Table 1. Accuracy comparison among different combinations with distinct datasets

	Moving⁺ dataset[b]					Extending dataset[b]					Mixed dataset[c]				
	CP	Lab	CT	BC	ALL	CP	Lab	CT	BC	ALL	CP	Lab	CT	BC	ALL
A1	1	1	1	0.75	0.93	0.29	0.67	0.67	0.83	0.63	1	0.83	0.83	0.71	0.85
A2	1	0.5	1	0.75	0.86	0.64	0.33	0.93	0.61	0.66	1	1	0.5	0.88	0.85
A3	1	0.75	1	0.5	0.86	0.14	0.56	0.8	0.5	0.5	0.88	1	0.89	1	0.92
A4	1	1	0.5	1	0.86	0.5	0.56	0.87	0.5	0.61	0.6	0.5	1	1	0.77
A5	0.75	1	1	0.75	0.71	0.29	0.22	0.93	0.78	0.52	1	0.5	1	1	0.92

[a]Randomly divided 80% and 20% as training data and test data separately.
[b]The same model as moving+ dataset and extending dataset as test data.

90%, and the best one achieves to 93% by A1 combination. In this case, TF-IDF as a weight vector can further improve the system performance, as shown in A1 and A2 results. It is worth to note that the intra- category difference is not vary large in moving+ dataset. Based on the semantic information from YOLOv5, our approach is proved to be effective for moving platform.

Keeping the same training model, we verify the performance of our approach on different test data. The second block on extending dataset shows the accuracy of different combinations. With different test conditions, it can be seen that the performances are mostly about 60%, which can prove the robustness of our approach to some extent. Among those results, CT is with the sound performance compared with other scenes. The main reason may be that the characteristic of CT is more distinctive than other scenes. Once some special objects such as plates and servicing windows are detected, it is easy to make the right decision. The best performance is achieved by A2, which is with all information including TF-IDF weight.

We further conduct experiments on mixed dataset to avoid the overfitting problem caused by limited number of videos in moving+ dataset. The best performance is achieved by A3 and A5, which is 92%. However, compared with performance on moving+ dataset, it can be found that with the increasing of dataset scale, the performance is a little declining. It is because that the extra data from extending dataset is different from those in moving+ dataset, which will cause the increasing divergence within category.

In summary, different combinations are with different performances. On three dataset conditions, the best combination is distinct. Advantage of TF-IDF does not meet our expectation and the performance is not stable. It may be caused by that the objects in each scene are not rich enough.

In order to analysis the details of best performance on each dataset, we give the confusion matrix in Fig. 8 It can be seen that on moving+ dataset, few samples in BC scene are misclassed into CP. The reason may be that there are some object list overlaps between campus and basketball courts. While for mixed dataset, although the amount of training data is increasing, the divergence also tends to expand. From subfigure (c) in Fig. 8, it can be seen that except confusion between CP and BC, there are also few misclassifications between Lab and CT. As for subfigure (b) in Fig. 8, the confusion is sharpened. It is easy to understand these results since the test data are downloaded from internet, in which the object list in each scene may be appear huge differences from training data. Although the performance is not as good as expected, the advantage of principal diagonal in confusion matrix is obvious.

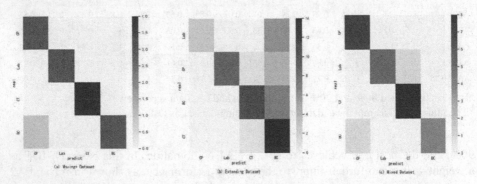

Fig. 8. Confusion matrix of best combination in Table 1 on each dataset.

6 Conclusion

In this paper, we proposed a semantic scene classification approach on moving platform. Based on YOLOv5 detection result, we can not only extract useful semantic information, but also overcome the weakness caused by the moving platform. By a semantic embedding layer, we combine the object confidence, location information with TF-IDF, a weight to enhance the effect of some special objects. With the help of the temporal handling ability in LSTM, our approach can further seal the temporal information into the final frame representation. On LSTM, our approach can identify a scene from semantic level. Experiments on three datasets proved the effectiveness of our approach for moving platform.

Acknowledgements. This work is partially supported by Shandong Provincial Natural Science Foundation (ZR2020KF022), the Special Fund for Science and Technology of Guangdong Province (2020S00055) and National Key R&D Program of China under Grant (2021YFE0193900).

References

1. Xie, L., Lee, F., Liu, L., Kotani, K., Chen, Q.: Scene recognition: a comprehensive survey. Pattern Recognition **102**, 107205 (2020)
2. Li, L. J., Su, H., Lim, Y., Fei-Fei, L.: Objects as attributes for scene classification. In: European Conference on Computer Vision, pp. 57–69. Springer, Berlin, Heidelberg (2010)
3. Cheng, X., Lu, J., Feng, J., Yuan, B., Zhou, J.: Scene recognition with objectness. Pattern Recognit. **74**, 474–487 (2018)
4. Oliva, A., Torralba, A.: Modeling the shape of the scene: a holistic representation of the spatial envelope. Int. J. Comput. Vis. **42**(3), 145–175 (2001)
5. Vogel, J., Schiele, B.: A semantic typicality measure for natural scene categorization. In: Joint Pattern Recognition Symposium, pp. 195–203. Springer, Berlin, Heidelberg (2004)
6. Wu, J., Rehg, J.M.: Centrist: A visual descriptor for scene categorization. IEEE Trans. Pattern Anal. Mach. Intell. **33**(8), 1489–1501 (2010)
7. Csurka, G., Dance, C., Fan, L., Willamowski, J., Bray, C.: Visual categorization with bags of keypoints. In Workshop on Statistical Learning in Computer Vision, ECCV, vol. 1(1–22), pp. 1–2 (2004)
8. Lowe, D.G.: Distinctive image features from scale-invariant keypoints. Int. J. Comput. Vis. **60**(2), 91–110 (2004)
9. Dalal, N., Triggs, B.: Histograms of oriented gradients for human detection. In: 2005 IEEE Computer Society Conference on Computer Vision and Pattern Recognition (CVPR'05), vol. 1, pp. 886–893. IEEE (2005)
10. Margolin, R., Zelnik-Manor, L., Tal, A.: Otc: a novel local descriptor for scene classification. In: European Conference on Computer Vision, pp. 377–391. Springer, Cham (2014)
11. Seong, H., Hyun, J., Kim, E.: FOSNet: an end-to-end trainable deep neural network for scene recognition. IEEE Access **8**, 82066–82077 (2020)
12. Huang, L., Cai, S., Zhuang, Y., Jing, C., Huang, Y., Tu, X., Ding, X.: A two-stage contrastive learning framework for imbalanced aerial scene recognition. In: ICASSP 2022-2022 IEEE International Conference on Acoustics, Speech and Signal Processing (ICASSP), pp. 3518–3522. IEEE (2022)
13. Jiang, P., Ergu, D., Liu, F., Cai, Y., Ma, B.: A Review of Yolo algorithm developments. Procedia Comput. Sci. **199**, 1066–1073 (2022)
14. Thuan, D.: Evolution of Yolo algorithm and Yolov5: The state-of-the-art object detention algorithm (2021)
15. Yu, Y., Si, X., Hu, C., Zhang, J.: A review of recurrent neural networks: LSTM cells and network architectures. Neural Comput. **31**(7), 1235–1270 (2019)

LIRS-ArtBul: Design, Modelling and Construction of an Omnidirectional Chassis for a Modular Multipurpose Robotic Platform

Artem Apurin[1] , Bulat Abbyasov[1(✉)] , Liaisan Safarova[1] ,
Alexandra Dobrokvashina[1] , Tatyana Tsoy[1] , Edgar A. Martínez-García[2] ,
and Evgeni Magid[1,3]

[1] Laboratory of Intelligent Robotic Systems, Intelligent Robotics Department, Institute of Information Technology and Intelligent Systems, Kazan Federal University, Kremlyovskaya Str. 35, Kazan 420111, Russia
abbyasov@it.kfu.ru
[2] Institute of Engineering and Technology, Department of Industrial Engineering and Manufacturing, Autonomous University of Ciudad Juarez, Zona Pronaf Condominio, Manuel Díaz H. No. 518-B, 32315 Chihuahua, Cd Juárez, Mexico
[3] Tikhonov Moscow Institute of Electronics and Mathematics, HSE University, Tallinn Str, 34, Moscow 123458, Russia

Abstract. Service robotics is a promising area of commercializing robotic solutions of various kinds, from education and medical services to entertainment and advertisement. It might be useful to construct a series of different specialized service robots that have a modular construction and share the same chassis. Such approach allows to reuse encapsulated locomotion libraries instead of their development from scratch for each model of a robot and easily add or replace particular robot modules depending on a target task or an operational environment. This paper provides a tutorial on developing an omnidirectional mecanum wheeled chassis for a modular multipurpose robotic platform. We describe a chassis design, modelling in Blender, selection of components, assembly process and basic locomotion software development. We used Gazebo simulator for robot behaviour emulation due to its support of the Robot Operating System (ROS). For control Raspberry PI 4 and Arduino Mega2560 modules were employed. The chassis model behavior was validated in virtual environments of Gazebo and, after assembling, in real world locomotion scenarios. The chassis will be further employed in development of several new in-house mobile platforms, which could serve for particular purposes within the service robotics field.

Keywords: Mobile robot · Mecanum wheels · Service robotics

1 Introduction

A rapid development of robotics provides new opportunities for integration of robotic systems into many areas of a human life including manufacturing [1], autonomous driving [2], agriculture [3], medical services [4], search and rescue operations [5], and other

A. Ronzhin et al. (Eds.): ICR 2022, LNCS 13719, pp. 70–80, 2022.
https://doi.org/10.1007/978-3-031-23609-9_7

areas. Service robotics [6, 7] is a promising area of commercializing robotic solutions of various kinds, from education [8] and medical services [9] to entertainment [10] and advertisement [11]. A special attention is paid for a human–robot interaction (HRI) while collaborating in a shared workspace [12]. The purpose of a service robot is to replace a person when performing routine or life-threatening tasks [13], which is especially important when a robot is located in an area that is inaccessible or dangerous for a human [14].

Over the past decades, the use of service robots in medical services automation scenarios [15] has become popular, including medication and vaccines delivery [16], comprehensive patient consulting [17] etc. The pandemic has clearly demonstrated that the medical field requires more workers, while performing simple but repetitive and labor-intensive tasks takes a significant time and effort [18]. Service robots allow to reduce a number of such routine tasks and free medical personal to perform more complicated tasks [19]. It is desirable to implement a full-fledged robotic ecosystem for a hospital environment considering disinfection robots, static patient health monitoring robots, drug and food delivery robots, nurse robots, informant robots, smart wheelchairs, and smart medical beds [20].

We are interested to develop a reliable, inexpensive, and multifunctional robotic chassis on mecanum wheels. In limited space or a large number of people environments each additional turn of a vehicle could lead to a collision, therefore the main advantage of mecanum wheels is the ability to move the vehicle in all directions [21]. In [22, 23] kinematics of the four-wheel omnidirectional platforms and robot hardware were described. In [24] a four mecanum wheels mobile platform for transportation of materials was equipped with Kinect, an IMU, a CCD camera, a laser rangefinder, bumpers, ultrasonic and photoelectric sensors. An omnidirectional platform for balance analysis IsiSkate was designed to reproduce a public transportation perturbation in a laboratory environment [25]. IsiSkate was equipped with force and inertial sensors intended for the evaluation of a human posture for static and dynamic equilibrium analysis of a human subject standing on it. A development of a 3 DOFs in motion and one DOF in steering omnidirectional wheels platform was described in [26]. Efficient omnidirectional wheel arrangements, main navigation issues and approaches that play an important role in the development of omnidirectional robots were reviewed in [27].

This article could serve as a tutorial on creating an omnidirectional robotic platform chassis. We describe a chassis design, modelling in Blender for Gazebo simulator, assembly process and basic locomotion software development. The robot software employs Robot Operating System (ROS) [28]. The chassis model behavior was validated in virtual environments of Gazebo and, after assembling, in real world locomotion scenarios.

2 Multipurpose Chassis Design and Modelling

The goal of this project was to construct an omnidirectional mecanum wheeled chassis for a modular multipurpose robotic platform, which could be further modified to serve different particular purposes. The chassis consist of two levels: a first level is a driving block, and a second level is a computational and sensory block. The first level contains wheels, motors, and batteries. The second level contains locomotion controllers and sensors. The idea behind was to encapsulated locomotion hardware and software libraries into this chassis so that it could be employed as a building block for further development of new mobile robots. Such modular construction allows to reuse encapsulated locomotion capabilities without their development from scratch. Using this chassis as a locomotion block, we are currently developing several mobile robots for particular tasks: a robot that has a capability to use elevators, a robot that has a capability to negotiate with doors, a robot for medication delivery, an educational robot for studying navigation and several others. For these robots a varying number of additional levels (one to three levels) will be placed on the top of the proposed two-level chassis.

Building a simulation robot model is an important stage for testing robot behavior and control algorithms in different environments [29, 30]. Varying sizes of robot part models allows to choose an optimal robot configuration within a required environment. The Blender modelling program was used to create a robot 3D model. In Blender model editor each component of the model (e.g., a wheel) is easily configurable.

Figure 1 shows a motor and a mecanum wheel model for a virtual robotic platform. A motor (Fig. 1 (left)) is 80 mm long with a diameter of 25 mm. A mecanum wheel (Fig. 1 (right)) has a diameter of 100 mm and 45 mm thick. Figure 2 shows a four-sided aluminum profile and an aluminum profile mounting bracket. Dimensions (length–width-height) of an aluminum profile (Fig. 2 (left)) are $400 \times 40 \times 165$ mm. Dimensions of a mounting bracket in Fig. 2 (right) is $30 \times 30 \times 30$ mm.

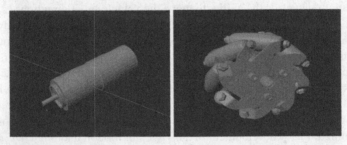

Fig. 1. Virtual robot modelling: a motor (left) and an omnidirectional wheel (right).

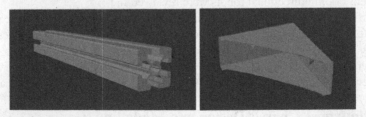

Fig. 2. Virtual robot modelling: a four-sided aluminum profile (left) and an aluminum profile mounting bracket (right).

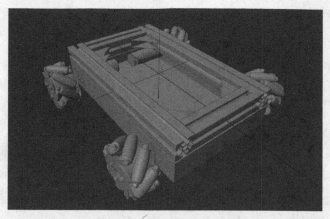

Fig. 3. Virtual robot modelling: assembled main part of the chassis.

Figure 3 presents an assembled 3D model of the omnidirectional chassis' main part, which contains four mecanum wheels, motors, fasteners for aluminum profiles and aluminum profiles. To improve ergonomics of the basic chassis, we added a plastic hull of a circular shape. It increases HRI safety and simplifies a path planning. Figure 4 (left) shows a first level of the chassis, which contains the basic chassis encapsulated into the hull. Two heavy high-capacity batteries are placed in an empty volume between the motors. Figure 4 (right) depicts a second level of the chassis, where a microcomputer, a microcontroller, USB hub connectors, a charging connector, power buttons and various sensors are located. Figure 5 presents the chassis' virtual 3D model in Gazebo simulator.

Fig. 4. Chassis' virtual 3D model with hull elements (left) and the second level (right).

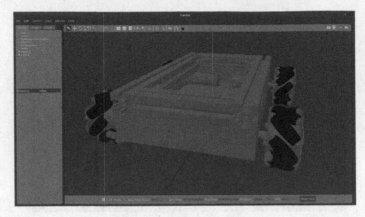

Fig. 5. Robot model in Gazebo.

3 Robot Construction

This section describes a real robot assembly process. The construction of the robot is a rectangular aluminum platform on mecanum wheels equipped with a raspberry Pi 4 microcomputer, a motor controller based on ATmega2560, two dual-channel motor drivers, one RC receiver, one remote controller and four DC motors with encoders (Fig. 6).

A mecanum wheel is a wheel with nine rollers along its circumference, located at an angle of 45 degrees to the axis of rotation of the wheel. This type of wheels allows the robot to move forward and backward, to the right and left, diagonally and rotate around Z-axis by changing the direction or speed of each wheel.

Raspberry Pi 4 model B was used as a microcomputer (Fig. 7 (left)). This low cost 1.5 GHz general-purpose computer has enough power to run ROS and compute sophisticated algorithms such as real-time simultaneous localization and mapping (SLAM). It has Quad core Cortex-A72 CPU with 8 GB of RAM and 4 USB ports for connection with external devices (e.g., Hokuyo Laser rangefinder (LRF, [31])).

Fig. 6. Omnidirectional robot: a robotic platform (left), a mecanum wheel (right).

MeBigDiv is a controller based on ATmega2560-16AU2 16 MHz with 8 KB of SRAM (Fig. 7 (right)). It is used for sending commands to motor drivers and gathering odometry from wheels. Two motor drivers (Fig. 8 (left)) are used to take a low-current control signal and then turn it into a higher-current signal that can drive a motor (Fig. 8 (right)). Motor drivers have overvoltage and undervoltage protection circuits. AB dual phase incremental encoders with basic pulse number 17 pulses per revolute (PPR) detect rotation angle pulses and convert angular motion or position of a shaft into an analog or digital code to identify a position or motion. The control board based on the ATmega2560 controller is connected via USB to the Raspberry Pi 4 microcomputer. The encoders are connected with a 4-wire daisy chain to the ATmega2560 board—two wires carry phase A and B signals, and the motor drivers are connected with a 10-wire daisy chain. The motor drivers can be powered from 9 to 24 V. The wiring diagram is shown in Fig. 9.

Fig. 7. Robot control boards: Raspberry PI 4 (left), MeBigDiv ATmega2560 (right).

Fig. 8. A robot motor driver (left) and a motor with an encoder equipped (right).

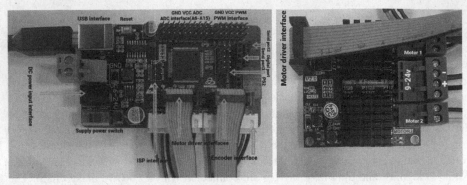

Fig. 9. Robot electrical circuit wiring diagram: Arduino ATmega2560 (left) Motor driver (right).

Ubuntu Mate 20.04 (Focal Fossa) is used as an embedded operating system in order to install ROS on Raspberry Pi 4. Ubuntu Mate is optimized for Raspberry Pi 4 and provides a stable Mate desktop environment, which runs faster than Xubuntu or Kubuntu. We used ROS Noetic version which runs under Ubuntu Mate. Packages rosserial arduino and rosserial created necessary software environment for data exchange between MeBigDiv and Raspberry Pi 4. A diagram of data exchange is shown in (Fig. 10).

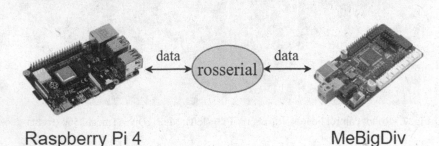

Fig. 10. Data exchange between MeBigDiv and Raspberry Pi 4 in ROS environment.

4   Implementation of a Motor Controller

4.1   Forward Kinematics

The required linear and angular velocity of the robot are set using a ROS message *geometry msgs/Twist*. The format of this message is as follows:

geometry msgs/Vector3::linear
float64 x

float64 y
float64 z
geometry msgs/Vector3::angular
float64 x
float64 y
float64 z

To calculate a rotation velocity of each motor, the implemented controller uses 3 variables: linear.x, linear.y, angular.z. The obtained values x, y, z set the linear velocity of the robot along the X, Y axes and the angular velocity along the Z-axis. Due to the design of the wheels, it is necessary to translate the received velocity values into the target rotation velocity for each wheel. Translation is carried out according to the following equations [32, 33]:

$$v_{LF} = (1/R_{wheel})(v_x - v_y - c \cdot v_z), \tag{1}$$

$$v_{RF} = (1/R_{wheel})(v_x + v_y + c \cdot v_z), \tag{2}$$

$$v_{LR} = (1/R_{wheel})(v_x + v_y - c \cdot v_z), \tag{3}$$

$$v_{RR} = (1/R_{wheel})(v_x - v_y + c \cdot v_z), \tag{4}$$

where v_{LF}, v_{RF}, v_{LR}, v_{RR} are velocities of left front, right front, left rear and right rear wheels respectively, R_{wheel} is wheel radius, v_x is a linear velocity along X-axis, v_y is a linear velocity along Y-axis and v_z is an angular velocity along Z-axis.

c value is a robot-specific coefficient calculated as:

$$c = \frac{s_{RL}}{2} + \frac{s_{FR}}{2}, \tag{5}$$

where s_{RL} is the distance between right and left wheels, s_{FR} is the distance between front and rear wheels.

There are 2 options for working with wheel velocities using encoders:

Converting the wheel velocity from rad/s to $pulses/s$;
Convert encoder values received per second from $pulses/s$ to rad/s.

The obtained values of wheel velocities expressed in rad/s must be converted to $pulses/s$.

$$v_{wheel} = \frac{v'_{wheel} \cdot PPR}{2 \cdot \pi}, \tag{6}$$

where v'_{wheel}—velocity measured in rad/s, PPR—pulses per revolution of encoder.

In order to make the robot drive at a desired velocity we used PIDv2 PID controller library. The library API takes an actual wheel velocity, a desired velocity and three coefficients—proportional, integral, and derivative which should be tuned to get an optimal response. The output is a PWM motor signal corrected by the PID correction function.

4.2 Odometry

Publishing odometry data over ROS system requires *nav_msgs/Odometry*. It is a special data structure that consists of information about robot pose and orientation, and coordinate frame names.

The default buffer size allocated by ROS for ATmega2560 controller is 512 bytes, a *nav_msgs/Odometry* message size is at least 694 bytes. Creating and transferring odometry data via *rosserial_arduino* on Arduino ATmega2560 requires increasing a buffer size. This is quite a difficult task, since increasing a size of the buffer requires recompilation of some ROS files due to *ros.h* changes. Moreover, changing an amount of memory used for *rosserial_arduino* can cause ROS system to become unstable.

The solution is creating a separate ROS node that runs on Raspberry Pi 4. Arduino code running on ATmega2560 calculates and publishes only actual velocities of the robot [34]:

$$\upsilon_x = (\upsilon_{LF} + \upsilon_{RF} + \upsilon_{LR} + \upsilon_{RR})/4, \tag{7}$$

$$\upsilon'_x = \frac{2 \cdot \pi \cdot R_{wheel} \cdot \upsilon_x}{PPR}, \tag{8}$$

$$\upsilon_y = (-\upsilon_{LF} + \upsilon_{RF} + \upsilon_{LR} - \upsilon_{RR})/4, \tag{9}$$

$$\upsilon'_y = \frac{2 \cdot \pi \cdot R_{wheel} \cdot \upsilon_y}{PPR}, \tag{10}$$

$$\upsilon_z = (-\upsilon_{LF} + \upsilon_{RF} - \upsilon_{LR} + \upsilon_{RR})/4 \cdot c, \tag{11}$$

$$\upsilon'_z = \frac{2 \cdot \pi \cdot R_{wheel} \cdot \upsilon_z}{PPR}, \tag{12}$$

where υ_{LF}, υ_{RF}, υ_{LR}, are velocities of left front, right front, left rear and right rear wheels respectiv. measured in pulses per second; υ_x, υ_y, υ_z are average of all velocities along X, Y and Z axes respectively measured in pulses per second; υ'_x, υ'_y, υ'_z are velocities along X, Y and Z. axes respectively measured in metres per second; PPR are pulses per revolution of encoder; R_{wheel} is wheel radius.

The separate ROS node running on Raspberry Pi 4 receives incoming calculated linear and angular velocities from Arduino ATmega2560, performs real time calculation (e.g., TF transformations) and publishes a *nav_msgs/Odometry* message.

The calculated X, Y and Z values are assigned to the corresponding elements of a *geometry_msgs/Vector3* message and then the message is published via *rosserial_arduino* to the odometry ROS node.

5 Conclusions

Building of specialized service robots could benefit from having a modular construction that shares the same chassis. A modular approach allows to reuse encapsulated locomotion libraries instead of their development from scratch for each model of a robot. This paper provided a tutorial on developing an omnidirectional mecanum wheeled chassis for a modular multipurpose robotic platform. We described the chassis design, modelling in Gazebo simulator, assembly process and basic locomotion software development. The chassis model behavior was validated in virtual environments of Gazebo and, after assembling, in real world locomotion scenarios. The chassis will be further employed in development of several new in-house mobile platforms, which could serve for particular purposes within the service robotics field.

Acknowledgements. The reported study was funded by the Russian Science Foundation (RSF) and the Cabinet of Ministers of the Republic of Tatarstan according to the research project No. 22-21-20033.

References

1. Gribkov, A., Morozkin, M., Kuptsov, V., Pivkin, P., Zelenskii, A.: Industry 4.0 concepts in the machine-tool industry. Russ. Eng. Res. **41**(7), 634–635 (2021)
2. Cheng, J., Zhang, L., Chen, Q., Hu, X., Cai, J.: A review of visual slam methods for autonomous driving vehicles. Eng. Appl. Artif. Intell. **114**, 104992 (2022)
3. Nguyen, V., Vu, Q., Solenaya, O., Ronzhin, A.: Analysis of main tasks of precision farming solved with the use of robotic means. In: MATEC Web of Conferences, vol. 113, pp. 02009. EDP Sciences (2017).
4. Kolpashchikov, D., Gerget, O., Meshcheryakov, R.: Robotics in healthcare. In: Handbook of Artificial Intelligence in Healthcare, pp. 281–306. Springer (2022)
5. Magid, E., Pashkin, A., Simakov, N., Abbyasov, B., Suthakorn, J., Svinin, M., Matsuno, F.: Artificial intelligence based framework for robotic search and rescue operations conducted jointly by international teams. In: Proceedings of 14th International Conference on Electromechanics and Robotics "Zavalishin's Readings", pp. 15–26. Springer (2020)
6. Belk, R.: Ethical issues in service robotics and artificial intelligence. Serv. Ind. J. **41**(13–14), 860–876 (2021)
7. Paulius, D., Sun, Y.: A survey of knowledge representation in service robotics. Robot. Auton. Syst. **118**, 13–30 (2019)
8. Gavrilova, L., Kotik, A., Tsoy, T., Martínez-García, E. A., Svinin, M., Magid, E.: Facilitating a preparatory stage of real-world experiments in a humanoid robot assisted english language teaching using gazebo simulator. In: 13th International Conference on Developments in eSystems Engineering (DeSE), pp. 222–227. IEEE (2020)
9. Sagitov, A., Tsoy, T., Li, H., Magid, E.: Automated open wound suturing: detection and planning algorithm. J. Robot. Netw. Artif. Life **5**(2), 144–148 (2018)
10. Morris, K.J., Samonin, V., Baltes, J., Anderson, J., Lau, M.C.: A robust in teractive entertainment robot for robot magic performances. Appl. Intell. **49**(11), 3834–3844 (2019)
11. Bustos, P., Manso, L.J., Bandera, A.J., Bandera, J.P., Garcia-Varea, I., Martinez-Gomez, J.: The cortex cognitive robotics architecture: use cases. Cogn. Syst. Res. **55**, 107–123 (2019)
12. Galin, R., Meshcheryakov, R.: Review on human–robot interaction during collaboration in a shared workspace. In: International Conference on Interactive Collaborative Robotics, pp. 63–74. Springer (2019)
13. Belanche, D., Casaló, L.V., Flavián, C., Schepers, J.: Service robot implementation: a theoretical framework and research agenda. Serv. Ind. J. **40**(3–4), 203–225 (2020)
14 Ha, Q P., La, H.M., Wang, S., Dalaguei, C.. Special issue on recent advances in field and service robotics: handling harsh environments and cooperation. Robotica 1–3 (2022).

15. Magid, E., Zakiev, A., Tsoy, T., Lavrenov, R., Rizvanov, A.: Automating pandemic mitigation. Adv. Robot. **35**(9), 572–589 (2021)
16. Cianchetti, M., Laschi, C., Menciassi, A., Dario, P.: Biomedical applications of soft robotics. Nat. Rev. Mater. **3**(6), 143–153 (2018)
17. Tan, S.Y., Taeihagh, A.: Governing the adoption of robotics and autonomous systems in long-term care in Singapore. Policy Soc **40**(2), 211–231 (2021)
18. Tavakoli, M., Carriere, J., Torabi, A.: Robotics, smart wearable technologies, and autonomous intelligent systems for healthcare during the covid-19 pandemic: An analysis of the state of the art and future vision. Adv. Intell. Syst. **2**(7), 2000071 (2020)
19. Savin, I., Ott, I., Konop, C.: Tracing the evolution of service robotics: Insights from a topic modeling approach. Technol. Forecast. Soc. Chang.**174**, 121280 (2022)
20. Brink, K.A., Wellman, H.M.: Robot teachers for children? Young children trust robots depending on their perceived accuracy and agency. Dev. Psychol. **56**(7), 1268 (2020)
21. Abd Mutalib, M.A., Azlan, N.Z.: Prototype development of meconium wheels mobile robot: A review. Appl. Res. Smart Technol. (ARSTech) **1**(2), 71–82 (2020)
22. Wu, X.B., Chen, Z., Chen, W.B., Wang, W.K.: Research on the design of educational robot with four-wheel omni-direction chassis. J. Comput **29**(4), 284–294 (2018)
23. Salih, J.E. M., Rizon, M., Yaacob, S., Adom, A. H., Mamat, M.R.: Designing omnidirectional mobile robot with mecanum wheel. Am. J. Appl. Sci., Citeseer (2006)
24. Qian, J., Zi, B., Wang, D., Ma, Y., Zhang, D.: The design and development of an omnidirectional mobile robot oriented to an intelligent manufacturing system. Sensors **17**(9), 2073 (2017)
25. Ma, J., Kharboutly, H., Benali, A., Amar, F.B., Bouzit, M.: Design of omnidirectional mobile platform for balance analysis. IEEE/ASME Trans. Mechatron. **19**(6), 1872–1881 (2014)
26. Song, J.B., Byun, K.S.: Design and control of a four-wheeled omnidirectional mobile robot with steerable omnidirectional wheels. J. Robot. Syst. **21**(4), 193–208 (2004)
27. Taheri, H., Zhao, C.X.: Omnidirectional mobile robots, mechanisms and navigation approaches. Mech. Mach. Theory **153**, 103958 (2020)
28. Quigley, M., Conley, K., Gerkey, B., Faust, J., Foote, T., Leibs, J., Wheeler, R., Ng, A.Y.: Ros: an open-source robot operating system. In: ICRA workshop on open-source software, vol. 3(5). Kobe, Japan (2009)
29. Takaya, K., Asai, T., Kroumov, V., Smarandache, F.: Simulation environment for mobile robots testing using ros and gazebo. In: 20th International Conference on System Theory, Control and Computing (ICSTCC), pp. 96–101. IEEE (2016)
30. Shabalina, K., Sagitov, A., Su, K.L., Hsia, K.H., Magid, E.: Avrora unior carlike robot in gazebo environment. In: International Conference on Artificial Life and Robotics, pp. 116–119 (2019)
31. Chebotareva, E., Safin, R., Hsia, K.H., Carballo, A., Magid, E.: Person-following algorithm based on laser range finder and monocular camera data fusion for a wheeled autonomous mobile robot. In: International Conference on Interactive Collaborative Robotics, pp. 21–33. Springer (2020)
32. Taheri, H., Qiao, B., Ghaeminezhad, N.: Kinematic model of a four mecanum wheeled mobile robot. Int. J. Comput. Appl. **113**(3), 6–9 (2015)
33. Gfrerrer, A.: Geometry and kinematics of the mecanum wheel. Comput. Aided Geom. Des. **25**(9), 784–791 (2008)
34. Maulana, E., Muslim, M. A., Hendrayawan, V.: Inverse kinematic implementation of four-wheels mecanum drive mobile robot using stepper motors. In: International Seminar on Intelligent Technology and Its Applications (ISITIA), pp. 51–56. IEEE (2015)

Comparison of Monocular ROS-Based Visual SLAM Methods

Liaisan Safarova[1] , Bulat Abbyasov[1](✉) , Tatyana Tsoy[1] , Hongbing Li[2] ,
and Evgeni Magid[1,3]

[1] Laboratory of Intelligent Robotic Systems, Intelligent Robotics Department, Institute of
Information Technology and Intelligent Systems, Kazan Federal University, Kremlyovskaya Str.
35, 420111 Kazan, Russian Federation
abbyasov@it.kfu.ru
[2] Department of Instrument Science and Engineering, Shanghai Jiao Tong University, Shanghai,
China
[3] Tikhonov Moscow Institute of Electronics and Mathematics, HSE University, Tallinn Str, 34,
123592 Moscow, Russian Federation

Abstract. Simultaneous Localization and Mapping (SLAM) is a robot navigation
approach used to estimate a movement of a sensor in an unknown environment.
SLAM application examples include urban search and rescue operations in high-
risk environments, visual surveillance and service robotics. Compared to laser-
range finders, visual sensors are more light weight, have less power consumption
and provide more vast amount of environmental information. Visual SLAM methods are based on visual information only and employ monocular, stereo or RGD-D
cameras as input sensors. Monocular SLAM methods are often preferred for a
robotic platform when cost, energy and system weight requirements are limited.
Calculation of errors and testing on ready-made datasets allow to check applicability of an algorithm in real-world scenarios with less efforts than experiments
with a real robot. Verification of a sensor position and robot trajectory estimation
accuracy is achieved by measuring Absolute Trajectory Error (ATE), Relative
Pose Error (RPE) and Root Mean Square Error (RMSE). This article presents
analysis and comparison of the most widely used Visual SLAM monocular algorithms built for Robot Operating System (ROS): ORB-SLAM2, ORB-SLAM3,
DSO and LDSO. The KITTI and Euroc MAV datasets were selected to evaluate
the algorithms' performance.

Keywords: Computer vision · Visual SLAM · ORB-SLAM3 · ORB-SLAM2 ·
LDSO · DSO

1 Introduction

Recent advances in robotics provide new opportunities for integration of robots systems
into multiple areas of a human life including autonomous driving [1] and transportation
[2], agriculture [3], manufacturing [4] and warehouse management [5], medical services
[6], search and rescue operations [7], human-robot interaction [8] and other areas. Mobile

A. Ronzhin et al. (Eds.): ICR 2022, LNCS 13719, pp. 81–92, 2022.
https://doi.org/10.1007/978-3-031-23609-9_8

robotics, its approaches and techniques play a significant role in all these areas, and one of promising areas is Simultaneous Localization and Mapping (SLAM). In robotics a SLAM method solves a major problem of finding a robot pose in an unknown environment [9]. In order to localize a robot within an environment a SLAM method uses only relative observations of environment landmarks to an incremental and real-time map building [10]. The map is used to compute a bounded estimate of the robot location within this map [11].

SLAM techniques use various sensors for gathering information of an unknown environment and can be implemented for laser range finders (LRF), monocular vision, stereo vision, and RGB-D cameras. SLAM is one on the key techniques that allow mobile robot navigation and autonomy, therefore there exist a broad number of comparative studies of various SLAM approaches, covering such cases as indoor environment navigation [12] and in particular visual SLAM for an indoor environment [13], stereo visual SLAM for planetary rovers [14], 2D and 3D SLAM for autonomous ground vehicles [15] and others.

Today, a 2D LRF SLAM is the most widely used SLAM approach that employs a LRF as a sensor together with wheel odometry data [16]. The high cost of LIDAR technology and cumulative mapping error caused by LRF measurements are the main drawbacks of 2D LRF SLAM [17]. Furthermore, robots can operate in rough and uneven terrain that is not suitable for 2D SLAM techniques because of lacking wheel odometry.

Compared to a 2D SLAM, Visual SLAM (vSLAM) technique relies on only a visual input from cameras [18]. vSLAM map building technique uses a visual sensor or several visual sensors, employing monocular, stereo or RGD-D cameras [19]. vSLAM methods rely on loop closure algorithm. The main goal of loop closure is to recognize a location repeatedly visited by a robot in order to solve the problem of position displacement with time [20]. A visual loop detection is mainly achieved by evaluating similarity between images. vSLAM has a great advantage in loop detection due to a volumetric amount of data obtained from images [21]. When the loop detection is performed successfully, image feature detection and matching algorithms are executed. Feature detection and matching techniques are used to detect features of target regions in image pairs (current and previous) and to match identical features. An internal optimization algorithm can reconfigure a trajectory and a map based on these data to reduce accumulated errors [22].

A monocular camera is a good visual sensor for vSLAM due to a sensor price, a light weight and an ability to provide reach information about an environment [23]. This paper presents a comparison of four modern and robust monocular vSLAM methods that were implemented in Robot Operating System (ROS): ORB-SLAM2, ORB-SLAM3, DSO and LDSO. ORB-SLAM2 and ORB-SLAM3 are feature-based approaches, DSO and LDSO are direct methods. The algorithms were evaluated on KITTI and Euroc MAV datasets. Absolute Trajectory Error (ATE), Relative Pose Error (RPE) and Root Mean Square Error (RMSE) metrics were used to validate sensor pose estimation accuracy and robot trajectory precision [24]. This work extends our previous works on comparative analysis of SLAM algorithms [11, 25, 26].

2 Vision-Based Monocular SLAM Approaches

2.1 Visual Motion Estimation

Visual odometry (VO) describes sensor motion estimation from images captured by a monocular camera. Existing VO methods can be classified into feature-based and direct methods [27]. A feature-based approach is detecting image feature points and matching them between subsequent frames. A direct method estimates a sensor motion by minimizing a photometric error over all pixels.

Direct methods. A direct method directly operates with pixel intensity and uses an alignment of two images by minimizing the photometric error [28]. This approach allows to determine how much a robot (a visual sensor) is shifted between two image frames. Direct methods are divided into three categories:

- Direct sparse data method does not require a calculation of descriptors and uses only a few number of pixels. It is the fastest map reconstruction method but can only calculate a sparse map representation.
- Semi-dense direct method processes pixels with gradients and discard pixels with non-obvious gradients.
- Dense direct method processes all image pixels.

This paper considers Direct Sparse Odometry (DSO) and Direct Sparse Odometry with Loop Closure (LDSO) direct methods. DSO uses the direct sparse data method. DSO partitions an image and selects pixels with different color intensities [29]. This leads to evenly distributed tracked points throughout the entire image. The disadvantage of DSO is a lack of the loop closure method [1]. LDSO method retains the main feature of the DSO method of evenly distributing tracked points on a map, while extending DSO by adding a loop closure algorithm and adding an ability to globally optimize the map [30].

Feature-based methods. A feature-based method needs to select a certain number of representative points from collected images. These points are called key or feature points [31]. Feature points are used to gain a visual sensor pose in environment. This paper considers ORB-SLAM2 and ORB-SLAM3 feature-based methods.

ORB-SLAM2 is a complete vSLAM system based on ORB feature point detection [32]. The vSLAM system can calculate a camera trajectory in real time. The method implementation also includes a real-time visual odometry estimation, a visual sensor tracking and a loop closure detection. ORB-SLAM2 is suitable for monocular, stereo, and RGB-D vision systems.

ORB-SLAM3 is an extension of ORB-SLAM2 and the most modern feature-based vSLAM method. The developed versatile vSLAM system can performing visual, visual-inertial and multi-map vSLAM that operates with a wide variety of sensors (monocular, stereo and RGB-D cameras [33].

ORB-SLAM3 has introduced new features over ORB-SLAM2: a fusion of visual and inertial sensors (so called visual-inertial vSLAM capability), a multi-map support and a fisheye camera support [34]. ORB-SLAM3 visual odometry estimation result is depicted in Fig. 1.

Fig. 1. Example of running ORB-SLAM3 on EuRoC dataset.

2.2 Datasets

The dataset is a collection of related sets of environment information. In computer vision field it is used for assessing the camera tracking accuracy within environments. For the comparison of the algorithms we employed two of the most popular datasets for vision testing: EuRoC and KITTI.

EuRoC dataset is visual-inertial data collected by onboard sensors of a micro-aircraft (MAV) [35]. The dataset contains synchronized stereo images, IMU measurements and accurate ground truth data. The EuRoC MAV dataset is a selection of eleven visual-inertial sequences recorded in three different rooms by two monocular cameras of a manually piloted MAV. In each environment, sequences become qualitatively more complex as a sequence number increases including such features as faster motion or poor lighting conditions (Fig. 2).

Fig. 2. The EuRoC dataset samples.

KITTI dataset is one of the most popular datasets used in mobile robotics and autonomous driving [36]. It contains hours of traffic scenarios recorded with a variety of sensors including high resolution RGB, grayscale stereo cameras and a 3D laser scanner. The KITTI dataset was labeled with eleven classes: building, tree, sky, car, sign, road, pedestrian, fence, pole, sidewalk, and cyclist. The samples of KITTI dataset is shown in Fig. 3.

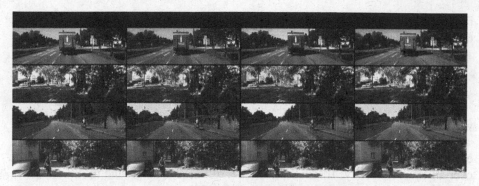

Fig. 3. The KITTI dataset samples.

2.3 Method Evaluation

We compared ORB-SLAM2, ORB-SLAM3, DSO and LDSO vSLAM methods by considering their localization accuracy. ATE and RPE are the two most important metrics used to evaluate the accuracy of vSLAM sensor pose estimation module. RPE is used to calculate the difference of pose changes that show local accuracy. ATE calculates the difference between a real value of a camera pose and a value estimated by vSLAM system. RMSE is used to quantify the quality of an entire trajectory [37]. In order to calculate evaluation metrics we used EVO utility [38].

EuRoC. EuRoC allows using absolute trajectory mean square error and relative position standard deviation by using entire ground truth camera trajectories. The criterion is RMSE of ATE that is a deviation of a trajectory estimate from a ground truth trajectory for assessing the quality of vSLAM systems. ATE is calculated as:

$$ATErmse = (1/n \sum_{i=0}^{n} ||Trans(E_i)||^2)^2, \tag{1}$$

where $Trans(E_i)$ represents a translation part of the ATE. Typically, mean, or median values are calculated. *ATErmse* of the trajectory is the average deviation from the ground trajectory per frame [39].

The relative pose error (RPE) measures the local accuracy of the trajectory over a fixed time interval (Δt). It is calculated as follows:

$$RPE(E1 : n, \Delta t) = \left(1/m \sum_{i=1}^{m} ||Trans(E_i)||^2\right). \tag{2}$$

The RPE metric combines rotational and translation errors into one dimension, while ATE only considers translation errors. As a result, RPE is always slightly larger than ATE. Rotational errors usually also show up in mistranslations and thus are indirectly captured by ATE. From a practical point of view, ATE has a rather intuitive visualization. However, both metrics are highly correlated [39].

KITTI. To evaluate the algorithms' performance on KITTI dataset we used *align RMSE*. The align RMSE represents a distance between two feature points. To calculate a square root of a squared error, we need to align a start and an end independently of each other and to calculate two relative transformations.

$$RMSEalign = \left(\sqrt{\sum_{i=1}^{n}(y_i - \widehat{y_i})^2} \right)/n, \tag{3}$$

where y_i is an observed value, $\widehat{y_i}$ is a corresponding predicted value.

In our analysis the combined error and the alignment error were calculated. These errors equally consider errors that were caused by a scale, a rotation, and a translation drift over an entire trajectory. Translational RMSE of tracked and ground truth trajectories was aligned to the start and end estimated points [28].

3 Comparative Analysis

3.1 EuRoC

We evaluated DSO, LDSO, ORB-SLAM2, and ORB-SLAM3 vSLAM methods on the EuRoC dataset across all sequences for each of the two camera streams, which were interpreted as single sequences with a same basis. Table 1 shows ATE RMSE (measured in meters) and RPE RMSE (measured in meters per second). The best results are indicated in bold.

Table 1. vSLAM algorithms evaluation results for EuRoC dataset.

		MH01	MH02	MH03	MH04	MH05
ORB-Slam2	ATE	0.041	**0.035**	0.041	**0.074**	**0.054**
	RPE	0.491	0.458	1.095	0.560	0.589
ORB-Slam3	ATE	**0.016**	0.085	**0.036**	0.075	0.088
	RPE	**0.148**	**0.212**	**0.401**	**0.156**	**0.112**
DSO	ATE	0.054	0.063	**0.209**	0.173	0.169
	RPE	0.132	0.134	0.711	**0.632**	0.199
LDSO	ATE	**0.044**	**0.044**	0.090	**0.136**	**0.127**
	RPE	**0.131**	**0.131**	**0.706**	0.642	**0.198**

Table 1. (continued).

		V1.01	V1.02	V1.03	V2.01	V2.02	V2.03
ORB-Slam2	ATE	0.054	0.054	0.091	0.047	0.051	0.096
	RPE	0.454	0.528	0.409	0.225	0.508	**0.477**
ORB-Slam3	ATE	**0.033**	**0.019**	**0.034**	**0.036**	**0.022**	**0.081**
	RPE	**0.198**	**0.070**	**0.186**	**0.140**	**0.205**	0.066
DSO	ATE	0.104	1.047	**0.584**	0.064	0.162	1.439
	RPE	**0.088**	0.137	**0.334**	**0.081**	0.306	0.087
LDSO	ATE	**0.099**	**1.013**	0.607	**0.058**	**0.106**	**1.266**
	RPE	0.089	**0.111**	0.375	**0.081**	**0.281**	**0.086**

For Table 1, a color representation of the measurements is shown in Fig. 4. These color-coded maps give a clearer presentation of tabular measurements. Since the error is calculated from the measurement data, color representations of error deviations are shown for each line: the closest values to a benchmark are lighter, the greater the deviation—the darker is a color tone.

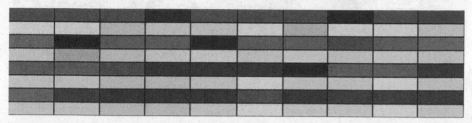

Fig. 4. Color-coded evaluation results for SLAM algorithms performed on EuRoC dataset.

3.2 KITTI

Table 2 represents a comparison of align ATE RMSE (in meters) of ORB-SLAM2, ORB-SLAM3, DSO and LDSO on KITTI dataset across all image sequence. For the direct and feature-based vSLAM methods the ATE values that are closest to the benchmark are highlighted in bold.

Table 2. vSLAM algorithms evaluation results for KITTI dataset.

	00	01	02	03	04	05
ORB-Slam2	5.33	-	21.25	1.51	1.62	4.85
ORB-Slam3	**1.259**	**10.15**	**4.58**	**1.332**	**0.211**	**0.855**
DSO	126.7	165.03	138.7	4.77	1.08	49.85
LDSO	**9.32**	**11.68**	**31.98**	**2.85**	**1.22**	**5.1**

Table 2. (continued).

	06	07	08	09	10
ORB-Slam2	12.34	2.26	46.68	6.6	8.8
ORB-Slam3	**0.667**	**0.503**	**3.858**	**1.967**	**1.09**
DSO	113.57	27.99	**120.17**	74.29	**16.3**
LDSO	**13.55**	**2.96**	129.02	**21.64**	17.3

Color representation of Table 2 is shown in Fig. 5. The lightest tones show results close to the benchmark, and the darkest tones show a high deviation. For example, the result of KITTI dataset (00 sequence) evaluation with feature-based methods shows that the closest align ATE RMSE value to the benchmark is a value obtained from ORB-SLAM3 method (highlighted in bold in Table 1). ORB-SLAM3 align ATE RMSE value evaluated represents with a lighter shade than the value obtained from ORB-SLAM2 method.

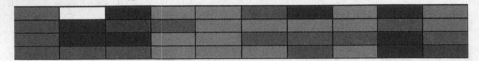

Fig. 5. Color-coded evaluation results for SLAM algorithms performed on KITTI dataset.

3.3 Visual SLAM Features

In order to determine the most appropriate algorithm, we considered the features that allow us to increase the reliability and the accuracy of algorithms that allow recreation of images in real time using one or more cameras. For example, ORB-SLAM2 has the ability to build a map in real time, has an implementation of the loop closing algorithm, and also has the ability to receive data from one or two cameras. ORB-SLAM3 includes all the features. DSO method has the ability to receive data from one or two cameras, and LDSO, in addition to receiving data from one or two cameras, also has an implementation of the loop closure algorithm.

The brief information about vSLAM features considered is shown in Table 3. Real-time mapping, Loop Closing, Multi Maps support and various sensor usage support are considered.

The Table 3 shows that ORB-SLAM3 is the most complete SLAM system that includes all these features.

Table 3. Comparison of vSLAM features.

Method	Real-time mapping	Loop closing	Multi maps	Mono	Stereo	Mono IMU	Stereo IMU
ORB-Slam2	+	+	-	+	+	-	-
ORB-Slam3	+	+	+	+	+	+	+
DSO	− (only VO)	−	−	+	+	−	−
LDSO	− (only VO)	+	−	+	+	−	−

3.4 Guidelines and Virtualization

Providing a well-written documentation helps other researchers to understand, make use of and contribute back to open source projects. Often vSLAM methods depend on special math and vision software packages and require a concrete version of Linux OS system. A well-written documentation provides a detailed installation manual and includes a getting started section that describes minimal reproducible tutorials.

Docker is an open source platform that enables developers to build and run containers with necessary software. It can be useful for creating Linux OS with vSLAM compiled with all necessary library dependencies. The container is properly configured and ready to be run in the same operating system as its host.

Table 4 shows that all vSLAM methods include good documentation and examples on how to use them on predefined datasets. But unfortunately, vSLAM methods authors do not provide ready-to-use Docker containers.

Table 4. Analysis of ROS-based monocular SLAM algorithms.

Method	Documentation	Examples of usage on datasets	Docker
ORB-Slam2	+	+	−
ORB-Slam3	+	+	−
DSO	+	−	−
LDSO	+	+	−

3.5 Summary

Table 1 shows that ORB-SLAM3 system is more accurate than ORB-SLAM2 due to a better recognition algorithm, which closes loops earlier and provides more intermediate image feature matches. Considering both measurements on EuRoC dataset 1 and measurements on KITTI dataset 2 the unambiguity of the results is clear (excluding some examples). The results indicated a natural superiority of ORB-SLAM3 algorithm over ORB-SLAM2 algorithm, which was the ORB-SLAM3's predecessor.

DSO and LDSO methods are highly accurate in the presence of complete photometric data and focused mainly on local accuracy. Therefore, DSO and LDSO are the most suitable methods for short range tasks. Feature-based ORB-SLAM2 and ORB-SLAM3 methods outperform direct methods in a global accuracy, making them a versatile solution for most SLAM tasks that require a long-term performance with stable and reliable results along all trajectories.

4 Conclusion

This article presented the comparison of four ROS-based open-source monocular Visual SLAM algorithms. The analysis showed that the direct DSO and LDSO methods are highly accurate in a presence of complete photometric data, and focus mainly on a local accuracy. Therefore, DSO and LDSO are the most suitable vSLAM approaches for vision tasks related to working at short distances and requiring a high accuracy in a local posture estimation. At the same time, feature-based methods ORB-SLAM2 and ORB-SLAM3 outperform direct methods in a global accuracy, making them a one-stop solution for most SLAM applications that require a long-term work with stable and reliable results throughout trajectories. Encounter detected objects ORB-Slam3 accuracy will be higher than of ORB-SLAM2, and LDSO outperforms DSO, which was its historical predecessor.

Acknowledgements. The reported study was funded by the Russian Science Foundation (RSF) and the Cabinet of Ministers of the Republic of Tatarstan according to the research project No. 22-21-20033.

References

1. Cheng, J., Zhang, L., Chen, Q., Hu, X., Cai, J.: A review of visual slam methods for autonomous driving vehicles. Eng. Appl. Artif. Intell. **114**(5), 104992–105009 (2022). https://doi.org/10.1016/j.engappai.2022.104992
2. Martínez-García, E.A., Torres-Córdoba, R., Carrillo-Saucedo, V.M., López-González, E.: Neural control and coordination of decentralized transportation robots. In: Proceedings of the Institution of Mechanical Engineers. Part I: Journal of Systems and Control Engineering, pp. 519–540. SAGE Publications Sage UK, England (2018). https://doi.org/10.1177/095965 1818756777
3. Iakovlev, R., Saveliev, A.: Approach to implementation of local navigation of mobile robotic systems in agriculture with the aid of radio modules. Telfor J. **12**(2), 92–97 (2020). https://doi.org/10.5937/telfor2002092I
4. Gribkov, A., Morozkin, M., Kuptsov, V., Pivkin, P., Zelenskii, A.: Industry 4.0 concepts in the machine-tool industry. Russ. Eng. Res. **41**(7), 634–635 (2021). https://doi.org/10.3103/S1068798X2107011X
5. Khazetdinov, A., Aleksandrov, A., Zakiev, A., Magid, E., Hsia, K.: RFID-based warehouse management system prototyping using a heterogeneous team of robots. In: Proceedings of the 23rd International Conference on Climbing and Walking Robots and Support Technologies for Mobile Machines (CLAWAR 2020), pp. 263–270. CLAWAR Association Ltd (2020). https://doi.org/10.13180/clawar.2020.24-26.08.32
6. Kolpashchikov, D., Gerget, O., Meshcheryakov, R.: Handbook of Artificial Intelligence in Healthcare. Springer (2022).
7. Bai, Y., Asami, K., Svinin, M., Magid, E.: Cooperative multi-robot control for monitoring an expanding flood area. In: 17th International Conference on Ubiquitous Robots (UR), pp. 500–505. IEEE (2020). https://doi.org/10.1109/UR49135.2020.9144931
8. Chebotareva, E., Hsia, K.-H., Yakovlev, K., Magid, E.: Laser rangefinder and monocular camera data fusion for human-following algorithm by PMB-2 mobile robot in simulated gazebo environment. In: Proceedings of 15th International Conference on Electromechanics and Robotics "Zavalishin's Readings". Springer, Singapore (2021).https://doi.org/10.1007/978-981-15-5580-0_29
9. Durrant-Whyte, H., Bailey, T.: Simultaneous localization and mapping: Part I. IEEE Robot. & Autom. Mag. **13**(2), 99–110 (2006). https://doi.org/10.1109/MRA.2006.1638022

10. Saeedi, S., Trentini, M., Seto, M., Li, H.: Multiple-robot simultaneous localization and mapping: A review. J. Field Robot. **33**(1), 3–46 (2016)
11. Mingachev, E., Lavrenov, R., Tsoy, T., Matsuno, F., Svinin, M., Suthakorn, J., Magid, E.: Comparison of ROS-based monocular visual SLAM methods: DSO, LDSO, ORB-SLAM2 and DYNASLAM. Lecture Notes in Artificial Intelligence. Springer (2020). https://doi.org/10.1007/978-3-030-60337-3_22
12. Filipenko, M., Afanasyev, I.: Comparison of various SLAM systems for mobile robot in an indoor environment. In: International Conference on Intelligent Systems, pp. 400–407. IEEE (2018). https://doi.org/10.1109/IS.2018.8710464
13. Ibragimov, I., Afanasyev, I.: Comparison of ROS-based visual slam methods in homogeneous indoor environment. In: 2017 14th Workshop on Positioning, Navigation and Communications (WPNC), pp. 1–6. IEEE (2017). https://doi.org/10.1109/WPNC.2017.8250081
14. Giubilato, R., Chiodini, S., Pertile, M., Debei, S.: An experimental comparison of ROS-compatible stereo visual SLAM methods for planetary rovers. In: 2018 5th IEEE International Workshop on Metrology for AeroSpace (MetroAeroSpace), pp. 386–391. IEEE (2018). https://doi.org/10.1109/MetroAeroSpace.2018.8453534
15. Sankalprajan, P., Sharma, T. Perur, H.D., Pagala, P.S.: Comparative analysis of ROS based 2D and 3D SLAM algorithms for autonomous ground vehicles. In: 2020 International Conference for Emerging Technology (INCET), pp. 1–6. IEEE (2020). https://doi.org/10.1109/INCET4 9848.2020.9154101
16. Santos, J.M., Portugal, D., Rocha, R.P.: An evaluation of 2D SLAM techniques available in robot operating system. In: The 2013 IEEE International Symposium on Safety, Security, and Rescue Robotics (SSRR), pp. 1–6. IEEE (2013). https://doi.org/10.1109/SSRR.2013.671 9348
17. Chen, Y., Zhang, M., Hong, D., Deng, C., Li, M.: Perception system design for low-cost commercial ground robots: sensor configurations, calibration, localization and mapping. In: 2019 IEEE/RSJ International Conference on Intelligent Robots and Systems (IROS), pp. 6663–6670. IEEE (2019). https://doi.org/10.1109/MRA.2017.2787230
18. Aqel, M., Marhaban, M., Saripan, M., Ismail, N.B.: Review of visual odometry: types, approaches, challenges, and applications. SpringerPlus **5**(1), 1–26 (2016). https://doi.org/10.1186/s40064-016-3573-7
19. He, M., Zhu, C., Huang, Q., Ren, B., Liu, J.: A review of monocular visual odometry. Vis. Comput. **36**(5), 1053–1065 (2020). https://doi.org/10.1007/s00371-019-01714-6
20. Taketomi, T., Uchiyama, H., Ikeda, S.: Visual SLAM algorithms: a survey from 2010 to 2016. IPSJ Trans. Comput. Vis. Appl. **9**(1), 1–11 (2017). https://doi.org/10.1186/s41074-017-0027-2
21. Macario Barros, A., Michel, M., Moline, Y., Corre, G., Carrel, F.: A comprehensive survey of visual SLAM algorithms. Robotics **11**(1), 24 (2022). https://doi.org/10.3390/robotics1101 0024
22. Williams, B., Cummins, M., Neira, J., Newman, P., Reid, I., Tardos, J.: A comparison of loop closing techniques in monocular SLAM. Robot. Auton. Syst. **57**(12), 1188–1197 (2009). https://doi.org/10.1016/j.robot.2009.06.010
23. Abbyasov, B., Lavrenov, R., Zakiev, A., Tsoy, T., Magid, E., Svinin, M., Martinez-Garcia, E.A.: Comparative analysis of ROS-based centralized methods for conducting collaborative monocular visual SLAM using a pair of UAVs. In: Proceedings of the 23rd International Conference on Climbing and Walking Robots and Support Technologies for Mobile Machines, pp. 113–120. CLAWAR Association Ltd (2020). https://doi.org/10.13180/clawar.2020.24-26. 08.12
24. Chen, W., Shang, G., Ji, A., Zhou, C., Wang, X., Xu, C., Li, Z., Hu, K.: An overview on visual SLAM: from tradition to semantic. Remote. Sens. **14**(13), 3010–3057 (2022). https://doi.org/10.3390/rs14133010

25. Buyval, A., Afanasyev, I., Magid, E.: Comparative analysis of ROS-based monocular SLAM methods for indoor navigation. In: Ninth International Conference on Machine Vision (ICMV 2016), pp. 305–310. SPIE (2017). https://doi.org/10.1117/12.2268809
26. Mingachev, E., Lavrenov, R., Magid, E., Svinin, M.: Comparative analysis of monocular SLAM algorithms using TUM and EUROC benchmarks. In: Proceedings of 15th International Conference on Electromechanics and Robotics "Zavalishin's Readings". Springer, Singapore (2021). https://doi.org/10.1007/978-981-15-5580-0_28
27. Krombach, N., Droeschel, D., Behnke, S.: Combining feature-based and direct methods for semi-dense real-time stereo visual odometry. In: The 14th International Conference on Intelligent Autonomous Systems (IAS), pp. 855–868. Springer (2016). https://doi.org/10.1007/978-3-319-48036-7_62
28. Cremers, D.: Direct methods for 3D reconstruction and visual SLAM. In: 2017 Fifteenth IAPR International Conference on Machine Vision Applications (MVA), pp. 34–38. IEEE (2017). https://doi.org/10.23919/MVA.2017.7986766
29. Engel, J., Koltun, V., Cremers, D.: Direct sparse odometry. IEEE Trans. Pattern Anal. Mach. Intell. **40**(3), 611–625 (2017). https://doi.org/10.1109/TPAMI.2017.2658577
30. Gao, X., Wang, R., Demmel, N., Cremers, D.: LDSO: Direct sparse odometry with loop closure. In: 2018 IEEE/RSJ International Conference on Intelligent Robots and Systems (IROS), pp. 2198–2204. IEEE (2018). https://doi.org/10.1109/IROS.2018.8593376
31. Kazerouni, I.A., Fitzgerald, L., Dooly, G., Toal, D.: A survey of state-of-the-art on visual SLAM. Expert. Syst. Appl. **205**(6), 117734–117751 (2022). https://doi.org/10.1016/j.eswa.2022.117734
32. Mur-Artal, R., Tardos, J.D.: ORB-SLAM2: an open-source SLAM system for monocular, stereo, and RGB-D cameras. IEEE Trans. Robot. **33**(5), 1255–1262 (2017). https://doi.org/10.1109/TRO.2017.2705103
33. Campos, C., Elvira, R., Rodrıguez, J.J.G., Montiel, J.M., Tardos, J.D.: ORB-SLAM3: An accurate open-source library for visual, visual–inertial, and multimap SLAM. IEEE Trans. Robot. **37**(6), 1874–1890 (2021). https://doi.org/10.1109/TRO.2021.3075644
34. Merzlyakov, A., Macenski, S.: A comparison of modern general-purpose visual SLAM approaches. In: 2021 IEEE/RSJ International Conference on Intelligent Robots and Systems (IROS), pp. 9190–9197. IEEE (2021)
35. Burri, M., Nikolic, P., Gohl, T., Schneider, J., Rehder, S., Omari, M. W., Achtelik, Siegwart, R.: The EuRoC micro aerial vehicle datasets. Int. J. Robot. Res. **35**(10), 1157–1163 (2016). https://doi.org/10.1177/0278364915620033
36. Geiger, A., Lenz, P., Stiller, C., Urtasun, R.: Vision meets robotics: the KITTI dataset. Int. J. Robot. Res. **32**(11), 1231–1237 (2013). https://doi.org/10.1177/0278364913491297
37. Zhang, Z., Scaramuzza, D.: A tutorial on quantitative trajectory evaluation for visual (-inertial) odometry. In: 2018 IEEE/RSJ International Conference on Intelligent Robots and Systems (IROS), pp. 7244–7251. IEEE (2018)
38. EVO Homepage, https://github.com/MichaelGrupp/evo, last accessed 20 Oct 2022
39. Sturm, J., Engelhard, N., Endres, F., Burgard, W., Cremers, D.: A benchmark for the evaluation of RGB-D SLAM systems. In: 2012 IEEE/RSJ International Conference on Intelligent Robots and Systems, pp. 573–580. IEEE (2012). https://doi.org/10.1109/IROS.2012.6385773

Evaluation of RGB-D SLAM in Large Indoor Environments

Kirill Muravyev[(✉)] ⓘ and Konstantin Yakovlev ⓘ

Federal Research Center "Computer Science and Control" of Russian Academy of Sciences, Vavilov Str. 44-2, 119333 Moscow, Russia
{muraviev,yakovlev}@isa.ru

Abstract. Simultaneous localization and mapping (SLAM) is one of the key components of a control system that aims to ensure autonomous navigation of a mobile robot in unknown environments. In a variety of practical cases, a robot might need to travel long distances in order to accomplish its mission. This requires long-term work of SLAM methods and building large maps. Consequently, the computational burden (including high memory consumption for map storage) becomes a bottleneck. Indeed, state-of-the-art SLAM algorithms include specific techniques and optimizations to tackle this challenge; still their performance in long-term scenarios needs proper assessment. To this end, we perform an empirical evaluation of two widespread state-of-the-art RGB-D SLAM methods, suitable for long-term navigation, i.e. RTAB-Map and Voxgraph. We evaluate them in a large simulated indoor environment, consisting of corridors and halls, while varying the odometer noise for a more realistic setup. We provide both qualitative and quantitative analysis of both methods uncovering their strengths and weaknesses. We find that both methods build a high-quality map with low odometry noise but tend to fail with high odometry noise. Voxgraph has lower relative trajectory estimation error and memory consumption than RTAB-Map, while its absolute error is higher.

Keywords: SLAM · RGB-D SLAM · RTAB-MAP · Voxgraph · Longterm autonomy

1 Introduction

Making a robotic systems fully autonomous is an important problem for modern researchers [1–4]. In order to operate autonomously, the system needs to know its position on the map (environment). In case of indoor or underground environment, global position estimation like GPS is unable to work, so a robotic system has to estimate its position using its own sensors. If the environment is unknown, the map is also need to be built. Therefore, for solving this problem, Simultaneous Localization and Mapping (SLAM) techniques are need.

Traditional SLAM methods like ORB-SLAM [5] build a metric map of the environment matching features extracted from input images or laser scans. They map only feature coordinates, leading to building a sparse map. Path planning in such map is difficult because a planner may create path between feature points through unmapped obstacles.

On the other hand, direct SLAM methods like LSD-SLAM [6] and learning based methods like DROID-SLAM [7] build dense map but require high computational costs to update the map, especially in large environments. So, using them in a real robotic system for long-term navigation is highly restricted.

A possible solution for dense mapping a large environment is utilizing stereo or depth information in feature-based methods and its reprojecting during SLAM process. Such technique is implemented in RTAB-Map method [8]. RTAB-Map builds a graph of key frames and involves a comprehensive memory management approach, which is detailly described in Sect. 4.1. The key frames are stored at three levels of memory that helps maintain large maps and effectively close loops.

Another technique of effective long-lasting SLAM and odometry error elimination is building a graph of small submaps instead of keyframes. A submap is a map of a short segment of the environment built by a SLAM algorithm. It has an anchor pose (e.g. pose of the robot at the time of entering the submap, or pose of the submap's centroid), and these poses are structured in a graph. Pose graph and map correction could be done using graph optimization and submap fusing techniques. Such strategy is implemented in Voxgraph [9] algorithm. In this work, we do empirical evaluation of Voxgraph and RTAB-MAP methods. We conduct a series of experiments in photo-realistic Habitat simulator [10] in our university building model with 100 m corridor, halls and rooms. We evaluate absolute and relative trajectory errors for both methods over trajectories of length up to 1 km. We provide detailed experimental analysis in Sect. 5.

2 Related Work

2.1 SLAM Algorithms

Simultaneous localization and mapping has long history of study and is widely researched. First SLAM methods [11] use extended Kalman filter (EKF) to estimate robot's trajectory from noised sensor data. More recent works [5, 12] extract features from input images and track robot motion matching these features. Also these methods use global optimization techniques like Bundle Adjustment [13] to perform loop closure (global trajectory and map optimization in case of re-visiting a previously visited place). ORB-SLAM2 method [14] includes feature extraction, tracking, local mapping, and loop closing parts, and achieves trajectory estimation error of approximately 1% on KITTI dataset [15]. However, this method builds sparse map (only feature points are mapped), which is not suitable for path planning.

Besides traditional feature-based SLAM methods, deep learning-based methods are also actively developing. In method [16] neural network is used for optical flow estimation in order to accurately estimate robot's position. In work [7] SLAM is performed by a fully learning-based pipeline, including feature extraction and bundle adjustment. Both these methods build dense map and have small error, however, they require powerful GPU to operate, so use of these methods in a mobile robotic system is difficult.

One of the most common classical SLAM methods is RTAB-Map [8]. It tracks robot motion and builds the map matching features extracted from images. It builds dense map using depth information from RGB-D, stereo or lidar data. The map is stored in 3D point cloud format and projected into 2D occupancy grid, which is convenient for path planning. In addition, RTAB-Map utilizes a complex memory management strategy, which helps make effective mapping and loop closing even in large areas. We use this method in our comparison.

For navigation in large environments, map decomposition into submaps is also used. Such decomposition helps effectively optimize map and trajectory, significantly reduce path-planning costs, and eliminate odometry error accumulation. In recent work [17] the map is represented as a graph of submaps, one submap for each room or hallway. For navigation, a graph of doors and passages is used. This approach reduces planning time in two orders of magnitude (0.5 s vs 67 s) in comparison with global metric map. However, despite planning effectiveness, this method requires high computational resources for doors detection to divide the map into submaps.

Another submap-based approach is Voxgraph [9]. Submaps are switched in a fixed period of time. For submap creation, Voxblox [18] method is used. Loop closure is performed in two levels: local (in Voxblox, using ICP [19] method), and global, using graph optimization methods. In work [20], Voxgraph managed to build proper map during exploration of a large indoor area with severe odometry drift. We used Voxgraph method in our experimental evaluation.

2.2 Navigation and Mapping in Large Areas

Navigation in large environments and mapping large areas is an important problem for industrial and service robots. There are some works for building a map up to city-scale size [21]. In work [21], pre-built point cloud maps and cloud global map data like OpenStreetMap are used. In work [17], a hybrid metric-topological approach is used to map large areas. With this approach, a robot successfully explored an indoor area of 1137 m2 with 3 x memory reduction comparing with a metric SLAM approach. Another metric-topological approach for large area navigation is proposed in work [22]. In that work, a global map is divided into submaps—cubes of fixed size. Each submap is built by a conventional feature-based SLAM. During loop closure, only submaps with significant changes are modified, the other submaps only change their position. Indoor and outdoor tests on a robot with 600 m and 1200 m trajectories show that the method is able to maintain and quickly update large maps.

2.3 Long-term SLAM Evaluation

SLAM quality estimation has prolonged history of study. There are many benchmarks for SLAM evaluation, like TUM [23], EuRoC [24], KITTI [15]. With these benchmarks, a lot of comparative analysis of SLAM systems is done [25–27]. However, most of these works evaluate SLAM algorithms in short trajectories and small environments. There are some benchmarks for long-term SLAM evaluation like OpenLORIS [28] and SLAM robustness evaluation research like [29]. These works examine mostly SLAM robustness to environmental conditions changes (like illumination, weather, etc.). In our work, we evaluate SLAM memory and computational effectiveness and robustness to odometry noise in case of long-term running.

3　Problem Statement

Consider a robot equipped with an RGB-D and a noisy odometry sensor in large indoor environment. It moves through the environment along certain trajectory. At each time step t, passing through position p_t, the robot receives image I_t, depth D_t, and odometry estimation $\hat{p} = p_t + \epsilon_t$, where ϵ_t is odometry noise.

The task is to estimate precisely robot's trajectory using noised odometry estimations, images and depths:

$$\tilde{p}_t = A(I_{0..t}, D_{0..t}, \hat{p}_{0..t}); E(p_{0..T}, \tilde{p}_{0..T}) \rightarrow min,$$

where E is an error metric.

We use three error metrics in our evaluation: absolute trajectory error ATE, relative translation error E_{trans}, and relative rotation error E_{rot}:

$$ATE(p_{0..T}, \tilde{p}_{0..T}) = \frac{1}{T+1} \sum_{t=0}^{T} ||p_t - \tilde{p}_t||_2;$$

$$E_{trans}(p_{0..T}, \tilde{p}_{0..T}) = \frac{1}{T} \sum_{t=1}^{T} \frac{\left\| M_{p_{t-1}}^{-1} p_t - M_{\tilde{p}_{t-1}}^{-1} \tilde{p}_t \right\|_2}{||p_t - p_{t-1}||_2};$$

$$E_{rot}(p_{0..T}, \tilde{p}_{0..T}) = \frac{1}{T} \sum_{t=1}^{T} \frac{\angle \left(M_{p_{t-1}}^{-1} p_t, M_{\tilde{p}_{t-1}}^{-1} \tilde{p}_t \right)}{||p_t - p_{t-1}||_2},$$

where M_p is the transformation matrix which transforms zero position and orientation into pose p; $||x||_2$ is L_2-norm of x, and $\angle (a, b)$ is the angle between vectors a and b.

4　Methods Overview

4.1　RTAB-MAP

RTAB-MAP [8] is a feature-based SLAM method, which takes stereo, RGB-D or laser scan data and builds 2D occupancy grid map and 3D point cloud map. This method is divided by odometry estimation, mapping, and loop closure. A scheme of the method is shown in Fig. 1.

For odometry estimation, RTAB-Map extracts features from images using BRIEF detector [30]. For memory and computational efficiency, RTAB-Map selects key frames from the input flow. New keyframe is added when previous keyframe and current frame has few feature matches (less than certain threshold). Robot motion is tracked by feature matching between current and previous keyframes using PnP RANSAC algorithm [31]. Estimated camera position is corrected using Local Bundle Adjustment method [32] and predictions from previous camera motion.

For mapping, local occupancy grids are used. These grids are received from input depth maps or laser scans. Local maps are fused into global map using a voxel filter. Global map is optimized with loop closures. The loop detection algorithm is based on

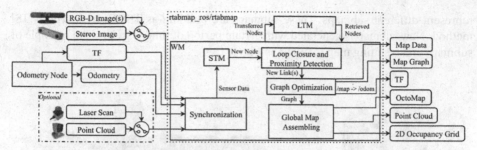

Fig. 1. Scheme of RTAB-MAP algorithm (from [8]).

feature matching on input frames (RGB images or laser scans). Features needed for loop closing are extracted using SURF algorithm [33]. The frames are stored as sets of features organized into kd-trees. For effective loop closure, keyframes are organized as a graph where links are constraints taken from keyframe neighborhood or loop detection. In the loop closure stage, this graph is optimized using g2o graph optimization technique [34].

To store the graph of keyframes, RTAB-MAP uses three levels of memory: working memory (WM), short-term memory (STM), and long-term memory (LTM). WM contains most useful frames, STM contains a sequence of last frames, and LTM contains all frames. Frames that have maximum number of similar features are moved from STM to WM. For loop closure, the frame, which is most similar to current, is used. The loop closure scheme is shown in Fig. 2.

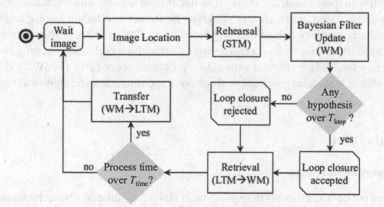

Fig. 2. Scheme of RTAB-MAP loop closure methodology (from [8]).

4.2 Voxgraph

Voxgraph [9] is a SLAM method, which takes odometry, and point cloud data as an input and builds pose graph and global map in Truncated Signed Distance Field (TSDF) format. A global map is building as a set of overlapping submaps. Different colors represent different submaps. These submaps are building as TSDFs by Voxblox [18] method. New submap is generated with certain period of time, e.g. 20 s. An example of submaps and resulting map is shown in Fig. 3.

Fig. 3. An example of Voxgraph map building (from [9]).

Voxgraph algorithm fuses submaps using submap pose graph. The nodes of the pose graph are sensor positions at start of each submap. The edges of the pose graph are constraints for optimization. They are divided into three kinds: odometry, loop closure, and registration constraints. An odometry constraint between neighbor submaps attaches transformation between these submaps to odometry change from start of the first submap to start of the second one. A loop closure constraint comes from loop closure hypothesis from an external loop closure source. It binds corresponding submaps. A registration constraint binds together a pair of overlapping submaps. Voxgraph algorithm optimizes pose graph with these constraints using non-linear least squares minimization technique.

Such graph-based approach lets Voxgraph be robust to odometry noise and significantly reduces memory consumption. According to [20], a robot is able to operate in large area for 10–15 min with severe odometry drift without collisions, keeping low CPU and memory load. With efficient external loop closure source like DBoW2 [35], Voxgraph is able to long-term operation without error accumulation and significant memory growth.

5   Evaluation

5.1   Experimental Setup

We carried out our experiments in large scene in Habitat simulator. The scene represented one store of university building, with a 100 m-long branched corridor, a wide hall and one classroom of size 6×15 m. Virtual agent navigated along a manually set route and was tasked to estimate its trajectory and build a map of the environment. The route was set as a sequence of waypoints, and navigation performed using Habitat's built-in ShortestPathFollower algorithm. We used two routes - the former had length 300 m and consisted of 12 points, the latter had length 1 km and consisted of 25 points. Linear and angular speed of agent were set to 1.5 m/s and 90 degrees/s respectively.

To model real odometry sensors, we noised ground-truth position with Gaussian noise. We used four degrees of noise – small (linear std 0.0015, angular std 0.003), medium (linear std 0.003, angular std 0.0075), large (linear std 0.0075, angular std 0.015), and extra-large (linear std 0.015, angular std 0.025). Linear noise was added to linear speed, angular noise was added to agent's angle. The noise updated every 10 s.

As an RGB-D sensor data, we used ground truth RGB and depth images from the simulator. Depth range was limited by 8 m. Both RGB and depth had resolution 320 × 240, and field of view 90 degrees. For RTAB-MAP, we used only mapping module, which was feed with noised odometry from simulator. We used RTAB-MAP in 3DoF mode, with extraction of 2000 features from each image and enable ray tracing. Height of the obstacle cells was set from 0.2 m to 1.5 m.

For Voxgraph, we set TSDF voxel size to 0.2, submap creation interval to 20 secs, and TSDF truncation distance to 0.8.

5.2 Results

We ran RTAB-Map and Voxgraph methods on 300 m and 1 km trajectories in Habitat simulator with four degrees of odometry noise: small, medium, large and extra-large. For each degree of noise, we ran both the algorithms 5 times and calculated average metric values and their standard deviation. The resulting metric values are shown in Table 1. RTAB-Map demonstrated smaller absolute trajectory errors than Voxgraph, however its translation error was comparable to Voxgraph's one, and its rotation error was significantly larger than that of Voxgraph. An example of estimated trajectories (300 m, extra-large drift) is shown in Fig. 4. We can see that Voxgraph's trajectory has bigger absolute deviation than RTAB-Map's one, however it is closer to ground truth relatively (see Fig. 5). This can be explained by large amount of whole graph optimizations during Voxgraph operation.

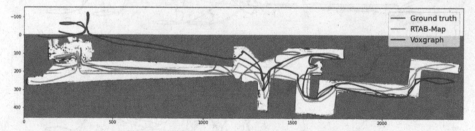

Fig. 4. Trajectories estimated by RTAB-Map (red) and Voxgraph (blue) compared to ground-truth trajectory (green). The background is the map built by RTAB-map, it has a fake corridor in the left part.

Memory consumption values for both algorithms are shown in Table 2. As seen in the table, RTAB-Map took up to 8.6 GB of RAM on 1 km trajectory, which can exceed memory limit on some on-board computers. On 300 m trajectory, RTAB-Map consumed about 3.6 GB of RAM, which is also a large volume. Voxgraph consumed approximately 5–6 times less memory on both trajectories – up to 0.57 GB on 300 m trajectory and up to 1.8 GB on 1 km trajectory with extra-large drift. Such difference in memory volume

Table 1. Evaluation of RTAB-Map and Voxgraph algorithms on 300 m and 1 km trajectories: average metric values and standard deviation of 5 runs. Etrans is the relative translational error, Erot is the relative rotational error (in degrees per meter), ATE is the absolute trajectory error. For all the metrics, lower is better.

Noise		300 m trajectory				1 km trajectory			
		Small	Medium	Large	X-large	Small	Medium	Large	X-large
RTAB-MAP	E_{trans} ($\pm$std)	0.017	0.030	0.072	0.153	0.021	**0.037**	**0.094**	0.187
		0.002	0.0004	0.001	0.007	0.0003	0.0006	0.001	0.004
	E_{rot} ($\pm$std)	0.071	0.106	0.181	0.276	0.213	0.308	0.571	1.29
		0.008	0.012	0.02	0.04	0.005	0.01	0.05	0.45
	ATE ($\pm$std)	0.99	**1.91**	**4.07**	**7.69**	**0.92**	**1.75**	**5.00**	**9.77**
		0.087	0.41	0.37	0.17	0.14	0.23	0.23	1.44
Voxgraph	E_{trans} ($\pm$std)	**0.015**	**0.027**	**0.065**	**0.122**	**0.020**	**0.039**	**0.094**	**0.176**
		0.0005	0.001	0.005	0.003	0.0003	0.0006	0.001	0.004
	E_{rot} ($\pm$std)	**0.033**	**0.073**	**0.152**	**0.229**	**0.031**	**0.071**	**0.181**	**0.316**
		0.002	0.004	0.013	0.021	0.001	0.003	0.033	0.029
	ATE ($\pm$std)	**0.93**	2.21	5.13	10.1	2.43	5.92	10.6	20.0
		0.05	0.15	0.32	0.26	0.04	0.06	1.87	0.97

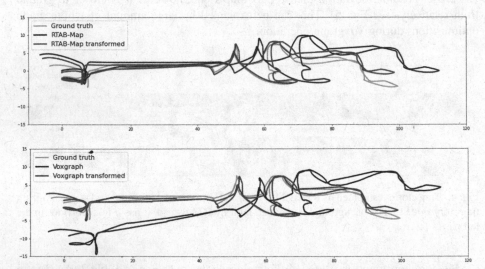

Fig. 5. Comparison of RTAB-Map's (top) and Voxgraph's (bottom) estimated trajectory. Red line denotes ground truth trajectory, black line denotes estimated trajectory, and blue line denotes estimated trajectory fitted into ground truth by a transform (translation, rotation, scaling). Voxgraph's trajectory was fitted more accurately; despite it has bigger absolute deviation.

Table 2. Memory consumption (in GB) of RTAB-Map and Voxgraph algorithms on 300 m and 1 km trajectories.

Noise	300 m trajectory				1 km trajectory			
	Small	Medium	Large	X-large	Small	Medium	Large	X-large
RTAB-MAP	3.6	3.5	3.6	3.7	6.3	6.2	8.5	8.6
Voxgraph	0.52	0.53	0.54	0.57	1.2	1.3	1.3	1.8

is explained by difference in the map type (TSDF vs voxel grid), and difference in the graph structure (graph of submaps, vs graph of key frames).

The built maps of both algorithms on 1 km trajectory are shown in Fig. 6. With small and medium noise degrees, both algorithms built maps close to the ideal, but with large and extra-large noises, both algorithms failed to build a consistent map.

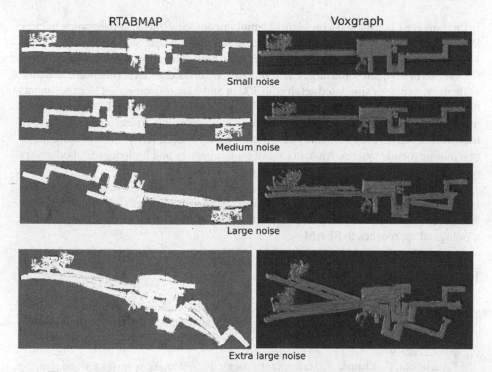

Fig. 6. Visual comparison of RTAB-MAP and Voxgraph maps on 1 km trajectory.

RTAB-Map built fake corridors in the middle part of the map, whereas Voxgraph built fake corridors in the left and the right parts of the map. So, RTAB-Map's loop closure started failing in long distances and severe odometry noises. Voxgraph, which has no built-in loop closure, also fails to fuse large map under severe odometry noise. We also tried Voxgraph with DBoW2 loop closure; this helped reduce number of "corridor bifurcation" cases, but did not eliminate all of them (see Fig. 7). The issue of interaction of Voxgraph and loop closure methods requires additional research.

Pure Voxgraph   Voxgraph with loop closure

Fig. 7. Voxgraph map without loop closure (left) and with DBoW2 loop closure (right). consumption may exceed RAM limit of a computer of a mobile robotic system.

6   Conclusion

In this paper, we considered a problem of simultaneous localization and mapping in large indoor environments. For our study, we chose keyframe-based SLAM method RTAB-Map and submap-based SLAM method Voxgraph, both of them are positioned as suitable for long-term navigation and large environments. We carried out experimental evaluation of them on an indoor simulated setup with 300 m and 1 km trajectories. The experiments have shown that the submap-based method Voxgraph overcomes RTAB-Map in terms of memory consumption and relative errors, but loses in absolute trajectory error. On long trajectories, RTAB-Map's memory consumption may exceed RAM limit of a computer of a mobile robotic system. Also, in case of long trajectory and high degree of odometry noise, both methods fail to build plausible map.

Our empirical evaluation has shown that long-term navigation in large environments is a challenging problem that is lacking a universal solution and needs additional research. The perspective fields of this research are memory-efficient loop closure methods, and topological approaches to SLAM.

References

1. Gonzalez, A.G., Alves, M.V., Viana, G.S., Carvalho, L.K., Basilio, J.C.: Supervisory control-based navigation architecture: a new framework for autonomous robots in Industry 4.0 environments. IEEE Trans. Ind. Inform. **14**(4), 1732–1743 (2017). https://doi.org/10.1109/TII.2017.2788079
2. Papachristos, C., Khattak, S., Mascarich, F., Alexis, K.: Autonomous navigation and mapping in underground mines using aerial robots. In: 2019 IEEE Aerospace Conference, pp. 1–8. IEEE (2019). https://doi.org/10.1109/AERO.2019.8741532
3. Tang, L., Wang, Y., Ding, X., Yin, H., Xiong, R., Huang, S.: Topological localmetric framework for mobile robots navigation: a long term perspective. Auton. Robot. **43**(1), 197–211 (2019). https://doi.org/10.1007/s10514-018-9724-7
4. Choi, J., Park, J., Jung, J., Lee, Y., Choi, H.T.: Development of an autonomous surface vehicle and performance evaluation of autonomous navigation technologies. Int. J. Control. Autom. Syst. **18**(3), 535–545 (2020). https://doi.org/10.1007/s12555-019-0686-0

5. Mur-Artal, R., Montiel, J.M.M., Tardos, J.D.: ORB-SLAM: a versatile and accurate monocular SLAM system. IEEE Trans. Robot. **31**(5), 1147–1163 (2015). https://doi.org/10.1109/TRO.2015.2463671

6. Engel, J., Schops, T., Cremers, D.: LSD-SLAM: Large-scale direct monocular SLAM. In: European Conference on Computer Vision, pp. 834–849. Springer (2014). https://doi.org/10.1007/978-3-319-10605-2_54

7. Teed, Z., Deng, J.: DROID-SLAM: Deep visual SLAM for monocular, stereo, and RGB-D cameras. Adv. Neural Inf. Process. Syst. **34**, 16558–16569 (2021). https://doi.org/10.48550/arXiv.2108.10869

8. Labbe, M., Michaud, F.: RTAB-map as an open-source Lidar and visual simultaneous localization and mapping library for large-scale and long-term online operation. J. Field Robot. **36**(2), 416–446 (2019). https://doi.org/10.1002/rob.21831

9. Reijgwart, V., Millane, A., Oleynikova, H., Siegwart, R., Cadena, C., Nieto, J.: Voxgraph: Globally consistent, volumetric mapping using signed distance function submaps. IEEE Robot. Autom. Lett. **5**(1), 227–234 (2019). https://doi.org/10.1109/lra.2019.2953859

10. Savva, M., Kadian, A., Maksymets, O., Zhao, Y., Wijmans, E., Jain, B., Straub, J., Liu, J., Koltun, V., Malik, J.: Habitat: a platform for embodied AI research. In: Proceedings of the IEEE/CVF International Conference on Computer Vision, pp. 9339–9347 (2019). https://doi.org/10.48550/arXiv.1904.01201

11. Smith, R., Self, M., Cheeseman, P.: A stochastic map for uncertain spatial relationships. In: Proceedings of the 4th International Symposium on Robotics Research, pp. 467–474 (1988)

12. Klein, G., Murray, D.: Parallel tracking and mapping for small AR workspaces. In: 2007 6th IEEE and ACM International Symposium on Mixed and Augmented Reality, pp. 225–234. IEEE (2007). https://doi.org/10.1109/ISMAR.2007.4538852

13. Triggs, B., McLauchlan, P.F., Hartley, R.I., Fitzgibbon, A.W.: Bundle adjustment – a modern synthesis. In: International Workshop on Vision Algorithms, pp. 298–372. Springer (1999). https://doi.org/10.1007/3-540-44480-7_21

14. Mur-Artal, R., Tardos, J.D.: ORB-SLAM2: An open-source SLAM system for monocular, stereo, and RGB-D cameras. IEEE Trans. Robot. **33**(5), 1255–1262 (2017). https://doi.org/10.48550/arXiv.1610.06475

15. Geiger, A., Lenz, P., Stiller, C., Urtasun, R.: Vision meets robotics: the KITTI dataset. Int. J. Robot. Res. **32**(11), 1231–1237 (2013). https://doi.org/10.1177/0278364913491297

16. Min, Z., Dunn, E.: VOLDOR-SLAM: For the times when feature-based or direct methods are not good enough. In: 2021 IEEE International Conference on Robotics and Automation (ICRA), pp. 13813–13819. IEEE (2021). https://doi.org/10.48550/arXiv.2104.06800

17. Gomez, C., Fehr, M., Millane, A., Hernandez, A.C., Nieto, J., Barber, R., Siegwart, R.: Hybrid topological and 3D dense mapping through autonomous exploration for large indoor environments. In: 2020 IEEE International Conference on Robotics and Automation (ICRA), pp. 9673–9679. IEEE (2020). https://doi.org/10.1109/ICRA40945.2020.9197226

18. Oleynikova, H., Taylor, Z., Fehr, M., Siegwart, R., Nieto, J.: Voxblox: Incremental 3D Euclidean signed distance fields for on-board MAV planning. In: 2017 IEEE/RSJ International Conference on Intelligent Robots and Systems (IROS), pp. 1366–1373. IEEE (2017). https://doi.org/10.48550/arXiv.1611.03631

19. Besl, P.J., McKay, N.D.: Method for registration of 3-D shapes. In: Sensor fusion IV: control paradigms and data structures, vol. 1611, pp. 586–606. Spie (1992). DOI: https://doi.org/10.1109/34.121791

20. Schmid, L., Reijgwart, V., Ott, L., Nieto, J., Siegwart, R., Cadena, C.: A unified approach for autonomous volumetric exploration of large scale environments under severe odometry drift. IEEE Robot. Autom. Lett. **6**(3), 4504–4511 (2021). https://doi.org/10.1109/LRA.2021.3068954

21. Niijima, S., Umeyama, R., Sasaki, Y., Mizoguchi, H.: City-scale grid-topological hybrid maps for autonomous mobile robot navigation in urban area. In: 2020 IEEE/RSJ International Conference on Intelligent Robots and Systems (IROS), pp. 2065–2071. IEEE (2020). https://doi.org/10.1109/IROS45743.2020.9340990

22. Schmuck, P., Scherer, S.A., Zell, A.: Hybrid metric-topological 3D occupancy grid maps for large-scale mapping. IFAC-PapersOnLine **49**(15), 230–235 (2016). https://doi.org/10.1016/j.ifacol.2016.07.738

23. Sturm, J., Engelhard, N., Endres, F., Burgard, W., Cremers, D.: A benchmark for the evaluation of RGB-D SLAM systems. In: 2012 IEEE/RSJ International Conference on Intelligent Robots and Systems, pp. 573–580. IEEE (2012). https://doi.org/10.1109/IROS.2012.6385773

24. Burri, M., Nikolic, J., Gohl, P., Schneider, T., Rehder, J., Omari, S., Achtelik, M.W., Siegwart, R.: The EuRoC micro aerial vehicle datasets. Int. J. Robot. Res. **35**(10), 1157–1163 (2016). https://doi.org/10.1177/0278364915620033

25. Bokovoy, A., Muraviev, K.: Assessment of map construction in vSLAM. In: 2021 International Siberian Conference on Control and Communications (SIBCON), pp. 1–6. IEEE (2021). https://doi.org/10.1109/SIBCON50419.2021.9438884

26. Mingachev, E., Lavrenov, R., Magid, E., Svinin, M.: Comparative analysis of monocular SLAM algorithms using TUM and EuRoC benchmarks. In: Proceedings of 15th International Conference on Electromechanics and Robotics "Zavalishin's Readings", pp. 343–355. Springer (2021). https://doi.org/10.1007/978-981-15-5580-0_28

27. Zhang, S., Zheng, L., Tao, W.: Survey and evaluation of RGB-D SLAM. IEEE Access **9**, 21367–21387 (2021). https://doi.org/10.1109/ACCESS.2021.3053188

28. Shi, X., Li, D., Zhao, P., Tian, Q., Tian, Y., Long, Q., Zhu, C., Song, J., Qiao, F., Song, L.: Are we ready for service robots? The openloris-scene datasets for lifelong SLAM. In: 2020 IEEE International Conference on Robotics and Automation (ICRA), pp. 3139–3145. IEEE (2020). https://doi.org/10.1109/ICRA40945.2020.9196638

29. Hong, Z., Petillot, Y., Wallace, A., Wang, S.: Radar SLAM: a robust SLAM system for all weather conditions. arXiv preprint arXiv:2104.05347 (2021). https://doi.org/10.48550/arXiv.2104.0534

30. Calonder, M., Lepetit, V., Strecha, C., Fua, P.: Brief: binary robust independent elementary features. In: European Conference on Computer Vision, pp. 778–792. Springer (2010). https://doi.org/10.1007/978-3-642-15561-1_56

31. Brachmann, E., Krull, A., Nowozin, S., Shotton, J., Michel, F., Gumhold, S., Rother, C.: DSAC-differentiable RANSAC for camera localization. In: Proceedings of the IEEE conference on computer vision and pattern recognition, pp. 6684–6692 (2017). https://doi.org/10.1109/CVPR.2017.267

32. Zhang, Z., Shan, Y.: Incremental motion estimation through local bundle adjustment (2001).

33. Bay, H., Tuytelaars, T., Gool, L.V.: SURF: speeded up robust features. In: European conference on computer vision, pp. 404–417. Springer (2006). https://doi.org/10.1007/11744023_32

34. Kummerle, R., Grisetti, G., Strasdat, H., Konolige, K., Burgard, W.: G2o: a general framework for graph optimization. In: 2011 IEEE International Conference on Robotics and Automation, pp. 3607–3613. IEEE (2011). https://doi.org/10.1109/ICRA.2011.5979949

35. Galvez-Lopez, D., Tardos, J.D.: Bags of binary words for fast place recognition in image sequences. IEEE Trans. Robot. **28**(5), 1188–1197 (2012). https://doi.org/10.1109/TRO.2012.2197158

Goal and Force Switching Policy for DMP-Based Manipulation

Andrey Gorodetsky[1], Konstantin Mironov[1,2](✉) (iD), Daniil Pushkarev[1],
and Aleksandr Panov[2,3] (iD)

[1] Moscow Institute of Physics and Technology, Institutskiy per. 9, 141701 Dolgoprudny,
Moscow Region, Russia
mironovconst@gmail.com
[2] AIRI Artificial Intelligence Research Institute, Kutuzovskii pr., 32/1, 121165 Moscow, Russia
[3] Federal Research Center "Computer Sciences and Control", Vavilova 44/2, 119333 Moscow,
Russia

Abstract. Effective solving of manipulation tasks is significant for collaborative
robots to act within human-oriented environments. It may be executed using classical or learning-based control methods. Classical methods are accurate; however,
they require complicated tuning of the regulators. Learning-based control provide
obtaining the parameters of the process model while training, but this model is
rough. We apply a combined approach to solving manipulation tasks, where the
robot moves to the target vicinity under learning-based control and then operates
the target under simplified classical control. On the first stage, control system
generates reference trajectory for execution using dynamic movement primitives
(DMP). The parameters of the DMP are determined by output of a neural network
and trained via policy optimization. On the second stage the forcing term of the
DMP is set to zero, while goal is defined by the simplified predictive control model.
We evaluate our approach on the tasks of reaching target point by end effector and
pushing elevator button with UR5 collaborative manipulator. Evaluation is made
in Isaac and URSim simulation taking in mind dynamics and functionality of the
robot. The approach is successfully reproduced on a real robot.

Keywords: Robotic manipulator · Dynamic movement primitives · Model
predictive control · Reinforcement learning · Neural dynamic policies

1 Introduction

Modern robotic systems are able to execute various collaborative tasks in human-oriented
environments, e.g. office buildings. Many of these tasks include operating certain objects
with a robotic manipulator [1–4]. Control methods for manipulation tasks may be classical (defining analytical process model and applying control actions influencing this
model) or learning-based (the process model is derived based on machine learning).
Defining the classical control model for each setup and task is a challenging process as it
requires careful choice and tuning of controller setting and parameters. On the contrary,

A. Ronzhin et al. (Eds.): ICR 2022, LNCS 13719, pp. 105–116, 2022.
https://doi.org/10.1007/978-3-031-23609-9_10

learning-based approaches allow the controller to avoid prior knowledge of complicated process models. Reinforcement learning (RL) is of particular interest: this is a way to obtain an optimal sequential decision-making process for solving a task by an agent (in our case, a robotic manipulator), which interacts with the environment. The inference of RL-based controllers provides fast execution of simple tasks; however, the obtained process model is not precise. Therefore, inference results may be not accurate enough. This lead to safety issues of end-to-end learning-based control in real environments, which require additional challenging methods for guaranteeing safety [5].

In this paper, we develop a combined approach to solving manipulation tasks. Our main contribution consists in the design of the two-step control algorithm, which includes RL-based movement to the surrounding of the target and further operation based on simplified model predictive control (MPC). This approach allows us to avoid the inaccuracy and unsafety of RL-based control and complicated tuning of MPC. We use dynamic movement primitives (DMPs) as a concept, which allows representing both modes of control in a similar way. In RL-based control, the parameters of the DMP are obtained from the neural network. Such an approach was proposed in [6] and called Neural Dynamic Policies (NDP). Here we evaluate practical accuracy of the concept and explore longer exploitation of each obtained DMP. In our MPC approach, parameters of the DMP are set in such a way that they reproduce the predictive model of the process. We call our approach "goal and force switching policy" (GFP) as we switch goal and forcing terms of the DMP during task execution.

We develop and evaluate an application of GFP for an example task of robotic button pushing, which is useful for various robotic applications, especially in human-oriented environments. The rest of the paper is organized as follows. Section 2 includes a brief overview of the related works. In Sect. 3 we describe the control model and the learning algorithm, developed within our approach. In Sect. 4, we design a solution for robotic pushing. Section 5 includes experimental evaluation of the proposed ideas, while Sect. 6 provides concluding remarks.

2 Related Works

The standard approach for executing robotic movements is the following. First, the sequence of required robotic positions is defined. Then, the robot trajectory between target positions is determined using a certain planning algorithm. After that, the planned motion is executed using PID regulators.

Among the classical control methods, Model Predictive Control is of great interest. MPC provides real-time optimization for the values of the control input over a specified time interval (prediction horizon). This optimization is based on the model of object dynamics. MPC may be applied for various challenging aspects of manipulation such as path planning [7], avoiding static and dynamic obstacles [8], or providing desirable interactions with the environment [2, 9]. Applying MPC to a multilink robotic manipulator is a challenging task for the following reason. The model of robot dynamics is nonlinear, which leads to high complexity of the process model and optimization procedure. To avoid this complication, the manipulator model is linearized. Most often the linearization method based on the Taylor series expansion is applied. This method was developed in [10, 11]. The authors of the recent work [12] have developed a computa-tionally cheap approach to manipulation (MPC with Integral Compensation). In this approach, the optimization and tuning of controller parameters is done offline, prior to control execution. Actual control input is defined in a reference of matrix additions and multiplications.

In Deep Reinforcement Learning, relatively simple continuous control tasks can be successfully solved by model-free algorithms [13–16]. These algorithms use pol-icy gradients to make updates of policy parameters in order to maximize RL objective. While some tasks can be efficiently solved using reactive behavior, e.g. by following simple rules, model-free algorithms suffer from relatively low sample efficiency. To improve sample efficiency or performance of an RL algorithm, one can introduce induc-tive biases in the form of domain knowledge about how the environment works, which will potentially help the agent make better decisions.

One of the common choices of a dynamical system that is used to describe the movement of robotic systems is Dynamic Movement Primitives (DMPs) [17, 18], which are a special case of a more general dynamical system [19, 20]. They require expert demonstrations for training or evaluation. Introducing a dynamical system to repre-sent movement primitives can be seen as introducing prior knowledge in the form of differential equations, which contain some knowledge about the physical laws of the environment. Introducing such parameterization may simplify a control problem for the policy by offering a temporal abstraction in the form of trajectory and by imposing some restrictions on the consecutive states that are a part of the same trajectory. DMP can be incorporated into the neural network policy in a differentiable way [6], which allows using any policy gradient RL algorithm to train it on raw data of agent-environment interaction.

Because of the complex objective functions, using MPC to solve an RL problem is a hard task. Usually, MPC is used in conjunction with a learned model of the environment in various settings. MPC as a high-performant policy is proposed in [21], which uses a model of the environment learned on interaction data. This algorithm does not update control policy parameters and recomputes control at each step using optimization. It learns the environment model in a supervised manner and can approximate arbitrary nonlinear dynamics.

MPC as a data collecting policy is used in [22]. This method is a model-based policy optimization algorithm that learns an ensemble of functions to approximate transition dynamics. MPC samples rollouts from the environment model, the policy is trained using a maximum-entropy objective on a mix of model and environment data. MPC as a control policy for learning dynamics model is used in [23]. The method performs model-based policy optimization with subsequent model-free fine-tuning. The algorithm uses a simple random-sampling shooting method together with an environment model to perform model-predictive control. Using parameter-free MPC as a control policy avoids policy degradation due to inaccuracies in the environment model. This method is extended in [24] by introducing optimization and filtering into the MPC loop and probabilistic ensembles to represent environment dynamics.

Our method uses MPC as a control policy in the last stage of the movement execution process to increase positioning accuracy.

3   DMP, MPC, and RL for Manipulation

Trajectories consist of elements of an agent's state space (two common choices—joint coordinates or gripper coordinates). Let y be the inner robot state, $\dot{y}$ is velocity, and $\ddot{y}$ is acceleration. Denoting the goal state as g, the DMP is described by the equation [6, 17]:

$$\ddot{y} = \alpha(\beta(g - y) - \dot{y}) + f(x), \tag{1}$$

where α, β are chosen to guarantee critical damping and smooth convergence to the goal state. f is a nonlinear function, which describes the shape of the trajectory. Evolution of x is described by:

$$\dot{x} = -a_x x. \tag{2}$$

Function f is implemented as an RBF system:

$$f(x, g) = \frac{\sum \psi_i w_i}{\sum \psi_i} x(g - y_0), \quad \psi_i = e^{(-h_i(x-c_i)^2)}, \tag{3}$$

where $i = [1..n]$. and n is the number of basis functions. Coefficients $c_i = e^{\frac{-i\alpha_x}{n}}$ are responsible for shift and $h_i = \frac{n}{c_i}$ for width of the basis functions. The trajectory of the dynamical system is determined by two parameters: the weights of the basis functions $w = w_1, \ldots, w_i, \ldots, w_n$ and the goal g.

If the vector of joint angles of the manipulator $\theta[k]$ at the moment $[k]$ is considered as inner state y, (1) will get the following view:

$$\ddot{\theta}[k] = DMP(g[k], \theta[k], \dot{\theta}[k], \alpha, \beta, f(x))$$
$$= \alpha(\beta(g[k] - \theta[k]) - \dot{\theta}[k]) + f(x). \tag{4}$$

Equations (2) and (3) represent the view of the forcing function, which was pro-posed in [17] and applied in [6]. Now let us denote another setting for Eq. (1) in order to insert there the predictive model from [12]. Two terms from (1) are the subject of modification: goal g and forcing function $f(x)$. In our learning-based solution, the values of g and $f(x)$ are defined by the neural network (see Sect. 4). For our MPC solution, we set $f(x) = 0$ (to avoid complication of the model) and denote g in such a way that Eq. (1) becomes a DMP-representation of MPC trajectory following.

Angular acceleration in MPC trajectory following [12] is defined based on the angular position and velocity at the moment k and on desired trajectory:

$$\ddot{\theta}[k|k+1] = K_{MPC}(\Theta_d[k|k+p] - \mathbf{I_a}\theta[k] - \mathbf{I_b}\dot{\theta}[k]), \tag{5}$$

$$\mathbf{I_{a(p \times n)}} = (\mathbf{I}, \mathbf{I}, \ldots \mathbf{I})^T, \mathbf{I_{b(p \times n)}} = (\mathbf{I}, 2\mathbf{I}, \ldots p\mathbf{I})^T \cdot \Delta t.$$

Here $\ddot{\theta}[k|k+1]$. is an acceleration between time moments k and $k+1$(assumed to be constant), Δt is time interval between k and $k+1$, I is identity matrix, p is prediction horizon, n is number of manipulator's DoF, $\Theta_d[k|k+p]$ is a vector of size $p \cdot n$ representing the desired reference of joint angles made at the moment k for next p steps. K_{MPC}

is defined based on the formulation and solution of the optimal control problem (see [12] for exact definition). Here we reformulate (5) based on the following two properties of K_{MPC}. First, K_{MPC} is n by $p \cdot n$ matrix consisting of $p \cdot n$ diagonal matrices of size by n. Let us call them $K_1, K_2, \ldots, K_p$. Second, for any diagonal matrix $K_1, K_2, \ldots, K_p$, the diagonal elements will be equal. Let us call their values $k_1, k_2, \ldots, k_p$. Taking in mind these properties (5) may be reformulated as follows:

$$\ddot{\theta}[k+1] = \sum_{i=1}^{p}(k_i \theta_d[k+i]) - \theta[k] \sum_{i=1}^{p} k_i - \dot{\theta}[k] \cdot \Delta t \cdot \sum_{i=1}^{p} ik_i. \quad (6)$$

This equation may be considered as a case of (4) with the following setup:

$$\alpha_{MPC} = \Delta t \cdot \sum_{i=1}^{p} ik_i, f_{MPC} = 0, \beta_{MPC}$$
$$= \frac{\sum_{i=1}^{p} k_i}{\Delta t \cdot \sum_{i=1}^{p} ik_i}, g_{MPC}[k] = \frac{\sum_{i=1}^{p}(k_i \theta_d[k+i])}{\sum_{i=1}^{p} k_i}. \quad (7)$$

Here $g_{MPC}[k]$ is redefined for eh step, while other parameters may be defined on the initialization stage. This setting is applicable for the situation when the desired trajectory is predefined and satisfying controller safety limits (as in [12]). As we propose to use it for local control of the manipulator in the small area, we can define the trajectory to be safe.

In the RL-based solution we use DMPs to model state-space trajectories that the agent predicts for further execution [6, 25]. The general idea is in parametrizing the action space of the agent's deep neural network policy by a parametric family of nonlinear differential equations and training it using the RL algorithm. Thus, the neural network makes predictions in the space of trajectories. The embedded dynamical system allows optimizing the parameters of the whole policy by end-to-end differentiation. The choice of the differential equation to represent the space of trajectories is due to the fact that its integral curves, which represent the trajectories of material objects in Euclidean space, are physically plausible.

To produce output, neural net Φ takes s and predicts w, g.

These w, g are used to solve the dynamical system (1) to obtain robot inner state $\{y, \dot{y}, \ddot{y}\}$. Thus, Neural Dynamic Policy (NDP) is defined as $\pi(a|s; \theta) \triangleq \Omega(\text{DE}(\Phi(s; \theta)))$, where $\text{DE}(w, g) \rightarrow \{y, \dot{y}, \ddot{y}\}$ means solving the differential Eq. (1).

During model inference, acceleration is computed from Eq. (1) using previous state $y_{t-1}, \dot{y}_{t-1}$:

$$\ddot{y}_t = \alpha(\beta(g - y_{t-1}) - \dot{y}_{t-1} + f(x_t, g). \quad (8)$$

Forward Euler method is used to integrate the equation:

$$\dot{y}_t = \dot{y}_{t-1} + \ddot{y}_{t-1}dt, y_t = y_{t-1} + \dot{y}_{t-1}dt \quad (9)$$

The integration process unrolls for m steps. Then one could apply m states y_t as action to the robot through inverse controller $\Omega(.)$, or to subsample trajectory into $k \in \{1, m\}$ actions. To update network parameters, we use proximal policy optimization (PPO) [15]. The loss is computed for such (s, a) pairs, that a is a k-th element of action sequence generated from s.

4   Solution for Pushing Task

In this section, we define the two-stage DMP-based control algorithm, which allow the manipulator to execute button pushing tasks. At the first "global" stage, RL-based DMP is applied to move the robot to the button surrounding. On the second "local" stage MPC-based DMP is applied to execute precised pushing motion. Example setup for the considered task is shown in Fig. 1. The task is executed by the Husky mobile robotic platform with mounted UR5 manipulator. Button location is determined by the computer vision system that is out of the scope of this article.

Fig. 1. Setup for an example task of robotic button pushing.

Ability of the robot to push buttons is useful for various applications such as calling the elevator [26–28], autonomous road crossing [29] or activating emergency alert in an industrial environment [30]. The task consists of two main subtasks: first, button positioning based on sensor input and, second, controlling pushing motion. The control method for pushing the button depends on the construction of the robot (Cartesian or joint-based). Some works consider Cartesian manipulators, e.g. [29–31], and methods from these works are not applicable for the setup from Fig. 1. The works using joint-based manipulators [26–28] are more relevant. In [26] a planar manipulator with three joints was applied. The transition from Cartesian coordinates of the button to respective joint angles was introduced, however the control of robotic motion from initial position towards the button was not considered. In [28], the camera was mounted on a gripper and the commands were defined in such a way that they provided convergence of the camera image to the desired view. Each iteration of the algorithm determined the current angular position of the button corners in the camera coordinates, calculated the desired position of the button at the image, determined the desired position of the manipulator, and moved toward the desired position. In [27], a humanoid robot with the 3DoF arm was used. Two stages of movement were introduced: movement into the button surrounding and further fine tuning towards the target position. For both stages the motion was considered as direct mapping from initial to the target joint position.

4.1 Trajectory for Button Pushing

We define the pushing task in the following way. As an input we have estimated Cartesian button coordinates $\tilde{x}_{tar}$ and current joint coordinates $\theta[k]$. First, we put our global target x_{tar} onto the normal to the button in such a way that the distance from x_{tar} to $\tilde{x}_{tar}$ is equal to $e_{pos} + e_{dmp.}$, where e_{pos} is the allowed error of positioning and $e_{dmp.}$ is the allowed error of RL-based DMP.

After that, RL-based DMP is applied to move the manipulator to the certain point $x[k]$ such that the distance between $x[k]$ and x_{tar} is less that e_{dmp}. Our task now is to define the trajectory, which let the robot push the button. First, the end effector moves from point $x[k]$ to the point on the normal to the button such that the distance from $\tilde{x}_{tar}$ is equal to e_{pos}. Then it moves along the normal till the contact with the button. In order to make the trajectory smooth, its first part should be the curve, such that the button normal is a tangent to this curve on a distance e_{pos} from $\tilde{x}_{tar}$. We choose the simplest case, when it is a parabola. The motion of the robot should not be too fast in order to avoid damage. We know that $x[k]$ is near the button normal and assume that the di. Since to $\tilde{x}_{tar}$ may be underestimated. Therefore, we can replace $\tilde{x}_{tar}$ with $\hat{x}_{tar} = \tilde{x}_{tar} + \Delta x$ where Δx is an error bias corresponding to e_{pos}. We define trajectory in such a way that the end effector moves along the straight line from $x[k]$ to $\hat{x}_{tar}$. This line is represented as a sequence of points $x[k], x[k+1], \ldots, x[k+p] = \hat{x}_{tar}$. The distance between the points is defined in such a way that provide required smoothness and slow motion. After that, the reference of $x[k], x[k+1], \ldots, x[k+p] = \hat{x}_{tar}$ is replaced with $\theta[k], \theta[k+1], \ldots, \theta[k+p] = \hat{\theta}_{tar}$. Using the method of calculating inverse kinematics from [12]. The defined reference of angular position is then used to calculate MPC-based goal term for a DMP controller according to (7).

4.2 Two-Stage Control Algorithm

The design of our algorithm is shown in Pseudocode 1 and Fig. 2. It consists of two serial loops: RL-based loop (lines 2–12 of the pseudocode) and MPC-based loop (lines 15–22 of the pseudocode). On each iteration of both loops, the control input is defined via forward Euler integration of DMP output (blue boxes on the scheme). The first loop provides the motion from initial position to the button surrounding. The goal and the forcing term of the DMP are derive from the neural network (green boxes on the scheme). After reaching the target surrounding DMP parameters are switched from RL-based to MPC-based. Pushing trajectory is determined as it is described in Sect. 4.2 (lines 13 and 14 of the pseudocode, and yellow boxes at the scheme). After that, the second loop is applied to push the button. End effector is moving along the line until the force sensor measures the fact of the push or until it reaches $\hat{x}_{tar}$.

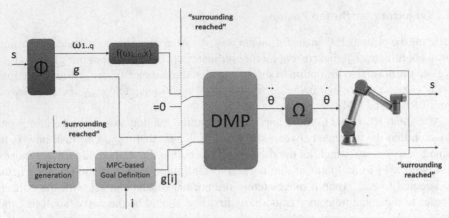

Fig. 2. Scheme of the controller.

Pseudocode 1 Solution for pushing task

Require: α_{MPC}, β_{MPC}, $\theta[1]$, q, p, x_{tar}, e_{dmp}, e_{pos}

1: k = 1
2: **while** button surrounding not achieved **do**
3:     once in T steps:
4:         $\{\omega_{1..n}, g[i]\}_{i=k..k+T} = \Phi(\theta[k])$
5:         $x = x(k)$
6:         $f = f(\omega_{1..n}, x)$
7:     **for** i=k,k+1,...,k+q-1 **do**
8:         $\ddot{\theta}[i+1] = DMP(\theta[i], g[k], \dot{\theta}[i], \alpha_{MPC}, \beta_{MPC}, f)$
9:         $\dot{\theta}[i+1] = \Omega(\ddot{\theta}[i+1], \dot{\theta}[k])$
10:        Execute $\dot{\theta}[i+1]$
11:    **end for**
12:    $k = k+q$
13: **end while**
14: Define $\hat{x}_{tar}$
15: $\{p, \Theta[k|k+p]\} = Trajectory(y[k], x_{tar}, e_{pos}, e_{dmp})$
16: **for** i = $k+1, k+2, ..., k+p$ **do**
17:    Define $g[k]$
18:    $\ddot{\theta}[k|k+1] = DMP(\theta[k], g[k], \dot{\theta}[k], \alpha_{MPC}, \beta_{MPC}, 0)$
19:    $\dot{\theta}[k+1] = \Omega(\ddot{\theta}[k|k+p], \dot{\theta}[k])$
20:    Execute $\dot{\theta}[k+1]$
21:    $k = k+1$
22:    **if** button_is_pushed **then** break
23: **end for**

5   Experiments

Experimental evaluation was done in two stages. At the first stage, RL-based solution was examined using MuJoCo and URSim simulation environments. At the second stage, algorithm 1 was evaluated in URSim and reproduced on a real manipulator.

The learning environment consists of a 6-DoF UR5 robotic arm model with the first three joints from the robot base being controllable by the agent and others fixed. The goal is to reach a specific point with the end effector. The goal is sampled uniformly in the sphere with a radius of 0.2 m centered on the point located 0.5 m in front of the robot base and 0.5 m above the floor. Each episode lasts 250 simulation steps of s each. The positioning error of less than 10 cm at the last step of the episode was considered a success. The agent acts in the space of increments of joints' coordinates. During training, we assume that the control system of the robot is capable of precisely positioning each joint within a 0.03 rad neighborhood of the current position in one simulation step. The agent rolls out the integrator for 35 steps and subsamples the sequence of length 3, each element of which is sequentially executed in the environment as an action. As an observation, the agent gets positions and velocities of the controllable joints, the position of the goal and the end-effector, as well as the current reference for the position control system. The reward function maps state to a negative distance from the end-effector to the goal.

Results show an average error of 3 cm (Fig. 3). We denote NDP, which generates an action sequence of length q as NDP-q, the same for PPO. In our experiments in the UR5 environment, NDP-3 reaches the performance level required to reach the 10 cm vicinity of the target point faster than PPO-1. However, in the long run, PPO-1 shows a smaller average error, but both PPO and NDP have too high position variance of the end effector for precise positioning and thus are switched for another control technique near the button. If we perform NDP update using state-action pairs from the same step [6], resulting performance degrades heavily compared to trajectory-cohesive update, described in Sect. 3.

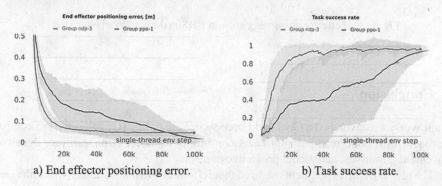

a) End effector positioning error.   b) Task success rate.

Fig. 3. NDP and PPO training performance in MuJoCo environment.

After training, we run the agent in URSim environment, which showed a terminal positioning error of less than 7 cm (Fig. 5). e_{dmp} was set to this value. e_{pos} was set to 4 cm according to the results from Sect. 5.B. The evaluation of the MPC-based local control in URSim showed that it provides successful motion along the defined trajectory. Execution of the same MPC-based algorithm for complete movement from initial position to the button failed as the controller could not find an inverse kinematic solution, providing unconstrained motion along the trajectory. The approach was reproduced on a real UR5 arm. The procedure may be seen in the supplementary video [32] (Fig. 4).

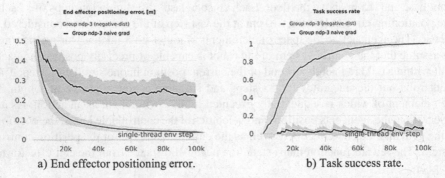

a) End effector positioning error.   b) Task success rate.

Fig. 4. NDP performance with naive and trajectory-cohesive parameters update.

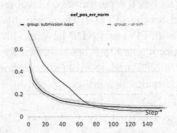

Fig. 5. End effector positioning error in URSim during model inference.

6   Conclusion

In our work, we developed a Goal and Force switching policy (GFP)—a hybrid control approach for robotic manipulation tasks combining reinforcement learning, dynamic movement primitives, and model predictive control.

The results of the experiments showed that RL-based DMPs are able to move the end effector to the vicinity of the target, and simplified MPC provides accurate execution of the trajectory within this surrounding. The proposed approach allowed us to execute an example task of pushing the elevator button, which could not be solved via the application of both approaches separately.

Acknowledgements. This work was supported by the Ministry of Science and Higher Education of the Russian Federation under Project 075-15-2020-799.

References

1. Yang, P.Y., Chang, T.H., Chang, Y.H., Wu, B.F.: Intelligent mobile robot controller design for hotel room service with deep learning arm-based elevator manipulator. In: 2018 International Conference on System Science and Engineering (ICSSE), pp. 1–6 (2018).
2. Mironov, K., Mambetov, R., Panov, A., Pushkarev, D.: Model predictive control with torque constraints for velocity-driven robotic manipulator. In: 2021 20th International Conference on Advanced Robotics (ICAR), pp. 107–112 (2021). https://doi.org/10.1109/ICAR53236.2021.9659428
3. Pushkarev, D., et al.: Door opening strategy for mobile manipulator with constrained configuration. In: Ronzhin, A., Meshcheryakov, R., Xiantong, Z (eds.) Interactive Collaborative Robotics (ICR). Lecture Notes in Computer Science (2023)
4. Aitygulov, E., Panov, A.I.: Transfer learning with demonstration forgetting for robotic manipulator. Procedia Comput. Sci. **186**, 374–380 (2021). https://doi.org/10.1016/j.procs.2021.04.159
5. Knuth, C., Chou, G., Ozay, N., Berenson, D.: Planning with learned dynamics: probabilistic guarantees on safety and reachability via Lipschitz constants. Robot. Autom. Lett. **6**(3), 5129–5136 (2021). https://doi.org/10.1109/LRA.2021.3068889
6. Bahl, S., Mukadam, M., Gupta, A., Pathak, D.: Neural dynamic policies for end-to-end sensorimotor learning. Adv. Neural Inf. Process. Syst. **33**, 5058–5069. Preprint at arXiv:2012.02788 (2020)
7. Tika, A., Gafur, N., Yfantis, V., Bajcinca, N.: Optimal scheduling and model predictive control for trajectory planning of cooperative robot manipulators. IFAC-PapersOnLine **53**(2), 9080–9086 (2020)
8. Li, W., Xiong, R.: Dynamical obstacle avoidance of task-constrained mobile manipulation using model predictive control. IEEE Access **7**, 88301–88311 (2019). https://doi.org/10.1109/ACCESS.2019.2925428
9. Wahrburg A., Listmann, L.: MPC-based admittance control for robotic manipulators. In: 55th Conference on Decision and Control (CDC), pp. 7548–7554. IEEE (2016). https://doi.org/10.1109/CDC.2016.7799435
10. Poignet, P., Gautier, M.: Nonlinear model predictive control of a robot manipulator. In: 6th International Workshop on Advanced Motion Control. Proceedings Cat. No. 00TH8494, pp. 401–406. IEEE (2000)
11. Hedjar, R., Toumi, R., Boucher, P. Dumur, D.: Feedback nonlinear predictive control of rigid link robot manipulators. In: Proceedings of the 2002 American Control Conference, Cat. No. CH37301, vol. 5, pp. 3594–3599. IEEE (2002)
12. Chen, Y., Luo, X., Han, B., Luo, Q., Qiao, L.: Model predictive control with integral compensation for motion control of robot manipulator in joint and task spaces. IEEE Access **8**, 107063–107075 (2020). https://doi.org/10.1109/ACCESS.2020.3001044
13. Haarnoja, T., Zhou, A., Abbeel, P. Levine, S.: July. Soft actor-critic: Off-policy maximum entropy deep reinforcement learning with a stochastic actor. In: International conference on machine learning, pp. 1861–1870. PMLR (2018).
14. Fujimoto, S., Hoof, H. Meger, D.: Addressing function approximation error in actor-critic methods. In: International Conference on Machine Learning, pp. 1587–1596. PMLR (2018)
15. Schulman, J., Wolski, F., Dhariwal, P., Radford, A. Klimov, O.: Proximal policy optimization algorithms. Preprint at arXiv:1707.06347 (2017)

16. Mnih, V., Badia, A.P., Mirza, M., Graves, A., Lillicrap, T., Harley, T., Silver, D. Kavukcuoglu, K.: Asynchronous methods for deep reinforcement learning. In: International conference on machine learning, pp. 1928–1937. PMLR (2016)

17. Ijspeert, A.J., Nakanishi, J., Hoffmann, H., Pastor, P., Schaal, S.: Dynamical movement primitives: learning attractor models for motor behaviors. Neural Comput. **25**(2), 328–373 (2013)

18. Schaal, S.: Dynamic movement primitives-a framework for motor control in humans and humanoid robotics. In: Adaptive Motion of Animals and Machines, pp. 261–280. Springer, Tokyo (2006)

19. Ratliff, N.D., Issac, J., Kappler, D., Birchfield, S., Fox, D.: Riemannian motion policies. Preprint at arXiv: 1801.02854 (2018)

20. Younes, A. Panov, A.I.: Toward faster reinforcement learning for robotics: using Gaussian processes. In: Artificial Intelligence, pp. 160–174. Springer, Cham (2019). https://doi.org/10.1007/978-3-030-33274-7_11

21. Williams, G., Wagener, N., Goldfain, B., Drews, P., Rehg, J.M., Boots, B. Theodorou, E.A.: Information theoretic MPC for model-based reinforcement learning. In: 2017 IEEE International Conference on Robotics and Automation (ICRA), pp. 1714–1721. IEEE (2017)

22. Morgan, A.S., Nandha, D., Chalvatzaki, G., D'Eramo, C., Dollar, A.M., Peters, J.: Model predictive actor-critic: accelerating robot skill acquisition with deep reinforcement learning. In: 2021 IEEE International Conference on Robotics and Automation (ICRA), pp. 6672–6678. IEEE (2021)

23. Nagabandi, A., Kahn, G., Fearing, R.S., Levine, S.: Neural network dynamics for model-based deep reinforcement learning with model-free fine-tuning. In: 2018 IEEE International Conference on Robotics and Automation (ICRA), pp. 7559–7566. IEEE (2018)

24. Nagabandi, A., Konolige, K., Levine, S., Kumar, V.: Deep dynamics models for learning dexterous manipulation. In: Conference on Robot Learning, pp. 1101–1112. PMLR (2020)

25. Zholus, A., Ivchenkov, Y., Panov, A.I.: Addressing task prioritization in model-based reinforcement learning. In: International Conference on Neuroinformatics, pp. 19–30. Springer, Cham (2022). https://doi.org/10.1007/978-3-031-19032-2_3

26. Wang, W.J., Huang, C.H., Lai, I.H., Chen, H.C.: A robot arm for pushing elevator buttons. In: Proceedings of SICE Annual Conference, pp. 1844–1848. IEEE (2010).

27. Tiyu, F.A.N.G., Huiwu, C.H.E.N., Jianjie, S.H.I., Jinping, L.I.: Positioning and pressing elevator button by binocular vision and robot manipulator. In: 2018 International Conference on Security, Pattern Analysis, and Cybernetics (SPAC), pp. 120–133. IEEE (2018).

28. Zhu, D., Min, Z., Zhou, T., Li, T., Meng, M.Q.H.: An autonomous eye-in-hand robotic system for elevator button operation based on deep recognition network. IEEE Trans. Instrum. Meas. **70**, 1–13 (2021). https://doi.org/10.1109/TIM.2020.3043118

29. Chand, A.N.: Design of an intelligent outdoor mobile robot with autonomous road-crossing function for urban environments. In: 2012 IEEE/ASME International Conference on Advanced Intelligent Mechatronics (AIM), pp. 355–362. IEEE (2012). https://doi.org/10.1109/AIM.2012.6265913

30. Meng, X., et al.: Contact force control of an aerial manipulator in pressing an emergency switch process. In: 2018 IEEE/RSJ International Conference on Intelligent Robots and Systems (IROS), pp. 2107–2113. IEEE (2018)

31. Wang, F., Chen, G., Hauser, K.: Robot button pressing in human environments. In: IEEE International Conference on Robotics and Automation (ICRA), pp. 7173–7180. IEEE (2018). https://doi.org/10.1109/ICRA.2018.8463180

32. Robotic button pushing based on dynamic movement primitives, https://youtu.be/8g13Kujqc zo2022/09/02. Accessed 11 Sept 2022.

Impedance Control of an Elastic Actuator with Strongly Coupled Structure

Igor Shardyko[(✉)] [ID], Vladislav Kopylov [ID], and Victor Titov [ID]

Russian State Scientific Center for Robotics and Technical Cybernetics, Tikhoretsky Pr. 21, 194064 Saint-Petersburg, Russia
i.shardyko@rtc.ru

Abstract. Compliance has become a widespread topic in industrial robotics in the last decades, both in hardware and in software . In terms of software, virtual compliance is applied widely, mostly the various implementations of impedance control algorithms. Concerning mechanics, series elastic actuators have gained a lot of attention, which are superior to the traditional rigid robotic joints in terms of shock robustness, interaction safety, torque control etc. In this article, one relatively rare case of such system is considered, i.e. a differential-drive robotic joint. This type of joint makes it possible to move the motors out of the joint unit and transmit motion regardless of the configuration of the joint axes. However, this layout leads to strong coupling between input and output joint angles. Introduction of elasticity further complicates the matter, as in general there is coupling in elastic torques as well. Hence, the control system should provide as much decoupling as possible to get satisfactory performance. A mathematical model of this joint has been designed as well as a control system based on elastic structure preserving impedance control. The latter has been verified by simulation in Simulink.

Keywords: Flexible joint robot · Control system · Differential-drive joint · Matlab · Simulink · Impedance control · Elastic structure preserving control · ESπ-control

1 Introduction

The application area of robotics is wide and deep, and includes a lot of various tasks in different environments. One of those tasks pertains to manipulation in hazardous cells, which requires great endurance to detrimental factors such as heat, radiation, etc. To meet the requirements, one can move the motors out of the arm into the stationary and isolated base of the manipulator, as considered in the recent paper [1]. It was also suggested to bring elasticity into the joints in order to increase interaction safety and obtain torque feedback. The necessity of torque feedback is caused by the task nature.

Basically, all robotic tasks can be divided into so-called contact and free tasks. Free tasks assume the positioning of objects without accounting for the interaction with the environment. The interaction may or may not happen, but if it does, then the motion is strictly precomputed and there is no need to measure interaction forces, e.g. when the object location is exactly known and the robot accuracy is sufficiently high.

A. Ronzhin et al. (Eds.): ICR 2022, LNCS 13719, pp. 117–129, 2022.
https://doi.org/10.1007/978-3-031-23609-9_11

However, this is not the case for a number of tasks in [1] for at least two reasons. First, the mechanical arm with distant location of the motors makes smooth motions not possible. Second and more important, the robotic arm should perform a lot of service tasks that cannot be described exactly, because the objects can be dislocated in the cell to some extent from their specified position. There can be technical means to identify the actual locations of the objects, but there still will be some errors. The straightforward way to overcome this problem is the implementation of torque feedback, and in [1] it was chosen to obtain it through the introduction of elastic elements, i.e. torsion springs, into the joins and certain placement of position sensors. Thus, the deformation of the springs can be measured, and the torque can be easily found based on the deformation and known spring stiffness.

But the hardware alone cannot solve the interaction task. The interaction itself can be described differently, which is primarily defined by the task. Some tasks require that exact force should be applied in certain directions, like in cutting or gluing [2] tasks. Other tasks require that the end effector tracks some predefined trajectory and in case of interaction with some external object it should behave in some desired way, which is guaranteeing safe and stable contact while trying to achieve the task objective. In [3] it was proposed to employ the notion of impedance to describe this interaction.

To briefly introduce a reader, basic principles can be defined as follows [4]. From a systems point of view, the input/output behavior of a linear continuous system of the type considered here is described by the ratio of two variables, effort (F) and flow $(v = \dot{x})$. For a mechanical system, effort is represented by force and torque, and flow is represented by linear and angular velocity. Motors and batteries are considered equivalent, in a system sense, both being effort sources. Similarly, a current generator or a rotating cam shaft are both flow sources. Passive elements are characterized by resistance (B), capacitance (K), and inertia (M). Resistance represents the proportional relationship between effort and flow, $B = F/v$, capacitance represents their integral relationship, $K = F \int v dt$, and inertia represents their differential relationship, $M = F/\dot{v}$. For linear, time-invariant continuous systems, the impedance Z may be defined as the ratio of the Laplace transform of the effort $F(s)$ to the Laplace transform of the flow $v(s)$. For nonlinear systems, the term impedance can still be used to describe the relationship between effort and flow. In this case, the impedance is operating point dependent. That is, the impedance of the nonlinear system is defined as the equivalent linear impedance for the system linearized about a particular operating point.

Hogan in his work [3] also introduced the notion of admittance, analyzed the duality of admittance and impedance and justified that a robot should represent the impedance side. However, later a lot of discussion was devoted to the different issues related to the choice and implementation of desired behavior. In practice, the impedance equation is typically chosen so as to enforce an equivalent mass-damper-spring behavior for the end-effector position displacement under an external force acting on the end effector [5]. This behavior is well illustrated with the scheme in Fig. 1 [6], where x is the current end-effector position, F_{ext} is the external force, $\Lambda_d, D_d,$ and K_d, are the desired virtual mass, damping and stiffness respectively.

Control algorithms, directed to make a robot behave in this way, are known as impedance control, which was proposed in [3] and gained extreme popularity since.

Plenty of subtopics appeared within the overall subject: force-based impedance control [7], motion-based impedance control [8], hybrid impedance control [4], and others. One important subtopic is impedance control of robots with elastic joints, e.g. [9].

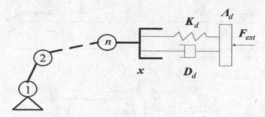

Fig. 1. The scheme of traditional impedance control in task space.

It is often sufficient and/or desired that virtual mass should be to equal actual mass, due to simplicity and easier stability analysis [10]. Then the impedance equation simply reflects damped elastic deformation, or Voigt model. Actually, there is also Maxwell model of plastic deformation that also represents impedance, and recently there have published a number of studies that implemented such a behavior [11]. The principal schemes of these models are depicted in Fig. 2. Certainly, other models can be built on the basis of these bricks, which can also comprise elements of mass in the branches [12].

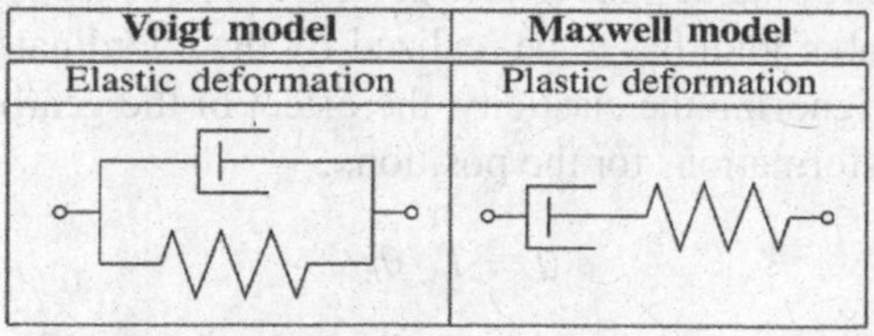

Voigt model	Maxwell model
Elastic deformation	Plastic deformation

Fig. 2. Principal schemes of elastic and plastic deformation.

Those seeking more information on the subject may refer to the review articles published recently. The application of impedance control is immense, but just to name a few: large workpiece assembly [13], grinding and polishing [14], quadruped legs [15], haptic devices [16], and much more.

Getting back to the robotic arm in question [1], there is another distinctive feature, i.e. the shoulder, the elbow and the wrist are represented by 2-DoF coupled, differentially-driven joints, which kinematic scheme is shown in Fig. 3. Similar solutions can be found in [17] and [18], where coupled and elastic joints are employed as well for an arm and a hand respectively and appropriate impedance controllers are proposed. However, a more appealing solution was recently presented in [19] to control the impedance of the elastic arm, only for a usual elastic-joint robot. In this article, we apply the abovementioned controller to control a single coupled joint in order to verify that the desired properties are reached. The development of the joint mathematic model and the controller is presented in Sects. 2 and 3 respectively. Next, the workability and some properties of the controller are verified in simulation in Sect. 4. Section 5 concludes the article.

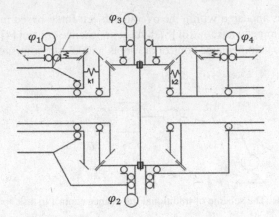

Fig. 3. Kinematic structure of the differential-drive joint.

2   Modeling of the Differential Joint

The differential gearbox has two inputs and two outputs, either positions/velocities or torques. This structure has a number of advantages, e.g. the torque of both motors can be used in the principal directions of motion, permitting there the increase of available torque for a given motor size. However, the strong coupling between the axes does not permit independent controller design for each actuator. As a consequence of the coupling, a movement of one robot joint has to be realized by the coordinated movement of two actuators, see Fig. 3. Ignoring the elasticity, the effect of the gearbox can be described by the following transformations for the positions.

$$\theta = T \cdot \theta_m \tag{1}$$

Correspondingly, the torques are related as:

$$\tau_m = T^T \cdot \tau \tag{2}$$

with

$$T = \begin{bmatrix} -\frac{1}{2} & -\frac{1}{2} \\ \frac{1}{2r} & -\frac{1}{2r} \end{bmatrix} \tag{3}$$

The motor position is denoted herein by θ_m, while θ is the same position expressed in link coordinates. It is important to note the difference between the motor position expressed in link coordinates θ and the link-side position, which will be denoted by q. While θ represents the same system state as θ_m only written in another coordinate system, q is a different state variable, representing the position of the link after the joint elasticity. It can also be expressed in motor or link coordinates. The coordinate system is denoted by a subscript; a missing subscript denotes link coordinates. Accordingly, τ and τ_m are the joint torques expressed in link and motor coordinates, respectively.

While the elasticity of a single-DoF joint stems merely from the harmonic drive gear, for the coupled joint one has the additional elasticity of the differential gear, i.e. two elastic sources, the springs $k1$ and $k2$. Still, the expressions (1)–(3) remain valid. But in elastic case actual output position q differs from θ, so the elastic joint model, neglecting structural damping and gravity and with assumptions of Spong [20], can be written as:

$$\begin{cases} M(q)\ddot{q} = K(\theta - q) = K(T \cdot \theta_m - q) = \tau \\ B_m \ddot{\theta}_m + \tau_m = B_m \ddot{\theta}_m + T^T \tau = u_m \end{cases} \tag{4}$$

The matrix $K \in R_{nxn}$ here is positive definite, B_m is a diagonal matrix containing the motors' inertia, $M(q)$ is the mass matrix of the rigid robot dynamics (load inertia). The motor torque vector um is the input quantity for the controller. In order to find the stiffness matrix, one should bring together output torques τ and deflections of the springs δ, while the latter should be expressed in terms of input angles θ and output angles q. Following the notation of Fig. 3, after some transformations, we obtain:

$$\delta_1 = \theta_{m1} + q_1 - r \cdot q_2 \tag{5}$$

$$\delta_2 = -\theta_{m2} - q_1 - r \cdot q_2 \tag{6}$$

After some transformations, considering linear elasticity, we find:

$$K = \begin{bmatrix} k_1 + k_2 & -r(k_1 - k_2) \\ -r(k_1 - k_2) & r^2(k_1 + k_2) \end{bmatrix} \tag{7}$$

The choice of variables φ in Fig. 3 is intentional, and it means that these values are measured by physical sensors. As $\varphi_1 = \theta_{m1}$ and $\varphi_4 = q_1$, the output torque can be as well written in terms of sensor variables:

$$M = C \cdot \varphi = \begin{bmatrix} -k_1 & r(k_1 - k_2) & rk_2 & -2k_2 \\ rk_1 & -r^2(k_1 + k_2) & r^2 k_2 & -2rk_2 \end{bmatrix} \begin{bmatrix} \varphi_1 \\ \varphi_2 \\ \varphi_3 \\ \varphi_4 \end{bmatrix} \tag{8}$$

It's important to notice that K is still symmetric (7), and therefore the controller design in principle may follow the lines of [21]. A model of the joint was designed in Simulink, which is shown in Figs. 4 and 5. The presented schemes are rather straight-forward. It's only worth mentioning that the elastic part $K(T\theta_m - q)$ is realized by the function in the block "Elastic Transform".

3 Controller Design

The development of impedance control algorithms mainly follows two paradigms: keeping the natural inertia or shaping it [22]. Accordingly, in the first case the closed-loop dynamics remains coupled while the controller is mostly uncoupled and in the second case it is vice versa. An exemplary method that shapes inertia is feedback linearization, e.g. through inverse dynamics [23]. Inertia keeping methods include classical approaches like PD + controller [24] as well as newly developed elastic structure preserving impedance control (ESπ) [19].

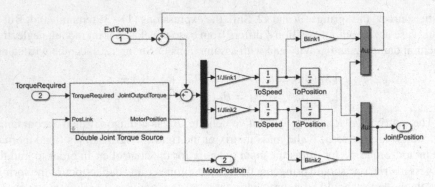

Fig. 4. Model of the 2-DoF joint.

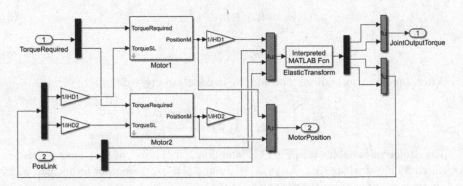

Fig. 5. Model of the actuator part of the joint along with elastic gearbox.

Feedback linearization provides more freedom in the controller design, but relies heavily on the knowledge of the model and requires more computational effort than inertia keeping. Keeping inertia restricts the controller design to some extent, but requires fewer coefficients to tune, and those coefficients have clear physical sense and thus give a way to specify interaction behavior intuitively. For that reason, we have chosen the ESπ method to control the coupled elastic joint. However, there are other methods, e.g., in the abovementioned project MIRO [21] a state feedback controller was designed through modal decomposition approach, i.e. through simultaneous diagonalization of inertia and stiffness matrices. This approach allows transforming a complex MIMO (multi-input, multi-output) system into a set of SISO (single input, single output) systems, simplifying the analysis and tuning of the controller. However, the resulting controller is not model-free and requires the measurement of joint torque and its rate of change.

From the other hand, ESπ algorithm is based on passivity properties. Our goal is to make the link part behave like a damped spring, so that the closed-loop equation takes form:

$$M\ddot{q} = K(\eta - q) - D_q\dot{q} - K_q(q - q_d) \qquad (9)$$

where η is some new equivalent motor variable, D_q and K_q are virtual damping and stiffness matrices. Comparing with (4), we get:

$$K(T \cdot \theta_m - q) = K(\eta - q) - D_q \dot{q} - K_q(q - q_d) = K(\eta - q) + n \qquad (10)$$

and

$$\theta_m = T^{-1}\eta + T^{-1}K^{-1}n \qquad (11)$$

Substituting (11) into the second line of (4), we get the new motor side equation:

$$B_m T^{-1}\ddot{\eta} + B_m T^{-1} K^{-1}\ddot{n} + T^T K(\eta - q) - T^T D_q \dot{q} - T^T K_q(q - q_d) = u_m \qquad (12)$$

Then we premultiply (12) by T^{-T} and introduce:

$$B = T^{-T} B_m T^{-1} \qquad (13)$$

in order to make the motor equation look more like the initial one (4). Now this equation reflects motor-side dynamics brought to the differential gearbox output:

$$B\ddot{\eta} + K(\eta - q) = T^{-T}u_m - B \cdot K^{-1}\ddot{n} - D_q\dot{q} - K_q(q - q_d) = \bar{u}_{link} = T^{-T}\bar{u}_m \qquad (14)$$

The new control input $\bar{u}_{link}$ can be reasonably set as:

$$\bar{u}_{link} = -D_\eta \dot{\eta} \qquad (15)$$

where D_η is the damping control matrix. Finally, the control torque takes form:

$$u_m = -T^T D_\eta \dot{\eta} - B \cdot K^{-1} D_q q^{(3)} - B \cdot K^{-1} K_q \ddot{q} - T^T D_q \dot{q} - T^T K_q(q - q_d) \qquad (16)$$

while the motor equation simplifies to

$$B\ddot{\eta} + K(\eta - q) = \bar{u}_{link} \qquad (17)$$

Referring back to [19], the transformation is displayed evidently on the scheme shown in Fig. 6. The authors consider a one-dimensional joint, but it is sufficient to show the concept. In our case, it's worth noticing that K is not always diagonal but always symmetric, however, it turns out that B is still diagonal after the transformation (13). Therefore, starting with the arguments in [19] and applying logic similar to [25] we set the control matrices as follows:

$$K_q = diag\{k_{p1}, k_{p2}\}, D_\eta = 2\gamma_1\sqrt{B \cdot K}, D_q = 2\gamma_2\sqrt{M \cdot K_q} \qquad (18)$$

where k_{p1}, k_{p2} set the desired virtual stiffness for roll and pitch respectively, while γ_1 and γ_2 are motor-side and link-side damping factors.

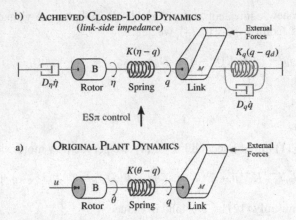

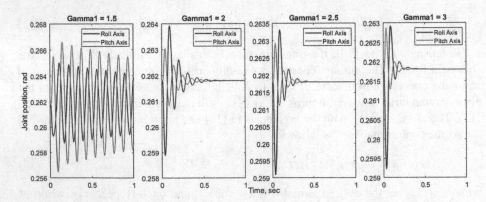

Fig. 6. Visual representation of the model transformation.

4 Simulation Tests

Simulations tests have been performed in Matlab-Simulink to verify the theoretical arguments. As the robotic arm in [1] assumes application of springs with relatively low stiffness in the range from 500 to 2000 N · m/rad, the case of interest would be to achieve high virtual stiffness, e.g. 20000 N · m/rad. If we stick to non-varying impedance in the supposed task, then it is important to define an appropriate range of damping factors to employ. Thus, the first part of tests includes a task of applying short-term ("impulse") external torque at the joint output. It was found out beforehand, that the application of roll torque makes greater effect on the joint, so we restricted ourselves with this type of load. We have performed two series of tests fixing either $\gamma_2 = 2$, or $\gamma_1 = 2$ and changing the values of the other factor. The results are shown in Figs. 7 and 8.

Fig. 7. The influence of the damping factor γ_1 on the impulse torque response ($\gamma_2 = 1.5$)

We have chosen $\gamma_1 = \gamma_2 = 2$ for the second part of tests as these values provide fast transient and good damping. In the second part, we have performed another three

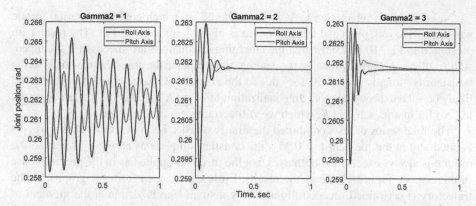

Fig. 8. The influence of the damping factor γ_2 on the impulse torque response ($\gamma_1 = 2$).

series of tests to investigate the behavior of the joint in different modes. The first task was a trajectory task without any external disturbances. The trajectory was chosen as a fifth order polynomial, achieving rotation of 10 degrees (0.1745 rad) in 0.5 s and starts at the moment t = 0.1 s. The model does not account for stiction, so it is expected that the oscillations damp faster in a physical system. The trajectory task was consecutively performed by the roll joint, by the pitch joint and by both joints together. Each time two stiffness layouts were in consideration: different stiffness with $k_1 = 500_2 = 1500$ N·m/rad, and equal stiffness $k_1 = k_2 = 1500$ N·m/rad. The results are depicted in Fig. 9, showing stable and well damped trajectory performance. There is evident coupling of axes if stiffness is different, as the resting axis in the first two graphs deviates from zero, and actually this error is closely connected to the dynamic error of the moving axis. This coupling vanishes though or becomes negligible if stiffness is equal.

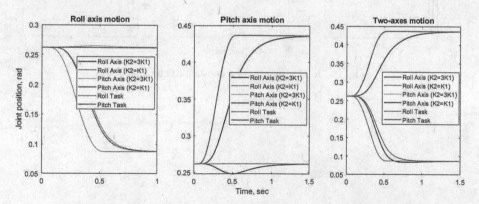

Fig. 9. Trajectory performance without external disturbance.

Next, a simple interaction task was considered, in which constant external torque was applied to roll, pitch and finally both axes of the joint at t = 0.01 s. The results are presented in Fig. 10 and show that the emerging oscillations are successfully damped, static deflection is proportional to the external torque and in the case of equal stiffness the transient is virtually non-oscillatory due to the absence of elastic coupling. This could likely be solved through double diagonalization of B and K in (21), like it was suggested in [26] for matrices M and K, which we will certainly try in the future.

The final series of tests combined the first two tasks, i.e. a trajectory task was performed and at the moment t = 0.25 s the constant torque was applied. This time the motion is always executed at both axes, but the torque is applied as in the previous case in three ways. Figure 11 shows the results. Little can be seen from the graphs, as the trajectory is performed successfully and only a small leap is visible at the moment of torque application. Again, static deflection is proportional to the external torque.

We should notice that the tasks have been deliberately chosen to prevent the control saturation because if the voltage or current of the motor exceed the limits the presented controller becomes senseless due to the strong coupling. This issue requires additional research. Otherwise, the tests show that this controller successfully damps the oscillations and represents the desired impedance behavior.

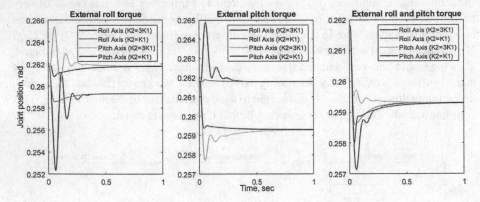

Fig. 10. Joint response for a constant torque load.

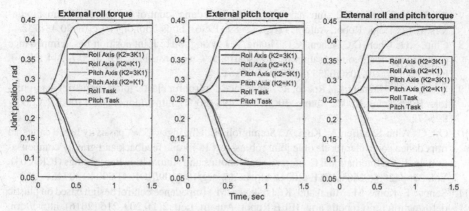

Fig. 11. Trajectory performance with external torque application.

5 Conclusion

In this paper, an impedance controller has been proposed for a coupled differential-drive 2-DoF joint within the elastic structure preserving framework. The simulations validated the performance of the controller. Further validation on the basis of the joint prototype is assumed to be presented in the future. However, a number of issues still remains, such as control saturation, motor inertia shaping, application of nonlinear spring. These issues will be addressed in future work as well as the design of the controller for a full robotic arm, in Cartesian task space and accounting for the derivatives of the trajectory.

Acknowledgments. This research is supported by the Ministry of Science and Higher Education of the Russian Federation. State assignment №075-01623-22-00 (FNRG-2022-0009, ID 1021060307688-8-2.2.2).

References

1. Kopylov, V., Dalyaev, I., Vasiliev, A., Titov, V.: Torque sensing in robotic joints with introduced elasticity for application in hazardous environments. In: Robotics and Artificial Intelligence (RAI), pp. 12–17 (2021)
2. Iturrate, I., Kramberger, A., Sloth, C.: Quick setup of force-controlled industrial gluing tasks using learning from demonstration. Front. Robot. AI, 354 (2021). https://doi.org/10.3389/frobt.2021.767878
3. Hogan, N.: Impedance control (An approach to manipulation) Part I, II, III. Trans ASME J. Dyn. Syst. Measur. Control **107**, 1–24 (1985)
4. Anderson, R.J., Spong, M.W.: Hybrid impedance control of robotic manipulators. IEEE J. Robot. Autom. **4**(5), 549–556 (1988). https://doi.org/10.1109/56.20440
5. Caccavale, F., Natale, C., Siciliano, B., Villani, L.: Six-dof impedance control based on angle/axis representations. IEEE Trans. Robot. Autom. **15**(2), 289–300 (1999). https://doi.org/10.1109/70.760350
6. Xiong, G., Chen, H., Zhang, R., Liang, F.: Robot-environment interaction control of a flexible joint light weight robot manipulator. Int. J. Adv. Robot. Syst. **9**(3), 76 (2012). https://doi.org/10.5772/51308

7. Bonitz, R.C., Hsia, T.C.: Internal force-based impedance control for cooperating manipulators. IEEE Trans. Robot. Autom. **12**(1), 78–89 (1996). https://doi.org/10.1109/70.481752
8. Chiu, S.H., Chen, C.C., Chen, K.T., Huang, X.J., Pong, S.H.: Joint position-based impedance control with load compensation for robot arm. J. Chin. Inst. Eng. **39**(3), 337–344 (2016). https://doi.org/10.1080/02533839.2015.1101617
9. Ferretti, G., Magnani, G., Rocco, P.: Impedance control for elastic joints industrial manipulators. IEEE Trans. Robot. Autom. **20**(3), 488–498 (2004). https://doi.org/10.1109/TRA.2004. 825472
10. Ott, C., Albu-Schaffer, A., Kugi, A., Stamigioli, S., Hirzinger, G.: A passivity based cartesian impedance controller for flexible joint robots-part I: Torque feedback and gravity compensation. In: IEEE International Conference on Robotics and Automation Proceedings (ICRA'04), Vol. 3, pp. 2659–2665. IEEE (2004). https://doi.org/10.1109/ROBOT.2004.1307462
11. Senoo, T., Koike, M., Murakami, K., Ishikawa, M.: Impedance control design based on plastic deformation for a robotic arm. IEEE Robot. Autom. Lett. **2**(1), 209–216 (2016). https://doi. org/10.1109/LRA.2016.2587806
12. Wandinger, D.: Enhancing classical impedance control concepts while ensuring transferability to flexible joint robots. Hochschule München (2020)
13. He, G., Shi, S., Wang, D., Liu, H.: A strategy for large workpiece assembly based on hybrid impedance control. In: 2019 IEEE International Conference on Mechatronics and Automation (ICMA), pp. 799–804. IEEE (2019). https://doi.org/10.1109/ICMA.2019.8816475
14. Zhou, H., Ma, S., Wang, G., Deng, Y., Liu, Z.: A hybrid control strategy for grinding and polishing robot based on adaptive impedance control. Adv. Mech. Eng. **13**(3), 1–21 (2021). https://doi.org/10.1177/1687814021100403
15. Tiseo, C., et al.: Hapfic: An adaptive force/position controller for safe environment interaction in articulated systems. IEEE Trans. Neur. Syst. Rehab. Eng. **29**, 1432–1440 (2021). https:// doi.org/10.1109/TNSRE.2021.3098062
16. Jeong, S., Tadano, K.: Force feedback on hand rest function in master manipulator for robotic surgery. In: 2021 IEEE/RSJ International Conference on Intelligent Robots and Systems (IROS), pp. 1815–1820. IEEE (2021). https://doi.org/10.1109/IROS51168.2021.9636632
17. Hagn, U., et al.: The DLR MIRO: a versatile lightweight robot for surgical applications. Indus. Robot Int. J. **35**(4), 324–336 (2008). https://doi.org/10.1108/01439910810876427
18. Chen, Z., Lii, N.Y., Wimboeck, T., Fan, S., Liu, H.: Experimental evaluation of Cartesian and joint impedance control with adaptive friction compensation for the dexterous robot hand DLR-HIT II. Int. J. Hum. Robot. **8**(4), 649–671 (2011). https://doi.org/10.1142/S02198436 11002605
19. Keppler, M., Lakatos, D., Ott, C., Albu-Schaffer, A.: Elastic structure preserving impedance (ESπ) control for compliantly actuated robots. In: 2018 IEEE/RSJ International Conference on Intelligent Robots and Systems (IROS), pp. 5861–5868. IEEE (2018). https://doi.org/10. 1109/IROS.2018.8593415
20. Spong, M.: Modeling and control of elastic joint robots. J. Dyn. Syst. Measur. Control **109**(4), 310–319 (1987). https://doi.org/10.1115/1.3143860
21. Le Tien, L., Schaffer, A.A., Hirzinger, G.: MIMO state feedback controller for a flexible joint robot with strong joint coupling. In: Proceedings 2007 IEEE International Conference on Robotics and Automation, pp. 3824–3830. IEEE (2007). https://doi.org/10.1109/ROBOT. 2007.364065
22. Dietrich, A., et al.: Practical consequences of inertia shaping for interaction and tracking in robot control. Control Eng. Pract. **114**, 1–17 (2021). https://doi.org/10.1016/j.conengprac. 2021.104875
23. Buondonno, G., De Luca, A.: September. A recursive Newton-Euler algorithm for robots with elastic joints and its application to control. In: 2015 IEEE/RSJ International Conference

on Intelligent Robots and Systems (IROS), pp. 5526–5532. IEEE (2015). https://doi.org/10.1109/ACCESS.2020.3018470

24. Slotine, J.J., Weiping, L.: Adaptive manipulator control: A case study. IEEE Trans. Automat. Control 33(11), 995–1003 (1988). https://doi.org/10.1109/9.14411

25. Shardyko, I., Samorodova, M., Titov, V.: Development of control system for a SEA-joint based on active damping injection. In: 2020 International Conference on Industrial Engineering, Applications and Manufacturing (ICIEAM), pp. 1–6. IEEE (2020). https://doi.org/10.1109/ICIEAM48468.2020.9111886

26. Keppler, M., Lakatos, D., Ott, C. Albu-Schäffer, A.: A passivity-based approach for trajectory tracking and link-side damping of compliantly actuated robots. In: 2016 IEEE International Conference on Robotics and Automation (ICRA), pp. 1079–1086. IEEE (2016). https://doi.org/10.1109/ICRA.2016.7487239

Door Opening Strategy for Mobile Manipulator with Constrained Configuration

Daniil Pushkarev[1], Konstantin Mironov[1,2]([✉]) [iD], Ilya Basharov[1] [iD],
Margarita Kichik[1] [iD], Sergey Linok[1] [iD], Dmitry Yudin[1,2] [iD], Muhammad Alhaddad[1] [iD],
and Aleksandr Panov[2,3] [iD]

[1] Moscow Institute of Physics and Technology, Institutskiy Per. 9, 141701 Dolgoprudny,
Moscow Region, Russia
[2] AIRI Artificial Intelligence Research Institute, Kutuzovskii Pr, 32/1, 121165 Moscow, Russia
[3] Federal Research Center "Computer Sciences and Control", Vavilova 44/2, 119333 Moscow,
Russia

Abstract. We address the task of robotic door opening in office environments.
This task is important for providing indoor mobility for collaborative mobile
manipulators. In our work, we mainly focus on the use of high-level control
opportunities and identification of the door parameters from visual and lidar data.
We develop a solution, which includes handle recognition, handle twisting, and
opening. The position of the handle is identified from stereo images by a neural-
network-based method. We divide the opening procedure into two stages: first,
handle twisting and slightly opening, and second, wide opening. The first stage is
implemented via high-level task-space control of the robotic arm, while the platform is static. The position of the door axis is identified during the slight opening
by fitting lidar data to the kinematic model. At the second stage, both the platform
and the arm are active. The trajectory of the platform is defined by the model
predictive planner in such a way that it avoids pushing the arm into a singular configuration, while the manipulator is operated via high-level impedance control. In
our experiments, a mobile manipulator composed from the wheeled platform and
the robotic arm was able to open office doors using the proposed approach.

Keywords: Mobile manipulator · Model predictive control · Interactive
manipulation · Object recognition

1 Introduction

The development of mobile manipulators in recent years has faced a number of new
robotic tasks and open issues. The ability to open standard doors is useful for the mobility
in human-intended environments [1]. It is also theoretically interesting as it requires
interaction with a large-size movable mechanical object (comparable to or larger than
the size of the robot).

There is a number of works on robotic door opening; however, it still may be considered a relevant scientific task. Door opening may be performed by various types of

© The Author(s), under exclusive license to Springer Nature Switzerland AG 2022
A. Ronzhin et al. (Eds.): ICR 2022, LNCS 13719, pp. 130–142, 2022.
https://doi.org/10.1007/978-3-031-23609-9_12

robotic systems e.g. manipulator on a wheeled platform [2–5] or humanoid robot [6, 7]. Control approaches for door opening can be divided into two groups: real-time compliance control methods [2, 8, 9] and planning the trajectory of a robotic system for door opening [3, 4, 6, 7].

The works in the first group consider the following task statement. The endeffector of the robot interacts with the door handle; resistance of the door is identified by the force and torque sensors. The task is to define control inputs based on these sensor data, which helps to move the door in the required direction without damage. This task requires fast communication with sensors and high performance of feedback processing. Communication and control frequency have an order of tens or hundreds Hz. The time of door opening is much longer then for opening by human (e.g., 20 s with 100 Hz communication in [9] and 35 s with 20 Hz in [8]).

The works in the second group aim to determine the trajectory (the reference of robot configurations), which allow the system to open the door. Derivation of control inputs is out of this task statement and can be executed by inner regulators of the robotic system. Obviously, two approaches may be combined, e.g., in [4] compliant controller is used to execute the trajectory, which is defined by the planner. Trajectory planning can be based on a heuristic search or on numerical optimization. The first approach is used in [3] where anytime repairing A* algorithm from [10] is applied to define the executable robot trajectory on a configuration graph. In [4], the sampling-based RRT algorithm was applied for motion planning. [6] claims that the sampling-based search is both overpowered (as the configuration space of door opening is not yet complicated for applying these techniques) and underpowered (as it requires post-processing to make the trajectory smoother) for door opening. Through these statements, the authors substantiate their approach based on the CHOMP [11] trajectory optimization. A bit later, [7] applied for this the TrajOpt [12] method, which is faster than CHOMP. The aforementioned works applied to a robotic system with complicated dynamics and required relatively long time either for trajectory definition or for motion execution and consider path and motion planning as two separated tasks. It seems promising to apply a holistic approach based on the nonlinear model predictive control (MPC), which provides trajectory optimization and a definition of related control inputs as a single operation.

We present a novel approach for wide door opening using a mobile manipulator. Trajectory planning is made for a wheeled platform while the control of the arm is defined to adjust the trajectory of the end-effector to the door opening trajectory under impedance of the door handle. This statement is a bit similar to [3], but contrary to this work, we, first, develop our own planner based on trajectory optimization and, second, apply high-level force control of the arm. The use of high-level force control simplifies the opening task; however, it is challenging as the arm must avoid singular configurations. We insert singularity avoidance into objectives and constraints for the optimization task. The wide opening of the door is predated by the door positioning and unlocking. Unlocking is implemented via simple high-level control rules, while the positioning of the door is based on machine vision. We have developed a complex neural solution for handle positioning from stereo camera images and estimate the door kinematic model based on lidar data. We have implemented and tested our approach on a mobile manipulator, which is shown in Fig. 1. It consists of the differential drive Husky platform [13] and

UR5 [14] the robotic arm with two-fingers gripper and stereo camera mounted on its end-effector. Compared with purely indoor mobile manipulators (e.g. TIAGo [15]) Husky has a relatively big footprint, which makes collision avoidance challenging and reduces effective workspace of the arm. The rest of the paper is organised as follows. In Sect. 2, we present our common view on the opening pipeline. The following three sections focused on the three main subtasks of the solution: recognition of the door handle (3), handle twisting and slightly opening with simultaneous identification of door kinematics (4), and wide opening (5). In Sect. 6, we present the experimental results, while Sect. 7 includes the concluding remarks.

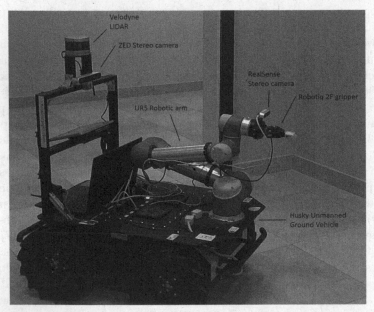

Fig. 1. Experimental mobile manipulator composed of a four-wheels platform and a robotic arm.

2   Common Architecture of the Solution

Following the STRL architecture for cognitive agents [16–18], we divide the components of the solution into strategic, tactical, and reactive layers. A strategic layer corresponds to high-level cognitive tasks, the tactical one corresponds to local perception and planning for executing high-level action, while the reactive one includes low-level data processing and control. We consider door opening as a single task, which is stated on the strategic layer and executed on the tactic and reactive layers. Common architecture is shown in Fig. 2. We divide the opening procedure into three stages:

1. Positioning of the door and wheelbase before opening. The spatial position of the door handle is identified from stereo images (Sect. 3; the handle recognition component is shown in Fig. 2).

2. Handle twisting and slightly opening via the manipulator (Sect. 4). The manipulator unlocks the handle and slightly opens the door (the handle twisting and slightly opening component is shown in Fig. 2). In the meantime, the kinematic model of the door is identified based on LIDAR data (the door state recognition component is shown in Fig. 2).
3. Door opening via the whole-body motion. The wheelbase and the manipulator are acting in order to open the door wide (Sect. 5).

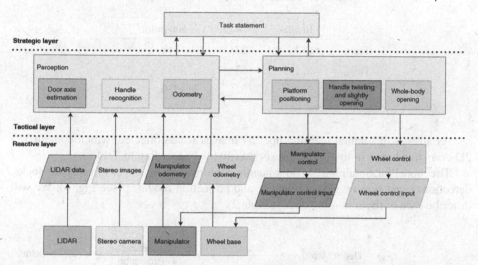

Fig. 2. Architecture of the solution components.

3 Recognition and Positioning of the Door Handle

This section describes in detail the method for determining the door handle position, as well as the collection and annotation of the necessary data for 2D detection and keypoint regression tasks. The dataset includes the markup of:

1. door handle localization data via 2D bounding boxes b_i,
2. each b_i contains inside six 2D keypoints $k_{ij}, j \in \{1, \ldots, 6\}$.

So, the dataset helps us solve two tasks simultaneously: 2D object detection and keypoint regression. To determine the position in 3D space, the door handle can be represented as a simplified skeleton model consisting of six keypoints.

Using the symmetry of an object, 1–2–3 points are assigned as «start» and 4–5–6 as the "end" of a handle. Points 2–3 and 4–5 are responsible for bending along the main axis 3–4 (Fig. 3). Photos of door handles are taken from different angles and scales. The dataset does not include information about keypoint visibility.

Fig. 3. Keypoints location overview on the created dataset.

Table 1. Distribution of the Train Test Split.

	Images	Boxes	Keypoints
Train	212	258	1548
Test	52	67	402
Total	264	325	1950

As a result of manual marking up, 264 images were collected, which contain 325 2D bounding boxes in total. The dataset was divided according to Table 1.

The model for obtaining 3D door handle coordinates consists of three main blocks: detection, regression of 3D coordinates, and projection modules (see Fig. 4). We will describe each of them in more detail (Table 2).

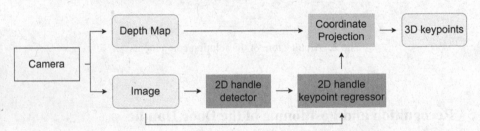

Fig. 4. Data pipeline to get 3D door handle keypoints.

Table 2. Methods evaluation.

Steps/Tasks	Detection	Regression	
Method	YOLOX-s [19]	HRNet [21]	HRNet-Lite [20]
Metric[a]	mAP: 0.82	PCK: 0.38	PCK: 0.31
FPS[b]	54	32	51

[a] Door handle test set
[b] NVIDIA TeslaV100

YoloX [19] was taken as a detection module. This high-performance anchorfree method tiny version works 23 FPS on Jetson Xavier NX with TensorRT optimization. Additionally, it has a good speed-accuracy trade-off. It has been trained with original instructions from authors with 50 epochs on TeslaV100 GPU. HRNetLite [20] was taken as a keypoint regressor module. This is an updated light-weight version of HRNet [21]. Thanks to the multi-scale architecture, the model enables one to cope well with the problems of rotating and obscuring keypoints. Using the MMPose framework [22], it has been trained in the 256×192 image scale with 20 epochs. To compensate the lack of data and make the keypoint regressor more robust, different augmentation techniques were applied.

1. Detection module. To make our method resistant to color changes, such as shadows, light environment, etc., we use RandomHSV. Also, since the manipulator needs to observe the handle from different sides, we apply image transformations as RandomFlip and RandomAffine. The latter includes RandomShear, RandomTranslation, RandomRotation. To make inference more robust, we apply MixUp and Mosaic augmentations.
2. Regression module. To accurately determine the skeleton of the handle, the following transformations were selected: RandomFlip and RandomAffine.

Using a depth map and an intrinsic matrix, we can obtain 3D coordinates:

$$
\begin{bmatrix} u \\ v \\ 1 \\ 1/z \end{bmatrix} = \frac{1}{z} \underbrace{\begin{bmatrix} K & 0 \\ 0 & 1 \end{bmatrix}}_{4 \times 4} \underbrace{\begin{bmatrix} R & t \\ 0 & 0 \end{bmatrix}}_{4 \times 4} \begin{bmatrix} x \\ y \\ z \\ 1 \end{bmatrix} \tag{1}
$$

where rotation matrix R, translation vector t, and the intrinsic matrix K make up the camera projection matrix. u, v is a camera coordinate system, and z, y, z is a world coordinate system.

4 A Strategy for the Slight Opening

Geometric appearance for the slightly opening procedure is shown at Fig. 5. At the beginning the only known information is the position of the handle center H in the coordinate system related to the robot base (it is got from the recognition component). This information is enough to perform three consecutive actions: first, capture the handle by the gripper at point H, second, twist the handle via compliant rotation of the gripper, and, third, slightly open the door by pulling the handle. Wide opening of the door require knowledge about the position of the door axis O and rotation radius r. This task is equivalent to estimating the transition between base-related and door-related coordinate systems. Estimation of the door axis is made from LIDAR data while slightly opening.

Some modern robotic arms, including UR5, are able to be controlled by forces in Cartesian task space (if joint configuration is not singular). Our common philosophy for operating a mobile manipulator is to use this ability as much as we can. This mode called "force mode" could be used for soft operations avoiding destruction of the objects and

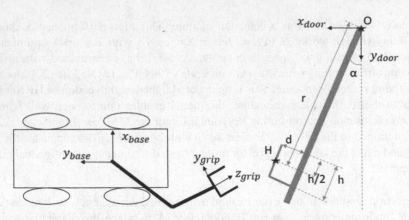

Fig. 5. Relative positions of the robot and the door.

dropping the control box in the safety block. It was used for gripping and twisting the handle. For the handle twist stage, forces were determined in the gripper frame: down pressure and small rotation force around z_{grip}. After that, the manipulator could be able to slightly open the door by pulling the handle toward the negative z_{grip}. At the final stage, the manipulator returns the handle to the original orientation, for which forces were given as reversed forces at the twist stage and iteratively checking the alignment of the yz_{grip} plane and xy_{base} plane.

The position of the door plane is obtained by solving the plane-popout task on the LIDAR pointcloud. A subset of the points near the handle are taken from the pointcloud. RANSAC is applied to fit the plane to these points. As a result, we get the parameters of the plane equation in base-related 3D coordinates. As we consider the plane to be vertical, this equation is reduced to the straight line equation in base-related planar coordinates. During the slight opening, several such estimations are made resulting in a set of line equations. By assuming that all these lines intersect in O, we can define a set of linear equations with unknown coordinates of O. Each equation looks as follows:

$$\cos \alpha_i x_{O(base)} + \sin \alpha_i y_{O(base)} = p_i \tag{2}$$

Here α_i and p_i are the door plane parameters for the single lidar measurement; specifically, α_i is the door opening angle with respect to robot base. If we have more than two such equations, we can estimate O by the least squares method.

5   Planning for the Whole-Body Opening Motion

The geometric appearance for the wide opening task is shown in Fig. 6. If we want to exploit the Cartesian force control of the arm, we should define the platform trajectory in such a way that it avoids the pushing arm into a singular configuration. The non-singular configuration requires that the position of the end-effector be within the certain limits. The end-effector must be within the black-dashed circle in Fig. 6. The center of the circle is at distance b forward to the robot base. If the base joint of the arm is rotated with a certain angle, then the center of the non-singular area is also rotated with this angle. The radius of non-singular area Δr_{max} is equal to approximately 30 cm for UR5 robotic arm. Another aspect of singularity avoidance is that the difference between the azimuth of the end-effector and the azimuth of the base joint must not exceed certain value φ (for UR5 $\varphi \approx 45°$). The singularity avoidance work as force that push end-effector from danger zone, strength determined from experiments. The opening trajectory of the wheeled platform should be defined in such a way that the point, which is b forwards to the robot base, is within the corridor between the two red-dash arcs. In this case, the end-effector pulling the door handle is within a non-singular area. Also, the angle between b-line and the door normal must not exceed φ. This angular constraint is harder to satisfy, but its violation is less critical. If the angular constraint is violated, but other constraints are satisfied, the arm may be switched to a fully compliant mode, which has no singularity restrictions. As the platform is moving through the planned path within the corridor, a compliant mode will allow the arm to open the door.

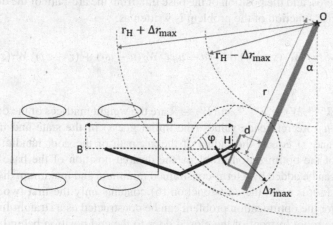

Fig. 6. Geometric singularity-avoidance constraints for wide-opening.

The motion planning for a wheeled platform is achieved by turning the planning task into a model-predictive control statement, which represents the optimization problem. A numerical solution is achieved with the "Acados" toolkit [21]. Let $s = [x, y, v, \theta]^T$ and $u = [a, w]^T$ be the state and the input vectors of the system. Here x, y and θ are the coordinates and orientation of the geometric center of the robot in the inertial frame of the door, v and a are the linear velocity and acceleration of the robot, and ω is the angular velocity of the robot. The kinematic model of the differential-drive platform is the following:

$$
\begin{aligned}
\{\dot{x}\} &= v cos\theta, \\
\{\dot{y}\} &= v sin\theta, \\
\{\dot{v}\} &= a, \\
\{\dot{\theta}\} &= \omega.
\end{aligned}
\tag{3}
$$

The optimization problem for the model (3) has a cost function, which should be minimized in the presence of constraints on s and u. For the planning of the motion of the mobile robot, it is suggested that the position of the base link of the manipulator should be as near as possible to the arc-path of the door handle; therefore, it is necessary to introduce the coordinates of the base link in the inertial door frame:

$$x_b = -b\cos(\theta) + x,$$
$$y_b = -b\sin(\theta) + y. \tag{4}$$

The position of the base link is given as:

$$z = \sqrt{x_b^2 + y_b^2} \tag{5}$$

The cost function of the studied problem consists of three terms: square deviations of the parameters of the state vector from the desired values, square values of the input vector from zeros, and the position of the base link from the arc-path of the door handle. The general cost function of the problem is written as:

$$J = \int_0^T (s - s_d)^T W_1(s - s_d) + +(u - u_d)^T W_2(u - u_d) + (z - z_d)^T W_3(z - z_d)d\tau, \tag{6}$$

where $W_1 \in \mathbb{R}^{n \times n}$, $W_2 \in \mathbb{R}^{m \times m}$ and $W_3 \in \mathbb{R}$ are the weight matrices of the optimization problem, s_d, u_d are reference values (the initial guess) of the state and input vector respectively, and z_d equals the radius of the arc-path of the door handle. In another formulation of the optimization problem, the desired position of the base link of the manipulator can be added by a term-constrained minimum and maximum distance from the arc-path. In this case, the cost function (6) contains only the first two terms. The initial guess for the optimization problem can be constructed as a straight line from the position of the robot in front of the closed door to the end position behind the opened door with angle $\pi/2$, so the end position of the initial guess is fixed with respect to the door frame. The change in scenarios of the initial guess depends on the initial position and orientation of the robot only. Figure 7 shows the initial and optimized path of the center point of the robot, in case that the initial posture of the robot is (-0.8, 0.8, -1.57) and the end posture is (0.8, 0.9, $-\pi$) where the handle is located at position (0.8, 0) for the closed door and at (0, 0.8) for the opened door.

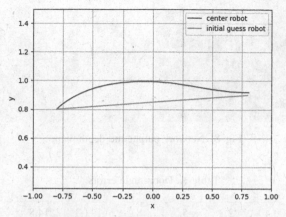

Fig. 7. Initial guess and optimized trajectory.

6   Experiments

The experimental evaluation was made in two stages. At the first stage, we validated the accuracy of identifying door and handle. At the second stage, the common pipeline was tested on a real mobile manipulator.

To obtain groundtruth data about the handle position and the door kinematics, we applied the ARUCO markers recognition module from OpenCV [24]. This module returns pixel coordinates of the marker's angles, which are then converted into 3D according to (1). Their 3D positions are used to define the door normal and transform between ARUCO-related, camera-related and robot-related coordinate systems. Distance between the marker and the center point of the door handle is measured manually. Thanks to augmentations the 2D keypoints, the regressor works in the most difficult situations. Using a depth map, the method can transform coordinates in 3D (Fig. 8). TensorRT implementation increases the processing speed, which enables one to work in real time. The comparison of 17 cases of positioning with the Aruco data showed that the standard deviation in positioning is equal to 9 mm. To validate the method of the door axis estimation, a set of experiments were conducted. We manually measured the angle of the door in several positions and recorded lidar scans to apply our algorithm. The results of the example procedure of axis estimation are given Table 3. As a result, we calculate the mean door angle error equal $1.2°$ and max door angle error equal $2.9°$. The LS estimation of the door axis based on lidar measurements provides accuracy improving up to 1–2 cm.

At the second stage of the experiments, the real robot was able to open the office door with an 0.8-m radius. The unlocking and slight opening stage took around 15 s, the wide opening for $90°$ – around 8 s. See the supplementary video [25] for the details.

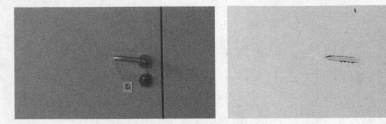

Fig. 8. Network output and depth map.

Table 3. Door angle errors, °.

Lidar angle, °	0.4	2.3	5.5	8	11.3	14.8	20	22.8
GT angle, °	0	2.9	5.8	8.7	11.5	14.5	17.5	20.5
Angle error, °	0.4	0.6	0.3	0.7	0.2	0.3	2.5	2.3
Axis error, cm	–	42	10	10	10	9	9	9
Lidar angle, °	25.6	29.7	32.1	35	38	41.2	44.5	47.5
GT angle, °	23.5	26.8	30	33.4	36.9	40.5	44.5	48.6
Angle error, °	2.1	2.9	2.1	1.6	1.1	0.7	0	0.9
Axis error, cm	8	7	6	4	3	3	1	1

7 Conclusion

In this work, we have developed a solution for robotic door opening based on LIDAR and stereo camera measurements. The opening motion of a mobile manipulator is determined by a combination of compliant control for the robotic arm in the task space and model predictive trajectory planning for the wheeled platform. Numerical experiments showed that the proposed methods for positioning the door handle and the axis satisfy accuracy requirements of a real robotic system. Our approach was implemented on a real mobile manipulator and enabled it to open standard doors in an office environment. These results may help to provide the mobility of mobile manipulators in office environments.

Acknowledgements. This work was supported by the Ministry of Science and Higher Education of the Russian Federation under Project 075–15-2020–799.

References

1. Mironov, K., Mambetov, R., Panov, A., Pushkarev, D.: Model predictive control with torque constraints for velocity-driven robotic manipulator. In: 2021 20th International Conference on Advanced Robotics (ICAR), pp. 107–112. IEEE (2021). https://doi.org/10.1109/ICAR53 236.2021.9659428

2. Chung, W., Rhee, C., Shim, Y., Lee, H., Park, S.: Door-opening control of a service robot using the multifingered robot hand. IEEE Trans. Indus. Electron. **56**(10), 3975–3984 (2009). https://doi.org/10.1109/TIE.2009.2025296

3. Chitta, S., Cohen, B., Likhachev, M.: Planning for autonomous door opening with a mobile manipulator. In: 2010 IEEE International Conference on Robotics and Automation, pp. 1799–1806. IEEE (2010). https://doi.org/10.1109/ROBOT.2010.5509475

4. Arduengo, M., Torras, C., Sentis, L.: Robust and adaptive door operation with a mobile robot. Intel. Serv. Robot. **14**(3), 409–425 (2021). https://doi.org/10.1007/s11370-021-00366-7

5. Zuo, W., Venkatraman, R., Song, G., Chen, Z.: A novel design of mobile robotic system for opening and transitioning through a watertight ship door. In: 2021 IEEE/RSJ International Conference on Intelligent Robots and Systems (IROS), pp. 1378–1383. IEEE (2012). https://doi.org/10.1109/IROS51168.2021.9635942

6. Zucker, M., Jun, Y., Killen, B., Kim, T.G., Oh, P.: Continuous trajectory optimization for autonomous humanoid door opening. In: 2013 IEEE Conference on Technologies for Practical Robot Applications (TePRA), pp. 1–5. IEEE (2013). https://doi.org/10.1109/TePRA.2013.6556358

7. Banerjee, N., Long, X., Du, R., Polido, F., Feng, S., Atkeson, C.G., Gennert, M., Padir, T.: Human-supervised control of the ATLAS humanoid robot for traversing doors. In: 2015 IEEE-RAS 15th International Conference on Humanoid Robots (Humanoids), pp. 722–729. IEEE (2015). https://doi.org/10.1109/HUMANOIDS.2015.7363442

8. Ding, L., Xia, K., Gao, H., Liu, G., Deng, Z.: Robust adaptive control of door opening by a mobile rescue manipulator based on unknown-force-related constraints estimation. Robotica **36**(1), 119–140 (2018). https://doi.org/10.1017/S0263574717000200

9. Stuede, M., Nuelle, K., Tappe, S., Ortmaier, T.: Door opening and traversal with an industrial cartesian impedance controlled mobile robot. In: 2019 International Conference on Robotics and Automation (ICRA), pp. 966–972. IEEE (2019). 10.1109/ ICRA.2019.8793866

10. Likhachev, M., Gordon, G.J., Thrun, S.: ARA*: Anytime A* with provable bounds on sub-optimality. Adv. Neural Inf. Process. Syst. **16** (2003)

11. Ratliff, N., Zucker, M., Bagnell, J.A., Srinivasa, S.: CHOMP: Gradient optimization techniques for efficient motion planning. In: 2009 IEEE International Conference on Robotics and Automation, pp. 489–494. IEEE (2009). https://doi.org/10.1109/ROBOT.2009.5152817

12. Schulman, J., et al.: Motion planning with sequential convex optimization and convex collision checking. Int. J. Robot. Res. **33**(9), 1251–1270 (2014)

13. Husky, U.G.V: Outdoor field research robot by Clearpath. https://clearpathrobotics.com/ husky-unmanned-ground-vehicle-robot/

14. The UR5: A flexible collaborative robot arm, https://www.universal-robots.com/products/ ur5-robot/

15. PAL Robotics, http://pal-robotics.com/robots/tiago/

16. Multilayer cognitive architecture for UAV control: Emel'yanov, S., Makarov, D., Panov, A.I., Yakovlev, K. Cogn. Syst. Res. **39**, 58–72 (2016). https://doi.org/10.1016/j.cogsys.2015.12.008

17. Panov, A.I.: Goal setting and behavior planning for cognitive agents. Sci. Tech. Inf. Process. **46**(6), 404–415 (2019). https://doi.org/10.3103/S0147688219060066

18. Panov, A.I.: Simultaneous learning and planning in a hierarchical control system for a cognitive agent. Autom. Remote Control **83**(6), 869–883 (2022). https://doi.org/10.1134/S0005117922060054

19. Ge, Z., Liu, S., Wang, F., Li, Z., Sun, J.: Yolox: Exceeding yolo series in 2021. arXiv:2107.08430 (2021)

20. Yu, C., Xiao, B., Gao, C., Yuan, L., Zhang, L., Sang, N., Wang, J.: Lite-hrnet: A lightweight high-resolution network. In: Proceedings of the IEEE/CVF Conference on Computer Vision and Pattern Recognition, pp. 10440–10450 (2021)

21. Sun, K., Xiao, B., Liu, D., Wang, J.: Deep high-resolution representation learning for human pose estimation. In: Proceedings of the IEEE/CVF conference on computer vision and pattern recognition, pp. 5693–5703. (2019)
22. MMCV Contributors. MMCV: OpenMMLab Computer Vision Foundation. https://github.com/open-mmlab/mmcv
23. Verschueren, R., et al.: ACADOS—A modular open-source framework for fast embedded optimal control. Math. Prog. Comput. **14**(1), 147–183 (2022)
24. ArUco Marker Detection, https://docs.opencv.org/3.4/d9/d6d/tutorial_table_of_content_aruco.html
25. Autonomous door opening by mobile manipulator, https://youtu.be/tuRkFwhmRws

Domain Randomization with Adaptive Weight Distillation

Shixuan Wang[1,2]($\boxtimes$) (iD), Fengge Wu[1,2] (iD), Yijun Lin[1,2], and Junsuo Zhao[1,2]

[1] Institute of Software, Chinese Academy of Sciences, Beijing 100190, China
wangshixuan20@mails.ucas.ac.cn
[2] University of Chinese Academy of Sciences, Beijing 100190, China

Abstract. Domain Randomization (DR) is one of the increasingly popular techniques for domain generalization, which learns a policy from simulation by randomizing domain parameters. However, integrating information from randomized domains into one policy may lead to high variance and an unstable training process. Thus, we draw on policy distillation, distilling multiple policies into a single policy to effectively reduce the high variance of the model. The following question is whether the importance of multiple tasks may affect the performance of the distilled policy. To address this issue, we propose an adaptive-weight distillation strategy depending on teacher policy performance called Domain Randomization with Adaptive Weight Distillation (DRAWD) to control the student policy to learn toward better-performing teacher policy. This way, DRAWD addresses the problem of the under-generalization of a single policy and the potential imperfect teacher of a multiple-policy ensemble. We compare DRAWD with two baselines on two Mujoco continuous control tasks. Our results show that the target domain performance of policies trained with DRAWD is better than the other two baselines on the metric of variance and average rewards of the task.

Keywords: Deep reinforcement learning · Domain randomization · Policy distillation · Multitask learning

1 Introduction

Deep reinforcement learning has been applied to robot control tasks with remarkable achievements [1]. However, like other machine learning methods, generalizing deep reinforcement learning to novel and unknown environments is one of the existing challenges. Compared to other machine learning techniques, the more challenging part of deep reinforcement learning is deploying to real-world environments, such as robot control, where discrepancies generally exist between simulation and the real world, also called the reality gap [2, 3]. A widely used method to improve the generalization capability of policies in deep reinforcement learning called domain randomization [1, 2], is to randomize the parameterized physical simulation environment during training so that the agent can adapt to variants of the environment, and the trained policy enables it to perform well in test domains. The randomized parameters are properties of physical environments, such as robot masses and friction coefficients. Each parameter follows a

A. Ronzhin et al. (Eds.): ICR 2022, LNCS 13719, pp. 143–154, 2022.
https://doi.org/10.1007/978-3-031-23609-9_13

specific distribution and is chosen for a domain by sampling randomly from the distribution. Suppose the distribution is rich enough and the random samples are large enough. In that case, the training domain will cover the situation of real-world environments or target domains.

However, the range of the distribution of the domain parameters is hard to configure. Generally, the distribution of parameters is set to be large, which may result in high variance and poor convergence [4]. Current research is divided into two directions to alleviate the issue. First, adapting the domain parameter distribution during learning are proposed [4–8]. The method automatically adapts domain parameter distribution in simulation based on sparse data from target domains. Second, the distillation technique is proposed to integrate multiple policies individually trained in different domains into a single policy [9, 10]. The variance of distilled policy can effectively reduce by mixing multiple models, and the policy enables to generalize target domains with good stability.

Nevertheless, this still leaves some imprecision, such as the inability to guarantee that trained teacher policies are optimal. If the teacher policies are suboptimal, or the training results are unsatisfactory, it will negatively impact the student policy to imitate. Considering that, each teacher policy needs to evaluate its performance to estimate how much to trust them for the student policy [11]. We observe that teacher policy training results strongly impact student policy performance. The student policy distilled from well-performed teacher policies in training domains has better sample efficiency and higher cumulative rewards than the student policy distilled from under-performed teacher policies in training domains, as shown in Fig. 1. Thus, when a training session yields superior and inferior teacher policies, we need to estimate them based on specific evaluation criteria and allocate distinct weights for each teacher to control the student policy's update direction.

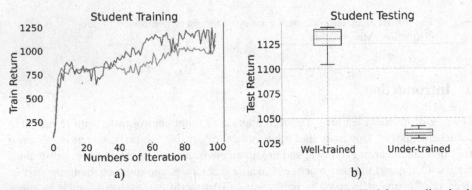

Fig. 1. Comparison of student performance in training and testing distilled from well-trained teachers and under-trained teachers. The student training return were obtained by exhaustively running PPO with 2000 steps, and both test results were obtained by evaluating the student policy with ten different rollouts: a) average return of student policy in training distilled from well-trained teachers (blue) and under-trained teachers(red); b) test return of student policy distilled from well-trained teachers and under- trained teachers (Color figure online).

Contributions: We advance the combination of domain randomization and policy distillation method by introducing Domain Randomization with Adaptive Weight Distillation (DRAWD). This algorithm automatically adapts teacher task weight based on teacher policy performance. Our work assigns weights to teacher policy tasks dynamically and evaluates teacher policy performance using cumulative rewards obtained by teacher policies in test domains as a progress signal. Finally, we validate the algorithm's feasibility in the open-source Mujoco physical simulation environment [13]. The experiment results show that DRAWD improves the performance in terms of generalization capability and stability, which reduces model variance and increases cumulative rewards of tasks.

2 Background

2.1 Domain Randomization in Deep Reinforcement Learning

Domain randomization method abstracts environments into various parameters, i.e., to parameterize simulation environments such that each parameter following a specific distribution is randomly sampled to simulate environments for a good variety of situations and thus reduce the deviation between training domains and target domains. Tobin et al. [2] firstly proposed to combine domain randomization and deep neural network, drawing domain randomization method into domain generalization of deep reinforcement learning. The core of domain randomization is to make policies trained in the simulated environments sufficiently so that they can be successfully applied to the target domain without further tuning.

A significant challenge that the domain randomization method faces is to design domain parameter distributions inclusive to cover the real-world situation as much as possible, leading to high model variance. In order to address this problem, some optimization methods that allow the algorithm to adapt the distributions of parameters have been incorporated automatically. Vuong et al. [8] used a bilevel optimization idea to make the domain parameter distribution adapt automatically. Muratore et al. [6] proposed Bayesian Domain Randomization, using bayesian optimization to optimize the domain parameter distribution, which can adapt the distribution based on the environments and avoid the problem of over-setting parameter distribution. Zhao et al. [10] combined domain randomization and policy distillation by distilling multiple policies trained in different domains to a single student policy.

Motivated by previous works, we use the distillation method to avoid high variance caused by training a single policy model. Instead, each teacher policy is trained alone in an individual domain with different randomized parameters. As a result, the policy can be trained in a broad range distribution with a reducing variance and a better generalization to the unknown target domains for the distilled control policy.

2.2 Policy Distillation

In deep reinforcement learning, massive neural networks are usually required to process high-dimensional input data. Policy distillation extracts knowledge to train a new network, which allows a huge network, namely teacher network, to be compressed into a smaller but more efficient network, namely student network, that retains a similar level of expertise as the original large network. The distillation concept was firstly proposed by Hinton et al. [15] and Rusu et al. [14] combined the distillation with policy network in reinforcement learning to achieve policy model compression. In multitask distillation, whether the teacher policy is optimal is crucial to the distillation results. Czarnecki et al. [11] mentioned that a teacher value function can be used to evaluate teacher policies for the problem of suboptimal teacher policies and leverage imperfect teachers to estimate the degree of trust in teacher policies. Lai et al. [16] argued that if teacher policies are suboptimal, the performance of the student model will be limited by teacher models, and therefore proposed that two student models extract knowledge from each other to improve training without using a pre-trained teacher model.

For the selection of distillation loss function, Rusu et al. [14] proposed three distillation methods, including negative log likelihood loss (NLL), mean squared error loss (MSE), and Kullback-Leibler (KL) divergence. By comparison, they concluded that KL divergence better represents the difference in distribution between teachers and students. Czarnecki et al. [11] similarly proposed three loss function design methods, including N-distill, Expected Entropy Regularized, and Teacher V reward, and concluded that the Expected Entropy Regularized loss function performs better by comparison. Our work chooses KL divergence as the basic term for the distillation loss function.

2.3 Multitask Learning

Policy distillation can be divided into single-task distillation and multitask distillation [14]. The difference depends on the number of teacher policies. In our work, in order to gain better generalization for the student policy, we adopt a multitask policy distillation approach to construct the algorithm model, where each teacher policy is trained in a separate environment with different domain parameters. However, in multitask learning, the performance may differ for each task. When a particular teacher policy is suboptimal, the performance of student policy will decrease accordingly. In order to minimize the impact of suboptimal teacher policies on student policy, we adaptively assign weights to the loss function of each teacher-student pair depending on the performance of teacher policies on the test domain, which allows the student policy to leverage different teacher policies when it is updated, so that the student policy enables to learn from well-performed teacher policies.

Many works have investigated the adaptive assignment of weights to loss functions in multitask learning. Kendall et al. [17] proposed that the performance of multitask learning models strongly depends on the associated weights of the loss function for each task. Some approaches propose that the weight of loss function between different tasks can be dynamically adjusted according to prescribed criteria or normalization requirements, such as GradNorm [18]. Some researchers proposed to learn from progress signals, namely the model's ability [19]. In [20], Graves et al. use an accuracy metric as a learning progress signal to find a stochastic policy for task curriculum learning. In our work, we use the returns of teacher policies in test domains as progress signals to supervise the learning of student policy and then dynamically compute task weights between different teachers during student training.

3 Problem Statement

We abstract a continuous control task as a Markov Decision Process (MDP), denoted as a tuple $M = (S, A, R, P, \gamma)$, where S is the state space, A is the action space, $R : S \times A \to R$ is the reward function, $P : S \times A \to S$ is the transition function, and γ is the discounted factor. The training environment, also called domain, is symbolized by its parameters ξ, which are vectors of all parameter instances of environments, such as mass, friction coefficient and link length. It is assumed that the parameter ξ satisfies a probability distribution predefined as $p(\xi)$. Different domain parameters affect the transition function of environments $P_\xi : S_\xi \times A_\xi \to S_\xi$. For a timestep t, the continuous state and action is denoted as $s_t \in S_\xi, a_t \in A_\xi$. In each episode, the agent draws an initial state s_0 from the distribution $\sigma_\xi(s_0)$ as the start of training. The agent is trained with the goal of learning an optimal stochastic policy $\pi_\theta(a|s)$ in reinforcement learning, which allows it to maximize curriculum rewards, also called the expected return. This value measures the performance of the policy, which is defined in (1):

$$J(\pi_\theta, \xi) = E_{s_0 \sim \sigma_\xi(s_0)} \sum_{t=0}^{T} \gamma^t r(s_t, a_t). \tag{1}$$

During the training process, the transition function generates the state s_{t+1} for the next time step according to the current state s_t and action a_t. The curriculum rewards are calculated according to the current state s_t and action a_t, which determines the updated direction of the gradient and then adjusts the parameters of the policy. We use trajectories to record all states, actions, and rewards across the entire training process, which is denoted as $\tau = \{s_t, a_t, r_t\}_{t=0}^{T}$, where $r_t = r(s_t, a_t)$. When the domain parameter vector is ξ, the goal of the task becomes to maximize the expected returns of current domain parameters, as shown in (3):

$$J(\theta) = E_{\xi \sim p(\xi)}[J(\pi_\theta, \xi)] \tag{2}$$

$$J(\theta) = E_{\xi \sim p(\xi)}\left[E_{\tau \sim p(\tau)} \sum_{t=0}^{T.} \gamma^t r(s_t, a_t)\right] \tag{3}$$

4 Domain Randomization with Adaptive Weight Distillation

DRAWD consists of two main steps: teacher policy training and student policy training. The domain parameters are randomly sampled in the training domain for teacher policy training. Then the large teacher policies with specific tasks are transferred to student policy by supervision during student policy training. The weights of teacher tasks are dynamically assigned as coefficients of the loss function based on the performance of the teacher policies in the test domains. The sketch of the algorithm is shown in Fig. 2, and the general overview of the algorithm is shown in Algorithm 1.

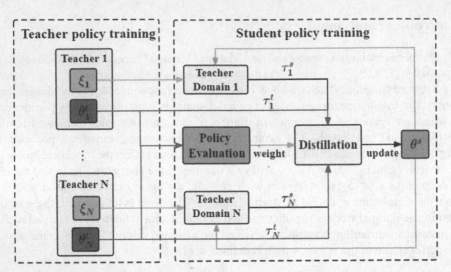

Fig. 2. Sketch of the Domain Randomization with Adaptive Weight Distillation algorithm. The method consists of two parts: teacher policy training and student policy training. The process of teacher training uses domain randomization to build multiple task models. The student policy training can be viewed as a combination of policy distillation and task weight evaluation.

Algorithm 1 Domain Randomization with Adaptive Weight Distillation

---

Input: domain parameter distribution $p(\xi)$, number of teachers N, iterations I, epochs E randomly
 1: Initialization: teacher policy parameters $\theta_{1:N}^t$ and student policy parameters θ^s
 2: **for** each teacher $n = 1 : N$ **do**
 3:     Sample a set of domain parameters ξ_n from $p(\xi)$ for teacher n
 4:     Train teacher n individually in its own environment $\theta_n^t \leftarrow \xi_n$
 5: **end for**
 6: **for** each iteration $i = 1 : I$ **do**
 7:     **for** each teacher $n = 1 : N$ **do**
 8:         Execute student policy θ_s in every teacher domain $\tau \leftarrow rollout(\pi_{\theta^s}, \xi_n)$
 9:         Test teacher n in test domain $KPI_n \leftarrow r_{test}(\theta_n^t) \leftarrow \theta_n^t$
10:     **end for**
11:     **for** each epoch $e = 1 : E$ **do**
12:         Compute each teacher-student pair distillation loss $_n = KL(\pi_{\theta_n^t}(\tau_n)\|\pi_{\theta^s}(\tau_n))$
13:         Compute the sum of all distillation loss $L = \sum_{n=1}^N w_n L_n$
14:         Update student policy θ^s using L
15:     **end for**
16: **end for**
Output: trained student policy parameters θ^s

During teacher policy training, we randomly initialize a set of N teacher policy networks $\theta_{1:N}^t$, and each teacher policy is deployed to a separate domain for individual training, called teacher domain. Each teacher domain randomizes different domain parameter vector ξ, and each element in the domain parameter vector is a parameter of the environment. The distributions of all domain parameters are abstracted into a distribution set $p(\xi)$, so the process of sampling every domain parameter in the distribution can be viewed as sampling the domain parameter vector ξ in the distribution set $p(\xi)$. The distributions of these parameters are predefined.

The student training process can also be referred to as policy distillation. Firstly, we collect the training data generated by teacher policies, i.e., the observation space of teacher domains. Then the student policy θ^s randomly initialized executes in the observation space of teacher domains and obtains N trajectories $\tau_{1:n}$. Subsequently, we gain the action distribution of each teacher during training. We regard each teacher-student pair as an individual task T_n and use KL divergence to metric the action distribution of each task, denoted as

$$L_n = KL(\pi_{\theta_n^t}(\tau_n) \| \pi_{\theta^s}(\tau_n)) \tag{4}$$

where $\pi_{\theta_n^t}$ is the n th teacher policy. For the loss function L_n of each task T_n, we assign a task weight w_n to leverage the relative importance of the task. The process of learning towards a better performing teacher policy is accomplished by minimizing the weighted sum of KL divergence of all teacher-student pairs to update the student policy parameters:

$$L_{total} = \sum_{n=1}^{N} w_n L_n \tag{5}$$

We select a key performance indicator (KPI) to measure the performance of every task Tn, denoted as $p \in [0, 1]$. KPI should be a meaningful metric, such as accuracy or average precision in regression tasks [12]. In our work, the average return of a teacher policy over a certain number of test domains is normalized as a KPI to measure the performance of the teacher policy. The normalization operation needs to reflect the difference in performance between different teacher policies, and the value should not be negative. Therefore, we chose the logarithmic function as the normalization function:

$$p_n = \frac{\log(R_n)}{\log(max(R))} \tag{6}$$

where R_n denotes the average return of the nth teacher policy in test domains, and $max(R)$ denotes the maximum average returns of all teachers. Another advantage of using a logarithmic function for normalization is that the KPI values of two teachers, even if their performance differs significantly, do not vary greatly, i.e., the KPI of the underperformed teacher does not approach zero. It ensures that the student policy can learn more from outperformed teachers and learn data from different teacher tasks with different domains without discarding training data from other suboptimal teacher policies, resulting in a reduced training sampling diversity.

KPI measures the performance of the teacher policy in test domains, with a larger KPI value for a well-performing teacher and a smaller KPI value for a suboptimal performing teacher. The task weight of the nth teacher w_n is the value of p_n after softmax output $w_n = softmax(p_n)$. With this transformation, the student policy can learn more knowledge from perfect teachers and less from imperfect teachers without losing the diversity of training domains, increasing the generalization and stability of the student policy.

5   Experiment

To validate the stability of DRAWD, we evaluate the policy in two continuous control task baselines on the Mujoco physics engine [13] of OpenAI: ant and half-cheetah, as shown in Fig. 3. We set domain parameters and distributions of simulated ant environment and half-cheetah environment as shown in Tables 1 and 2.

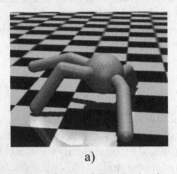
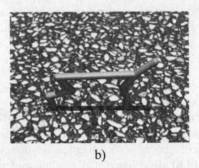

a)   b)

Fig. 3. Illustrations of the 3D simulated environments used to evaluate the method. The ant (a) and half-cheetah (b) tasks present more challenging variants when varying the environment.

Table 1. Ant environment domain parameter distribution.

Parameter	Distribution
Wind condition	$w \sim U(-5\epsilon, 5\epsilon)$
Gravity constant	$g \sim$ $U(g_0(1 - 0.5\epsilon), g_0(1 + 0.5\epsilon))$
Sliding friction	$sf \sim$ $U(sf_0(1 - 0.5\epsilon), sf_0(1 + 0.5\epsilon))$
Torsional friction	$tf \sim$ $U(tf_0(1 - 0.5\epsilon), tf_0(1 + 0.5\epsilon))$
Rolling friction	$rf \sim$ $U(rf_0(1 - 0.5\epsilon), rf_0(1 + 0.5\epsilon))$
Density	$d \sim$ $U(d_0(1 - 0.5\epsilon), d_0(1 + 0.5\epsilon))$

We compare our DRAWD with the following prior methods as baselines:

- Uniform Domain Randomization (UDR) [2]: UDR randomly samples a new set of domain parameters from the distribution at every iteration and updates the policy based on the generated rollouts by the parameters. Therefore, the policy continuously faces new domain instances, leading to increased robustness against mismatch between different domains but lower stability.

- Distilled Domain Randomization (DiDoR) [9]: DiDoR combines domain randomization and policy distillation, aiming at reducing the high variance of the model and learning a robust policy that can be deployed successfully in the real world. In contrast to UDR, DiDoR trains several teachers individually, and each teacher is trained in one domain, which means the parameters of each teacher stay fixed during training. Different from DRAWD, DiDoR sets the same weight for each teacher during distilling progress, and DRAWD adapts the weight of every teacher based on the teacher's performance.

Table 2. Half Cheetah environment domain parameter distribution.

Parameter	Distribution
Total mass	$m \sim N(14, 1.4)$
Tangential friction	$tf \sim U(tf_1(1 - 0.5\epsilon), tf_1(1 + 0.5\epsilon))$
Torsional friction	$tf \sim U(tf_2(1 - 0.5\epsilon), tf_2(1 + 0.5\epsilon))$
Rolling friction	$rf \sim U(rf_1(1 - 0.5\epsilon), rf_1(1 + 0.5\epsilon))$

We use Proximal Policy Optimization (PPO) [21] with GAE [22] as the policy update method and the feedforward neural network as the policy network. We train all methods with similar hyper-parameters to facilitate a fair comparison, as shown in Table 3. To represent the level of randomization, we use a randomization coefficient $\epsilon \in (0, 1)$ to control the diversity of domains and change the range of distribution in test domains by changing the value of ϵ. As training parameter distribution, we take $\epsilon = 0.2$ for the two tasks. From the return curves shown in Figs. 4a and 4c, DRAWD performs better than the other two baseline methods, as reflected in the sampling effectiveness and convergence.

Table 3. Hyperparameters for all policies training.

Parameter	Value
Algorithm	PPO with GAE
Policy	FNN 64–64 with relu hidden-layer and tanh output-layer
Sample step	5000 steps
Value function	FNN 32–32 with relu hidden-layer
Discount factor γ	0.98

(continued)

Table 3. (*continued*)

Parameter	Value
Lambda	0.97
Learning rate	1e-4 for critic, 7e-4 for PPO
Iteration	200 for teacher, 50 for student
Batch size	64
PPO clip ratio	0.1
Teacher number	5

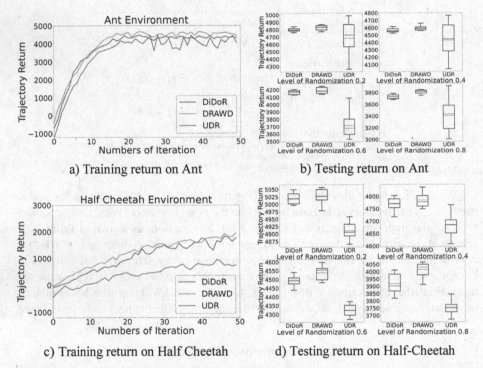

a) Training return on Ant   b) Testing return on Ant

c) Training return on Half Cheetah   d) Testing return on Half-Cheetah

Fig. 4. Summary of training and generalization result on Ant and Half-Cheetah environments; (a) and (c) are training return comparison across three methods; (b) and (d) compares the three methods by changing the level of randomization. The red line represents the median return and the blue line represents the average return of ten test domains.

We evaluate the generalization performance of the method proposed above, as shown in Figs. 4b and d, by simulating unknown domains with different randomization coefficients ϵ. The experiment results show that DRAWD gains higher median and higher average return than the baselines. Moreover, multiple teachers distill to a single student policy can effectively reduce the variance of the model, depending on higher variance in UDR than the other two methods across two tasks. As for DiDoR and DRAWD, we can see that the student policy obtains higher returns in test domains with DRAWD in two environments, even if the level of randomization changes. It leads to the conclusion that adaptively weighting teacher policies according to teacher policy performance can improve student policy performance and stability.

6 Conclusion

Domain generalization to an unseen domain in reinforcement learning is of vital importance, and domain randomization is an important branch of research in domain generalization. In this work, we focus on the common existing problems of domain randomization while transferring from source domain to target domain and make improvement to it. We propose Domain Randomization with Adaptive Weight Distillation, a method automatically computing multitask weights in distillation depending on the teacher's performance. DRAWD combines multitask learning and distilled domain randomization. After experimental comparison, DRAWD provides improved performance and stable generalization in unknown domains than the method without adaptive weights, implying that our hypothesize is correct.

For future research, we will focus on real-world applications based on our research results, such as robot arms, to more convincingly verify the generalizability of our work. In the future, our goal is to apply domain generalization to the posture control of satellite.

References

1. Andrychowicz, O.M., et al.: Learning dexterous in-hand manipulation. Int. J. Robot. Res. **39**(1), 3–20 (2020). https://doi.org/10.1109/IROS.2016.7759557
2. Tobin, J., Fong, R., Ray, A., Schneider, J., Zaremba, W., Abbeel, P.: Domain randomization for transferring deep neural networks from simulation to the real world. In: 2017 IEEE/RSJ international conference on intelligent robots and systems (IROS), pp. 23–30. IEEE (2017). https://doi.org/10.1109/IROS.2017.8202133
3. Koos, S., Mouret, J.B., Doncieux, S.: The transferability approach: Crossing the reality gap in evolutionary robotics. IEEE Trans. Evol. Comput. **17**(1), 122–145 (2012). https://doi.org/10.1109/TEVC.2012.2185849
4. Mehta, B., Diaz, M., Golemo, F., Pal, C. J., Paull, L.: Active domain randomization. In: Conference on Robot Learning, pp. 1162–1176. PMLR (2020). https://doi.org/10.48550/arXiv.1904.04762
5. Tiboni, G., Arndt, K., Kyrki, V.: DROPO: sim-to-real transfer with offline domain randomization (2022). https://doi.org/10.48550/arXiv.2201.08434
6. Muratore, F., Eilers, C., Gienger, M., Peters, J.: Data-efficient domain randomization with bayesian optimization. IEEE Robot. Autom. Lett. **6**(2), 911–918 (2021). https://doi.org/10.1109/LRA.2021.3052391
7. Mozian, M., Higuera, J. C. G., Meger, D., Dudek, G.: Learning domain randomization distributions for training robust locomotion policies. In: 2020 IEEE/RSJ International Conference on Intelligent Robots and Systems (IROS), pp. 6112–6117. IEEE (2020). https://doi.org/10.1109/IROS45743.2020.9341019

8. Vuong, Q., Vikram, S., Su, H., Gao, S., Christensen, H. I.: How to pick the domain random-ization parameters for sim-to-real transfer of reinforcement learning policies? (2019). https://doi.org/10.48550/arXiv.1903.11774

9. Brosseit, J., Hahner, B., Muratore, F., Gienger, M., Peters, J.: Distilled domain randomization. (2021). https://doi.org/10.48550/arXiv.2112.03149

10. Zhao, C., Hospedales, T.: Robust domain randomised reinforcement learning through peer-to-peer distillation. In: Asian Conference on Machine Learning, pp. 1237–1252. PMLR (2021). https://doi.org/10.48550/arXiv.2012.04839

11. Czarnecki, W.M., Pascanu, R., Osindero, S., Jayakumar, S., Swirszcz, G., Jaderberg, M.: Distilling policy distillation. In: The 22nd International Conference on Artificial Intelligence and Statistics, pp. 1331–1340. PMLR (2019). https://doi.org/10.48550/arXiv.1902.02186

12. Guo, M., Haque, A., Huang, D.-A., Yeung, S., Fei-Fei, L.: Dynamic Task Prioritization for Multitask Learning. In: Ferrari, V., Hebert, M., Sminchisescu, C., Weiss, Y. (eds.) ECCV 2018. LNCS, vol. 11220, pp. 282–299. Springer, Cham (2018). https://doi.org/10.1007/978-3-030-01270-0_17

13. Todorov, E., Erez, T., Tassa, Y.: Mujoco: A physics engine for model-based control. In: 2012 IEEE/RSJ International Conference on Intelligent Robots and Systems, pp. 5026–5033. IEEE (2012). https://doi.org/10.1109/IROS.2012.6386109

14. Rusu, A.A., et al.: Policy Distillation (2015). https://doi.org/10.48550/arXiv.1511.06295

15. Hinton, G., Vinyals, O., Dean, J.: Distilling the knowledge in a neural network. 2, 7 (2015). https://doi.org/10.48550/arXiv.1503.02531

16. Lai, K.H., Zha, D., Li, Y., Hu, X.: Dual policy distillation (2020). https://doi.org/10.48550/arXiv.2006.04061

17. Kendall, A., Gal, Y., Cipolla, R.: Multi-task learning using uncertainty to weigh losses for scene geometry and semantics. In: Proceedings of the IEEE Conference on Computer Vision and Pattern Recognition, pp. 7482–7491 (2018). https://doi.org/10.1109/CVPR.2018.00781

18. Chen, Z., Badrinarayanan, V., Lee, C. Y., Rabinovich, A.: Gradnorm: Gradient normaliza-tion for adaptive loss balancing in deep multitask networks. In: International conference on machine learning, pp. 794–803. PMLR (2018). https://doi.org/10.48550/arXiv.1711.02257

19. Kumar, M., Packer, B., Koller, D.: Self-paced learning for latent variable models. In: Advances in Neural Information Processing Systems, Vol. 23 (2010)

20. Graves, A., Bellemare, M. G., Menick, J., Munos, R., Kavukcuoglu, K.: Automated curriculum learning for neural networks. In: International Conference on Machine Learning, pp. 1311–1320. PMLR (2017). https://doi.org/10.48550/arXiv.1704.03003

21. Schulman, J., Wolski, F., Dhariwal, P., Radford, A., Klimov, O.: Proximal policy optimization algorithms (2017). https://doi.org/10.48550/arXiv.1707.06347

22. Schulman, J., Moritz, P., Levine, S., Jordan, M., Abbeel, P.: High-dimensional continuous control using generalized advantage estimation (2015). https://doi.org/10.48550/arXiv.1506.02438

Numerical Solution of the Inverse Kinematics Problem on the Example of a 6-DOF Robot

Georgy Karabanov[1]([✉]), Alexander Selyukov[2], and Oleg Krakhmalev[3,4,5] [iD]

[1] Moscow State University of Technology, STANKIN", Vadkovsky Lane 3a, 127055 Moscow, Russia
gosha.100@bk.ru
[2] The Bauman Moscow State Technical University, 2Nd Baumanskaya Str. 5, Room 1, 105005 Moscow, Russia
[3] Financial University Under the Government of the Russian Federation, 4-Th Veshnyakovsky Passage 4, 109456 Moscow, Russia
[4] Moscow State University of Food Production, Volokolamsk Highway 11, 125080 Moscow, Russia
[5] Bryansk State Technical University, Boulevard 50 Years of October 7, 241035 Bryansk, Russia

Abstract. A geometric model has been created for the selected 3D model 6-DOF the robot. It is a mathematical model using matrices of transformation of homogeneous coordinates. For matrices of transformation of homogeneous coordinates using special differentiation matrices partial derivatives has been obtained and Jacobi matrix corresponding to selected geometric model has been formed. Rotation matrix reflecting working member orientation in space using aircraft angles has been obtained. These angles are a variation of Euler angles. The Gauss method has been chosen as the numerical method for solving the systems of linear equations. Based on the Gauss method, an algorithm for solving the inverse kinematics problem and software implementing it has been developed. When developing the software, object-oriented programming tools were used. The software has been verified using a 3D model of the real industrial robot. The software has been tested on an Intel Core i5-2430M microprocessor running the Windows 10 operating system. Results of studies has been presented by values of given and actual coordinates corresponding to trajectory of 6-DOF robot movement, orientation of its working member and operating time of the algorithm for different number of iteration steps.

Keywords: 6-DOF Robot · 3D Model · Homogeneous coordinates · Inverse kinematics problem · Software

1 Introduction

Industrial robots are one of the components of automated production systems used in flexible automated production. Industrial robots can improve labor productivity and the level of quality of products.

An industrial robot is a machine whose main purpose is to move its working member in space along a given trajectory.

An important characteristic of an industrial robot is the number of degrees of freedom (DOF) of its manipulation system (MS). For the 6-DOF robot, the number of degrees of freedom is six, respectively. The working space of an industrial robot is determined by the combination and mutual arrangement of links in its MS. It is usually assumed that the first three kinematic pairs realize movement of the working member along a given trajectory, and the remaining three realize orientation of the working member in space.

Object of study of this paper is MS of 6-DOF robots, which are open kinematic chains consisting of links interconnected by kinematic pairs of the fifth class [1]. To describe the structure of MS of robots, a graph method is used based on the concept of a tree structure [2]. When studying the motion of 6-DOF robots, two main kinematics problem are considered: forward and inverse.

The forward kinematics problem is to determine the position and orientation of the robot working member relative to the absolute coordinate system by the known vector of generalized coordinates and given geometric parameters [3].

The inverse kinematics problem is to determine generalized coordinates by a given position and orientation of the robot working member in an absolute coordinate system. In this case, the structure of the MS of robot determined by its kinematic scheme is taken into consideration.

The inverse kinematics problem can be solved offline or online. In the first case, the time is not limited. When programming robots online, the time of solving the problem must be taken into account, but for different cases the permissible time varies.

Previously, studies have been conducted on modeling the dynamics of 6-DOF robots [4 and 5]. The purpose of this paper is to develop an algorithm for numerically solving the inverse kinematics problem and software that implements this algorithm. When developing software, it is necessary to use object-oriented programming tools, because this will improve the structure of the software and the possibility of its further development.

To achieve this purpose, highlight the following tasks:

1. The choice of a mathematical apparatus for solving the inverse kinematics problem.
2. Development of a numerical-iterative method algorithm for solving the inverse kinematics problem.
3. Software development using object-oriented programming tools.
4. Software verification based on the use of a 3D model of the industrial robot and the presentation of results in a convenient form for analysis.

2 Development of the Geometric Model

The geometric model of the MS of robot is a mathematical model that allows to determine the position of the robot and its working member in the absolute coordinate system.

In the studied MS of robot, all kinematic pairs are rotational; the number of links is six. To describe the position of the 3D model of the robot in space, the method of two related coordinate systems can be used [6].

The motion of the MS of robot is considered in an inertial coordinate system rigidly connected to a fixed base. The origin of this coordinate system has been placed at the center of the first kinematic pair (see Fig. 1).

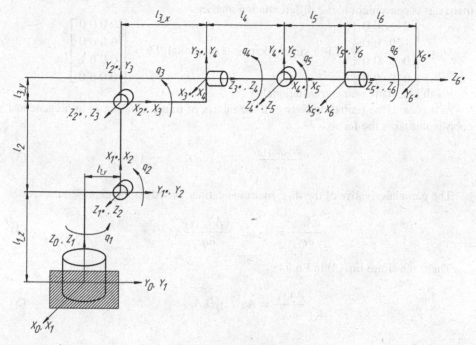

Fig. 1. Kinematic scheme.

The position of the MS of robots in space can be described by means of matrices of transformation of homogeneous coordinates having dimension (4×4). For example, the matrix of transformation of homogeneous coordinates from a local coordinate system associated with the k-th link to an absolute coordinate system is a sequence of matrix products $A_{(i-1), i}$, where $i = (1, \ldots, k)$ [6–8]:

$$A_{0,k} = \prod_{i=1}^{k} A_{(i-1),i}. \tag{1}$$

Accordingly, $A_{0,6*} = A_{0,6} A_{6,6*}$. Overall form of the matrix $A_{0,6*}$:

$$A_{0,6*} = \begin{bmatrix} a_{11} & a_{12} & a_{13} & a_{14} \\ a_{21} & a_{22} & a_{23} & a_{24} \\ a_{31} & a_{32} & a_{33} & a_{34} \\ 0 & 0 & 0 & 1 \end{bmatrix} =$$

$$= \begin{bmatrix} \cos(X_0, X_{6*}) & \cos(X_0, Y_{6*}) & \cos(X_0, Z_{6*}) & X_{6*} \\ \cos(Y_0, X_{6*}) & \cos(Y_0, Y_{6*}) & \cos(Y_0, Z_{6*}) & Y_{6*} \\ \cos(Z_0, X_{6*}) & \cos(Z_0, Y_{6*}) & \cos(Z_0, Z_{6*}) & Z_{6*} \\ 0 & 0 & 0 & 1 \end{bmatrix}. \tag{2}$$

To solve the inverse kinematics problem based on a system of equations performing coordinate transformations, it is necessary to form a Jacobi matrix. This requires partial derivatives of matrices for each generalized coordinate. For the convenience of programming this operation, instead of calculating the derivative of each element of the matrix, it is convenient to use differentiation matrices:

$$D_i = \begin{bmatrix} 0 & -1 & 0 & 0 \\ 1 & 0 & 0 & 0 \\ 0 & 0 & 0 & 0 \\ 0 & 0 & 0 & 0 \end{bmatrix}, \text{ if i-th kinematic pair is rotational, } D_i = \begin{bmatrix} 0 & 0 & 0 & 0 \\ 0 & 0 & 0 & 0 \\ 0 & 0 & 0 & 1 \\ 0 & 0 & 0 & 0 \end{bmatrix},$$

if i-th kinematic pair is translational.

In this case, the partial derivative of the matrix of transformation of homogeneous coordinates takes the form:

$$\frac{\partial A_{(i-1),i}}{\partial q_i} = A_{(i-1),i} D_i. \tag{3}$$

The partial derivative of the $A_{0,k}$, matrix is defined based on the expression:

$$\frac{\partial A_{0,k}}{\partial q_i} = A_{0,(i-1)} \frac{\partial A_{(i-1),i}}{\partial q_i} A_{i,k} \tag{4}$$

Then, substitute Eq. (3) in Eq. (4):

$$\frac{\partial A_{0,k}}{\partial q_i} = A_{0,(i-1)} D_i A_{i,k}. \tag{5}$$

3   Formation of the Jacobi Matrix

By applying the matrices of transformation of homogeneous coordinates, the absolute coordinates of the point M of the k-th link in the absolute coordinate system given by the radius vector $\bar{r}_M^{(0)}$, can be determined from the equation:

$$\bar{r}_M^{(0)} = A_{0,k} \bar{r}_M^{(k)}, \tag{6}$$

where $\bar{r}_M^{(k)}$ a radius vector defining the local coordinates of the point M given in the coordinate system associated with the k-th link.

Analytically, determine the relationship between the generalized coordinates and the six selected parameters by differentiating the position function:

$$d\bar{r}^{(0)} = \sum_{i=1}^{k} \frac{\partial A_{0,k}}{\partial i} \bar{r}^{(k)} dq_i. \tag{7}$$

Replacing differentials with small increments of generalized Δq_i coordinates, for the selected MS of robot, obtain:

$$
\begin{bmatrix}
\bar{i}_0 \frac{\partial A_{0,6}}{\partial q_1}\bar{r}^{(6)} & \cdots & \bar{i}_0 \frac{\partial A_{0,6}}{\partial q_6}\bar{r}^{(6)} \\
\bar{j}_0 \frac{\partial A_{0,6}}{\partial q_1}\bar{r}^{(6)} & \cdots & \bar{j}_0 \frac{\partial A_{0,6}}{\partial q_6}\bar{r}^{(6)} \\
\bar{k}_0 \frac{\partial A_{0,6}}{\partial q_1}\bar{r}^{(6)} & \cdots & \bar{k}_0 \frac{\partial A_{0,6}}{\partial q_6}\bar{r}^{(6)} \\
\bar{i}_0 \frac{\partial A_{0,6}}{\partial q_1}\bar{j}_6 & \cdots & \bar{i}_0 \frac{\partial A_{0,6}}{\partial q_6}\bar{j}_6 \\
\bar{i}_0 \frac{\partial A_{0,6}}{\partial q_1}\bar{k}_6 & \cdots & \bar{i}_0 \frac{\partial A_{0,6}}{\partial q_6}\bar{k}_6 \\
\bar{j}_0 \frac{\partial A_{0,6}}{\partial q_1}\bar{k}_6 & \cdots & \bar{j}_0 \frac{\partial A_{0,6}}{\partial q_6}\bar{k}_6
\end{bmatrix}
\begin{bmatrix}
\Delta q_1 \\ \Delta q_2 \\ \Delta q_3 \\ \Delta q_4 \\ \Delta q_5 \\ \Delta q_6
\end{bmatrix}
=
\begin{bmatrix}
\Delta X \\ \Delta Y \\ \Delta Z \\ \Delta e_{X_0,Y_6} \\ \Delta e_{X_0,Z_6} \\ \Delta e_{Y_0,Z_6}
\end{bmatrix},
\tag{8}
$$

where $\bar{i}_0 = \begin{bmatrix}1\,0\,0\,0\end{bmatrix}, \bar{j}_0 = \begin{bmatrix}0\,1\,0\,0\end{bmatrix}, \bar{k}_0 = \begin{bmatrix}0\,0\,1\,0\end{bmatrix}, \bar{j}_6 = \bar{j}_0^T, \bar{k}_6 = \bar{k}_0^T$, is a basis vectors, $\Delta e_{X_0,Y_6}, \Delta e_{X_0,Z_6}, \Delta e_{Y_0,Z_6}$ is an angles between corresponding axes.

Let's write Eq. (8) in symbolic form:

$$
\{J\}\{\Delta q\} = \{\Delta X\},
\tag{9}
$$

where $\{J\}$ is a Jacobi matrix of dimension (6×6), $\{\Delta q\}$ is a vector of increment of homogeneous coordinates, $\{\Delta X\}$ is a vector of increment of position and orientation of robot working member.

To form the last three rows of the Jacobi matrix, need to know the orientation of the robot working member in space. To do this, three non-diagonal elements of the $A_{0,6*}$ matrix are selected, which are cosines of the angles between the axes, in this case it is elements a_{12}, a_{13} and a_{23} [9, 10].

The three angular coordinates specifying the orientation expand the position vector of the working member and allow it to be multiplied with the inverse Jacobi matrix. However, these angles do not have sufficient clarity, so will use aircraft angles for visualization and analysis.

The α angle (yaw angle) determines the deviation of the position of the robot working member from the X_0Z_0 plane, the β angle (pitch angle) determines the deviation from the horizontal coordinate plane X_0Y_0, and the γ angle (roll angle) is the angle of rotation of the working member around its own axis Z_{6*}.

The sequence of rotations by these angles can be represented by sequentially multiplying the corresponding rotation matrices:

$$
M_{\alpha\beta\gamma} =
\begin{bmatrix} 1 & 0 & 0 \\ 0 & 0 & 1 \\ 0 & -1 & 0 \end{bmatrix}
\begin{bmatrix} C\alpha & 0 & -S\alpha \\ 0 & 1 & 0 \\ S\alpha & 0 & C\alpha \end{bmatrix}
\begin{bmatrix} 1 & 0 & 0 \\ 0 & C\beta & S\beta \\ 0 & -S\beta & C\beta \end{bmatrix}
\begin{bmatrix} C\gamma & S\gamma & 0 \\ -S\gamma & C\gamma & 0 \\ 0 & 0 & 1 \end{bmatrix},
\tag{10}
$$

where $C\alpha$, $C\beta$, $C\gamma$, $S\alpha$, $S\beta$, $S\gamma$ is a cosines and sines of corresponding angles.

Then:

$$
M_{\alpha\beta\gamma} =
\begin{bmatrix}
C\alpha C\gamma - S\alpha S\beta S\gamma & C\alpha S\gamma + S\alpha C\gamma S\beta & -C\beta S\alpha \\
S\alpha C\gamma + C\alpha S\beta S\gamma & S\alpha S\gamma - C\alpha C\gamma S\beta & C\alpha C\beta \\
C\beta S\gamma & -C\beta C\gamma & -S\beta
\end{bmatrix}.
\tag{11}
$$

The resulting rotation matrix reflects the orientation of the coordinate system associated with the working member relative to the absolute coordinate system. Therefore, the elements of the $M_{\alpha\beta\gamma}$ matrix are equal to the corresponding elements of the matrix $A_{0,6}*$.

Then, it is possible to express the aircraft angles from the resulting matrix $M_{\alpha\beta\gamma}$:

$$\alpha = \arcsin\left(\frac{a_{13}}{-\cos(\beta)}\right), \beta = -\arcsin(a_{33}), \gamma = \arccos\left(\frac{a_{32}}{-\cos\beta}\right). \tag{12}$$

4   The Algorithm for Solving the Problem

To solve Eq. (9) by the numerical method, the determinant of the Jacobi matrix must be unequal to zero, i.e. its service coefficient must be sufficiently high [11, 12]. This is achieved by examining the working space of the MS of robot and selecting a trajectory in it.

For ease of calculation and programming, will choose the Gauss method [13].

For each next step of the algorithm, the solution obtained in the previous step is used:

$$\left\{J\left(q^k\right)\right\}\left\{\Delta q^k\right\} = \left\{\Delta X^k\right\}, \tag{13}$$

$$\left\{\Delta X^k\right\} = \left\{X^{k+1}\right\} - \left\{X^k\right\}, \tag{14}$$

$$\left\{q^{k+1}\right\} = \left\{q^k\right\} + \left\{\Delta q^k\right\}, \tag{15}$$

where $\{\Delta q_k\}$ is a solving Eq. (9) at the k-th iteration step, $\{q_k\}$ is a vector of generalized coordinates corresponding to this solution.

Let us make a flowchart of the solution algorithm, where L is an array of vectors that determine the shape of the links, N is a required number of iteration steps, q_0 is a generalized coordinates at the initial moment of movement, X is an absolute coordinate of the final link (see Figs. 2–4).

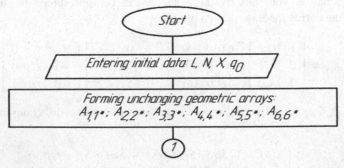

Fig. 2. Flowchart of algorithm.

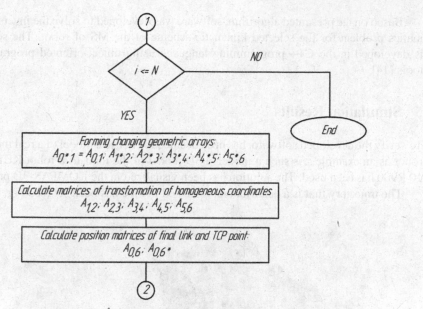

Fig. 3. Flowchart of algorithm.

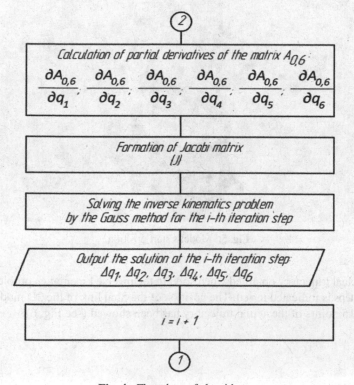

Fig. 4. Flowchart of algorithm.

Based on the presented algorithm, software was developed to solve the inverse kinematics problem for the selected kinematic scheme of the MS of robot. The software is developed in the C++ programming language using object-oriented programming tools [14].

5   Simulation Results

To verify the developed software, has been decided to choose a model of a real industrial robot as an example. As such a model, a 3D model of the industrial robot KUKA KR 10 R900 has been used. The solution has been visualized in the KOMPAS-3D program.

The trajectory that is a quadrilateral indicated in blue has been set (see Fig. 5):

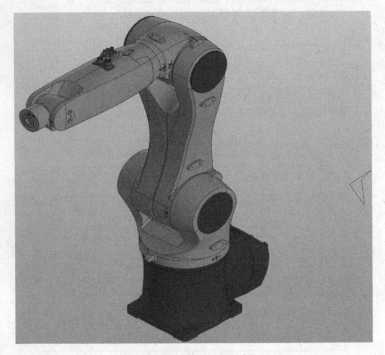

Fig. 5. Model's start position.

The actual trajectory obtained when solving the inverse kinematics problem for 400 iteration steps is indicated in red. The position of the final link of the 3D model at the 1, 2, 3, 4 and 5 points of the actual trajectory has been showed (see Fig. 6):

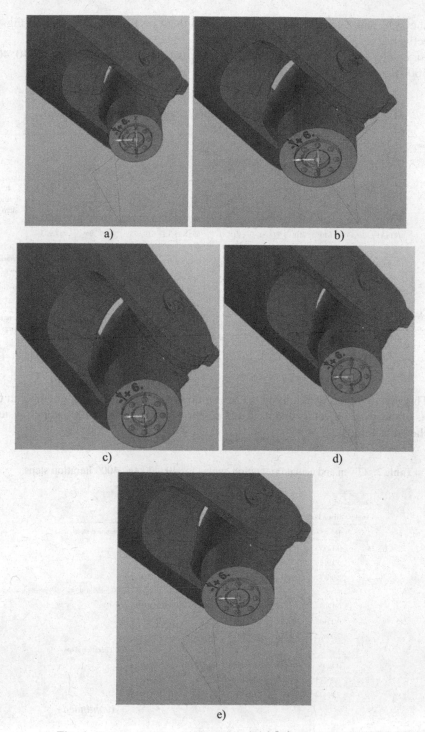

Fig. 6. Trajectory point: (a) 1st; (b) 2nd; (c) 3rd; (d) 4th; (e) 5th.

The X, Y, and Z axes in Fig. 6 correspond to the X_{6*}, Y_{6*} and Z_{6*}, axes in Fig. 1, respectively.

For ease of analysis, the coordinates of the actual and given trajectories for 40, 400 and 4000 iteration steps are shown in Table 1:

Table 1. Actual and given trajectories for 40, 400 and 4000 iteration steps.

Trajectory Coordinate	Given					Actual					
	Point №										
	1	2	3	4	5	1	2	3	4	5	40 iteration steps
X	−59.182	−40	−10	−20	−59.182	−59.182	−39.6957	−9.2131	−19.3262	−58.3401	
Y	573.95	520	600	580	573.95	573.95	519.356	599.136	578.63	572.353	
Z	718.81	655	640	710	718.81	718.81	655.125	639.405	709.306	717.903	
	1	2	3	4	5	1	2	3	4	5	400 iteration steps
X	−59.182	−40	−10	−20	−59.182	−59.182	−39.9717	−9.92385	−19.9354	−59.1	
Y	573.95	520	600	580	573.95	573.95	519.935	599.913	579.863	573.79	
Z	718.81	655	640	710	718.81	718.81	655.014	639.942	709.932	718.72	
	1	2	3	4	5	1 .	2	3	4	5	4000 iteration steps
X	−59.182	−40	−10	−20	−59.182	−59.182	−39.997	−9.99217	−19.9933	−59.1736	
Y	573.95	520	600	580	573.95	573.95	519.993	599.991	579.986	573.934	
Z	718.81	655	640	710	718.81	718.81	655.001	639.994	709.993	718.801	

The aircraft angles determining the orientation of the robot working member at the points of the given trajectory and its actual position for 40, 400 and 4000 iteration steps are shown in Table 2.

Table 2. Given and actual orientation angles for 40, 400 and 4000 iteration steps.

Orientation Angle	Given Point №					
	1	2	3	4	5	40 iteration steps
α	0.1205	0.0768485	0.0332153	−0.010418	−0.054051	
β	0.25193	0.208297	0.164663	0.12103	0.077397	
γ	2.06472	2.10835	2.15198	2.19562	2.23925	
	1	2	3	4	5	400 iteration steps
α	0.1205	0.0768485	0.0332153	−0.010418	−0.054051	
β	0.25193	0.208297	0.164663	0.12103	0.077397	
γ	2.06472	2.10835	2.15198	2.19562	2.23925	
	1	2	3	4	5	4000 iteration steps
α	0.1205	0.0768485	0.0332153	−0.010418	−0.054051	
β	0.25193	0.208297	0.164663	0.12103	0.077397	
γ	2.06472	2.10835	2.15198	2.19562	2.23925	

(*continued*)

Table 2. (*continued*)

Orientation						
Angle	Actual Point №					
	1	2	3	4	5	40 iteration steps
α	0.1205	0.0720493	0.0287328	−0.012583	−0.0578433	
β	0.25193	0.208601	0.165049	0.1226	0.0837845	
γ	2.06472	2.07271	2.11225	2.15053	2.19029	
	1	2	3	4	5	400 iteration steps
α	0.1205	0.0763984	0.0327927	−0.010606	−0.054409	
β	0.25193	0.208323	0.164703	0.121209	0.078097	
γ	2.06472	2.07114	2.11071	2.15014	2.18944	
	1	2	3	4	5	4000 iteration steps
α	0.1205	0.0768038	0.0331733	−0.0104365	−0.0540867	
β	0.25193	0.208299	0.164667	0.121048	0.0774677	
γ	2.06472	2.07099	2.11057	2.15011	2.18936	

To solve inverse kinematics problem using the Intel Core i5-2430M microprocessor, running the Windows 10 operating system, performed in 1, 14 and 118 ms for 40, 400 and 4000 iteration steps, respectively.

6 Conclusion

The paper presents a developed algorithm for solving the inverse kinematics problem for a 6-DOF robot and software that implements this algorithm using the Gauss method to solve systems of linear equations. The results of the solution for the given trajectory, obtained using the developed software, has been illustrated using the selected 3D model of the real industrial robot KUKA KR 10 R900 in the figures and are presented in the tables. The dependence of the accuracy and operating time of the algorithm on the number of iteration steps has been showed.

Subsequently, the obtained results can be used to assess the position errors and orientation of the robot working member in space, develop methods for reducing these errors and further study the dynamics of the MS of robot.

References

1. Shigley, J.E., Pennok, G.R., Uicker, J.J.: Theory of Machines and Mechanisms. Oxford University Press, New York (2011)
2. Lynch, K.M., Park, F.C.: Modern Robotics Mechanics. Planning and Control. Cambridge University Press, England (2017)
3. Yang, D., Liu, L., Wang, J., Chen, K.: Forward kinematics analysis by using homogeneous transformation matrix. Mach. Des. Res. **18**(2), 20–22 (2002)
4. Krakhmalev, O., et al.: Mathematics model for 6-DOF joints manipulation robots. Mathematics **9**(21), 1–11 (2021)
5. Krakhmalev, O., et al.: Parallel computational algorithm for object-oriented modeling of manipulation robots. Mathematics **9**(22), 1–12 (2021)

6. Krakhmalev, O.N., Petreshin, D.I., Fedonin, O.N.: Mathematical models for base calibration in industrial robots. Russ. Eng. Res. **37**(11), 995–1000 (2017). https://doi.org/10.3103/S10 68798X17110089

7. Zudilova, T.V., Ivanov, S.E.: Mathematical modeling of the robot manipulator with four degrees of freedom. Glob. J. Pure Appl. Math. **12**(5), 4419–4429 (2016)

8. Roberts, L.G.: Homogeneous Matrix Representation and Manipulation of n-Dimensional Constructs. Lincoln Laboratory, Massachusetts Institute of Technology (1965)

9. Siciliano, B., Sciavicco, L., Villani, L., Oriolo, G.: Robotics Modelling. Planning and Control. Springer, London (2009)

10. Sciavicco, L., Siciliano, B.: Modelling and Control of Robot Manipulators. Springer, London (2000)

11. Miteva, L., Pavlova, G., Trifonov, R., Yovchev, K.: Manipulability analysis of redundant robotic manipulator. In: 21st International Conference on Computer Systems and Technologies, pp. 135–140. Association for Computing Machinery, New York (2020)

12. Yang, D.C., Lai, Z.C.: On the dexterity of robotic manipulators: Service Angle. ASME J. Mech. Trans. Autom. Des. **107**(2), 262–270 (1985)

13. Anghel, C.: Application in programs of Gauss numerical method for solutions of linear equation systems. In: Proceedings of International Conference on Sebes IV, p. 121. (2004)

14. Shapira, Y.: Mathematical Objects in C++ Computational Tools in a Unified Object-Oriented Approach. Taylor & Francis Ltd, London (2017)

Experimental Study of the Sensitivity Adjustment Technique for Exoskeleton Arm

Artem Sukhanov[✉] [iD], Ivan Ermolov [iD], Maxim Knyazkov [iD], Eugeny Semenov [iD], and Filipp Belchenko [iD]

Ishlinsky Institute for Problems in Mechanics of the Russian Academy of Sciences, Prospekt Vernadskogo, 101-1 Moscow, Russia
sukhanov-artyom@yandex.ru

Abstract. Manipulating objects during the working day affects a person's fatigue, his muscle tone changes. Therefore, when applying biofeedback algorithms based on an electromyogram technique, it is important to take into account the dynamics of such changes and research the possibility of adapting the control system to the psychophysical state of the operator. This technique is being developed as part of the study of the remote control possibility of a robotic platform designed for cleaning ship hulls. The use of this control technique may also be relevant in human-machine systems designed to manipulate heavy objects, for example, during loading and unloading operations at docks or assembly operations. The study considers the possibility of using the operator's electromyogram as a source signal for exoskeleton motor control. This paper shows the features of the variation in the electromyogram envelope during the implementation of rapid movements and the effect of muscle deactivation on the attenuation of the amplitude of the electromyogram envelope on the example of the biceps brachii muscle of the operator. The results of the application of the method of adjusting the sensitivity of the active exoskeleton control system to the operator's actions, previously developed within the project, are shown.

Keywords: Exoskeleton · Electromyogram · Control · Experimental Study · Bezier curves

1 Introduction

Interest in bio-control of wearable robotic devices has been growing in recent years. This is primarily due to the development of electroencephalogram (EEG) and electromyogram (EMG) processing methods, the use of optimal control techniques and machine learning methods.

The use of information about the signal dynamics set directly by the peripheral nervous system leads to the design of prospect interfaces for human-machine systems that perceive natural human impulses to motion [1, 2]. Thus, it becomes possible to implement intuitive control of mechatronic drives that are part of wearable robotic devices. This, in turn, leads to an increase in the efficiency of control such devices and integration of robotic systems into human life.

A. Ronzhin et al. (Eds.): ICR 2022, LNCS 13719, pp. 167–178, 2022.
https://doi.org/10.1007/978-3-031-23609-9_15

2   Control System

2.1   Structure

The nervous system of a human in the process of planning the movement of his limbs generates a control signal characterized by a frequency and amplitude of voltage determined for the action being performed. The signal comes to the muscle groups, where a motion signal is formed from it, controlling muscle contraction [3].

Perceptual devices detect the value of muscle activity and transmit it for processing to the controller, where the signal is filtered and transformed. Then the algorithm of relative motion of the exoskeleton links is formed. The controller sets the required movement speed to the exoskeleton device actuators. Depending on the result of the algorithm, either the current position of the links is stabilized, or the movement of the links of the exoskeletal device set.

At the same time, the current readings of the angular encoder data and the speed of relative movement of the links are monitored from the control system and from the operator, whose nervous system perceives tactile data from the interaction of human limbs with the structural elements of the exoskeleton and performs visual perception of the current action for further motion planning.

Figure 1 shows a structural model of the exoskeletal system, which reflects the functional relationships between the elements of the system and gives an idea of the organization of the control system in the exoskeletal device.

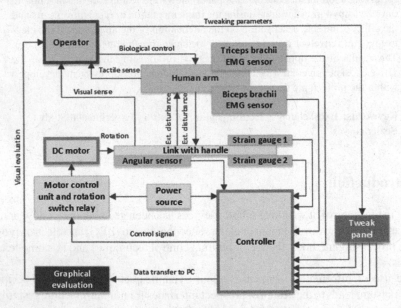

Fig. 1. The technical scheme of the system.

In many works related to the R&D of a control system for mechatronic drives in complex robotic devices (exoskeletons, active prostheses), which are driven by the activity of the electrical potential of human muscles, it is said about the formation of the speed of movement of the drive. However, these works do not take into account the dynamics of acceleration and braking of the drive along with the dynamics of the processes taking place in the motor units of muscle groups, namely the processes of activation and deactivation of muscle fibers.

Estimating the situation, the operator decides to use his muscular apparatus, forming an action potential on the motor neuron that exceeds a certain amplitude threshold and is sufficient to start the ion exchange of a muscle cell with the periocellular space.

Depending on the number of motor neurons involved, the total volume of ions involved in the intersection of muscle cell membranes may vary, thus setting the intensity of contraction and quantitatively reflecting the desire to create an effort when moving a limb. At the same time, a potential difference arises in the muscle tissue, which can be evaluated and used for processing as information about the current activity of the muscle.

By converting the allotted biopotential according to certain algorithms, it is possible to generate a control signal for a mechatronic drive integrated into the exoskeleton joint and driving its link. At the same time, the excited muscle tissue begins to contract, since the processes of interaction of actin and myosin proteins are started due to the penetration of ions into the cell. By contracting, the muscle sets the operator's limb in motion, thereby allowing the operator to be evaluated by the visual channel. At the same time, the following happens:

1. An electric pulse releases $Ca2+$ ions from the L-system;
2. $Ca2+$ binds troponin and opens the active centers of the actin protein;
3. Myosin heads attach to actin;
4. The legs of the myosin heads tilt at an angle of 45 degrees, pulling up the myosin relative to the actin filaments, detach and reattach to the next active centers of actin. Each attachment and detaching comes with an expenditure of ATP energy. The mechanism continues as long as there is $Ca2+$ and ATP [4].

2.2 Sensitivity Adjustment Method

A single muscle works exclusively for contraction. Therefore, in order to fully control the movement of the limb (at least in one plane), two antagonist muscles are necessary. In our study, we consider the biceps brachii, the antagonist of which is the triceps brachii (Fig. 2). Working in pairs, these muscles compensate for each other's movements, thereby allowing you to control the movement of the forearm in the elbow. Thus, it is important to take into account the simultaneous contribution of both muscles to movement control. However, after contraction, the muscle fibers should relax [4, 5]. At the same time, there is an outflow of reaction products from the cells of motor units, which also affects the readings of biopotential sensors.

In a relaxed muscle, calcium channels are closed, but according to the law of supercompensation, ions reappear in the periocellular space, forming a current that is read by biopotential sensors and can be interpreted by the control system as a signal to action. If one implements mechatronic drive control using information about the biopotentials of antagonist muscles, it is extremely necessary to take into account the accumulated information about the state of the system at a certain time buffer and, analyzing it, already make a decision on control compensation. Among the methods that can be applied to compensate for the control signal are dynamic changes in the dead zone level [6, 7], as well as dynamic changes in the sensitivity of the system to control signals.

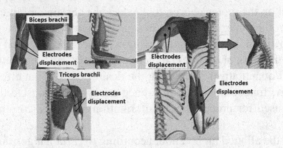

Fig. 2. Location of the elbow joint electrodes.

Thus, the adjusted value of the parameter of the total amplitude of the electromyogram envelope $EMG_{corrected}$ must be transmitted to the control system (1).

$$EMG_{corrected} = aEMG_{filtered}, \tag{1}$$

where $EMG_{filtered}$ is the value of the parameter of the total amplitude of the electromyogram envelope that has passed primary filtering. In this case, the variable a is a parameter that depends on the sensitivity of the sensors to changes in the amplitude of the electromyogram. For the implementation of slow movements it is extremely important to monitor the dynamics of the electromyogram amplitude at its relatively small values.

Thus, in order to make an estimate for small amplitude deviations, it is necessary to scale the incoming value with a coefficient exceeding one. However, in this case, sudden movements corresponding to large amplitude of the electromyogram will be interpreted incorrectly and it is possible to go beyond the limits of control restrictions.

On the other hand, finding this coefficient in the range from 0 to 1 will reduce the influence of noise, but in this case it is not possible to get the maximum speed of the drive. In this work, an algorithm is proposed by which it is possible to combine the advantages of establishing the conversion coefficient of the control value for low and high speeds. To do this, it is proposed to change the control value non-linearly. That is, in this case we will get the next (2):

$$EMG_{sum} = EMG_{corr.bic} + EMG_{corr.tric}, \tag{2}$$

where $EMG_{corr.bic}$ and $EMG_{corr.tric}$ are the corrected values of the obtained EMG data from the biceps brachii and triceps brachii sensors of the operator, respectively. At the same time, a nonlinear law of correction of the control parameter was implemented for the control system using the Bezier curves technique. This technique was chosen because it allows one to build a continuous curve inside a given area with control points (see Fig. 3) and at the same time allows one dynamically changing the shape of the curve.

So, for example, if one takes as a basis the construction of a cubic curve described by a system of equations in parametric form (3):

$$\begin{cases} x = x_1(1-t)^3 + 3tx_2(1-t)^2 + 3t^2x_3(1-t) + t^3x_4 \\ y = y_1(1-t)^3 + 3ty_2(1-t)^2 + 3t^2y_3(1-t) + t^3y_4 \\ \qquad t \in [0,1] \end{cases} \tag{3}$$

then, if the coordinates $x_1 = 0$, $y_1 = 0$, $x_4 = 255$, $y_4 = 255$ are known, one can create the necessary curve by specifying only coordinates of two points- $T1[x_2, y_2]$ and $T2[x_3, y_3]$. Figure 3 shows examples of the functional dependencies of the adjusted EMGcorr parameter on the EMG parameter formed on the basis of data obtained from the EMG sensor.

In this figure, one can see that by changing the coordinates of points $T1[x_2, y_2]$ and $T2[x_3, y_3]$, one may adjust the sensitivity of the output value (in this case, this is the adjusted parameter of the operator's muscle biopotential data) to the change in the input value (in this case, this is the data obtained directly during the measurement and passed the primary filtering).

Thus, applying the proposed technique of sensitivity adjustment to the exoskeleton control system, it is possible to implement various modes of its operation. For example, if the coordinates of the point $T1$ and the coordinates of the point $T2$ are numerically identical, respectively, then the functional dependence of the corrected value on the measured value will set into a linear one (Fig. 3a).

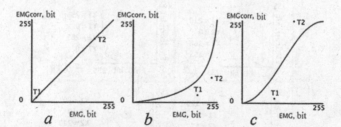

Fig. 3. Examples of setting the sensitivity of the control system.

Figure 3b shows that when the biopotential signal changes in the region close to zero, the corrected value changes slowly, which allows getting rid of the influence of noise at weak signals and set more smooth control of the movement of the exoskeleton. In the presence of a high biopotential corresponding to the operator's desire to increase the speed of movement of the exoskeleton link, the adjusted value changes faster, this allows implementing a fast positioning mode [8, 9].

In Fig. 3c, one can see the situation that is characterizes the slow mode of operation of the exoskeleton. This mode is used when accuracy of movement is important. This dependence can be divided into three sections. The first section, characterized by a weak signal, is described similarly to the area close to zero from Fig. 3b. In this area, weak noise, interference, and small fluctuations in the biopotential signal are filtered. The second section has a characteristic close to linear, and the last section reduces the influence of random signal fluctuations at high speeds or under smooth muscle tetanus.

3   Experimental Study

In the laboratory of Robotics and Mechatronics of the IPMeh RAS, different situations were tested. These situations characterize various manipulations both without an object and with an object of known mass. The Fig. 4 depicts the process of conducting experiments.

Fig. 4. Experiment sets (moving object (left) and catching object (right)).

The first stage of the experiments was organized in order to clarify the features of the behavior of the envelope electromyogram when the arm moves on the bend in the elbow. Figure 5 shows the settings of the coordinates of *T1* and *T2* points for further experiments.

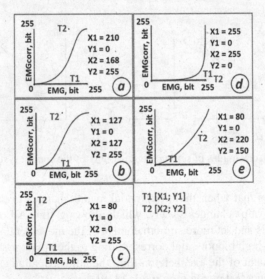

Fig. 5. Experiment settings.

These settings will be used in the relevant experiments further. By shifting the coordinates *X* of points *T1* and *T2*, we only change the threshold of sensitivity of the system. MyoWare sensors were used as biopotential sensors, and a microcontroller based on a high-performance ARM processor platform was used to ensure a high polling frequency. The duration of the experiments was limited to 3 s. Before setting up the experiment, the sensitivity of the system was set, namely the coordinates of points *T1* and *T2* in the algorithm for constructing the Bezier curve. Data on the current biopotential was obtained at a frequency of 100 Hz. After obtaining the first set of data, the Kalman filter was applied to them [10], and then the transformation took place according to the proposed Bezier curve method. The first experiment is slow flexion–extension at the elbow without a load with 1 approach in 3 s.

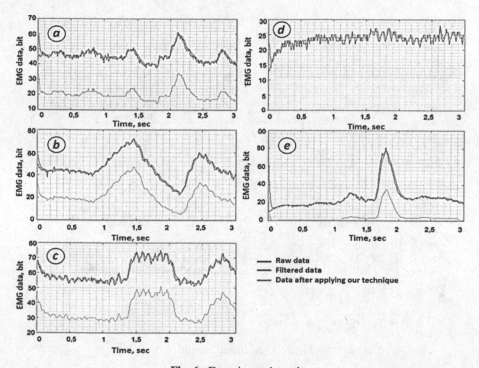

Fig. 6. Experiment 1 results.

It can be seen that the settings of the upper right graph convert the signal to zero. For slow movements, this setting will not work. Among these results, the upper left and central left graph with the corresponding settings of coordinates *T1* and *T2* can be considered preferable. It can be seen (Fig. 6) that the central area of the sensitivity adjustment graph is close to linear in its shape, thus it allows to implement the usual "operating mode", which does not lead to significant changes in the signal shape but allows you to reduce the influence of small noises on control.

The second experiment involved rapid flexion-extension at the elbow without load with 3 approaches in 3 s (Fig. 7). At this stage, one can see the effect of supercompensation is a biological law formulated by Karl Weigert (German pathologist). It consists in the fact that the body, in response to the waste of substances or the loss of tissues (within certain limits), reacts with the formation of new substances and tissues of the same kind, in an amount exceeding the lost. Here, the settings corresponding to the central right graph will be the most preferred. Here there is a stronger suppression of weak signals, which gives a clearer picture of the beginning of the urge to action. At the same time, the more curved the sensitivity adjustment graph is, the less the effect of supercompensation will be noticeable, which can be removed in the control system by setting the dead zone. However, it is worth noting that with sufficiently fast movements, the amplitudes of the electromyogram overlap. This is due to the fact that the muscle has not yet fully passed the relaxation stage and there is still a current of ions in the periocellular space.

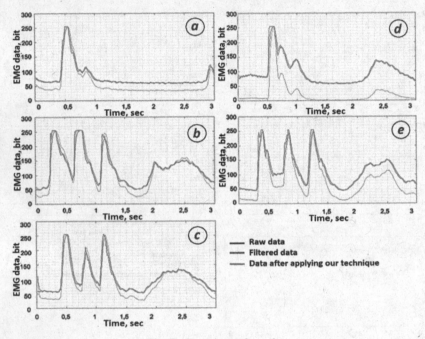

Fig. 7. Experiment 2 results.

The third experiment was set while the settings of coordinates *T1* and *T2* were similar—slow flexion-extension at the elbow with a load of 10 kg 1 approach in 3 s (Fig. 8). In this experiment, there is a load, and therefore a greater number of motor units are involved. Therefore, one can notice an increase in the frequency of signal changes. Shifting the coordinates of points *T1* and *T2* on the sensitivity adjustment graph to the right side of the graph allows you to get an adjusted signal in the end, which will have a more pronounced amplified amplitude component.

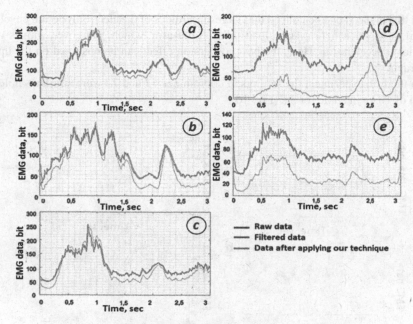

Fig. 8. Experiment 3 results.

The fourth experiment set involved rapid flexion-extension at the elbow with a load of 10 kg 3 approaches in 3 s (Fig. 9).

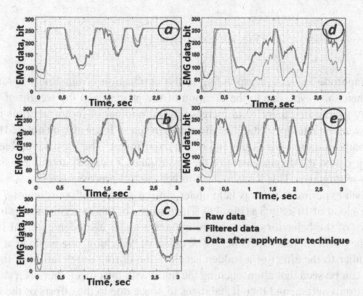

Fig. 9. Experiment 4 results.

In this mode, it can be noticed that large amplitudes of the electromyogram envelope prevail here, since here a large load falls on the arm, which, moreover, moves with significant acceleration. Here, the best conversion effect can be observed on the upper left graph.

In the fifth experiment the settings of coordinates *T1* and *T2* were similar – holding a load of 10 kg in static for 3 s (Fig. 10).

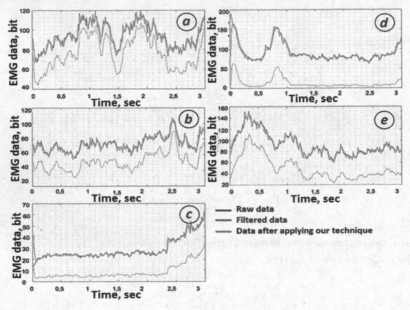

Fig. 10. Experiment 5 results.

The amplitude values corresponding to the application of maximum force are not observed here, however, due to the duration of the process and the weight of the load, it is clearly visible that there is an increase in the number of motor neurons involved, which indicates an attempt to stabilize the object in space. It can also be noticed the effect of supercompensation towards the end of the experiment. The most favorable settings here can be called the displacement of the coordinates *T1* and *T2* to the left side of the sensitivity setting area. This leads to a smoother control process.

The sixth experiment set was held under similar settings of coordinates *T1* and *T2* – catching a load of 10 kg in 3 s (Fig. 11). The purpose of this experiment was to find out the features of the behavior of an electromyogram under a sudden external influence. Here are the results of this experiment. The effect of "catching" the payload at the same time is similar to the effect of a sudden acceleration during acceleration of the load in motion. It can be seen that after touching the hand with the object, there is a sharp jump in the electromyogram, and then it stabilizes in space due to the efforts of the biceps.

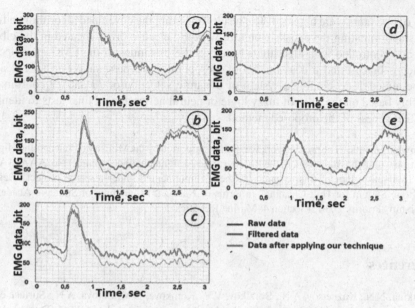

Fig. 11. Experiment 6 results.

The seventh experiment was conducted to reveal the behavior of the rate of change of the electromyogram, which can be used to identify the intensity of the operator's intention (Fig. 12).

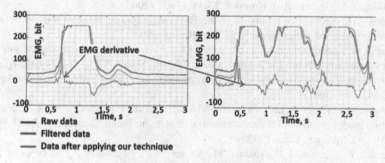

Fig. 12. Experiment 7 results.

By the numerical value of this value, we can tell how strong the operator's desire to influence the object was. Negative acceleration in this case can be considered as the cessation of movement, thereby allowing you to get rid of the effect of reverse ion current when relaxing the muscle.

4 Conclusion

As part of the work, it was possible to obtain various data for several operators, on the basis of which reference values of the control system parameters for calibration for a group of operators were obtained. The results of testing the developed algorithm on full-scale stand imitating the exoskeleton arm with the electric drive, located in the elbow joint, and controlled with algorithms based on the dynamics of the EMG envelope of the biceps brachii and triceps brachii of the operator are presented. Further research will be aimed at developing a system of dynamic selection of $T1$ and $T2$ coordinates (possibly based on the rules of fuzzy logic or neural network) and final tests to identify the effectiveness of the proposed method.

Acknowledgments. The present work was partly supported by the Ministry of Science and Higher Education within the framework of the Russian State Assignment under contract No. AAAA-A20-120011690138-6. Part of this research has been implemented under research project "Design of Robotic System for Hull Cleaning" in terms of National Programme of Strategic Academic Leadership "Priority 2030" (Section 4: Marine Robotics).

References

1. Rukina, N.N., Kuznetsov, A.N., Borzikov, V.V., Komkova, O.V., Belova, A.N.: Surface electromyography: its role and potential in the development of exoskeleton. Mod. Technol. Med. **8**(2), 109–117 (2016)
2. Verdugo Latorre, R., Matamala, J.M.: Clinical neurophysiology standards of EMG instrumentation: twenty years of changes (2019)
3. Cifrek, M., Medved, V., Tonković, S., Ostojić, S.: Surface EMG based muscle fatigue evaluation in biomechanics. Clin. Biomech. **24**(4), 327–340 (2009)
4. Dimitrova, N.A., Dimitrov, G.V.: Interpretation of EMG changes with fatigue: facts, pitfalls, and fallacies. J. Electromyogr. Kinesiol. **13**(1), 13–36 (2003)
5. De Luca, C.J.: Spectral compression of the EMG signal as an index of muscle fatigue. In: Electrophysiological Kinesiology, p. 57. IOS Press (1993)
6. De Sapio, V.: An approach for goal-oriented neuromuscular control of digital humans in physics-based simulations. Int. J. Human Fact. Modell. Simul. **4**(2), 121–144 (2014)
7. Valderrabano, V., et al.: Muscular lower leg asymmetry in middle-aged people. Foot Ankle Int. **28**(2), 242–249 (2007)
8. Gradetsky, V.G., Ermolov, I.L., Knyazkov, M.M., Semenov, E.A., Sukhanov, A.N.: Switching operation modes algorithm for the exoskeleton device. In: Smart Electromechanical Systems, pp. 131–142. Springer, Cham (2020)
9. Gradetsky, V., Ermolov, I., Knyazkov, M., Semenov, E., Sukhanov, A.: Features of human-exoskeleton interaction. In: Robotics: Industry 4.0 Issues & New Intelligent Control Paradigms, pp. 77–88. Springer, Cham (2020)

Gait Synthesis of a Home Quadruped Robot

Dmitry Dobrynin$^{(\boxtimes)}$ [ID]

Federal Research Center for Computer Science and Control RAS, 44/2, Vavilova 119333, Russia
`rabota51@mail.ru`

Abstract. Quadruped robots have high adaptability and high dynamics, which provides excellent maneuverability and adaptability to the environment. Robots have learned to walk on difficult terrain, overcome various obstacles in the form of stairs and bumps. There were walking robots capable of running like animals. Home walking robots have a high appeal because they mimic the behavior of pets. Gait planning is an important component of a walking robot's control system. This article suggests a rules-based approach to gait synthesis. The article presents a robot model and its mathematical model. The robot gait control system is considered. The synthesis of the gait of a home robot is made using elementary foot movements. The calculation of elementary movements is carried out using a kinematic model of the leg. The issues of stability of the robot when walking are considered The article provides examples of various gaits of a home robot - wave gaits, irregular gait and rotation of the robot body in place. The proposed gait construction principle allows you to change the robot's gaits as needed, as well as to build complex models of robot movement. A simulation of the robot's movement using synthesized gaits was carried out.

Keywords: Quadruped robot · Control system · Walking robot

1 Introduction

Walking robots are an important area of modern research in the field of robotics. The walking robot is able to adapt to difficult terrain. Therefore, its patency is higher than robots with wheels or tracks. A quadruped robot is simpler in design than a hexapod robot, and has better stability and load capacity than a robot with two legs. Walking robots can be effective when used in an open area and in a complex environment of industrial facilities. Home walking robots are more maneuverable than their wheeled counterparts, and can become our friends and assistants.

Since the 1980s, Raibert's MIT-Leg lab team has conducted extensive research on quadruped robots. Over the past time, a number of classical theories have been developed that have significantly advanced research in the field of quadruped robots. Currently, typical quadruped robots are: BigDog [1], LittleDog [2] and Spotting [3] from Boston Dynamics; MIT Cheetah [4] from the Massachusetts Institute of Technology, ANYmal [5] from the Swiss Federal Institute of Technology Zurich; HyQ [6] from the Italian Institute of Technology, Unitree [7] from a Chinese company Unitree Robotics.

A. Ronzhin et al. (Eds.): ICR 2022, LNCS 13719, pp. 179–188, 2022.
https://doi.org/10.1007/978-3-031-23609-9_16

The most important component of the control system of a walking robot is gait planning. Currently, this field of research is rapidly developing. The traditional method of gait planning is planning based on the kinematic model of a quadruped robot. Matsuoka [8] proposed a method for controlling a central pattern generator (CPG) to simulate biological spontaneous rhythmic movement. CPG control was mainly based on a simplified single-layer CPG model with feedback to implement gait control. This method has been actively used by other researchers [9]. A detailed overview of this method is given in [10].

Early studies of the gaits of walking robots provided an understanding and mathematical formulation of the usual gaits found in nature in insects and animals. A detailed review is given by Gonzalez in [11].

Currently, the main directions in the field of gait research are increasing the speed of movement of robots, increasing stability and increasing cross–country ability in difficult areas with restricted areas. To move a walking robot through difficult terrain, the robot must choose a fulcrum for each of its steps. This gait was called a free gait. McGee and Frank [12] analyzed the free gait in detail, and then the researchers used the free gait to conduct significant research on the passage of difficult terrain. To implement a free gait, various methods are used – training neural networks, optimizing the position of the center of gravity, etc. An overview of some methods can be found in [13, 14].

A home robot should be able to move in a difficult environment: in rooms with furniture and various objects, along corridors, possibly stairs. The surfaces on which the home robot moves are usually flat surfaces. However, due to the difficult situation, simple wave gaits are not enough for such movements. Research in this area has shown that non-periodic and even free gaits are necessary for such movements. The speed of movement of a home robot in such conditions is not a priority factor. It is much more important to ensure the stability of the robot's gaits and patency in a tight space. Limitations on the complexity of the home robot control system leads to the idea of limiting oneself to a set of non-periodic (intermittent) and wave gaits. The problem is the coupling of different gaits with each other, ensuring the movement of the robot without long stops, the stability of the robot and providing small computational costs for the implementation of the movement.

This paper proposes a rule-based approach to gait synthesis. The gait of a home robot can be synthesized from elementary foot movements. These movements are calculated in advance so as to ensure the stability of the robot's movement. The use of repetitive elementary movements will reduce the requirements for the necessary computing power for the control system.

2 Model of Home Robot

The appearance of the home robot is supposed to be made similar to a dog (Fig. 1a). To do this, it has four legs, each of which has three degrees of freedom. The robot also has a head with several degrees of freedom and a tail. These design elements are needed to animate the emotional state of the work. They are not considered in this paper.

The robot leg has a simple design (Fig. 1b). The leg design contains three drives that allow you to move the foot touch point in three dimensions. The M_1 drive deflects the

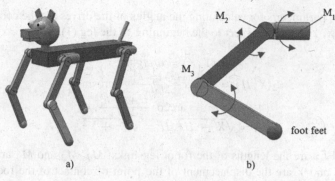

a)   b)

Fig. 1. a) Robot model; b) model of robot's leg

leg from the vertical position. It is fixed on the robot body. The M_2 drive is located close to it, deflecting the leg forward or backward. The M_3 knee joint drive bends the leg. It is located in the knee. This increases the mass that the M_2 drive moves. Potentially, this leads to a limitation of the speed of movement of the leg. Dynamixel type drives are supposed to be used as drives. They have a low speed of movement, which is not sufficient for rapid movements of the legs. However, this design is easy to implement, so it is quite justified for a home robot.

The mathematical model of the robot's leg is shown in Fig. 2.

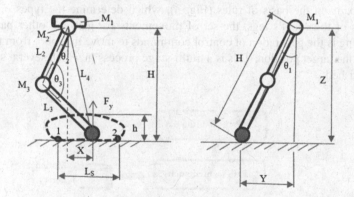

Fig. 2. Mathematical model of robot's leg

In general, the robot's leg is deflected from the vertical position. The slope of the leg plane is determined by the angle θ_1. The calculation of angles θ_2 and θ_3 for drives M_2 and M_3 is similar to the equations presented in [15].

The initial parameters for calculating the angles of the drives are the coordinates of the fulcrum (X, Y, Z) with respect to the beginning of the leg (1).

$$\theta_1(Y, Z) = arctg \frac{Y}{Z},$$
$$\theta_2(X, H) = \arccos \frac{L_2^2+L_4^2-L_3^2}{2L_2L_4} - \arcsin \frac{X}{L_4},$$
$$\theta_3(X, H) = \arccos \frac{L_2^2+L_3^2-L_4^2}{2L_2L_3},$$
$$L_4 = \sqrt{X^2 + H^2}, H = \sqrt{Z^2 + Y^2}.$$

(1)

Here: L_2 and L_3 are the lengths of the robot leg links; M_1, M_2 and M_3 are the robot leg drives; X and Y are the displacement of the point of contact of the foot from the projection of the beginning of the foot in the plane of the support surface; Z is the height of the beginning of the foot from the surface, H is the distance from the beginning of the leg to the point of contact in the plane of the leg; h is the height of the leg lift above the surface; Ls is step length.

To simplify the calculations, we will assume that the robot body retains a horizontal position during movement. Since the home robot must move on flat surfaces, this assumption is quite justified.

3   Motion Planning

A path planning and step generation system is used to generate robot movements. This system is built on the basis of rules (Fig. 3), which determine the types of possible movements of the robot's legs, the set of movements for gait and other parameters. Path planning is the generation of control commands to move the robot from the initial position to the target position. This is a multi-stage process in which several stages can be distinguished:

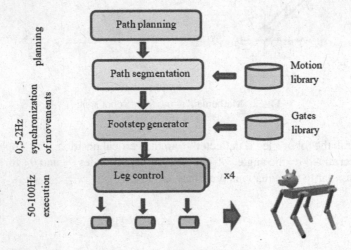

Fig. 3. Process of gait generation

Path segmentation splits the path into separate sections with their own types of gaits. For example, the beginning of movement, moving forward, stops, turns, the end of movement. When splitting, a library of geometric representations of gaits is used. The development of this component of the control system is a separate complex task and is not considered in this paper.

Footstep generator implements a specific character of the robot's movement (gait), using smaller primitives of the movement of individual legs. His task is to start the process of moving individual elements of the legs and synchronize it in time.

Leg control controls the movement of the leg drives, carrying out a given control process in time. This is the most time-critical part of the control system. Control commands to the drives must be issued at a frequency of 50 to 100 Hz and must be strictly synchronized.

This approach makes it possible to implement wave periodic gaits in fairly simple ways to move forward or backward, intermittent gaits to make turns.

4 Stability of Robot

Since the speed of movement of the home robot is chosen small, and the robot moves on flat surfaces, we can limit ourselves to the classical criterion of static stability S_{SM} [11]. The stability of the robot is determined by the position of the projection of the center of gravity (COG) on the support surface. The robot will be statically stable if the horizontal projection of its center of gravity lies inside the reference polygon (Fig. 4). For a robot with four legs, the reference polygon can be either a quadrilateral or a triangle.

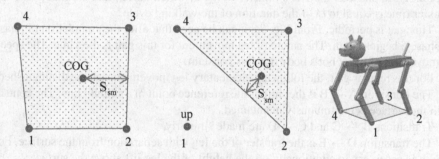

Fig. 4. Static stability of robot

To ensure a margin of stability, the distance from the projection of the COG center of gravity to the edge of the reference polygon must be at least the specified value (Fig. 4).

To ensure the stability of the robot, we will use stable types of gaits. Their stability is tested at the modeling stage.

The basic idea of such gaits is that the static stability of S_{SM} should be provided for each phase of the gait.

5   Gate Generation

Theoretical studies conducted earlier by [11] have shown that the number of possible gaits of a quadruped robot is 4! (24 in total), which is quite large. The number of statically stable gaits is significantly less. They can be determined by the criterion of static stability.

To form the gait, we will use the splitting of the trajectory of the movement of the foot into different sections. Two main phases can be distinguished when performing a step: the reference phase and the transfer phase. In the reference phase, the robot's foot contacts the surface. When the robot body moves, the reference point is stationary relative to the surface. However, at the same time it moves relative to the robot body. The laws of change of the drive angles when moving the reference point along a straight line are nonlinear and are determined by Eqs. (1).

In the transfer phase, it is necessary to move the reference point of the robot's leg back in relation to the direction of movement. To perform the step, we chose a piecewise elliptical trajectory of the foot movement [15]. In it, it is possible to distinguish the phase of lifting the foot, moving back in a straight line and lowering the foot to the surface. Let's look at the examples of the process of gait formation.

Figure 5a shows an example of a regular gait with alternate transfer of legs. The diagram of the pivot point transfer is shown on the right. The origin of the coordinates corresponds to the projection of the beginning of the leg on the support surface (Fig. 2). In phase 1, the leg 1 is transferred back. This corresponds to moving the fulcrum from point D to point A in the right diagram. This element of movement requires its own trajectory of movement of the leg. In the remaining phases, the foot support point 1 moves in a straight line relative to the robot body. This corresponds to the transition from point A to point D. In phase 2, there is a transfer of leg 2, which takes place similarly. The leg transfer time is equal to ¼ of the duration of the walking cycle.

This gait is periodic. From Fig. 5a, it can be seen that after the completion of phase 4, phase 5 begins again. The nature of leg movement for this gait is the same. The speed of movement of the robot's body remains constant.

For this regular gait, the following elementary leg movements can be distinguished:

The transition A → B is the shift of the reference point in a straight line. The contact with the surface is continuously maintained.

Transitions B → C and C → D are made similarly.

The transition D → E is the transfer of the leg with separation from the surface. For him, it is necessary to additionally set the height of the leg lift above the surface.

Thus, in order to perform a regular gait (Fig. 5a), only four elementary leg movements are necessary. A regular gait with alternate shifting of the leg can be used to move in a straight line. Note that the stability of such a gait is low, since the projection of the center of gravity is located near the diagonal side of the reference triangle (Fig. 4).

Figure 5b shows an example of a regular gait with simultaneous transfer of two legs. It can be noticed that this gait has two phases. In each phase, one diagonal pair of legs is transferred. This gait has only two elementary movements: shift A → B and transfer B → A.

Note that this gait is not statically stable, since when transferring two diagonal legs, the reference polygon turns into a line (Fig. 4). The gait can be dynamically stable if the

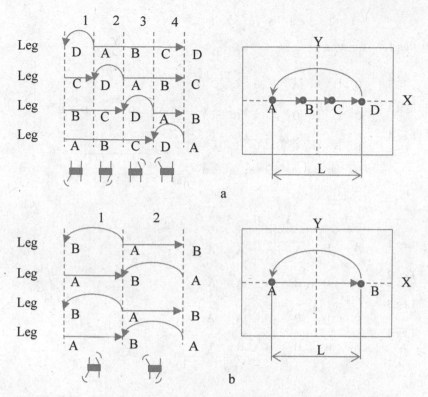

Fig. 5. a) regular gate, alternate rearrangement of legs; b) regular gate, moving by twos

legs move quickly enough. In this case, the robot body does not have time to tip over due to the large inertia. In our case, when using slow drives, such a gait will not work.

To increase the stability margin, it is necessary to mix the projection of the center of gravity closer to the center of the reference triangle. To do this, you can use the discontinuous gaits described in [11]. One leg is carried when all the other legs are on the surface. At the same time, the robot's body remains stationary, which ensures the static stability of the robot. The body is set in motion by all supporting legs, while the legs move simultaneously.

In Fig. 6a a possible variant of such a gait is shown.

Unlike the previous cases, the legs move from one point to another with a stop at the end point. Figure 6b shows a rotation option. In phase 1, the reference points of the robot's legs move along the arcs of the circle relative to the center of rotation CR. Note that in this case, each leg must move along its own trajectory. In Fig. 6b on the right shows an approximate view of the trajectories for leg 1. After turning the body, the robot stops. The following phases of movement are necessary for alternately transferring the legs to the initial positions. After completing all phases, the robot is ready for a new move.

To perform elementary displacements, the dependences of the angles θ_1, θ_2 and θ_3 on time are calculated using Eqs. (1). Next, for each obtained dependence of the rotation

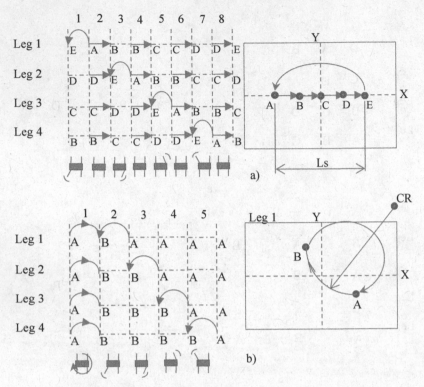

Fig. 6. a) discontinuous gate; b) rotate from center of rotation (CR)

angle of the drive on time, a Bezier polynomial is constructed. With this method of representing the dependence of the rotation angle on time, it is possible to obtain a compact representation while maintaining the necessary accuracy. When controlling, the leg controller uses the previously calculated Bezier polynomial to calculate the angle for each stroke of the drive control. The calculation of the polynomial has a low computational complexity and can be implemented on simple microcontrollers.

The pairing of different gaits occurs according to the same principle as the synthesis of gait. For example, to start moving using the periodic gait shown in Fig. 5a, it is necessary to bring the positions of the legs in accordance with the beginning of phase 1. To simplify the task, an intermediate state can be introduced, for example, when the robot stands motionless on four legs. From this position, the legs are alternately transferred to the phase 1 position, then sets the speed. At the end of walking, it is necessary to stop and move the legs to an intermediate position.

Thus, the coupling of the robot's gaits and poses is also a set of elementary movements.

6   Experiments

The proposed method of synthesizing the gait of a walking robot was tested on a simulator (Fig. 7). Experiments have shown acceptable stability of the robot when moving.

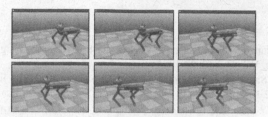

Fig. 7. Simulation of robot's gate

For the experiments, the sets of elementary movements necessary for the formation of gait were formed manually. Each elementary movement was set by the coordinates of the points of the beginning and end of the movement of the foot reference point. The coordinates were calculated relative to the beginning of the leg (Fig. 2). The formation of the angle change functions during movement was calculated using Eqs. (1). The calculated dependences of the change in the angles of the drives on time in the form of coefficients of Bezier polynomials were recorded in the gait library (Fig. 3).

The stability of elementary movement was calculated using the S_{SM} criterion when modeling gait. The footstep generator set the functions of changing the angles of the drives and synchronized them in time. After calculating the angles of the drives, they were sent to the robot simulator.

7   Conclusion

The development of sets of movements of a home robot and its poses is a separate interesting task. The robot's poses should reflect its emotional state. Together with the position of the body, it is important to take into account the position of the head, tail (Fig. 1), sounds and other visual characteristics.

Obviously, the set of movements of a home robot should be quite rich. Movements should include moving in a straight line, various turns, poses for expressing emotions, etc. At the same time, the number of elementary movements and gaits will be large. To effectively manage such a volume of data, it is necessary to develop special software tools.

Special cases are cases of rebalancing. For example, a home robot may fall on its side. In this case, the control system must determine the current position of the robot's body, then select a pose suitable for restoring the vertical position. Walking robots, unlike wheeled machines, can change the shape of their body and get up when tipping over. Conducting research in this direction is an interesting task.

The use of gait synthesis from elementary movements makes it possible to obtain a compact description of gait. This method allows you to pair different poses and gaits with each other, and ensure the movement of a walking robot without long stops. This method uses repetitive elementary movements of the robot's legs. This approach will reduce the requirements for the necessary computing power for the control system of a home robot.

References

1. M Raibert K Blankespoor G Nelson R Playter 2008 Bigdog, the rough-terrain quadruped robot IFAC Proc. Vol. 41 2 10822 10825
2. MP Murphy A Saunders C Moreira AA Rizzi M Raibert 2011 The littledog robot Int. J. Robot. Res. 30 2 145 149
3. SC Niquille 2019 Regarding the pain of spotmini: or what a robot's struggle to learn reveals about the built environment Archit. Des. 89 1 84 91
4. Bledt, G., Powell, M.J., Katz, B., Di Carlo, J., Wensing, P.M., Kim, S.: MIT Cheetah 3: design and control of a robust, dynamic quadruped robot. In: 2018 IEEE/RSJ International Conference on Intelligent Robots and Systems (IROS), pp. 2245–2252. IEEE (2018)
5. Hutter, M., Gehring, C., Jud, D., Lauber, A., Bellicoso, C.D., Tsounis, V., Hwangbo, J., Bodie, K., Fankhauser, P., Bloesch, M., Diethelm, R.: Anymal-a highly mobile and dynamic quadrupedal robot. In: 2016 IEEE/RSJ International Conference on Intelligent Robots and Systems (IROS), pp. 38–44. IEEE (2016)
6. C Semini NG Tsagarakis E Guglielmino M Focchi F Cannella DG Caldwell 2011 Design of HyQ–a hydraulically and electrically actuated quadruped robot Proc. Inst. Mech. Eng., Part I: J. Syst. Control. Eng. 225 6 831 849
7. Specification for robot Unitree B1 from Unitree, https://www.unitree.com/products/B1, last accessed 2022/10/24
8. K Matsuoka 1987 Mechanisms of frequency and pattern control in the neural rhythm generators Biol. Cybern. 56 5 345 353
9. J Shao D Ren B Gao 2018 Recent advances on gait control strategies for hydraulic quadruped robot Recent. Pat. Mech. Eng. 11 1 15 23
10. AJ Ijspeert 2008 Central pattern generators for locomotion control in animals and robots: a review Neural Netw. 21 4 642 653
11. PG Santos De E Garcia J Estremera 2006 Quadrupedal Locomotion: An Introduction to the Control of Four-legged Robots Springer London
12. RB McGhee AA Frank 1968 On the stability properties of quadruped creeping gaits Math. Biosci. 3 331 351
13. J He J Shao G Sun X Shao 2019 Survey of quadruped robots coping strategies in complex situations Electronics 8 12 1414
14. Y Shao Y Jin X Liu W He H Wang W Yang 2021 Learning free gait transition for quadruped robots via phase-guided controller IEEE Robot. Autom. Lett. 7 2 1230 1237
15. Dobrynin, D., Zhiteneva, Y.: Step path simulation for quadruped walking robot. In: International Conference on Interactive Collaborative Robotics, pp. 50–61. Springer, Cham (2021)

Modeling Biomorphic Robotic Fish Swimming: Simulations and Experiments

Ilya Mitin[1,2], Roman Korotaev[1,2], Nikolay Tschur[3], Innokentiy Kastalskiy[1,2], Susanna Gordleeva[1,2], Sergey Lobov[1,2], and Victor Kazantsev[1,2,3(✉)]

[1] Immanuel Kant Baltic Federal University, Nevskogo Str. 14 A, 236016 Kaliningrad, Russia
kazantsev@neuro.nnov.ru
[2] Lobachevsky State University, Pr. Gagarina 23, 603022 Nizhny Novgorod, Russia
[3] Russian State Scientific Center for Robotics and Technical Cybernetic, Tikhoretsky Pr. 21, 194064 Saint-Petersburg, Russia

Abstract. We present a fish robot implementing a thunniform type of movement in aquatic medium. The shape of the robotic fish body was copied from tuna fish using 3D model constructed from a photograph. The robot is equipped with a flexible tail whose oscillations provide translational motion in a water pool. We designed a control system imitating a simple CPG (central pattern generator), propulsion system implementing a simple form of muscle contraction activity and build experimental setup to monitor functional characteristics of the robot movement. We analyze how these characteristics including motion speed and energy consumption depend on the parameters of the oscillating tail, e.g. shape of the tail, frequency and amplitude of the oscillations. The fish robot demonstrated rather effective performance and can be further optimized. We also developed a simulation model of the fish swimming. The model includes exact copy of the geometry of the robotic fish body comprising rigid compartments and oscillating tail. Virtual robot movement in the water medium is modeled by numerical solutions of hydrodynamic and robot body biomechanics equations. In numerical experiments we calculated kinematic parameters of fish movement and visualized hydrodynamic flows at different stages of movement. Detailed simulation showed good qualitative agreement with experimental swimming in real water environment.

Keywords: Biomorphic robotics · Fish robot · Neuromorphic system · Control · Propulsion system · Locomotion · Central pattern generator (CPG)

1 Introduction

Biomorphic robotics has attracted great attention of researchers from different areas of science and technologies. Such robots reproduce basic mechanisms of movement of living animals including surface walking or crawling, flying in air or swimming in an aquatic medium. On the one hand, it is still a focus of fundamental research of how animal biomechanics and movement control are organized. On the other hand, fantastic performance of animal movement in terms of maneuverability and energetic efficiency

A. Ronzhin et al. (Eds.): ICR 2022, LNCS 13719, pp. 189–198, 2022.
https://doi.org/10.1007/978-3-031-23609-9_17

has attracted engineers targeting to design biomorphic robotic systems reproducing the functionality of living prototypes.

Fishes look like one of the simplest natural prototypes to be reproduced in biomorphic robotics [1]. Unlike in walking or flying animals the problem of balance relative to gravity field does not actually exist for fishes. In other words, movement control system needs to provide only locomotion in 3D aquatic medium. In nature fishes are excellent swimmers covering long distances reaching rather high cruising speed and demonstrate significant maneuvering skills. Take, for instance, tuna fish cruising with the speed up to 120 km per hour or a pike attacking with acceleration of 25g [1]. Note, that energy consumption of animals taken from biochemical metabolism stay at very low values (dozen of watts) for such exiting performance. Major factors providing such performance are believed to be biomechanics of movement and organization of its control. Obviously, that the main fish driving forces are tail oscillations. A number of peripheral fins provide mostly fine tuning in the fish movement during maneuvering. Depending on the type of the oscillations fish movement biomechanics can be divided on several types. The subcarangiform type of movement is characterized by a wave propagating from the head to the tail with just slightly increasing amplitude. Typical representatives of this group are salmon and cod. With the carangiform type of movement changes in the wave amplitude becomes noticeable (take, for example, mackerel and barracuda fish). Thunniform locomotion is characterized by the head staying almost at rest, and the oscillations starts approximately from the middle of the body and takes its maximum at the tail fin [2, 3]. Organization of motor control of the fish movements are determined by complex interaction of three body systems: the central nervous system (the brain and the spinal cord), the peripheral nervous system (nerves projecting to muscles and sensory neurons) and the musculoskeletal system. Central nervous system is responsible for solving "strategic" tasks of generating agile locomotion patterns and processing multi-modal sensory information. Robust oscillation and wave patterns are generated by central pattern generators (CPGs) located in the cord and driving actuator system (e.g., muscles). CPGs represent neural circuits capable to generate coordinated rhythmic activity even without sensory feedback and descending drive [4–9]. They provide basic locomotion patterns by producing rhythm and coordination. Feedbacks modulate these patterns to fit current environment conditions.

2 Recent Works

Many fish robot solutions have been proposed in recent decades. According to classifications of natural prototypes fish robots can be also divided following the locomotion patterns. For thunniform locomotion, oscillatory tail fin movement generates thrust and yields robot's translational motion. Obviously, that thunniform locomotion providing fast movement, has attracted primary interest in technological engineering. One of the first tuna-mimetic robot, RoboTuna, was proposed by MIT [10, 11]. Based on Robo-Tuna, the Vorticity Control Unmanned Undersea Vehicle (VCUUV) providing simple maneuverability and up-down motion was developed [12]. Along with multi-joint robot body design different solutions with a soft body was further proposed [1, 13, 14]. Electromagnetic-driven multi-joint bionic fish design and different control strategies was proposed in [15].

Strategic task in the development of underwater robots (not only biomorphic ones) is to achieve maximal performance in robot functionality, particularly, in speed and maneuverability with minimal energy consumption. In biomorphic solutions, the shape of the body and the geometry is fixed by "natural evolution" with a number (rather large) of dynamic variables, such as tail fin amplitude, frequency, order and phases of activation other fins. For each shape design, the key task is to compute and experimentally validate the dependences of the robot performance on dynamic parameters finding optimal values, if exist. Note, that even for thunniform robots whose propulsion system is quite simple dealing with tail oscillations optimal values can be quite sensitive to hidden parameters of the tail oscillations. In particular, it was recently shown that tail flexibility and stiffness could significantly influence on cruising speed [16]. The later research included a simulation model that could effectively predict characteristics of robot's functionality depending on model parameters.

In this paper we used our biomorphic robot implementing the thunniform locomotion (Fig. 1) described earlier in details in [17]. A 3D digital model of the robot shape was used in a novel mathematical model simulating swimming of particularly this robot in a water environment. In simulations and in real physical experiments presented in full in [17] here we calculated characteristics of robot's performance depending on the model parameters and compare the results.

a)   b)

Fig. 1. a) A picture of tuna fish; b) 3D digital model of biomorphic thunaform robot used in simulations and in physical experiments.

3   Methods

To imitate thunniform (tuna) and carangiform (horse mackerel) locomotion, a robot with a rigid body and a flexible tail can be used, since oscillations start approximately from the middle of the body. To create a robot using, for example, a subcarangiform type of swimming (salmon), it will be necessary to use a flexible body that deforms when moving. Contrariwise, the use of a rigid case greatly facilitates the installation of internal electronics and the manufacture of the case itself.

We developed a robotic fish prototype implementing thunniform locomotion. The shape of the body replicated its natural prototype, e.g. tuna fish (Fig. 1). We used standard

3D printing technology to elaborate vessel hull. General device layout is illustrated in Fig. 2.

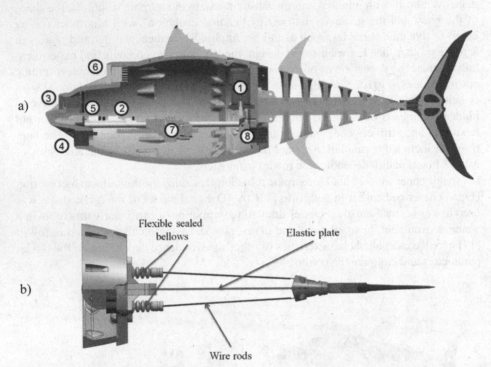

Fig. 2. Robotic fish system components: *1*. Servo. *2*. Control boards for motion control and data processing from sensors and on-board systems. *3*. Camera. *4*. Ultrasonic rangefinder camera (one of four is shown in the diagram). *5*. Sensor system including pressure sensor (planned range up to ~ 6 atm.), temperature sensor, gyroscope, accelerometer, magnetometer. *6*. LED spotlight. *7*. Immersion system (based on ballast tank). *8*. Sealed connector Not included in the scheme: Batteries, lead ballast, side fin servo drives; b) Schematic view of the bionic tail drive.

Thunniform locomotion was implemented by servo drive connected with two wire rods providing flexor/ extensor muscle like dynamics. In the result robotic fish demonstrates translational motion in the swimming pool. Control system permit to vary tail oscillation amplitude and frequency.

Experimental setup is schematically shown in Fig. 3. Translational movement of the robotic fish is recorded by video camera. Robot's trajectory is digitized and processed to calculate the translational speed of the body. Detailed description of the setup construction and remote-control system used in experiments can be found in [17].

In simulations we used custom-made software program based on ANSYS that permit to generate accurate 3D replica of the body of the robot used in experiments accounting all geometrical proportions, mass distribution parameters, inertial parameters and others needed to complete Navier-Stokes equations built in the software package. Method used in modeling the dynamics of biomorphic underwater robots was presented and tested

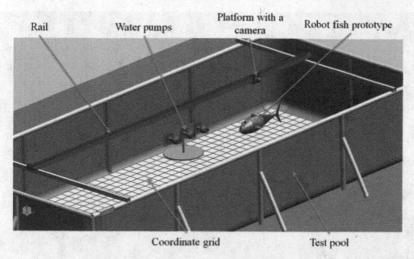

Rail   Water pumps   Platform with a camera   Robot fish prototype

Coordinate grid   Test pool

Fig. 3. Schematic view of experimental setup [17].

in work [18]. To simulate the dynamics of a fish-like robot, a surface and mesh deformation algorithm was developed accounting for fish-like deformation, similar to that observed in the experiment. The equations of robot dynamics and fluid dynamics were solved together. This approach permitted to obtain detailed data on the dynamics of the movement of a fish-like robot, such as the amplitude of fluctuations in the course of roll and trim, as well as their average values. It was also possible to compute macro characteristics of movement such as average speed of the body to compare with experimental results.

To estimate energetic efficiency in experiments we used the following method. Useful output energy is defined by the distance traveled by the robot. Input energy corresponds to energy value consumed by the servo, which is directly proportional to movement of the servo shaft. A quantity estimating the energetic efficiency coefficient, E, is defined as (see [17] for details):

$$E = \frac{v1000}{2\alpha F},$$

where v[m/s] is the movement speed, α[rad] is the tail oscillation angle and F[Hz] is the tail oscillation frequency.

4 Results

Figure 4 illustrates swimming of the biomorphic robot model visualized from numerical simulation. Tail oscillations result in direct translational motion of the robotic fish. Vortices of the flow that appeared due to the oscillations can be also visualized. Note that rigid head part of the fish robot demonstrates low amplitude oscillations, which, however, does not affect much the water flow.

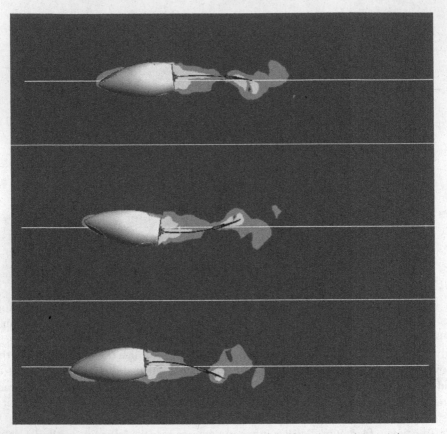

Fig. 4. Consequent snapshots of the fish robot swimming (from top to bottom) in computer simulation illustrating its translational motion in aquatic medium.

Following the simulations, we calculated basic kinematic characteristics of the swimming. Figure 5a illustrates typical acceleration profile of the robot started from zero initial conditions. After several seconds, it reached the stationary value of the velocity for a chosen set of dynamic characteristics (tail oscillation amplitude and frequency). As expected in a simple kinematic model it is a sigmoidal function with monotonically decreasing acceleration values.

In physical experiments, a plate with a plotted coordinate grid with a cell size of 100×100 mm was placed at the bottom of the pool. At each step of the experiment the robotic fish was launched with the specified (fixed during one iteration) control parameters of the amplitude and frequency of tail oscillations. After starting and gaining speed, the layout moving against the background of the coordinate grid was shot with a camera. According to the obtained video data, the speed and nature of the movement of the model were determined at various parameters of the amplitude and frequency of tail oscillations. Figure 6 illustrates measurement and speed detection errors obtained over more than ten trials for each experimental point. The vertical bars show the error of the mean (standard deviation multiplied by the root of the number of repetitions).

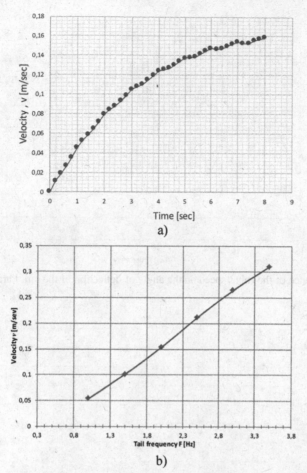

Fig. 5. Fish robot velocity versus time. Parameter values: tail frequency, $F = 2$ Hz, tail amplitude, $\alpha = 0.52$ rad; b) Fish robot velocity versus tail oscillation frequency.

Next, we calculated swimming performance characteristics estimating the energy consumption (see, Methods). Figure 7 illustrates that this quantity decrease with increasing tail amplitude. It was somewhat expected because more tail amplitude provided more vortices during swimming (Fig. 4).

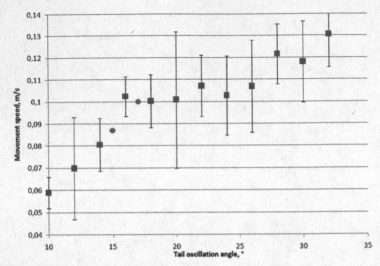

Fig. 6. Dependence of the robot speed on the angle of deflection of the tail. Parameter values: F = 4.92 Hz

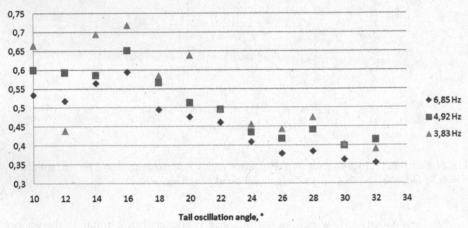

Fig. 7. Robot swimming efficiency (ratio of robot movement to servo rotation, see Methods for details)

5   Conclusion

We developed a research platform comprising simulation model, robot working prototype and experimental setup to investigate the dynamics of thunniform locomotion of underwater fish robot. First results of computer simulation showed good qualitative agreement with experimental swimming in real water environment. Quantitative differences between the parameters of real and virtual swimming, e.g. higher frequency is needed in experiments to achieve the same values of velocity, can be explained by the following reasons. In the model there are no rods running from the servo to the tail fin. The surface of the design model does not have technological holes for fasteners. Another essential point in the experiment is the wire running from the operátor to the model, on which floats are attached to maintain its neutral buoyancy. This wire, despite the small cross-section (three separate conductors with a diameter of 1 mm), can make a significant contribution to the hydrodynamic resistance of the robot. Furthermore, the model did not accounted waves reflected from the walls of the swimming pool. It can also affect ideal swimming.

In spite of these difficulties the thunniform fish robot demonstrated rather effective performance and can be further optimized to improve its functionality.

Acknowledgements. This work was funded by the Russian Science Foundation (grant No. 21-12-00246).

References

1. Du, R., Li, Z., Youcef-Toumi, K., Valdivia y Alvarado, P.: Robot Fish. Bio-inspired fishlike underwater robots. Springer Berlin, Heidelberg (2015). https://doi.org/10.1007/978-3-662-46870-8
2. Dewar, H., Graham, J.: Studies of tropical tuna swimming performance in a large water tunnel. III. Kinematics. J. Exp. Biol. **192**(1), 45–59 (1994). https://doi.org/10.1242/jeb.192.1.45
3. J Donley K Dickson 2000 Swimming kinematics of juvenile Kawakawa Tuna (Euthynnus Affinis) and Chub Mackerel (Scomber Japonicus) J. Exp. Biol. 203 20 3103 3116 https://doi.org/10.1242/jeb.203.20.3103
4. S Grillner 1995 Neural networks that co-ordinate locomotion and body orientation in lamprey Trends Neurosci. 18 6 270 279 https://doi.org/10.1016/0166-2236(95)80008-P
5. O Kiehn 2016 Decoding the organization of spinal circuits that control locomotion Nat. Rev. Neurosci. 17 4 224 238 https://doi.org/10.1038/nrn.2016.9
6. S Grillner A Manira El 2020 Current principles of motor control, with special reference to vertebrate locomotion Physiol. Rev. 100 1 271 320 https://doi.org/10.1152/physrev.00015.2019
7. S Grillner 2006 Biological pattern generation: the cellular and computational logic of networks in motion Neuron 52 5 751 766 https://doi.org/10.1016/j.neuron.2006.11.008
8. J Yu M Tan J Chen J Zhang 2014 A survey on CPG-inspired control models and system implementation IEEE Trans. Neural Netw. Learn. Syst. 25 3 441 456 https://doi.org/10.1109/TNNLS.2013.2280596
9. AJ Ijspeert 2008 Central pattern generators for locomotion control in animals and robots: a review Neural Netw. 21 4 642 653 https://doi.org/10.1016/j.neunet.2008.03.014
10. Barrett, D.S.: Propulsive efficiency of a flexible hull underwater vehicle. Massachusetts Institute of Technology, Department of Ocean Engineering, USA (1996)
11. DS Barrett M Triantafyllou D Yue MA Grosenbaugh MJ Wolfgang 1999 Drag reduction in fish-like locomotion J. Fluid Mech. 392 183 212 https://doi.org/10.1017/S0022112099005455
12. J Anderson N Chhabra 2002 Maneuvering and stability performance of a robotic tuna Integr. Comp. Biol. 42 1 118 126 https://doi.org/10.1093/icb/42.1.118
13. Mazumdar, A., Valdivia y Alvarado, P., Youcef-Toumi, K.: Maneuverability of a robotic tuna with compliant body. In: 2008 IEEE International Conference on Robotics and Automation, pp. 683–688. IEEE, Pasadena, CA, USA (2008). https://doi.org/10.1109/ROBOT.2008.4543284

14. S Du Z Wu J Wang S Qi J Yu 2021 Design and control of a two-motor-actuated tuna-inspired robot system IEEE Trans. Syst., Man, Cybern.: Syst. 51 8 4670 4680 https://doi.org/10.1109/TSMC.2019.2944786

15. Z Wang L Wang T Wang B Zhang 2022 Research and experiments on electromagnetic-driven multi-joint bionic fish Robotica 40 3 720 746 https://doi.org/10.1017/S0263574721000771

16. Zhong, Q., Zhu, J., Fish, F., Kerr, S.J., Downs, A.M., Bart-Smith, H., Quinn, D.B.: Tunable stiffness enables fast and efficient swimming in fish-like robots. Sci. Robot. **6**(57), eabe4088 (2021). https://doi.org/10.1126/scirobotics.abe4088

17. Mitin, I., Korotaev, R., Ermolaev, A., Mironov, V., Lobov, S.A., Kazantsev, V.B.: Bioinspired propulsion system for a thunniform robotic fish. Biomimetics **7**(4), 215 (2022). https://doi.org/10.3390/biomimetics7040215

18. Tschur, N.A., Glazunova, E.V.: Numerical simulation of dynamics and fluid dynamics for biomimetic underwater robots. Robot. Tech. Cybern. **10**(2), 104–112 (2022). (In Russian). https://doi.org/10.31776/RTCJ.10203

Complex User Identification and Behavior Anomaly Detection in Corporate Smart Spaces

Dmitriy Levonevskiy$^{(\boxtimes)}$ ⓘ, Anna Motienko ⓘ, and Mikhail Vinogradov ⓘ

St. Petersburg Federal Research Center of the Russian Academy of Sciences, 14Th Line V.I. 39, 199178 St. Petersburg, Russia
`levonevskij.d@iias.spb.su`

Abstract. This research deals with the task of detecting security anomalies and incidents in corporate smart spaces equipped with physical access control systems that support simultaneous implementation of various user identification and/or authentication methods and are often integrated with corporate cyber-physical and robotic systems. This approach allows gathering auxiliary data related to user behavior and thus detecting a wider range of security-related situation, such as entry and exit mismatches, usage of another person's passes, and even faults and failures of the access control system itself, as well as achieving the higher reliability of user identification. For this purpose, an architectural solution for a system that uses RFID identification and face recognition was built. A corresponding data model was proposed. Using this data model and its implementation (for example, using relational databases and object-relationship mappings), the gathered data can be processed in order to detect potentially anomalous situations and security incidents. Then, the description and classification of such situations was given, and the delays of operation were measured during the experiment. The measurement shows that the delays allow experiencing the process of interaction as being one continuous flow. The tasks of future research were also specified.

Keywords: Cyber-physical systems · Physical access control system · Human-robot interaction · Smart space · Physical security · User identification · Authentication · User behavior · Security anomalies · Data modeling

1 Introduction

Physical access control systems (PACS) have become an integral part of corporate governance in various organizations. Such systems allow optimizing the workflow as well as increasing the security level and labor discipline. Access control is a security feature that limits the sets of users who can access the organization resources and facilities. This is the basic concept of protection, which minimizes the danger to the organization. Control over the organization staff is carried out by collecting and processing information about the time when employees arrive to and leave the organization, as well as about their movement inside the facilities. According to [1], PACS is an electronic system that controls the ability of people or vehicles to enter a protected area by means of authentication

© The Author(s), under exclusive license to Springer Nature Switzerland AG 2022
A. Ronzhin et al. (Eds.): ICR 2022, LNCS 13719, pp. 199–209, 2022.
https://doi.org/10.1007/978-3-031-23609-9_18

and authorization at access control points. Access control systems delimit the rights of access to the premises (zones, territories) of certain categories of staff and restrict the access of those who do not possess required rights.

An important element of the system functioning is the identification of security incidents and anomalies in the organization, checking compliance with the work schedule. For these tasks, network systems are more effective than stand-alone systems (an alternative to door locks), as they have more features: they can set up access to the premises on a schedule, control the work schedule and integrate with video cameras, security and fire systems, or with the corporate cyber-physical environment [2], for example, in providing targeted digital signage [3]. Such systems can interact with corporate cyber-physical and robotic systems for various purposes, for instance, personalized assistance and guidance. Network systems are connected to a computer and controlled remotely. In the presented article, we are talking about the developed system for controlling and managing access to the organization based on face recognition of employees and visitors and RFID identification that also focuses on post-processing of security data.

Usage of multiple identification methods and integrating PACS into corporate smart spaces extends the ability to detect a wider range of security anomalies. In the considered case, combining face recognition and RFID allows detecting the situations of using someone else's RFID cards, etc. The approach also takes advantage from the different capabilities of the identification methods: for example, face recognition can be performed without active human participation, in various zones and places and by means of stationary systems or mobile robots, which allows gathering auxiliary data that describe user location and behavior.

The following tasks must be solved for successful identification of security anomalies in organizations:

1. Architectural solutions for user identification and authentication, including the combined approach, should be provided.
2. Models for data storage and processing should be developed.
3. Security incidents and anomalies should be described and classified.
4. An approach for identifying potential security violations and anomalies should be proposed.

2 State of the Art

Physical access control systems (PACS) are widely used in various organizations. A lot of solutions are known, just a little of them are mentioned in [4], and their development belongs mostly to the field of engineering.

The problem of data post-processing in PACS has been much less studied. A large volume of logs contains useful information that is often not used or underused. This information can be examined in a similar way to how computer network traffic [5] or remote shell actions [6] are examined for anomalous user activity, that can be a sign of a security incident.

Anomaly detection consists in discovering data that do not fit the rest of the dataset. Anomaly detection can be used in various domains, for example in intrusion detection system, for finding instances of fraud, or for finding out if a safety critical system is running in an abnormal way before any major harm is done [7]. Thus, this will allow identifying potentially dangerous situations, which may include both facts of violations and cases of incorrect functioning of the PACS itself.

Work [8] considers the issue of cloud architectures for PACS. This allows collecting data more efficiently for subsequent analysis, but data analysis algorithms are not considered.

In [9], an approach to anomaly detection based on the analysis of PACS logs is considered. The approach allows clustering users according to their behavior and assessing how atypical user behavior is regarding her/his group. The authors analyze the count of location access (including successes and denials), count of weekday/weekend access, count of day/night access cases and employees' job roles and departments.

In [10], the analysis of logs for forensic purposes is considered. The clustering results are checked for anomalies based on a score that considers some factors such as the total members in a cluster, the frequency of the events in the log file, and the inter-arrival time of a specific activity. The authors also propose a method for visualizing events.

Work [11] pays attention to the anomalous behavior of users, but in this research the apparatus of graphs is applied. Emphasis is placed on the frequency of access to the organization facilities.

It should be noted that the authors of these articles and tools do not take into account specific methods and technologies of identification, authentication, authorization, combined application of such methods and technologies, assessment of their reliability and issues of working with heterogeneous data that are generated by the joint use of various techniques.

There are also tools for generating analytics and visualizing data in PACS, for example, Splunk [12], which also allows detecting simple anomalous situations (for instance, mismatches in the number of entries and exits using the same card). Again, this is a tool for PACS using a single identification method.

This research, in contrast, deals with the task of detecting security anomalies and incidents in PACS that support combined implementation of various user identification and/or authentication methods.

3 Materials and Methods

3.1 System Architecture

The principal difference in the proposed architecture is the support of multiple user identification methods. As an example we will consider the prototype under research in SPC RAS that implements two identification methods: RFID (Radio Frequency Identification) and face recognition.

RFID is the most reliable and simple way to identify and authenticate users by means of RFID cards with unique identifiers at the stationary turnstile. At the same time, this method of identification has a significant drawback, as the system cannot verify that a particular card is used by its legitimate owner.

Face recognition can be used as an auxiliary identification method to increase the identification accuracy and obtain extra data. For this purpose a software for detecting and identifying faces was developed that uses deep learning model FaceNet characterized by high recognition accuracy and possibility of real-time operation. Also, an approach to generation of synthetic data for learning on the basis of generation nets was implemented [13, 14]. A face recognition system can be installed both on a stationary device or a mobile robot.

The general PACS architecture is shown in Fig. 1 and consists of the following subsystems:

1. RFID identification subsystem that:

   a. stores the valid RFIDs in the local database;
   b. saves an event in the form < RFID reader ID, card ID, timestamp > to the local buffer if a RFID card was used;
   c. if the data processing server is available:

      (1) keeps the RFID database up-to-date using the data processing server API;
      (2) transmits events from the buffer to the data processing server;
      (3) receives commands to open the turnstile, to show access granted/denied signals, as well as to alter the local configuration;

   d. if the data processing server is not available:

      (1) keeps the event data in the local buffer;
      (2) opens the turnstile and shows access granted/denied signals according to the local configuration and RFID database contents;

2. Face recognition subsystem that:

   a. stores and keeps up-to-date the local employee database (IDs and vectors);
   b. receives the video stream from cameras;
   c. identifies employees and visitors in the video stream;
   d. transmits the recognized person ID, position and direction to the data processing server;

3. Data processing server that:

   a. obtains from the management server and transmits to the RFID subsystem the current configuration, including sets of active RFIDs;
   b. obtains from the management server and transmits to the face recognition subsystem employee IDs and vectors;
   c. receives RFID event data from the RFID subsystem;
   d. receives data of the recognized users from the face recognition subsystem;
   e. decides to grant or deny access and sends corresponding commands to the RFID subsystem;
   f. transmits all collected event data to the management server for accounting;

4. Management server that:

   a. stores employee and visitor information;
   b. stores PACS device data and configuration;
   c. enables the system administrator adding, editing and deleting the user and device data;
   d. provides the data processing server with the up-to-date user and device data;
   e. stores the event logs;
   f. visualizes the event logs for the authorized users;
   g. carries out data analytics;
   h. generates reports.

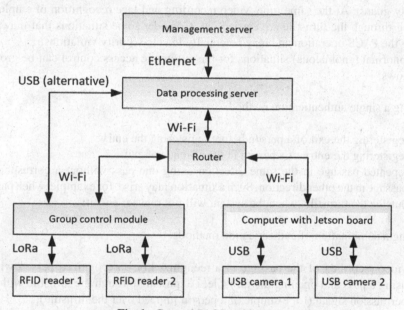

Fig. 1. General PACS architecture.

Figure 2 shows a sample scenario of RFID subsystem functioning in case when this subsystem uses the internal ID database along with the server API to keep the database up to date. The scenario is described in the BPMN notation.

3.2 Data Model

Heterogeneous data generated by PACS modules that implement different identification methods need to be consolidated into a global database for further processing. For this purpose, a data model is constructed. In its simplest form, such model can be represented as a specification of classes, their properties, and class relationships. On Fig. 3 this model is provided in the form of a UML class diagram. The main types of objects (classes) are: a registered event (LogEvent) and in particular a PACS event (PACSLogEvent), a device (Device) and in particular a PACS device (PACSDevice), a user (Employee) that belongs to an organization department (Subdivision). Any user's (employee's, visitor's) data is stored in the database, so it is possible to identify the user by different methods (EmployeeIdentification).

Using this data model and its implementation (for example, using relational databases and object-relationship mappings), we can process the gathered data in order to detect anomalous situations that are described in the next section.

3.3   Anomaly Classification

Passage through the turnstile is possible in two modes, when the passage control is carried out by the system, or the passage control is carried out by a person (watchman, security guard). At the same time, video recording and face recognition of employees passing through the turnstile are carried out. Consider some situations that may arise during the PACS operation and may potentially lead to security violations.

Abnormal (anomalous) situations for the automatic access control can be grouped as follows:

- using a single authentication method:

  - registering the exit of a person before registering the entry;
  - registering the entry of a person in the absence of exit;
  - repeated passage in the same direction using one pass without a corresponding passage in the other direction. Such a situation may arise, for example, when passing outside the turnstile, when the system will not register a visit;

- using a combination of authentication methods:

  - video recording of the passage of a recognized or unrecognized person without using a pass and opening the turnstile, i.e. passing through the turnstile without a permission signal (for example, if a person jumped over the turnstile);
  - using a pass without corresponding video registration of a user (this situation may have various causes, including using another employee's pass, inaccurate face recognition, etc.);
  - discrepancy between the personal data received from the employee's pass and the data obtained after face recognition from installed cameras, which may indicate that someone passed through the turnstile using the pass of another person.

Let us also consider the scenarios for the manual access control mode in case when a guard controls the passage manually in addition to the system. Thus, anomalous situations, in addition to those described above, include the following:

- passing through the turnstile with a pass, exiting in manual mode and vice versa;
- manual entry or exit without face recognition.

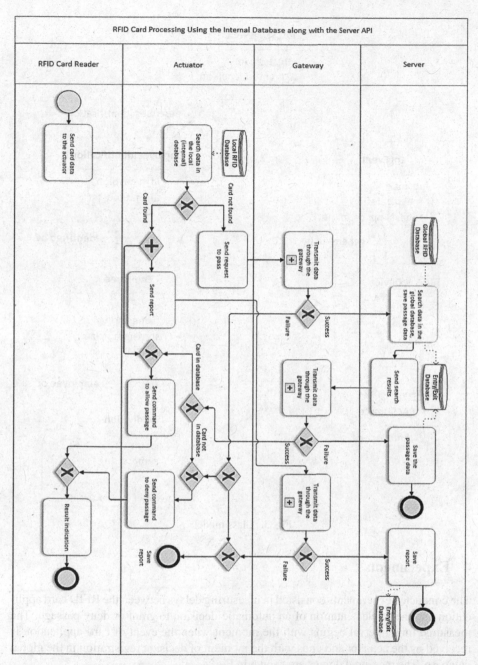

Fig. 2. BPMN diagram for the RFID identification-subsystem.

For each situation described above, its presence or absence within a certain period of time are checked with specific database queries

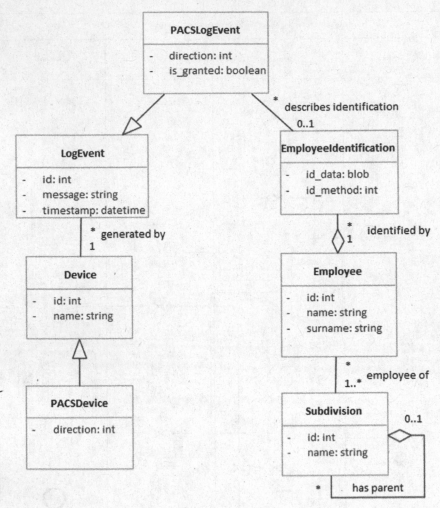

Fig. 3. Class model.

4   Experiments

The conducted experiments consisted in measuring delays between the RFID card application and the implementation of an automatic decision to grant or deny passage. The measured time interval begins with the moment when the event of card application is received by the actuator and ends with the moment of decision registration in the global database. The measured delays are shown in Fig. 4.

Also, processing times of queries to detect sample behavior anomalies were carried out. Average processing times for user authentication and a sample anomaly detection task are given in Table 1. As a sample anomaly we considered a situation of presence of an exit event for a user when the corresponding entry event is missing, so the corresponding

SQL query to the database was built and executed. Authentication takes more time due to the need of physical module operation and data transmission.

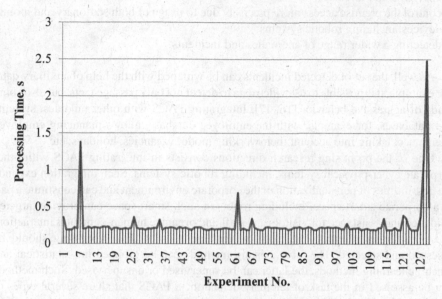

Fig. 4. Processing times for user authentication

Table 1. Average data processing times.

Operation	Average time, seconds	RMS
User authentication	0.26	0.24
Anomaly detection (entry/exit mismatch)	0.06	002

Thus, the considered processes are completed in a reasonable amount of time and meet the criterion of experiencing the interaction as being one continuous flow with delays less than 1 s [15].

5 Conclusion

The task of detecting security incidents and anomalies in PACS based on combined use of different types of user identification is insufficiently researched nowadays. We considered an implementation of PACS that performs employee identification using both RFID and face recognition, and introduced the architecture of such system, some scenarios of its functioning, and a data model.

Application of PACS that combine several methods of identification will allow:

- achieving the higher reliability of user identification;
- collecting additional and redundant data for the purpose of anomaly detection, analytics, and forensics;
- control the premise access more precisely due to usage of both stationary and mobile devices, including robotic systems;
- detecting a wider range of anomalies and incidents.

As well, the set of detected incidents can be widened with the help of auxiliary data. For example, it is possible to use video data to detect not only passage facts, but also some kinds of aggressive behavior [16, 17]. Integrating PACS with other modules, systems and databases, for example, with the employee database, allows managing employee attendance, taking into account their working mode, vacancies, holidays, etc.

One of the promising research directions consists in integrating PACS with other corporate cyber-physical systems, including robotic systems. Such integration expands the possibilities of personalization of the corporate environment and can constitute a part of a corporate smart space. Including robots in such smart space can provide targeted guidance and assistance for visitors and staff and organize human-computer interaction.

As a further research, the mathematical methods of data processing should be assessed and selected. The most existing methods can be grouped into statistical and machine learning methods, the latter can be supervised or unsupervised. Such methods can be assessed in the task of anomaly detection in PACS that share several types of user identification. Implementation of such methods along with multiple authentication points in the organization will make possible to get a solution like the one described in [11], but the difference of such work will consist in combined application of authentication methods. This will allow increasing the accuracy of situation identification and explore user behavior more widely. At the same time, approaches to preprocessing and preparation of datasets for these methods should be developed.

References

1. Security and privacy controls for information systems and organizations. NIST special publication 800-53 Revision 5. https://doi.org/10.6028/NIST.SP.800-53r5
2. Vatamaniuk, I., Levonevskiy, D., Saveliev, A., Denisov, A.: Scenarios of multimodal information navigation services for users in cyberphysical environment. In: Ronzhin, A., Potapova, R., Németh, G. (eds.) Speech and Computer. SPECOM 2016. Lecture Notes in Computer Science, vol. 9811, pp. 588–595. Springer, Cham (2016). https://doi.org/10.1007/978-3-319-43958-7_71
3. K Sandkuhl A Smirnov N Shilov 2019 Providing targeted digital signage: possible solutions SPIIRAS Proc. 18 4 831 857 https://doi.org/10.15622/sp.2019.18.4.831-857
4. Best access control systems of 2022, https://www.techradar.com/news/best-access-control-systems, last accessed 2022/08/21
5. Chen, A., Fu, Y. Zheng, X., Lu, G.: An efficient network behavior anomaly detection using a hybrid DBN-LSTM network. Comput. & Secur. **114** (2022). https://doi.org/10.1016/j.cose.2021.102600
6. XG Tian LZ Gao CL Sun MY Duan EY Zhang 2006 A method for anomaly detection of user behaviors based on machine learning J. China Univ. Posts Telecommun. 13 2 61 78 https://doi.org/10.1016/S1005-8885(07)60105-8

7. Jakub, B., Branišová, J.: Anomaly detection from log files using data mining techniques. In: Information Science and Applications, pp. 449–457 (2015). https://doi.org/10.1007/978-3-662-46578-3_53

8. F Antonolpoulos EGM Petrakis S Sotiriadis N Bessis 2018 A physical access control system on the cloud Procedia Comput. Sci. 130 318 325 https://doi.org/10.1016/j.procs.2018.04.045

9. Poh, J.P., Lee, J.Y.C., Tan, K.X., Tan, E.: Physical access log analysis: An unsupervised clustering approach for anomaly detection. In: Proceedings of the 3rd International Conference on Data Science and Information Technology, pp. 12–18 (2020). https://doi.org/10.1145/3414274.3414285

10. H Studiawan C Payne F Sohel 2017 Graph clustering and anomaly detection of access control log for forensic purposes Digit. Investig. 21 76 87 https://doi.org/10.1016/j.diin.2017.05.001

11. Geepalla, E., Asharif, S.: Analysis of physical access control system for understanding users behavior and anomaly detection using Neo4j. In: Proceedings of the 6th International Conference on Engineering & MIS 2020, Article 81, pp. 1–6. Association for Computing Machinery, New York, USA (2020). DOI: https://doi.org/10.1145/3410352.3410817

12. PACS log analysis using Splunk, https://habr.com/ru/company/tssolution/blog/345412/, last accessed 2022/11/21

13. Bengio, Y., Courville, A.C., Goodfellow, I.J., Mirza, M., Ozair, S.: Generative adversarial nets. In: Advances in Neural Information Processing Systems, vol. 2, pp. 2672–2680 (2014). https://doi.org/10.48550/arXiv.1406.2661

14. D Malov M Letenkov 2019 Method of synthetic data generation and architecture of face recognition system for interaction with robots in cyberphysical space Robot. Tech. Cybern. 7 2 100 108 https://doi.org/10.31776/RTCJ.7203

15. Henty, S.: UI response times. https://medium.com/@slhenty/ui-response-times-acec744f3157. Accessed 21 Aug 2022

16. Uzdiaev, M., Vatamaniuk, I.: Investigation of manifestations of aggressive behavior by users of sociocyberphysical systems on video. In: Proceedings of the Computational Methods in Systems and Software, LNNS, vol. 231, pp. 593–604. Springer, Cham (2021). https://doi.org/10.1007/978-3-030-90321-3_49

17. G Algazin D Algazina 2022 Modeling the dynamics of collective behavior in a reflexive game with an arbitrary number of leaders Inform. Autom. 21 2 339 375 https://doi.org/10.15622/ia.21.2.5

Model and Method of Resource-Saving Tasks Distribution for the Fog Robotics

Anna Klimenko[(✉)] [iD]

Institute of IT and Security Technologies, Kirovogradskaya Str. 25, 117534 Moscow, Russia
anna_klimenko@mail.ru

Abstract. In the current paper the question of the resource-saving tasks distribution is under consideration. Fog robotics, integrating fog computing and robotics, transfers the issues of the fog computing to the new subject area, as well as modern robots require more and more computing power. Tasks offloading to the fog spotlights the problem of assigning the task to those fog nodes, which failure rate decrease is acceptable. However, the models and methods of such task relocation problem are not presented in the literature, as well as the questions of devices reliability in the fog are not considered. In this paper a new model of task distribution is proposed, which allows to estimate the expediency of the task assigning to the node from the resource-saving point of view. Every node chooses: to process the data or to transmit them to the next node, which is situated farer from the data source. With the transfer of the data processing to the node of the low computational resources, its reliability can be improved by means of workload distribution through the extra-time, which appears due to the data transfer time reduction. Some selected simulation results are presented and discussed as well.

Keywords: Fog · Robotics · Tasks · Distribution · Reliability

1 Introduction

The increase of the computational complexity of the tasks, which robots within the robotic complex have to process, has spotlighted the questions of scalability, battery constraints and storage capabilities of the robotic equipment. This question has been solved partially by the cloud robotics concept, which presupposes the possibility to offload the edge devices, sending tasks to the cloud [1–3].

However, the usage of the "cloud" concept has the following drawbacks and challenges [4]:

- Large distance between the cloud and edge devices causes propagation and transmission delays.
- Large computational load on a single cloud server causes processing and queuing delays.
- Increased number of smart devices has hindered meeting the bandwidth requirements.

A. Ronzhin et al. (Eds.): ICR 2022, LNCS 13719, pp. 210–222, 2022.
https://doi.org/10.1007/978-3-031-23609-9_19

- Enormous number of smart devices will bring scalability, speed, and computational issues.
- Wireless medium between cloud and smart devices brings resource management issues.
- Security is a very critical thread, as the cloud is exposed to the whole world over the public internet.
- Computing offloading every-time at cloud causes a loss in energy and battery lifetime, and so on.

Fog (and edge-) computing, complementing the cloud one, provides the acceptable solutions for the large and geographically distributed IIoT projects, transferring the data processing to the fog – or to the edge of the network. Within the Internet of Robotic Things concept, where the interaction between the robots, sensors, gateways and other user devices takes place, there is a possibility to offload the computational tasks to the other devices on the edge, to transfer tasks to the fog nodes or to upload them to the cloud. There are a lot of published papers which consider the problems of scheduling, resource allocation, network load balancing within the distributed robotic systems [5–7]. The objective functions considered are various as well, including system latency minimizing, energy consumption minimizing, etc. However, the question of the edge and fog devices computational resource saving is not considered in the literature, except [8–10], while the time of expedient device exploitation does matter.

In the current paper we connect the term of "expedient time of device exploitation" with the reliability function of the computational node. Reliability function and failure rate describe the computational resource of the device and the expediency of its usage. Within the large distributed robotic system every device performing data processing loses its computational resource depending on its workload [10]. So, having a goal to extend the acceptable reliability level time period, the tasks offloading – in the edge or to the fog – must be performed on the basis of some methodology.

The main contributions of this paper are:

- the model of quantitative estimation of the task offloading effect;
- the resource-saving task distribution method which improves the device failure rate and reliability function.

2 Fog Robotics: State of the Art

Fog Robotics was introduced and coined in the studies [11–13].

The basic elements of the fog robotics concept are: Fog Robot Server, Cloud and sub Fog Robot Server. According to the description of the concept, Fog Robot Server perform the general functions of the Cloud-fog-broker, which are to make a decision whether the computational tasks must be transferred to the cloud or to be performed by the sub fog robot servers (which are similar to the fog nodes).

There are several studies which propose some new methods and application areas for the fog robotics concept, which are:

- to enhance human-robot interaction [12, 14, 15];

- object recognition/grasp planning in surface decluttering [16];
- industrial robotic systems implementation [17];
- coordination of robot movements [5].

Fog robotics benefits are discussed comprehensively in the study [18], where some experimental results of cloud- and fog-robotics comparison are presented and estimated. The main contribution of this study is the estimates of the system latency under conditions of the cloud data processing and under the fog one. It is shown that the ratio between time of information exchange between the edge device and the AWS cloud is more than 10 times.

Yet, the role of the fog robotics is not to decrease system latency only. Avoiding the network congestion within the constrained time period makes it possible to distribute computational workload through the time period and so to increase the reliability function values.

So, it seems to be expedient to put the data processing to the fog robot servers (or to the fog nodes nearby). While the most part of the papers are devoted to the latency problem, the area of the computational resource saving has not been considered, and the question "where to put the data processing tasks to enhance the device exploitation period" is still demands some additional efforts.

The basic architectures of the fog robotics system are considered as is shown in the Fig. 1.

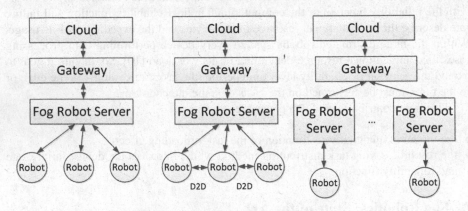

Fig. 1. Fog Robotics basic architectures

One can see that the architecture with the Device-to-Device (D2D) interaction can maintain the edge computations, while the architecture with multiple fog robot servers presuppose the active information exchange between fog robot servers. Anyway, the possibility to process the data via edge computing poses a question of the optimal task distribution to minimize the failure rate of the computational node and to enhance one's exploitation period.

3   Problem of Resource-Saving Computations

The general problem, which is solved by the FRS, is to distribute the computational workload through the fog. The same problem is solved by the cloud-fog broker within the fog computing concept in a way shown in the Fig. 2.

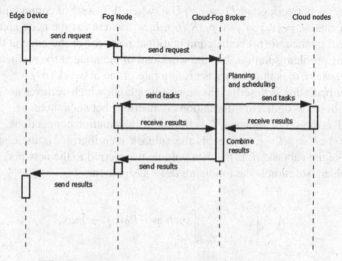

Fig. 2. The interaction between edge, fog and cloud

In case of D2D interaction and the possibility to implement the edge computing concept within the group of robots, the similar question arises which of the neighbor robots can share their resources to process the data and to decrease the network load. In the current paper the question of the leader election in the robotic group is out of the scope, so, we'll consider the resource-saving problem as: which device must be used for the data processing to get the acceptable failure rate and reliability function degrading?

Consider the following important equations. Reliability function value depends on the failure rate, while failure rate is connected to the device temperature and workload:

$$\lambda = \lambda_0 \cdot 2^{\frac{\Delta T}{10}} \tag{1}$$

where λ is a resulting failure rate, λ_0 is the failure rate under conditions of unloaded device, ΔT is the temperature difference between the temperature of unloaded device and the temperature of loaded one.

In the study [9] the rate is determined, which connects the node temperature and the workload.

$$\lambda = \lambda_0 \cdot 2^{\frac{kD}{10}} \tag{2}$$

Consequently, the reliability function is determined as follows:

$$P(t) = e^{-\lambda t} = e^{-\lambda t 2^{\frac{kD}{10}}} \tag{3}$$

where D is the node workload.

The problem of the resource-saving task distribution can be formulated as follows.

Consider the FRB, which receives the user task and data to solve. The problem is to schedule the task within the formed fog nodes community so, as $P_0(\tau) \to max$, where $P_0(\tau)$ is the overall reliability function value of the fog nodes community, including CFB, τ is the moment of the user operation completion.

Consider the network graph $G = <V, U>$, where V is a set of computational nodes, R is a set of ribs. $V = \{v_i\} = \{<i, p_i, R_i(t_0), L_i>\}$, where i is the node identifier, p_i is the node performance, $R_i(t_0)$ is the computational resource of the node at the moment of scheduling problem solution, L_i is the workload of the node at the moment of t_0.

$U=\{u_j\}$, where u_j is the data transmission rate of the network rib j.

The user operation is described as an acyclic graph, which vertexes are assigned to tasks, and ribs are assigned to information connections between them.

Where T is the set of subtasks, C is the set of information connections.

$T=\{t_i\}=\{<i, w_i, d_i>\}$, where i is the subtask identifier, w_i is the computational complexity of the subtask, d_i is the data volume transferred to the network.

The problem solution is the following tasks assignment:

$$A = \begin{vmatrix} t_{ij} & \dots \\ & \dots \\ \dots & t_{nm} \end{vmatrix} \text{ such as}: P_0(\tau) \to max, \tag{4}$$

where $P_0(\tau) = \prod P_0(\tau), P_j(\tau) = e^{-\lambda t 2^{\frac{kD}{10}}}$, $P_0(\tau)$ is the reliability function value; D is the node workload; k is the coefficient of node temperature increase depending on the current workload, t_{ij} is the moment of assignment of task i to the node j.

The constraint for this problem is as follows: $\tau \leq t_{const}$, that is the user operation completion time must be less than the declared time for this operation.

It must be mentioned that with the emergency of the new computational task the new portion of the workload is unavoidable for one of the fog nodes. But the FRS can make a choice, what to do: to perform the task or to transmit the data to the next node, increasing the distance between the data source and the data processor.

Then, assume the case when the tasks to solve are generated one by one, via requests, and can be distributed through the nodes as they arrive. So, the problem formulated can be solved in a "greedy" way with the following step: to assign the task to that node, for which it would be better to process the data instead of data transfer to the other node.

4   The Model of Tasks Distribution Effect

Consider the node workload as follows:

$$D = \frac{w_i}{p_j \cdot t_{const} \cdot x} \tag{5}$$

where w_i is the computational complexity of the task, x is time fraction for the data transfer of the node.

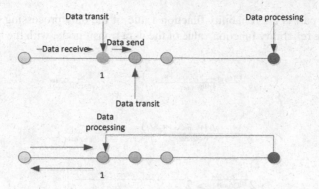

Fig. 3. Data processing transfer

. Consider the situation shown in Fig. 2, where the data transmission to the cloud is considered (Fig. 3).

Then, the reliability function is estimated as follows:

$$P(t) = e^{-\lambda t} = e^{-\lambda_0 t 2^{\frac{kD}{10}}} = e^{-\lambda_0 t 2^{\frac{kw}{10pt_{const}x}}} \qquad (6)$$

where x is the fraction of time needed for the full user operation completion, that is used for data transfer. The computational complexity depends on the value of data to be transferred.

$$P(t) = e^{-\lambda_0 t 2^{\frac{k\xi(d)}{10pt_{const}x}}} \qquad (7)$$

The average residual life is described as follows:

$$R = \frac{1}{\lambda} = \frac{1}{\lambda_0 2^{\frac{k\xi(d)}{10pt_{const}x}}} \qquad (8)$$

Next, consider the situation when the node №1 processes the data and sends the result to the user. This is described by the following equation:

$$P(t) = e^{-\lambda_0 t 2^{\frac{k\left(w_{receive}+w_{process}+w_{send}\right)}{10pt_{const}}}} \qquad (9)$$

Considering the fact that within the data transfer the node receives and sends the same data volume, we bring equations to the following form:

$$P(t) = e^{-\lambda_0 t 2^{\frac{k2w_{receive}}{10pt_{const}x}}} \qquad (10)$$

The next stage of the current research is to get the analytical interrelation between the x, $w_{receive}$, $w_{process}$, w_{send} parameters. The following inequality must be solved:

$$e^{-\lambda_0 t 2^{\frac{k\left(w_{receive}+w_{process}+w_{send}\right)}{10pt_{const}}}} > e^{-\lambda_0 t 2^{\frac{k2w_{receive}}{10pt_{const}x}}} \qquad (11)$$

where the left part is the reliability function value of the data processing node and the right part is the reliability function value of the data transit node, with the fixed value of t.

$$e^{-\lambda_0 t2 \frac{k\left(w_{receive}+w_{process}+w_{send}\right)}{10pt_{const}}} > e^{-\lambda_0 t2 \frac{k2w_{receive}}{10pt_{const}x}} \tag{12}$$

$$-2^{\frac{k\left(w_{receive}+w_{process}+w_{send}\right)}{10pt_{const}}} > -2^{\frac{k2w_{receive}}{10pt_{const}x}} \tag{13}$$

$$2^{\frac{k2w_{receive}}{10pt_{const}x}} > 2^{\frac{k\left(w_{receive}+w_{process}+w_{send}\right)}{10pt_{const}}}. \tag{14}$$

Exponentiate the Eq. (14) with $10^{\frac{pt_{const}}{k}}$:

$$2^{\frac{2w_{receive}}{x}} > 2^{w_{receive}+w_{process}+w_{send}}. \tag{15}$$

Comparing the indexes, the following interrelation is formed:

$$w_{receive} + w_{process} + w_{send} < 2\frac{2w_{receive}}{x}. \tag{16}$$

So, the data processing shift to the particular node is expedient when the computational complexity of the data receiving, sending and processing is less than the division of two computational complexities of the data receiving by time fraction of data transfer through the node.

5 The Method of Resource-Saving Task Distribution

Consider the situation when the fog-cloud broker receives some data, and the decision must be made about the further data transfer or about the data processing on the node. Also consider the information provisioning system on the basis of the distributed ledger. This system maintains the information about the nearby nodes stored locally on the node. All the fog devices have the sufficient memory, and the communication environment is stable and sufficient too.

The state of the fog device is described by the following tuple:

$$S_i = \; < p_i, W_i, edge\_dist, \{< br\_dist, br\_id >\}, \{vmin_j, br\_id\}, \tau >, \tag{17}$$

where p_i is the node performance, W_i is the overall computational complexity of the tasks which are being performed by the node, $edge\_dist$ is the distance between the node and the edge of the network in hops, $\{<br\_dist, br\_id>\}$ is the distances between the current node and the FRSs of one domain, $\{v\,min_j, br\_id\}$ is the minimum network bandwidth between the node and FRSs, τ is the time of device exploitation, t_{const} is the time of planned task completion.

The basic method of resource-saving task distribution includes the following stages.

1. The RFS is tested by the following estimation: $w_{recive} + w_{process} + w_{send} + w_f < \frac{2w_{receive}+w_f}{x}$. w_f is the overall computation complexity of the tasks being solved by the FRS. If the unequality is fair the following condition must be checked: $t_{receive} + t_{process} + t_{send} \leq t_{const}$.

If both inequalities are fair, then the FRS is assigned to the task. Otherwise, move to the stage 2.

2. FRS checks the ledger of node states S, selecting the neighbor nodes with the distance of 1 hop.
3. For each S_i check the following:

$$Y = \frac{t_{receive} + t_{process} + t_{send} + t_{broker\_transit\_data} + t_{broker\_transit\_result}}{t_{const}}$$

Y is the time constraint variable and estimates the time needed for the task performing paying attention to the data transmission time.

a. Check the inequality for the selected nodes:

$$w_{receive} + w_{process} + w_{send} + W_i < \frac{2w_{receive} + W_i}{x}$$

b. If the inequality is fair, put S_i to the candidates list.
c. Select the node with the maximum Y (the maximum of useful workload).

4. If there are no acceptable solutions in the list, the FRB begins to check the nodes within the distance of 2 hops from it paying attention to the data transit time increase. Repeat a-c stages.
5. If there are no candidates, return to the 1 hop distance nodes and select the node with the maximum of the residual resource (reliability function).

Such a decision can be a controversial issue, because the additional workload can worsen the reliability function of the node selected. Yet, selecting the node within the distance in 1 hop, we eliminate the intermediate nodes, and so decrease their workload, which is generated by the data transmission.

6 Simulation Results

Consider the following simplified network structure, as is shown in Fig. 4. There are the following nodes in the picture: edge device (robot), fog robot server, two for nodes, which can be used for the workload distribution, and a cloud device. The performances of the nodes are shown in the Fig. 5 as well. Also we consider the network channels as homogeneous ones. In the following simulation the Eq. (6) will be calculated, and the fairness of the statement about the expediency of the data processing on the particular node will be checked by means of reliability function estimation. The major variables and the experimental plan are presented in the Table 1.

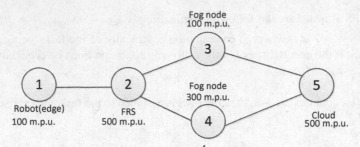

Fig. 4. Example network structure (m.p.u = modeling performance unit)

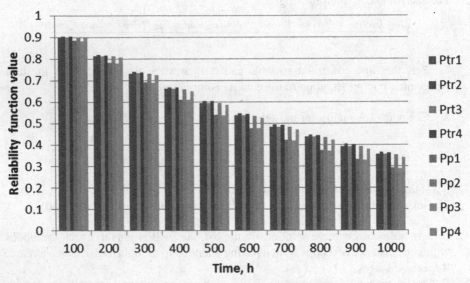

Fig. 5. Simulation №1. Low data transfer

Table 1. The plan of the experiment

N	$W_{receive}$	W_{send}	$W_{process}$	T_{decl}	Fairness of Eq. (15)
1	50	50	300	50	–
2	350	100	100	50	+
3	500	100	300	50	+
4	1000	100	300	50	+

In the Table 2 one can see that with the relatively small amount of input data and relatively complex data processing procedure, the eq. $w_s + w_p + w_r < 2w_r/x$ is not fair for all nodes.

Table 2. Values of the Eq. (15)

$w_s+w_p+w_r$	$2w_r/x$
400	105.26
400	105.04
400	104.38
400	104.38

The simulation of the reliability function of the nodes proves the inexpediency to put the data processing to the nodes. It is beneficial for every edge- and fog- node to transmit data to the cloud than to process it. It can be seen that the plots of reliability function of the data transfer trends (Ptr1, Ptr2, Ptr3, Ptr4) are better than values of the data processing trends.

The experiment 2 generates the following Table 3 of values for the nodes:

Table 3. Values of the Eq. (15).

$w_s+w_p+w_r$	$2w_r/x$
550	875.00
550	859.95
550	817.75
550	817.75

The values in the table are such as it is more beneficial for the nodes to process the data than to transmit it. The reliability function values are shown in the Fig. 6.

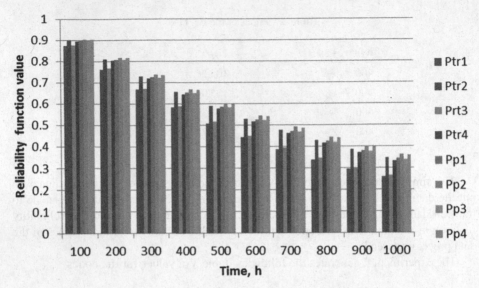

Fig. 6. Experiment №2. Increase of the data transfer

Then, with the following increase of the data volume to be transferred through the network, the following graphs are generated (experiments 3 and 4, Fig. 7, 8).

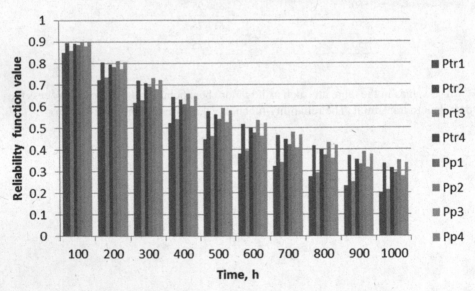

Fig. 7. Experiment №3. Further increase of the data transfer

It can be seen that with the increase of the input data for transferring the difference between the reliability function values can be esteemed as up to 25%.

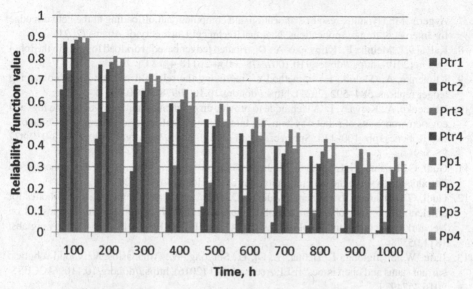

Fig. 8. Experiment №4. The maximum of the data transfer values

7   Conclusion

Fog robotics is one of the popular and fast growing trends. However, very little attention has been paid to such up-to-date question as device exploitation time and the resource saving computing, connected to the devices reliability. In this paper a model of the effect of the workload distribution estimation is presented, as well as the new method to distribute the computational task through the fog nodes. The method proposed implements the resource-saving strategy and based on the "greedy" rule of workload distribution. Simulation results prove the fairness of the model and method proposed.

References

1. Chueshev, A., Melekhova, O., Meshcheryakov, R.: Cloud robotic platform on basis of fog computing approach. In: International Conference on Interactive Collaborative Robotics, pp. 34–43. Springer (2018)
2. Hu, G., Tay, W.P., Wen, Y.: Cloud robotics: architecture, challenges and applications. IEEE Network **26**(3), 21–28 (2012). https://doi.org/10.1109/MNET.2012.6201212
3. Chaari, R., Cheikhrouhou, O., Koubaa, A., Youssef, H., Nguyen, T.: Dynamic computation offloading for ground and flying robots: Taxonomy, state of art, and future directions. Comput. Sci. Rev. **45**, 100488 (2022). https://doi.org/10.1016/j.cosrev.2022.100488
4. Rabeea, B.: Fog computing enabling industrial internet of things: state-of-the-art and research challenges. Sensors 19(21), 4807 (2019). https://doi.org/10.3390/s19214807
5. Xiang, X., Ziqi, C., Zhenhua, X., Jianhua, W.: A scalable resource management architecture for industrial fog robots, pp. 67–77 (2021). https://doi.org/10.1007/978-3-030-89095-7
6. Bhalekar, B., Saikrishna, P.: Control algorithms for a mobile robot application in a fog computing environment. In: Proceedings of the 2019 3rd International Conference on Automation, Control and Robots, pp. 30–36. https://doi.org/10.1145/3365265.3365283

7. Avgeris, M.: Dynamic resource allocation and computational offloading at the network edge for Internet of things applications. National Technical University of Athens (2021)
8. Kalyaev, I., Melnik, E., Klimenko, A.: Distributed ledger based workload logging in the robot swarm (2019). https://doi.org/10.1007/978-3-030-26118-4_12
9. Klimenko, A., Melnik, E.: A method of improving the reliability of the nodes containing ledger replicas, 584–592 (2021). https://doi.org/10.1007/978-3-030-90318-3_47
10. Klimenko, A., Kalyaev, I.: A technique to provide an efficient system recovery in the fog- and edge-environments of robotic systems In: International Conference on Interactive Collaborative Robotics, pp. 100–112. Springer, Cham (2021). https://doi.org/10.1007/978-3-030-877 25-5_9
11. Gudi, G., Krishna, S. L., Suman, O., Jesse, C., Johnston, B., Williams, M.: Fog robotics: An introduction to solve the general limitations of the cloud robotics (2017)
12. Gudi, G., Krishna, S.L., Suman, O., Jesse, C., Johnston, B., Williams, M.: Fog robotics for efficient, fluent and robust human-robot interaction. In: 17th International Symposium on Network Computing and Applications (NCA), pp. 1–5. IEEE (2018). https://arxiv.org/abs/1811.05578
13. Jiafu, W., Shenglong, T., Hehua, Y., Di, L., Shiyong, W., Athanasios, V.: Cloud robotics: current status and open issues. IEEE Access 4, 1–1 (2016). https://doi.org/10.1109/ACCESS.2016.2574979
14. Kolpashchikov, D., Gerget, O., Meshcheryakov, R.: Robotics in healthcare. In: Handbook of Artificial Intelligence in Healthcare, vol. 212, pp. 281–306 (2021)
15. Galin, R., Meshcheryakov, R.: Human-robot interaction efficiency and human-robot collaboration. In: Robotics: Industry 4.0 Issues & New Intelligent Control Paradigms, pp. 55–63. Springer, Cham (2020)
16. Tanwani, A., Mor, N., Kubiatowicz, J., Gonzalez, J., Goldberg, K.: A fog robotics approach to deep robot learning: application to object recognition and grasp planning in surface decluttering (2019). https://arxiv.org/abs/1903.09589
17. Salman, S., Struhár, V., Papadopoulos, A., Behnam, M., Nolte, T.: Fogification of industrial robotic systems: research challenges. In: Proceedings of the Workshop on Fog Computing and the IoT, pp. 41–45 (2019). https://doi.org/10.1145/3313150.3313225
18. Gudi, G., Krishna, S. L., Johnston, B., Williams, M.: Fog robotics: a summary, challenges and future scope. Preprint at https://arxiv.org/abs/1908.04935 (2019)

Intelligent-Geometric Control Architecture for Extinguishing Fires by a Group of UAVs

Mikhail Khachumov[1,2,3]($\boxtimes$) (iD) and Vyacheslav Khachumov[1,2,3] (iD)

[1] PSI RAS, Petra Pervogo Str. 4a, 152024 Veskovo, Russia
khmike@inbox.ru
[2] RUDN University, Miklukho-Maklaya Str. 6, 117198 Moscow, Russia
[3] FRC CSC RAS, Vavilova Str. 44/2, 119333 Moscow, Russia

Abstract. The article is devoted to solving cutting-edge scientific problem of creating models and methods for increasing the autonomy of unmanned aerial vehicles (UAVs) during fire-fighting operations in an uncertain environment. We show the necessity of using vehicles, both capable to monitor the fire hazard situation and to participate directly in fire extinguishing. A novel three-level hierarchical control architecture for UAVs is proposed, aimed at joint application of precise geometric and adaptive intelligent control methods providing operational reliability and ability to effectively plan motion and behavior in complex external conditions. A model problem of extinguishing a fire by a group of intelligent UAVs capable of exchanging information, choosing leaders, and autonomous planning of actions under wind disturbances in the presence of no-fly zones is considered and solved. To conduct experiments and test an intelligent-geometric approach, we use mathematical models of vehicle's dynamics and onboard rotary camera stabilization in the form of transfer functions integrated into a single control system. In accordance with the proposed architecture, the solution to the problem of controlling a UAV group involved in putting out a large-scale fire under uncertainty was simulated in the MATLAB Simulink system.

Keywords: Fire monitoring · Firefighting · UAVs · Geometric control · Intelligent control · Hierarchical architecture · Tasks distribution · Motion planning · Uncertain environment

1 Introduction

1.1 Motivation

The considerable scale of natural fires in the regions of the Russian Federation leads to a strong need for the development of theory, algorithms, and tools for fire-hazard monitoring and prompt responding to emergencies [1]. One of the cutting-edge challenges is to create optimized models and methods for delivering extinguishing agents to multiple fire spots in hard-to-reach and remote areas. The urgency of the problem is based on the high environmental and economic losses associated with fires and the opportunities to minimize the scale of the damage through real time area monitoring and taking rapid

© The Author(s), under exclusive license to Springer Nature Switzerland AG 2022
A. Ronzhin et al. (Eds.): ICR 2022, LNCS 13719, pp. 223–235, 2022.
https://doi.org/10.1007/978-3-031-23609-9_20

response measures. For example, only in the Yaroslavl region, for the first four months of 2020 about 1,000 fires were recorded which caused serious damage, and in April 2021 an extremely difficult situation was formed, which required up to 80 calls of firefighters per day.

Recently, unmanned aerial vehicles (UAVs) have been attracted to extinguish fires in an uncertain environment, which requires development of special intelligent software [2]. We can list the following major challenges to be solved: 1) automatic detection of fire-hazard situations and tracking fire dynamics along with measuring the size of the fire area; 2) optimal path planning for monitoring the required territories given by reference points considering air disturbances, obstacles, and no-fly zones; 3) forming coalitions to solve collaborative tasks in case of multiple fire spots. Despite the existence of a considerable number of papers concerning state-of-the-art approaches in the research field, the problem of using UAV teams under conditions of uncertainty to solve specific challenges, such as fire monitoring and extinguishing, remains unresolved.

1.2 Related Works

Paper [3] provides a comprehensive overview of research conducted between 2008 and 2021 on UAV-based forest fire extinguishing operations. The survey showed key areas of concern and gaps in this field of study. Among them the complexity of coordination in UAV teams, the lack of evaluation of fire extinguishing systems, the complexity of handling multiple spot fires, and poor management of extinguishing resources.

The use of UAVs leads to the development of special software for planning optimal paths to monitor given territories, timely detection of fires, and transmission of data to decision makers [4]. The problem of firefighting is complicated by the presence of disturbances, obstacles, and uncertainties. Therefore, the issue of developing intelligent path planning and following algorithms that can cope with dynamic environmental changes becomes extremely important [5]. Paper [6] discusses a new improved D*Lite algorithm to plan a safe and effective path in real time in the complex forest environment. However, the authors do not consider UAV dynamic model and wind loads that affect its trajectory, as well as major motion control issues. We note research considering important special cases of path planning problem for polygon areas [7] and intelligent algorithms for traveling salesman problem [8].

Optimal area coverage with multiple UAVs is considered as one of the most important issues in firefighting. To address this problem the authors of papers [9, 10] adopted particle swarm optimization (PSO) algorithm that is used to determine the solution in many optimization problems. However, this approach has some disadvantages, for example drones converge on each other, which limits the area covered and additionally, the swarm suffers from momentum, so it is difficult for the swarm to immediately change direction. Despite the efficiency of the PSO algorithm in many applications of multi-robot systems, it is ineffective when fire spreads to multiple places.

Significant research is presented in paper [11], which discusses a novel task planning approach for a UAV team in a forest fire fighting mission considering obstacles and simultaneous arrival. The proposed task allocation algorithm assumes that all UAVs carry different fire-fighting resources and can communicate with each other. However, the study is not complete and full-scale due to the following assumptions: 1) the aerodynamic and attitude of UAVs are not considered; 2) the obstacles and targets are static 3) simulation is made in unperturbed environment.

Essential formation control problem of multiple UAVs for forest fire monitoring and detection is discussed in [12]. According to search stage, UAVs team keeps certain configuration until a fire is detected. In this case, the leader UAV sends new formation reconfiguration commands and the whole team will reconfigure its formation shape according to new data, following the fire elliptic trajectory.

A multi-robot system approach requires a complex coordination process and increasingly complex software and hardware capabilities [13]. One of the main problems in performing a firefighting task in a forest is direct communication between team members in order discuss and make decisions among themselves. To make joint decisions team members exchange information with a central node or with ground stations. In systems with centrally controlled robots the absence of one or more robots will significantly affect available decisions and its reliability.

Despite the existence of a significant number of papers in the field of firefighting, the scientific literature lacks specific task and path planning algorithms for UAV teams. Much more attention should be paid to the problem of controlling UAVs in uncertain and perturbed environment. We note the necessity of conducting full-scale experiments and close to real modelling using perturbations, affecting the mission.

1.3 Main Contributions

In this paper, a novel concept of an intelligent-geometric control proposed in paper [14] is adopted to solve firefighting tasks. We consider hierarchical architecture of a complex control system combining the advantages of geometric and intelligent control theories. The scientific novelty of the study is determined by the new methods developed in the framework of intelligent-geometric control for task planning, controlling, and modelling UAVs motion in uncertain environment under disturbances. It is expected that the use of these methods can significantly increase the autonomy, reliability, and efficiency of UAVs participating in firefighting mission.

We propose an approach to solve the problem of extinguishing a fire by a team of UAVs capable of exchanging information, choosing a leader, and autonomously planning actions. To reach the firefighting spots we propose path planning models based on the novel concept of pursuing a pseudo target considering collision avoidance. Particular attention is paid to conducting experiments in conditions close to real, considering mathematical models of a UAV, camera, and wind loads.

2 Intelligent-Geometric Architecture for Extinguishing Fires

In the present paper, the concept of "geometric control" is associated with the solution of several trajectory optimization problems in relation to UAVs (as a physical or virtual objects). For example, the proposed approach to solving the trajectory tracking problem is associated with the introduction and pursuing of an ideal pseudo object, which involves using the theory of differential games. It is required a strict calculation of movement to a meeting point (with another object), which belongs to geometric invariants such as the Apollonian circle or sphere [15]. To construct an optimal control in ideal conditions (without disturbances) we use Pontryagin's maximum principle [14].

In the presence of external disturbances and obstacles, the problem of controlling UAVs is even more complicated and, in our opinion, can be successfully solved by integrating geometric and intelligent control methods. In particular, we apply goal-seeking behavioral strategies based on production rules that imitate the actions of a human operator, frame-based microprograms allowing to adapt to various operating conditions, as well as fuzzy semantic networks to obtain a formal map of the area.

For putting out large-scale fires with a group of UAVs we propose to use three levels of abstraction, each of which solves its own control problems (see Fig. 1).

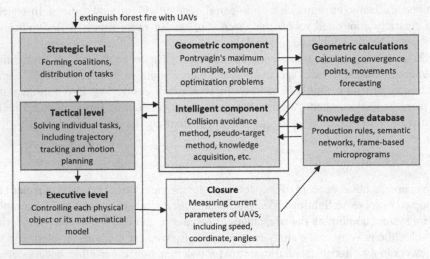

Fig. 1. Intelligent-geometric control system for extinguishing large-scale fires.

At the strategic level, the problems of forming coalitions, distribution of tasks and roles are being solved. At the tactical level, specific tasks given for separate vehicles are performed, in particular, tracking a given trajectory under wind disturbances, dynamic motion planning in the presence of obstacles under uncertainty. Specific control commands are generated and transmitted to the executive level for processing by UAVs. For expanding knowledge base, we use the proposed intelligent technology of the automatic knowledge extraction in the process of vehicles functioning.

3   Task Allocation Problem

3.1   Formulation of the Problem

At a strategic level, we consider the problem of task allocation for a group of drones in the process of extinguishing a large-scale forest fire.

Let be given:

- n sources (UAVs) with a_i units of a homogenous resource $\sum\limits_{i=1}^{n} a_i = Z_1$,
- m destinations (fire spots) with b_j units of demand $\sum\limits_{j=1}^{m} b_j = Z_2$,
- cost $c_{ij} > 0$ for transporting a unit of commodity from point i to point j.

The objective is to minimize the total cost of transportation, so it is required to find $x_{ij} \geq 0$ (the amount of commodity transported from point i to point j) such that

$$\sum_{i=1}^{n} \sum_{j=1}^{m} c_{ij} x_{ij} \to min. \tag{1}$$

If $Z_1 = Z_2$ we get the Monge-Kantorovich problem, which belongs to P-complexity class and is solved by linear programming or special methods. There are several well-known algorithms to solve problem (1) that minimize the total cost of transportation. Often the solution is split into stages, where at first the basic plan is determined by the minimum cost method, and on the second step the potential method is applied. Let us note significant research [16], where an algorithm with running time $O(nm^2(\log n + m \log m))$ is proposed. Paper [17] discusses an algorithm, each step of which requires considering the coefficients of only two rows (or columns) of a cost matrix. The method does not require a large amount of RAM and is suitable for large-scale transportation problems of any type.

For rapidly changing situations, for example, when extinguishing large-scale fires under conditions of time pressure, heuristic methods are of urgent interest. The task is to extinguish several fire spots by a team of UAVs provided that each UAV has some water supply and for each fire spot there is a demand for water (or other extinguishing agent). The amount of water b_j necessary to extinguish each fire sport j significantly exceeds the water reserves a_i, of each UAV i, i.e. $a_i < b_j$. Each element c_{ij} of the cost matrix corresponds to the Euclidean distance between UAV i and fire spot j. The UAV team needs to put out all fires, while minimizing the total cost of movements.

The intelligence of UAVs is determined by the ability to independently form coalitions, select a leader, and solve trajectory problems under disturbances.

3.2 Proposed Solution

In this paper, the problem of extinguishing fires is solved using a multi-agent approach. UAVs as agents receive information in the form of data messages from each other and from the environment. This approach is widely used in modeling a changing environment, when participants don't have complete information about the world.

Suppose we have a group of n UAVs denoted as $P = \{p_1, \ldots, p_n\}$. At the time of planning some of the agents may no longer have a supply of water that was spent on extinguishing previous fires. Information on the coordinates, volume of fires and the required amount of water is transmitted to agents. A set of active fires we denote as F_{act}. The following algorithm is proposed to solve task allocation problem:

1. All agents which have reserves of water P_{act} receive a list of active fires, information about their location and the amount of water necessary to extinguish them.
2. Each agent p_i informs all other agents from P_{act} about the total amount of water N_i it has, and the number of steps needed to reach each fire spot from F_{act}.
3. An agent with the largest volume of water acts as a leader p_{N^0} and finds a fire spot from F_{act}, that can be reached in a minimum number of steps N. Then it generates a list $(P_{act,N})$ of all agents that can reach the selected fire spot in the same number of steps. UAVs in $(P_{act,N})$ are sorted in descending order of water volume.
4. If the total volume of water available to agents from $(P_{act,N})$ exceeds the volume needed to extinguish the selected fire, then the leader p_{N^0} informs agents $p_{N^1}, p_{N^2}, \ldots$ p_{N^k} that they are included in the coalition under its control. Some agents may refuse to be included in the coalition, while other UAVs move towards the selected fire.
5. If the total volume of water available to team $(P_{act,N})$ is insufficient, then the leader UAV increases N and again finds a team of UAVs $(P_{act,N+1})$.
6. If the total volume of water available to team $(P_{act,N+1})$ is sufficient, then the leader informs the required agents from $(P_{act,N+1})$ about their inclusion in the coalition and gives an order to move towards the target. Otherwise, the leader tries to extinguish another spot from F_{act}, which can be reached in a number of steps exceeding N.
7. UAVs from P_{act} that don't have current tasks again select the leader and the cycle repeats. Thus, if the volume of water for some agent was not completely used up, then it can participate in the next coalition.

One can assign some agent as a permanent leader, in order not to make a dynamic selection for each fire spot. This could be justified when we use heterogeneous UAVs with various hardware capabilities. It is advisable to select as a leader the UAV with the best computing capabilities.

4 Tactical and Executive Levels

4.1 Trajectory Tracking and Target Tracking Problems

At the strategic level, the flight route is calculated for each UAV in the group, which is then transferred to the tactical level. When moving along a given route in an uncertain environment, UAV's trajectory is affected by external factors, including disturbing wind loads, physical obstacles, no-fly zones, and possible collisions. Each UAV is equipped with an onboard camera to monitor and track fires.

A novel approach to solve trajectory tracking problem is associated with the intro-duction of a pseudo target that implement a "reference" trajectory motion. It comes down to optimization problem of pursuing an evader (pseudo target) with the use of intelligent-geometric control approach. We assume that an ideal trajectory of each UAV $p_i P$ is given by the motion of the reference target $c_i C$, $C = \{c_1, \ldots, c_n\}$ along the given path. Each UAV pursues its own target guided by the selected strategy and the ability to control speed $v_{pi}[v_{min}; v_{max}]$, pitch $\theta_{pi}[\theta_{min}; \theta_{max}]$ and yaw $\psi_{pi}[\psi_{min}; \psi_{max}]$. The desired time T_i of traveling the whole path for each UAV is known. The presence of wind loads and obstacles $o_k O$, $O = \{o_1, \ldots, o_l\}$ leads to considerable deviation of a UAV from its ideal path. We consider a geometric model of a vehicle as a sphere of radius R (with some safety margin). Suppose that $p_i(t)$, $c_i(t)$, $o_k(t)$ are the coordinates of UAV p_i, reference target c_i and obstacle o_k at the instant t. Safety distance is determined by expressions $d(p_i(t), p_j(t)) \geq 2R, d(p_i(t), o_k(t)) \geq 2R, \forall i, j, k$.

Trajectory tracking problem. For each UAV p_i in a group, the problem consists in synthesizing the control $U_{pi}(t) = (v_{pi}(t), \theta_{pi}(t), \psi_{pi}(t))$, t $[0, T_i]$ under above given constraints, such that

$$\sum_{i=1}^{n} \int_{t=0}^{T_i} d(p_i(t), c_i(t))dt \to min. \tag{2}$$

To solve problem (2) we use geometric control methods (Pontryagin's maximum principle, methods of complex motion control and stabilization, control methods based on analysis of scene participants' movement, etc.) and intelligent control methods (including complex strategies implemented by sets of rules, behavior planning based on frame-based microprograms using fuzzy semantic networks, etc.) within a single robotic system with imposed control restrictions functioning in conditions of uncertainty. To comply with the safety requirements when drones are moving in a group, we use collision avoidance rules proposed in [18]. Also, we use special obstacles avoidance algorithm introduced in paper [19] that provides an ability to move under uncertainty toward the location of the target by the locally optimal route.

Another important issue is to track some object or region (for example, fire spot) with an onboard camera under disturbances. The problem is formulated as follows.

Target tracking problem. Let $f_i(t)$ and $r_j(t)$ be the coordinates of a fire spot f_i and the center of the observed (by the video camera of UAV p_j) region r_j, and $d(f_i(t), r_j(t))$ the distance between them at time instant t. For each p_j, the problem lies in constructing the camera actuators control $(\alpha_j(t), \beta_j(t))$ over the time interval $[0, T_j]$ under perturbations and control constraints, such that

$$\int_{t=0}^{T_j} d(f_i(t), r_j(t))dt \to min. \tag{3}$$

To solve problem (3), we adopt an approach based on the method of precise aiming of PTZ-camera (Pan Tilt Zoom) at a given point proposed in paper [20] and simulate the problem of fire zone tracking using models of video camera and wind loads.

4.2 UAV and Video Camera Models

UAV's dynamic model is defined by the transfer functions (TFs) that describe the automatic control system with an autopilot. We use an aircraft-type model that was obtained from the equations of UAV motion under wind loads. Figure 2 shows a general stabilization scheme of a yaw angle in the MATLAB Simulink with the following notation:

- ψ_G, ψ_C are the given and current values of the yaw angle,
- $W_{DA}(s) = \frac{1}{(ks+1)}$ is the TF of the direction actuator, where k is a parameter,

- $W_{\omega_{gy}/\Delta\delta_D}(s) = \frac{b_{\omega_{gy}}^{(0)}s^3 + b_{\omega_{gy}}^{(1)}s^2 + b_{\omega_{gy}}^{(2)}s + b_{\omega_{gy}}^{(3)}}{s^4 + a_{B_1}s^3 + a_{B_2}s^2 + a_{B_3}s + a_{B_4}}$ is the TF from the rudder to the yaw angular speed, where a, b with various subscripts are the dynamics parameters,

- $W_{\omega_{gy}/w_z}(s) = \frac{b_{\omega_{gy}/w_z}^{(0)}s^3 + b_{\omega_{gy}/w_z}^{(1)}s^2}{s^4 + a_{B_1}s^3 + a_{B_2}s^2 + a_{B_3}s + a_{B_4}}$, is the TF from wind to the yaw angular speed, w_z is the wind component generated by the function $R_t(\tau)$,

- k_ψ is the transfer ratio of the autopilot from the yaw angle; $k_{\omega_{gy}}$ is the transfer ratio of the autopilot from the angular yaw speed; s is the Laplace transform parameter.

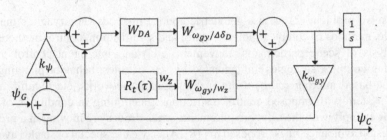

Fig. 2. Block diagram of a control system for a yaw angle.

We assume that a UAV carries out its movement in the yaw plane, while observing some object (fire spot). For testing we have selected a rotary PTZ-camera which ensures effective surveillance over a given area. Transition from one observation point to another is achieved by rotation in azimuth ($0 \div 360$ degrees) and elevation ($0 \div 90$ degrees). To simulate aiming of a camera at a region of interest in MATLAB Simulink we use control schemes for its horizontal (see Fig. 3a) and vertical (see Fig. 3b) actuators.

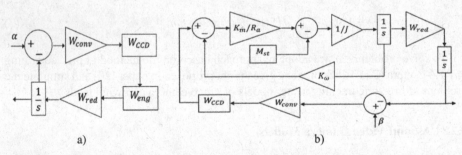

a)   b)

Fig. 3. Block diagrams of control systems for camera actuators: a) horizontal; b) vertical.

The control systems have following elements:

- $W_{eng} = \frac{k_{eng}}{p(T_M p + 1)}$ is the TF of the engine, where k_{eng} is the transfer number and T_M is the electromechanical constant,

- W_{red}, W_{conv} are TFs of the reducer and converter, M_{st} is the static torque of the engine shaft,

- $W_{CCD} = \frac{K_{g.c.}(T_{\omega p}p+1)}{T_{\omega 1}p+1}$ is the TF of the consistent corrective device (CCD), where $K_{g.c.}$ is the gain coefficient, $T_{\omega 1}, T_{\omega p}$ are constants, reflecting its inertial properties,
- R is the armature resistance, K_m is the electromagnetic ratio, J is the moment of inertia of the engine shaft.

The considered TFs are integrated into a single simulating system and serve as the basis for conducting experimental studies of trajectory problems in the presence of obstacles and wind loads.

5 Experiments

Let us consider the problem of optimal assignment of a group of drones to the given set of fire spots mentioned in Sect. 3. Suppose that a group of drones p_i, $i = \overline{1, 20}$ with water reserves a_i (see Table 1) are used to extinguish 5 fire spots.

Table 1. The number of resources available to UAVs.

i	1	2	3	4	5	6	7	8	9	10	11	12	13	14	15	16	17	18	19	20
a_i	9	15	10	30	4	36	7	30	34	3	10	4	20	18	35	34	12	6	17	24

The obtained solution is presented in Table 2, which shows the amount water necessary to extinguish each fire, identification numbers of UAVs and the number of resources involved in extinguishing fire spots by each UAV.

Table 2. The resulting solution of the task allocation problem.

Fire spot	Required volume of water	UAV coalitions (IDs and involved resources)
1	60	16:**7**, 19:**17**, 6:**36**
2	90	10:**8**, 16:**25**, 17:**12**, 5:**4**, 7:**7**, 9:**34**
3	75	1:**2**, 11:**10**, 12:**4**, 14:**18**, 16:2, 2:**15**, 20:**24**
4	50	1:**7**, 15:**13**, 4:**30**
5	70	13:**20**, 15:**22**, 18:**6**, 8:**22**

Here, the total cost of transportation is 1685. After putting out the first fire, UAVs No. 6 and No. 19 have completely exhausted their supply of water, and therefore do not take part in further actions. UAV No. 16 still has 27 units of water left and thus can take part in the elimination of the next fire.

To illustrate the first stage of solving the problem, we will simulate the extinguishing of the first fire site in a disturbed air environment with no-fly zones (see Fig. 4). Figure shows initial locations of UAVs (marked with blue color), no-fly zones indicated as polygons, fire spots (marked with red color) and obtained UAVs' trajectories. Modeling is performed in the MATLAB Simulink system using the abovementioned methods for planning and performing trajectory motion, ensuring safety when moving in a group and avoiding obstacles (no-fly zones). Figure 4 demonstrates the influence of wind loads and no-fly zones on the real UAV trajectory, and that the strategies and rules embedded in the intelligent-geometric control system successfully cope with the tasks.

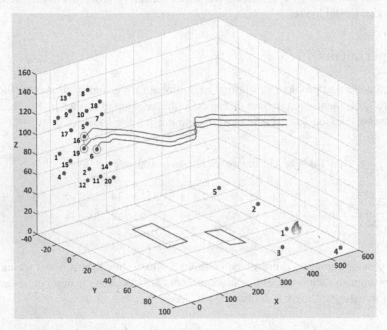

Fig. 4. Extinguishing of the first fire site in a complex environment.

During the movement a UAV monitors the fire spot with the help of a rotary camera. The simulation of the monitoring system and calculation of its main indicators have been carried out. The difference between the given and actual angles for the horizontal drive of the camera is shown in Fig. 5.

Here, the maximum discrepancy between the angles after stabilization does not exceed 0.25 degrees. As it shown in Fig. 5 the divergence between the center of the region observed by the camera and the coordinates of the fires spot does not exceed 10 m.

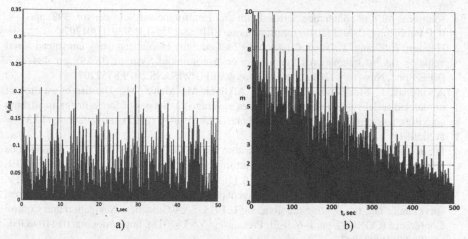

Fig. 5. Main indicators of a rotary camera. The x-axis shows the simulation time t (in seconds). The y-axes show: a) 0, deg is the deviation of the camera angle (in degrees); b) m is the deviation from the observed target (in meters).

6 Conclusion

In this paper, the task of extinguishing a large-scale fire by a group of intelligent UAVs loaded with water tanks is considered. The problems of forming coalitions and optimizing the distribution of functions between vehicles are solved. A novel hierarchical architecture is proposed, which is designed for combining geometric and intelligent control methods to cope with complex missions under uncertainty performed by a group of UAVs. We consider methods and models of intelligent-geometric control needed to solve application tasks such as dynamic motion and behavior planning in a disturbed environment with obstacles.

Experiments on implementation and controlling of UAVs movement to fire spots in an environment with no-fly zones and wind disturbances are conducted. Studies confirmed prospects of the intelligent-geometric theory and showed the feasibility of using the developed methods to form coalitions and organize goal-seeking behavior in uncertain conditions. "UAV– video camera" system allowing to track fire spots is described and its major characteristics are explored. In future, to speed up the processes of problems solution within the framework of the developed technologies, it is advisable to apply the hardware platform that supports parallel and pipelined computing.

Acknowledgements. The study was supported by a Grant from the Russian Science Foundation, № 22-11-20001 (https://rscf.ru/en/project/22-11-20001/) and a Grant in the form of a subsidy from the regional budget to organizations of the Yaroslavl region.

References

1. Ostapenko, A., Morkovin, V., Manmareva, V., Mammaiev, D.: Risk analysis in the management of forest fire in Russia. In: Forest ecosystems as global resource of the biosphere: calls, threats,

solutions. In: IOP conference Series: Earth and Environmental Science, vol. 392, pp. 1–9. IOP Publishing, Bristol (2019). https://doi.org/10.1088/1755-1315/392/1/012074

2. Hossain, F., Zhang, Y., Yuan, C.: A survey on forest fire monitoring using unmanned aerial vehicles. In: 3rd International Symposium on Autonomous Systems (ISAS), pp. 484–489. IEEE Press, New York (2019). https://doi.org/10.1109/ISASS.2019.8757707

3. Alsammak, I., Mahmoud, M., Aris, H., Alkilabi, M., Mahdi, M.: The use of swarms of unmanned aerial vehicles in mitigating area coverage challenges of forest-fire extinguishing activities: a systematic literature review. Forests 13(5), 1–31 (2022). https://doi.org/10.3390/f13050811

4. Islam S., Razi, A.: A path planning algorithm for collective monitoring using autonomous drones. In: 53rd Annual Conference on Information Sciences and Systems, pp. 1–6. IEEE Press, New York (2019). https://doi.org/10.1109/CISS.2019.8693023

5. Zhang, L., Liu, Z., Zhang, Y., Ai, J.: Intelligent path planning and following for UAVs in forest surveillance and fire fighting missions. In: IEEE CSAA Guidance, Navigation and Control Conference (CGNCC), pp. 1–6. IEEE Press, New York (2018). https://doi.org/10.1109/GNCC42960.2018.9018877

6. Luo, Z., Zhang, Y., Mu, L., Huang, J., Xin, J., Liu, H., Jiao, S., Xie, G., Yi, Y.: A UAV path planning algorithm based on an improved D lite algorithm for forest firefighting. In.: Chinese Automation Congress, pp. 4233–4237. IEEE Press, New York (2020). https://doi.org/10.1109/CAC51589.2020.9327111

7. Jiao, Y., Wang, X., Chen, H., Li, Y.: Research on the coverage path planning of UAVs for polygon areas. In: 5th IEEE Conference on Industrial Electronics and Applications, pp. 1467–1472. IEEE Press, New York (2010). https://doi.org/10.1109/ICIEA.2010.5514816

8. Xu, Y., Che, C.: A brief review of the intelligent algorithm for traveling salesman problem in UAV route planning. In: 9th International Conference on Electronics Information and Emergency Communication (ICEIEC), pp. 1–7. IEEE Press, New York (2019). https://doi.org/10.1109/ICEIEC.2019.8784651

9. Innocente, M., Grasso, P.: Self-organising swarms of firefighting drones: harnessing the power of collective intelligence in decentralised multi-robot systems. J. Comput. Sci. 34 80–101 (2019). https://doi.org/10.1016/j.jocs.2019.04.009

10. Ghamry, K., Kamel, M., Zhang, Y.: Multiple UAVs in forest fire fighting mission using particle swarm optimization. In: 2017 International Conference on Unmanned Aircraft Systems (ICUAS), pp. 1–7. IEEE Press, New York (2017). https://doi.org/10.1109/ICUAS.2017.7991527

11. Zhang, C., Hu, B., Yan, F.: Multiple UAVs forest fire fighting using a hierarchical task planning method. In: 2nd International Conference on Electronics, Communications and Information Technology, pp. 760–765. IEEE Press, New York (2021). https://doi.org/10.1109/CECIT53797.2021.00138

12. Ghamry, K., Zhang, Y.: Cooperative control of multiple UAVs for forest fire monitoring and detection. In: 12th IEEE/ASME International Conference on Mechatronic and Embedded Systems and Applications (MESA), pp. 1–6. IEEE Press, New York (2016). https://doi.org/10.1109/MESA.2016.7587184

13. Farinelli, A., Iocchi, L., Nardi, D.: Multirobot systems: a classification focused on coordination IEEE Trans. Syst. Man Cybern. 5(34), 2015–2028 (2004). https://doi.org/10.1109/TSMCB.2004,832155

14. Khachumov, M.: Tactical level of intelligent geometric control system for unmanned aerial vehicles. In: Ronzhin, A., Shishlakov, V., (eds.) Proceedings of 15th International Conference on Electromechanics and Robotics "Zavalishin's Readings". Smart Innovation, Systems and Technologies, vol. 187, pp. 55–67. Springer, Heidelberg (2020). https://doi.org/10.1007/978-981-15-5580-0_4

15. Ramana, M.V., Kothari, M.: Pursuit-evasion games of high speed evader. J. Intell. Rob. Syst. **85**(2), 293–306 (2016). https://doi.org/10.1007/s10846-016-0379-3

16. Brenner, U.: A faster polynomial algorithm for the unbalanced Hitchcock transportation problem. Oper. Res. Lett. **36** 408–413 (2008). https://doi.org/10.1016/j.orl.2008.01.011

17. Petrunin, S.: On solving transport problems of large dimensions. Civil Aviation High Technologies (Nauchnyi Vestnik MGTU GA) 131, 183–185 (2008)

18. Khachumov, M.: Solution of the problem of group pursuit of a target under perturbations (spatial case). Sci. Tech. Inf. Process. **187**, 435–443 (2018). https://doi.org/10.3103/S01476 88218060047

19. Khachumov, M., Khachumov, V.: The problems of route and motion planning for an autonomous flight vehicle in uncertain environment. In: 2018 Moscow Workshop on Electronic and Networking Technologies, pp. 1–6. IEEE Press, New York (2018). https://doi.org/10.1109/MWENT.2018.8337168

20. Khachumov, M.: Controlling flight vehicle motion and onboard video camera for tracking a dynamic target. In: 2017 International Multi-Conference on Engineering, Computer and Information Sciences, pp. 221–226 (2017). https://doi.org/10.1109/SIBIRCON.2017.810 9875

Approach to Automated Collection of Stones from Agricultural Lands by Means of a Heterogeneous Group of Robotic Systems

Roman Iakovlev$^{(\boxtimes)}$ (iD)

St. Petersburg Federal Research Center of the Russian Academy of Sciences, 39, 14th Line, 199178 St. Petersburg, Russia
iakovlev.r@mail.ru

Abstract. Within the development of robotic agricultural systems aimed at automating production processes, the actual task is to develop an approach to the detection and collection of extraneous objects, which is characterized by a high level of autonomy, a wide working area and the ability to perform tasks in a continuous mode. In this work, an approach to automated collection of stones from the territory of agricultural lands, based on the use of a group of heterogeneous robotic systems (RS), was proposed. Testing of the proposed approach was performed in the virtual environment Gazebo on the example of a simulated area of terrain with irregular topography. The final evaluation of the effectiveness of the proposed solution, averaged over all selected land sectors, was 77.2%. According to the results of the experiment, the proposed solution allows not only successfully perform tasks of stone collection on large agricultural objects in a continuous mode, but also carry out autonomous identification of potential areas where performing the appropriate operations is essential. Such potential areas are identified based on the analysis of the values of NDVI index in the observed area.

Keywords: Robotic means · Unmanned aerial vehicles · UAV · Heterogeneous RS · Stone collecting · Image-based detection · NDVI · SpineNet · Mask R-CNN

1 Introduction

Today, the quality and yield of crops directly depend not only on the presence of diseases, pests, weeds, and other harmful factors of biogenic origin on the territory of agricultural land, but also on the presence of other potentially harmful objects in the territory [1]. The presence of such extraneous objects as boulders and large pebbles significantly affects the quality of execution and the cost of individual agricultural operations, in particular, the presence of stones in the cultivated area significantly reduces the efficiency of mechanized preparation and treatment of agricultural areas. These foreign objects in combination with factors of biogenic origin are the cause of 40% of global crop losses [2].

To date, there are a number of innovative directions, the integration of which into the agroindustry has the potential to solve the problem of automated removing of extraneous

A. Ronzhin et al. (Eds.): ICR 2022, LNCS 13719, pp. 236–248, 2022.
https://doi.org/10.1007/978-3-031-23609-9_21

objects from agricultural lands. One of these areas is the introduction of robotic precise farming systems in agricultural facilities. Due to the integration of modern autonomous robotic systems (RS) and support of intelligent data analysis, it becomes possible to implement operations for the collection and remove of extraneous objects from cultivated land in an automated mode, which will not only optimize the basic production processes, reduce costs, but also increase the overall sustainability of the execution of production operations of agricultural enterprises. Thus, the present study is devoted to developing an approach to solving the problem of automated collection of extraneous objects and, in particular, stones from the territory of agricultural lands by RS.

2 Related Works

In general, the development of an approach to the collection of extraneous objects by means of RS, first of all, involves solving the problem of detecting the corresponding objects in the territory under study. To date, a number of approaches are known, the application of which allows directly or indirectly obtain an assessment of the territory for the presence of contamination by potentially harmful objects. In particular, in [3] the concept of hardware-software complex was proposed, which includes a set of scanning devices and a data processing server. Scanning devices include both CCTV cameras placed in the monitored area, and UAV groups, complete with RGB cameras and GPS. Groups of UAVs, while patrolling the territory, take targeted photos of the terrain. The collected data are sent to a server where the segmentation of the obtained images takes place and the presence of diseases and foreign inclusions among the target crops is detected. Application of a similar approach can take place in the assessment of agricultural areas for the presence of extraneous objects, but has a number of limitations. The most important of which is the need for accurate positioning of RS over the scanned area at a sufficiently short distance. Taking into account this limitation, scanning of large areas becomes a rather resource-intensive process.

The papers [4–6] consider the possibility of using biophysical parameters and vegetation indices, such as CPA and NDVI, to monitor areas in order to assess the condition of target crops and identify noxious weed inclusions. The authors propose to use UAVs to collect data through aerial photography of the assessed area. The collected data include both multispectral and RGB images, which allows to obtain dense point clouds, three-dimensional models as well as multispectral orthomosaics for the scanned areas at the post-processing stage. The proposed solutions make it possible to obtain sufficiently accurate data on the presence and condition of vegetation in the evaluated area, but can also potentially be applied to solve the problem of detecting inclusions of extraneous objects by identifying zones with reduced or atypical vegetation.

In the precise agriculture, approaches based on the use of machine learning models also find application [7–9]. Within the problem of detecting contamination of an area by potentially harmful objects, solutions that propose to use deep learning models for the detection of extraneous objects are of particular interest. Some papers [10, 11] propose to use convolutional neural networks to detect weeds in UAV images. The application of the method proposed in [10] achieved values of 0.9445 for the accuracy metric and 0.91 for the Kappa coefficient in the task of weed detection on the test dataset. The authors of the solution [2] proposed a system for detecting weeds and stones in strawberry and pea fields based on an improved Faster R-CNN. When evaluating the prediction quality of the resulting system, an average accuracy of 0.947 and a Kappa coefficient value of 0.89 were achieved. However, it should be noted that when using such solutions, based on the detection of objects by UAV means, a number of significant limitations arise. Thus, when detecting contamination of the surveyed area by such objects as rocks, it is important to take into account their size, the resolution of the scanning equipment, as well as the altitude of the UAV flight. Due to the limited capabilities of onboard equipment, as well as the low battery capacity of UAVs, direct detection of extraneous inclusions from the air is possible only for extremely small areas, which limits the applicability of these solutions.

Since the system of collection of extraneous objects, characterized by a high degree of autonomy and the possibility of use on real agricultural objects, must have a relatively high autonomous operation time, the ability to independently monitor the area and identify regions of interest, as well as be characterized by a sufficiently high payload capacity of the final robotic agents. Accordingly, the organization of such a system exclusively on the basis of a group of homogeneous UAVs is impossible due to the low payload capacity and autonomous operation time of the corresponding RS. Profiling of UAVs, as well as inclusion in the system of a number of ground-based robotic agents with large capacity and autonomous operation time will allow to significantly expand the effective operating range of the corresponding class of systems.

Thus, this study proposes an approach to automated collection of stones from the territory of agricultural lands by means of a heterogeneous group of RSs. The number of robotic agents is proposed to include a group of UAVs focused on the biophysical analysis of the surveyed territory using multispectral sensors, as well as a group of ground-based RSs implementing visual detection of extraneous objects, as well as direct stone collection through the use of a number of profile methods, as well as a set of specialized machine learning models. Further, let us consider the proposed approach in more detail.

3 Developed Approach to Automated Collection of Stones from the Territory of Agricultural Lands by Means of Heterogeneous Group of RSs

The approach developed in this study is designed to implement an automated collection of stones from the territory of agricultural lands using a group of autonomous robotic agents. The proposed approach includes the following main stages:

1. Construction of cartograms of territory contamination by extraneous objects:

   - Identification of potential regions of interest based on NDVI index values;
   - Monitoring of temporal variability of NDVI index values within potential regions of interest (sectors);
   - Assessment of sector pollution levels by foreign objects;

2. Prioritizing stone collection operations in the surveyed area;
3. Executing stone collection operations using ground RSs.

At a considerable distance of the fixing video camera (aerial photography), direct detection of stones is extremely difficult, because in the case of, for example, arable land such objects are usually characterized by relatively small size. Thus, within the proposed approach at the first stage is the identification of potential regions of interest and localization of areas of alleged contamination by extraneous objects with the use of UAVs.

The realization of this stage is based on the division of the base orthophotomap into sectors of a given scale. Thus, n independent sectors Ai with areas S_i $(i = 1...n)$ are formed. Then averaged values of NDVI index NDVIi for each sector A_i are estimated by means of UAV technical vision. In general case $NDVI_i = \frac{\iint NDVIdA_i}{S_i}$. However, taking into account the given altitude of the UAV flight and the limited resolution of the sensor devices, the expression above can be approximated as follows:

$$NDVI_i = \frac{\sum_{j=1}^{m} P_{ij}}{m},$$

where P_{ij} is the j-th segment of sector A_i for which the eigenvalue of NDVI index was obtained, m is the number of segments included in sector A_i. To estimate NDVI index values, a method presented in [12] is used. Thus, for each sector A_i of the surveyed area, the estimated values of NDVI index at a given moment of time can be obtained.

Identification of potential regions of interest is based on the analysis of the dynamics of NDVI index values for different sectors over time. In the context of solving the problem of detecting extraneous objects and, in particular, stones, the spring vegetation period, when the density of green mass has not yet reached high values, is of the greatest value. Accordingly, a set of associated averaged NDVI index values $NDVI_{iT}$ is generated for each sector Ai during a given time period T:

$$NDVI_{iT} = \{NDVI_{it}|t = \overline{1, T}\}.$$

On the basis of the obtained values, the growth rate of NDVI index for each of the sectors A_i can be estimated:

$$r_i = \frac{\sum_{t=1}^{t=T-1}\left(NDVI_{i(t+1)} - NDVI_{it}\right)}{T - 1},$$

where r_i is the average growth rate of the NDVI index for sector A_i.

According to the results of the evaluation above, the conclusion about whether sector A_i belongs to the set of potential regions of interest Reg can be made on the basis of the following expression:

$$A_i \in Reg, \text{если} \begin{cases} r_i < r_{mean} \\ NDVI_{iT} < NDVI_{meani}, \\ NDVI_{iT} < NDVI_{ibase} \end{cases}$$

where r_{mean} is the median value of the NDVI index growth rate by sector, $NDVI_{meanT}$ is the median of the final NDVI index values by sector, $NDVI_{ibase}$ is the year-averaged historical NDVI index value for sector A_i over a similar period (if available).

Thus, for each segment A_i of the studied area the conclusion about its belonging to the set of potential regions of interest (areas contaminated by extraneous objects) Reg is formed. For each A_k sector included in the Reg set the process of monitoring of this sector by UAV means is repeatedly initiated, but at lower altitudes, which allows obtaining more detailed information about NDVI index values in different parts of this sector. Based on the results of such detailed assessment a P_k set of NDVI index values associated with different segments of the studied sector A_k is formed:

$$P_k = \{\ NDVI_{km} | m = \overline{1, M}\},$$

where M is the number of segments in A_k sector, formed according to the results of detailed analysis of this sector by UAV means ($M > m$), $NDVI_{km}$ is the NDVI index value, associated with the m-th segment of A_k sector.

In the next step, a histogram of NDVI index values distribution is drawn for each A_k sector from the Reg set. Estimation of dispersion of NDVI index values over this sector can be obtained as follows:

$$D(P_k) = \frac{\sum_{m=1}^{M}(NDVI_{km} - E(P_k))^2}{M}.$$

The high value of the obtained $D(P_k)$ estimates indicates significant variability of the obtained NDVI index values between separate segments of the observed sector and signals about the increased probability of the presence of extraneous objects in the corresponding area. According to the obtained $D(P_k)$ estimates, all A_k sectors from the set Reg can be divided into the following groups G in terms of the assumed level of contaminate: 0 is no contaminate; 1 is insignificant contaminate; 2 is medium contaminate; 3 is heavy contaminate; 4 is very heavy contaminate. Thus, assignment of some A_k sector to one of the groups above can be realized according to the following expression:

$$A_k \in G_0, if : \left|\sqrt{D(P_k)}\right| \cong 0;$$

$$A_k \in G_1, if : 0 < \left|\sqrt{D(P_k)}\right| \leq 0.1;$$

$$A_k \in G_2, if : 0.1 < \left|\sqrt{D(P_k)}\right| \leq 0.2;$$

$$A_k \in G_3, if : 0.2 < \left|\sqrt{D(P_k)}\right| \leq 0.35;$$

$$A_k \in G_4, if : \left|\sqrt{D(P_k)}\right| > 0.35.$$

The proposed grouping makes it possible to make a mapping of the territory contaminate, i.e. not only to identify zones of potential contaminate by extraneous objects, but also to assess the level of alleged contaminate and accordingly prioritize the tasks of their elimination.

In terms of localization of zones of alleged contaminate within each target A_k sector as such zones should be considered, first of all, segments, the value of the NDVI index for which is less than $E(P_k)$. In this case, the lower the index value for some segment, the higher the probability of the presence of extraneous objects in it. Thus, at this stage a sectoral map of contaminate of the surveyed area with the indication of the assumed levels of contaminate of individual sectors is formed.

The next step of the proposed approach is to prioritize stone collection operations in the surveyed area. The basic prioritization at the sector level is achieved by ranking the sectors according to their assigned G-groups, based on the assumed level of contamination. In general, stone collection tasks are conditionally independent at the sector level, but, if necessary, ranking within each individual group can be based on the weighted average NDVI index values obtained for these sectors in the previous step: preference should be given to sectors where the $E(P_k)$ score is the lowest.

Next, let us consider the issue of prioritizing stone collection operations at the level of each individual sector A_i. Prioritization of operations implies determination of the most priority segments of sector A_i for stone collection. In general, the priority of segment directly depends on the supposed level of its contaminate (supposed number of stones on its territory), which increases when the NDVI index for this segment decreases. However, at this stage while forming the priorities, not only expediency of performance of operation on a certain segment, but also energy and time costs of RS to reach the segment should be taken into account. Thus, the question of prioritization of stone collection operations at the level of an individual sector can be presented as a multi-criteria optimization problem, where the criteria for the efficiency of its solution are:

1. Maximization of a number of collected stones per time unit;
2. Minimization of the aggregate trajectory of RS performing the corresponding operations.

Let's give a formal interpretation to the criteria presented above. Maximization of the number of stones collected per unit time can, without loss of meaning, be interpreted as minimization of the specific stone collection time T':

$$T' = \frac{\Delta T}{\Delta Q} \to min,$$

where ΔT is the time of the stone collection operation, ΔQ is the expected number of stones collected during the time ΔT.

In turn, the minimization of the cumulative trajectory of the RS during the operation can be represented as follows:

$$S' = \frac{\Delta S}{\Delta T} \to min,$$

where ΔT is the time of stone collection operation, ΔS is the length of the aggregated RS trajectory. In this case, as a basic algorithm for generating RSs trajectories we consider the method of Coverage Path Planning (CPP) to build a path in each individual segment [13] and a variation of the method RRT (Rapidly-Exploring Random Trees) to build a global path between the exit and entry points of different segments, as well as the start and end coordinates LRLHD-A* [14].

Thus, the task of prioritizing stone collection operations at the individual sector level can be formulated as follows:

$$H(T', S') \to min.$$

The search for one of the pareto-optimal solutions to this problem can be carried out using a wide toolbox of target programming methods. Thus, the results of this stage are used to determine the sub-optimal trajectory of RS movement during the execution of the stone collection operation in a given sector A_i.

At the final stage the operations of collecting stones are considered. During the stone collection operations, the RS, moving along the trajectory defined at the previous stage, analyzes the surrounding space in order to detect extraneous objects by the RS onboard camera [15]. Within the proposed solution, the SpineNet neural network model is used as the architectural basis, and the Mask R-CNN neural network model as the object detector [16]. Based on the results of the detection of a extraneous object (stone) in the surrounding space, the RS makes an assessment of the spatial position of this object.

At the next step, based on the data obtained by the vision aids and onboard sensors of the RS, the key points for grabbing the object are evaluated in accordance with the solution presented in paper [17]. The information obtained with respect to the optimal grabbing points is transmitted to the control system of the RS gripper mechanism. This control system calculates the trajectory of the RS manipulator to reach the specified grabbing points. The gripping process is performed using the feedback system implemented by using tactile sensors installed on the RS gripper mechanism [18, 19]. After successful grabbing of the target object, the RS arm moves this object to the basket located on the board, after which the RS continues to perform the operation and search for extraneous objects in the surrounding space.

Next, the results of an experimental evaluation of the quality of the stone collection task solution performed according to the approach proposed in this study will be considered.

4   Results

Let us consider the results of evaluating the quality of stone collection task execution by means of a heterogeneous group of RSs, obtained using proposed approach. An example of the territory obtained in such a way is shown in Fig. 1.

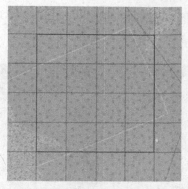

Fig. 1. An example of the territory generation results by means of the modeling complex (top view)

The experiment is based on simulation of a series of stone collection operations in a virtual environment Gazebo. The results of these operations serve as the basis for evaluating the effectiveness of the proposed approach. For carrying out of the experiment with use of computer model, generation of some terrain during the early vegetation period is carried out. After that, extraneous objects (stones) are put on it by means of the virtual environment.

This Figure shows the generated area and the operator-defined region of interest (blue frame) within which the scenario will be executed. The operator-defined region of interest is divided into 16 sectors of equal area. Table 1 below contains information on the number of stones added to each of these sectors during terrain modeling.

Table 1. Number of foreign objects (stones) placed by sectors during terrain modeling

	Column 1	Column 2	Column 3
Row 1	455	7 640	58
Row 2	73	517	749
Row 3	692	1 373	17 632
Row 4	399	481	6 318

Under the conditions of simulated environment, the values characterizing NDVI index in separate sectors of the region of interest are set inversely proportional to the number of stones applied to the corresponding sector, taking into account the normalizing factor. The contaminate map formed in such a way for the surveyed area (Fig. 1) is shown in Fig. 2a.

As can be seen in Fig. 2a, according to the data of the contaminate cartogram: 3 of 16 observed sectors have no contaminate by extraneous objects at all, 7 sectors are classified as a category of insignificant level of contaminate, 3 sectors have an average level of contaminate, 2 is high and 1 very high. Thus, according to the developed approach, stone collection operations will be independently initiated for 6 sectors with the highest level of pollution.

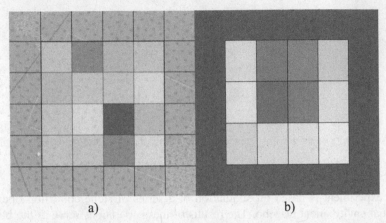

a)   b)

Fig. 2. Cartogram of contaminate by extraneous objects a) for whole surveyed area b) detailed for segment with a highest contaminate level

Next, as part of the experiment, we will evaluate the effectiveness of single extraneous objects collection operation on the example of the sector with a highest contaminate level. The distribution of extraneous objects among the 12 segments of the studied sector is as follows: $456_{1,1}$, $913_{1,2}$, $865_{1,3}$, $324_{1,4}$, $505_{2,1}$, $985_{2,2}$, $902_{2,3}$, $467_{2,4}$, $673_{3,1}$, $445_{3,2}$, $516_{3,3}$, $589_{3,4}$. The corresponding simulated values of the NDVI index in these segments of the sector are shown in Fig. 2b.

Proceeding from the NDVI index values by segments of the considered sector, it can be concluded that, according to the given scenario, a high concentration of extraneous objects is characteristic of six segments.

Next, let us consider the formation of a sub-optimal route of the stone collection operation in this sector. Using the covering trajectory method and a variation of the RRT method mentioned above (LRLHD-A*), the search for the pareto-optimal solution of the minimization problem of the function $H(T', S')$ was carried out:

$$H(T', S') = T' * S', \forall T', S'.$$

To solve this problem within the present experiment the Nash arbitrage scheme was used. According to the obtained solution the execution of the stone collecting operation will include bypassing only four segments (1.2, 1.3, 2.2, 2.3), characterized by the smallest values of NDVI index in the given sector. The resulting trajectory of the RS movement during the implementation of the corresponding operation is presented in Fig. 3.

As can be seen, despite the use of the covering trajectory method, the experiment did not achieve complete coverage of a number of segments. The imperfections of the resulting trajectory of RS movement is due to the presence of local obstacles on the path of RS along the calculated route. Nevertheless, it should be noted that despite the presence of obstacles and limited passability of ground RS, the final coverage ratio of the target segments was more than 81%. Separately, it should be noted that the trajectories of the exit to the start and end points of the operation have significant differences from the trajectories of movement within the target segments, since outside the target segments when RS moves, the key criterion for generating a trajectory is optimization of energy costs, taking into account local drops in altitude and the topography of the sector.

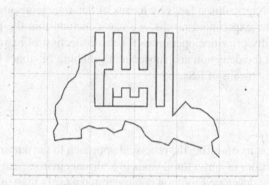

Fig. 3. The resulting trajectory of the ground RS during the considered stone collection operation.

At the final stage of the experiment, the final evaluation of the effectiveness of the stone collection operations is carried out. Within the considered operation, stone collection was carried out on the target segments of the sector. Numerical results of the conducted operation are presented in Table 2.

Table 2. Numerical results of the performed stone collection operation on the target segments of the sector under consideration

	Initial number of stones	Number of collected stones
Segment No. 1.2	913	542
Segment No. 1.3	865	599
Segment No. 2.2	985	837
Segment No. 2.3	902	791
Segment No. 1.2	913	542

The average percentage of detected and collected stones in the considered segments was 76%. The total operating time before leaving the working area was 252 min. The final consolidated estimate of the effectiveness of the proposed approach, obtained by averaging the estimates of the effectiveness of operations performed on all target sectors of the study area, was 77.2%. It should be noted that for the sectors with a lower concentration of stones (sectors No. 2.4, 3.2, 4.4), the percentage of detected and collected stones was slightly lower and on the average was 74.3%. The obtained results can be explained by the fact that during the process of grabbing objects the position and angle of observation of the scene by RS's sensors are changing, thus for the given area additional information about the presence of extraneous objects can be obtained, which has a limited positive effect on the resulting share of detected and respectively captured objects. Thus, we can conclude that the developed approach in general is characterized by a relatively high accuracy in solving the problem of automated·collection of stones from the territory of agricultural lands by means of heterogeneous group of RSs.

According to the experiment results, we can conclude that the proposed solution allows to successfully prioritize operations for the collection of extraneous objects, as well as to carry out the detection and subsequent grabbing of stones on the territory of agricultural lands by means of RSs.

5 Conclusion

According to the results of testing the proposed approach to the automated collection of stones from the territory of agricultural lands in a virtual environment on the example of a simulated area, the developed solution demonstrated a fairly high quality of execution of the relevant operations. The final evaluation of the effectiveness of the proposed approach, averaged over all selected sectors, was 77.2%. Thus, the proposed solution allows not only to execute successfully stone collecting tasks on large agricultural objects in a continuous mode, but also to carry out autonomous identification of potential areas, where it is required to perform the appropriate operations, based on the analysis of the values of NDVI index in the surveyed area.

Within the further research on the basis of the proposed approach it is planned to implement an automated system for collecting of extraneous objects on the basis of a group of heterogeneous RSs and test it on one of the existing agricultural facilities of the Northwestern Federal District of the Russian Federation.

References

1. Pinaki, M., Tewari, V.K.: Present status of precision farming: a review. Int. J. Agric. Res. 5(12), 1124–1133 (2010). https://doi.org/10.3923/ijar.2007.1.10
2. Khan, S., Tufail, M., Khan, M.T., Khan, Z.A., Anwar, S.: Deep learning-based identification system of weeds and crops in strawberry and pea fields for a precision agriculture sprayer. Precision Agric. 22(6), 1711–1727 (2021). https://doi.org/10.1007/s11119-021-09808-9
3. Kitpo, N., Inoue, M.: Early rice disease detection and position mapping system using drone and IoT architecture. In: 2018 12th South East Asian Technical University Consortium (SEATUC), vol. 1, pp. 1–5. IEEE (2018). https://doi.org/10.1109/SEATUC.2018.8788863
4. Suab, S.A., Syukur, M. S., Avtar, R., Korom, A.: Unmanned aerial vehicle (UAV) derived normalised difference vegetation index (NDVI) and crown projection area (CPA) to detect

health conditions of young oil palm trees for precision agriculture. In: The International Archives of Photogrammetry, Remote Sensing and Spatial Information Sciences, vol. 42, pp. 611–614 (2019). https://doi.org/10.5194/isprs-archives-XLII-4-W16-611-2019

5. Ghazal, M., Al Khalil, Y., Hajjdiab, H.: UAV-based remote sensing for vegetation cover estimation using NDVI imagery and level sets method. In: 2015 IEEE International Symposium on Signal Processing and Information Technology, pp. 332–337. IEEE (2015). https://doi.org/10.1109/ISSPIT.2015.7394354

6. Daroya, R., Ramos, M.: NDVI image extraction of an agricultural land using an autonomous quadcopter with a filter-modified camera. In: 2017 7th IEEE International Conference on Control System, Computing and Engineering, pp. 110–114. IEEE (2017). https://doi.org/10.1109/ICCSCE.2017.8284389

7. Su, J.: Wheat yellow rust monitoring by learning from multispectral UAV aerial imagery. Comput. Electron. Agric. **155**, 157–166 (2018). https://doi.org/10.1016/j.compag.2018.10.017

8. Escalante, H.J., Rodríguez-Sánchez, S., Jiménez-Lizárraga, M., Morales-Reyes, A., De La Calleja, J., Vazquez, R.: Barley yield and fertilization analysis from UAV imagery: a deep learning approach. Int. J. Remote Sens. **40**(7), 2493–2516 (2019). https://doi.org/10.1080/01431161.2019.1577571

9. Tamouridou, A.A.: Application of multilayer perceptron with automatic relevance determination on weed mapping using UAV multispectral imagery. Sensors **17**(10), 2307 (2017). https://doi.org/10.3390/s17102307

10. Bah, M. D., Hafiane, A., Canals, R.: Deep learning with unsupervised data labeling for weed detection in line crops in UAV images. Remote Sens. **10**(11), 1690 (2018). https://doi.org/10.3390/rs10111690

11. Huang, H.: A semantic labeling approach for accurate weed mapping of high resolution UAV imagery. Sensors **18**(7), 2113 (2018). https://doi.org/10.3390/s18072113

12. Astapova, M., Saveliev, A., Markov, Y.: Method for monitoring growth of microgreens in containers using computer vision in infrared and visible ranges. In: Agriculture Digitalization and Organic Production, pp. 383–394. Springer, Singapore (2022). https://doi.org/10.1007/978-981-16-3349-2_32

13. Vasquez-Gomez, J.I., Marciano-Melchor, M., Valentin, L., Herrera-Lozada, J.C.: Coverage path planning for 2D convex regions. J. Intell. Rob. Syst. **97** (1), 81–94 (2019). https://doi.org/10.1007/s10846-019-01024-y

14. Zakharov, K.S., Saveliev, A.I.: Smoothing the curvature of trajectory of ground robot in 3D space. Proc. Southwest State Univ. **24**(4), 107–125 (2020). (In Russ.). https://doi.org/10.21869/2223-1560-2020-24-4-107-125

15. TPU object detection and segmentation framework, https://github.com/tensorflow/tpu/tree/master/models/official/detection, last accessed 2022/07/21

16. Du, X., Lin, T.Y., Jin, P., Ghiasi, G., Tan, M., Cui, Y., Song, X.: Spinenet: Learning scale-permuted backbone for recognition and localization. In: Proceedings of the IEEE/CVF Conference on Computer Vision and Pattern Recognition, pp. 11592–11601 (2020). https://doi.org/10.48550/arXiv.1912.05027

17. Iakovlev, R.N., Rubtsova, J.I., Erashov, A.A.: Comparative evaluation of approaches for determination of grasp points on objects, manipulated by robotic systems. Mekhatronika, Avtomatizatsiya, Upravlenie **22**(2), 83–93 (2021). (In Russ.). https://doi.org/10.17587/mau.22.83-93

18. Erashov, A., Krestovnikov, K.: Algorithm for controlling manipulator with combined array of pressure and proximity sensors in gripper. In: Electromechanics and Robotics. Smart Innovation, Systems and Technologies, vol. 232, pp. 61–71 (2022). https://doi.org/10.1007/978-981-16-2814-6_6
19. Erashov, A., Kamynin, K., Krestovnikov, K., Saveliev, A.: Method for estimating time of wireless transfer of energy resources between two robots. Inform. Autom. **20**(6), 1279–1306 (2021). https://doi.org/10.15622/ia.20.6.4

Method for Planning a Coverage Trajectory for a Group of UAVs Marking Out Zones for Installing Seismic Modules

Valeriia Lebedeva[1], Roman Iakovlev[1]([✉]), Vitaliy Bryksin[2], and Vadim Agafonov[3]

[1] Laboratory of Autonomous Robotic Systems, St. Petersburg Federal Research Center of the Russian Academy of Sciences (SPC RAS), St. Petersburg Institute for Informatics and Automation of the Russian Academy of Sciences, 14th Line VI 39, 199178 St. Petersburg, Russia
lakovlev.r@mail.ru
[2] Institute of Applied Informatics and Mathematical Geophysics I. Kant BFU, Nevskogo Ul. 14 A, 236016 Kaliningrad, Kaliningrad Oblast, Russia
[3] Seismic Instruments and Software, Likhachevsky Proezd 4/1, Office 101, Dolgoprudny, Moscow Region 141701, Russia

Abstract. Today, the task of planning the trajectory of covering the area with a group of unmanned aerial vehicles (UAVs) remains relevant. This paper presents a method for planning the coverage trajectory when a group of UAVs performs aerial monitoring of the terrain in order to mark out the zones for installing seismic modules. The developed method allows solving the problem of constructing high-precision three-dimensional maps of vast territories by a group of UAVs due to the effective distribution of group agents over various parts of the global trajectory of terrain coverage. The proposed solution not only takes into account the current parameters of the UAV, the distance to the segments of the covering trajectories, but also ensures the minimization of the total time of the aerial monitoring mission. According to the results of experiments, using the proposed method, the average error in reconstructing maps of simulated areas using the ADNN metric was 13.01 cm. In the future, the proposed solution can be modified by introducing new algorithms for the decomposition of the global coverage trajectory, as well as methods for smoothing the covering trajectories.

Keywords: Coverage Trajectory · Group of UAVs · Mapping · Path planning

1 Introduction

Currently, the pace of research and development in the field of unmanned aerial vehicles (UAVs) and unmanned aerial systems (UAS) is constantly increasing due to their autonomy, as well as the ability to install various payloads on board, which, combined with the relatively low cost of production, allows the use of systems of this class for solving a wide range of applied problems. These features have made UAVs a valuable class of robotic systems used in civil and military applications, including fields of seismic geology and seismic exploration. Usually, 3D seismic surveys involve placing acquisition modules on a uniform grid with a specified spacing. However, at present, a significant part of seismic exploration works is performed in hard-to-reach territories characterized by complex topography and a set of different types of land surface areas (waterlogged or extremely dry areas, water bodies, etc.). Even deployment of a seismic exploration system itself on such territories is rather difficult then the precise placement of sensors on a uniform grid is almost impossible. As the accuracy of receiving sensors installation is extremely important for modern methods of seismic data processing, planning a seismic experiment should involve a preliminary detailed observation of the terrain to select the optimal points for sensors placement. This task can be effectively performed by the UAVs. A number of articles are directly related to the research and development of UAV control systems, solving applied problems in the field of seismogeology, seismic exploration and assessment of the consequences of earthquakes caused by tectonic processes. In most of recent works UAVs are considered as ideal agents for detecting subtle surface changes, ground ruptures, rock fractures, fault and fracture movement in natural and man-made structures. Definitely UAV have a number of advantages compared with other means of aerial monitoring [1, 2]. UAVs do not require additional infrastructure, such as an airfield with a runway and airspace management facilities. UAVs provide high-resolution multi-channel heterogeneous data recording, are capable of flying vertically and in limited geometric subspaces to refine identified areas of interest. By hovering at a certain point, UAVs can provide a stable recording of processes occurring in hard-to-reach places, e.g. deformations during volcanic eruptions and lava movement. In particular, in the work [3] were analyzed options for the use of different types of UAVs (aerostats, fixed wing aircrafts, multirotor, hybrid) for geological research. The study showed that the selected multirotor UAV provided video recording and subsequent reconstruction of a spatial orthophotomap, allowing structuring of objects of 5–10 cm in size. As a result, the proposed solution provided documentation of many more fractures than previously were mapped during the investigation of the Theistareykir geothermal area in northern Iceland. The use of UAV to assess damage and make decisions about rebuilding residential areas after an earthquake is discussed in [4]. A video survey in the village of Castelluccio di Norcia in Italy, which was affected by the 2016 earthquake, made it possible to construct a spatial model with an accuracy of 40 cm and assess the level of damage to buildings.

To date, a lot of specialized solutions to many industrial problems by means of single UAVs have been proposed, including the field of seismogeology and seismic exploration [4, 5]. At the same time, the development of applied systems based on groups of UAVs is a particularly relevant area of research, due to the higher performance of these solutions in terms of task execution time, as well as their increased adaptability and fault tolerance [6]. However, today, modern systems based on several UAVs still have a number of problems in such areas as multi-channel communication and group control [7]. Particularly the problem of planning the trajectory of terrain coverage when a group of UAVs performs specialized flight tasks is also relevant [8]. Thus, this paper proposes a method for planning the coverage trajectory when a group of UAVs performs aerial monitoring of the terrain in order to mark the zones for installing seismic modules.

2   Related Works

Currently, there are a significant number of methods for planning the trajectories of a group of robots that provide coverage of a given area [9, 10]. The vast majority of modern trajectory planning strategies are based on the concept of cellular decomposition of the workspace. The task of planning the coverage trajectory of a given area by agents is no exception, where it is required to find the optimal paths for a group of UAVs that survey the area with specialized vision sensors (lidar, RGB camera, multispectral camera), while ensuring full coverage of the working space [11].

In a number of papers, authors propose different methods for dividing the work area into sectors for constructing a coverage trajectory. In [12], authors conducted a study in search of an efficient algorithm for partitioning the workspace into sectors and compared the differences between the absence of decomposition, exact and approximate methods of cell decomposition. In the case of exact decomposition methods, the free workspace is subdivided into cells of the target scale, while the center of each resulting cell is considered as a waypoint on the adjacency graph. The problem of complete coverage in this case is solved by searching through the graph to determine the order in which cells are traversed [13]. Approximate decomposition involves splitting a given area depending on the obstacles registered on it, or chaotic splitting into convex polygons if the area is a non-convex polygon. After slicing the area, the planner builds covering trajectories on each resulting sections using known motion patterns such as back and forth or spiral movement [14, 15]. This type of terrain decomposition is often used in systems with several agents, where each agent is assigned its own sections of operation [16, 17].

In systems based on groups of UAVs, the methods mentioned above are also used in solving the problem of constructing a coverage trajectory, where there is an additional task of distributing sections of the decomposed workspace between the agents of the group. A number of relevant approaches use exact decomposition principles in combination with auction-based algorithms to allocate coverage sections to agents [16]. In [18] an alternative solution based on the CGM (column generation model) was demonstrated, the proposed method potentially allows taking into account the limited energy resources of the UAV, however, the authors presented only the results of basic model experiments, which does not allow us to evaluate the effectiveness and real application potential of this solution.

In general, despite the ability to preliminarily take into account static obstacles and the relatively high accuracy of covering trajectory generation, methods based on the principles of decomposition of the area are characterized by a relatively high computational complexity and, accordingly, a low speed of calculating the covering trajectory. At the same time, in the case of methods that use the principles of approximate decomposition, there is an additional task to determine the points of entry and exit to sections, as well as to construct the trajectories of the movement of agents when moving between the selected sections of the area. In the case of methods using full decomposition, the coverage trajectories are often characterized by a large number of turns and, accordingly, a high frequency of agent orientation changes, which complicates aerial monitoring missions. According to [19], to improve the quality of building maps of the area, it is necessary that the agent does not change orientation when photographing sections of the area, since this simplifies the process of three-dimensional reconstruction and image stitching, as it facilitates the search for singular points in adjacent images. Thus, exact decomposition methods cannot be used in solving the problem posed in the framework of this study, since they have a negative impact on the results of image stitching and, accordingly, on the quality of three-dimensional scene reconstruction.

In the absence of decomposition, the area is not divided into sections, and the trajectory itself is built according to the principle of back and forth or spiral movement [20, 21], providing coverage of the entire working area. The main advantage of such approach is its low computational complexity, which makes it possible to calculate the trajectory for a group of UAVs in real time. The main disadvantage is the inability of such methods to preventively take into account static obstacles in the process of constructing a trajectory. But it can be leveled by using dynamic obstacle recognition methods and methods for correcting the UAV local trajectory based on data from onboard sensor equipment [22].

Thus, according to the purpose of this work of this work, a method for planning the coverage trajectory when a group of UAVs perform aerial monitoring of the terrain in order to mark out the zones for installing seismic modules is proposed. The proposed solution does not use terrain decomposition methods and it is based on the back and forth motion pattern combined with local trajectory planning algorithms for agents to avoid obstacles. Next, consider the proposed method for planning the coverage trajectory for a group of UAVs in detail.

3   The Developed Method for Planning the Coverage Trajectory in Aerial Monitoring of the Terrain by a Group of UAVs

The developed method for planning the coverage trajectory for monitoring a given territory by a group of UAVs in order to identify the contamination zone for installing seismic sensors. During aerial monitoring of the area, the UAV follows a continuous and smooth trajectory that evenly covers the given area, and at the same time avoid areas and zones of no interest, access to which is limited. During the movement of the UAV along the trajectory, continuous collection of photographic material is carried out. Consecutive images must have a specified overlap percentage. The greater the degree of overlap, the higher the accuracy of the resulting terrain map is. The quality of the terrain map will also be better if images of adjacent terrain are taken at the same time. Otherwise, the risk of uncorrelated shadows or obvious visual differences increases, which will complicate the process of terrain reconstruction and reduce the quality of the results of aerial monitoring [23].

This paper presents a method for constructing a coverage trajectory without preliminary exact decomposition of the working space into sections. The absence of an accurate decomposition makes it possible to reduce the time for calculating the global trajectory, as well as to use the result obtained to form the target trajectories of the movement of each of the agents involved. The main feature of the developed method is that the global trajectory, built on the basis of the back and forth motion pattern. Then the global coverage trajectory is divided into non-intersecting segments, each of which is assigned a separate agent. In this case, the distance between the formed sections depends on the parameters of the sensors installed on board and the specified percentage of overlap. In other words, not the entire workspace is subjected to decomposition, but only the gen-erated global trajectory. This step allows to significantly reduce the time for calculating individual UAV trajectories, which is critically necessary in the tasks of planning and distributing routes between agents in near real time.

According to this work, it is assumed that there is a group of k multi-rotor UAVs covering a polygonal convex region in the space R^2, defined by a set of points P. In order to have comparable measurements within the scanned polygonal area, all UAVs must reach the same operating height, and the distance between the rows of the coverage trajectory must be constant. To avoid collisions when entering operating positions, each UAV is assigned different takeoff points, different altitude of the mission start points and different return to launch points (RTL), as shown in Fig. 1.

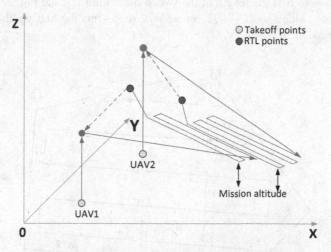

Fig. 1. Illustration of the general scheme of the mission.

According to the general mission scheme (Fig. 1), each involved UAV reaches a given individual height, after it makes a transition to the mission starting point, where it performs the back and forth movement along a section of the global trajectory, after which it returns to the mission initiation point. As mentioned earlier, the assigned paths of each UAV are continuous. It is assumed that each UAV involved is equipped with identical onboard sensors (depth camera, RGB camera, ultrasonic sensors or lidar) ori-ented perpendicular to the horizontal XY plane. The proposed method for planning the coverage trajectory for aerial monitoring of the terrain by a UAV group consists of the following key steps:

1. Calculation of the coverage trajectory for the area based on the back-and-forth motion pattern;
2. Decomposition of the global covering trajectory into connected sets of waypoints (trajectory segments) distributed among the agents of the group depending on the current position of the agents and UAV characteristics.

At the first step, to create a global back and forth trajectory, it is necessary to determine the required distance d between two adjacent rows. The calculation of this distance depends on the required percentage of image overlap and the parameters of the onboard sensors installed on the UAV. Let v characterize the percentage of vertical overlap of frames, and w will correspond to the camera frame width at the target UAV flight altitude. In such a case, the sought distance between adjacent rows, denoted as d, is the (vertical) distance between two frames. Given the required percentage of vertical overlap of frames, the distance d can be calculated as follows:

$$d = w \cdot (1 - v). \tag{1}$$

The number of turns n that must be performed in the area depends on the values of d, w and ls, where ls is the length of the sweep direction [21], see Fig. 2. Let's define an intermediate value $z = ls - w/2$, where $w/2$ represents the half width of the UAV camera coverage area.

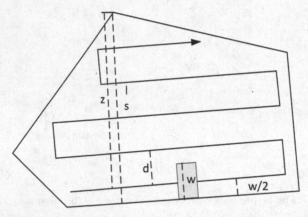

Fig. 2. Schematic illustration of the parameters required to calculate the number of turns within the global coverage trajectory.

Since the parameter d characterizes the distance separating the rows of the global trajectory, accordingly, the value equal to the ratio of z to d will indicate the number of rows needed to cover the polygonal area of interest using the back and forth pattern. However, if the distance between the bottom row and the top vertex of the region ($z \bmod d$) is greater than $w/2$, the polygon in question will not be completely covered by the number of rows equal to z/d, and accordingly the correct number of rows in the trajectory will be equal to $z/d + 1$. Each segment of the resulting global trajectory corresponds to exactly two turning points, so the total number of turns within the global coverage trajectory can be determined according to the following expression:

$$n = \{2z \backslash d, \text{ if } z \bmod d \le w/2 \, 2(z \backslash d + 1), \text{ if } z \bmod d > w/2. \tag{2}$$

As we can see, the number of turns on the trajectory depends strictly on the value of z, since the distance d is set when the task is formulated and remains unchanged during the mission. The parameter z, in turn, depends on the length of ls and on the value of w. This implies the conclusion that at a constant target operating height of the UAV, the number of turns on the trajectory is determined by the length ls and to reduce the number of turns, the length ls should be minimized. In other words, it is necessary to determine the optimal line sweep direction. The calculation of the optimal line sweep direction is a well-known and already solved problem and can be performed according to the algorithm presented in [21]. Accordingly, the construction of the coating trajectory is carried out by applying the back and forth pattern motion along the optimal line sweep direction [24, 25], after which the found trajectory is smoothed by the cubic interpolation method. The resulting trajectory is an adjacency graph consisting of an array of coordinates of waypoints with the previously calculated distance from each other. Thus, according to the results of the first stage of the proposed method, the optimal reciprocating trajectory of the coverage of the study area is formed.

At the next step of the developed method, the global covering trajectory is decomposed into related sets of waypoints (trajectory segments) distributed among the agents of the group, taking into account the current parameters of the UAV, distances to the formed segments, and the total expected time of the mission. To perform this step, this paper proposes to use the strategy of routing and distribution of trajectories between the agents of the group, implemented in the BINPAT [26] algorithm. This algorithm allows you to successfully generate sets of waypoints and distribute them among agents depending on the distance to the coverage area, as well as the assigned flight altitude and UAV characteristics.

An important parameter in the formation and distribution of waypoint sets is the total time to complete the mission. Assuming a constant average speed for each UAV, the total mission time T_k over the coverage area for a group of k UAVs can be modeled as follows [26]:

$$T_k = \sum_{i=1}^{N} \sum_{j=1}^{N} \frac{D_{ij}}{V_{ij}^k} M_{ij}^k + Hd^k, \text{ where } Hd^k = \frac{h_m^k + \Delta h^k}{V_a^k} + \frac{h_m^k + \Delta h^k}{V_d^k}. \quad (3)$$

Within the above expression, D_{ij} represents the cost of the flight distance between two nodes, V_{ij}^k represents the UAV flight speed. The binary variable M_{ij}^k determines whether the k-th UAV moves from point i to j. Hd^k is the delay caused by having different assigned altitudes for the UAV. The value of Hd^k depends on the assigned mission altitude (h_m^k), ascent rate (V_a^k), descent rate (V_d^k), and the difference between assigned altitudes and mission altitudes (Δh^k) of those involved agents. The total mission time will be equal to the maximum operation time of the kth UAV, taking into account the restrictions associated with the continuity of the trajectories of each of the agents.

Thus, the proposed method builds the global coverage trajectory minimizing the total mission execution time, taking into account the current parameters and the position of the UAVs involved, which potentially allows you to effectively solve the problem of building high-precision three-dimensional maps of vast territories by the group of UAV. The following describes the evaluation of the implementation of the proposed method for planning the coverage trajectory when a group of UAVs perform aerial monitoring of the area.

4 Experiments

To evaluate the effectiveness of the proposed solution, a number of experiments were carried out on the formation of three-dimensional maps of the area based on data from the onboard depth cameras of the group of UAVs. As part of the experiment, the accuracy of mapping of the area was evaluated. It is necessary, because the accuracy of the available height cartogram of the area has one of the main roles in marking the zones for the placement of seismic sensors.

The experiment was carried out in the Gazebo simulator using the ROS software package. An Intel RealSense D455 [27] camera was installed on the UAV as a depth sensor. As part of the experiment, a depth camera was chosen to build an actual elevation map of the area, since it has a relatively low cost, sufficient visibility range (up to 10 m), and the accuracy of building a map reaches 10–15 cm. In order to use the data from the depth camera obtained during the experiment, the results were recorded in bag-files of the ROS system. For the mapping, the Cartographer software package was used. It makes possible to restore the terrain height map based on various data sets in post-processing mode. Within the framework of the ROS software package, there are no differences between the data obtained from the recorded bag-file and the UAV data received in real time. The ROS bag files contain all the necessary data from the UAV moving along the terrain coverage trajectories, which were generated based on the method proposed in this paper.

Experimental testing of the developed solution for constructing area coverage trajectories for the implementation of aerial monitoring missions was carried out in the Gazebo simulator with subsequent processing of the obtained data using the Cartographer software package. The group of agents involved consisted of four multi-rotor UAVs (iris). An example of the original terrain model is shown in Fig. 3a, and the corresponding results of generating a terrain map using the developed solution are shown in Fig. 3b.

a)   b)

Fig. 3. An example of simulation: a) the original model of the terrain map b) the results of generating the terrain map using the developed solution.

As a result of a series of experiments, several reconstructed maps of areas were obtained. The map data was presented in the form of an Occupancy Grid. The occupancy grid is a two-dimensional interpretation of a map in space. The occupancy grid is a grid, each cell of which is characterized by a certain state. A cell can assume one of three states:

occupied, free, and unknown. In the experiments carried out, the occupancy grids of the reconstructed maps were changed so that their cells had only two values: occupied (black) and free (white), since such a transformation makes possible to significantly simplify the process of comparing maps. To compare the original maps with the obtained results using the developed solution, the maps were aligned and the difference metrics were calculated. Alignment was performed using the ICP (Iterative Nearest Point) [28] algorithm, which allows you to find such a transformation that minimizes the error of the sum of distances from each point of the map built by Cartographer to the nearest neighboring point on the reference map. As a difference metric in this paper, we used the metric described in [29], which calculates the average distance to the nearest neighbor (ADNN) as the sum of all distances divided by the number of occupied cells:

$$ADNN = \frac{\sum_{i=1}^{N} Nearest\_Neighbour(occupied\_grid\_cell(i))}{N}, \tag{4}$$

where N is the number of occupied cells.

As a result of the experiment with ten different areas, the average value of the recovery error calculated using the ADNN metrics was determined relative to the original simulated areas. The resulting deviation of the reconstructed maps from the original models in the framework of the experiment averaged 13.01 cm. In conclusion, the proposed solution provides a high quality of generation of terrain coverage trajectories and makes it possible to successfully carry out missions for aerial monitoring of the certain area by the group of UAVs in order to form high-precision three-dimensional maps of the area in various domains [30].

5 Conclusion

In order to increase the level of automation of seismic work, a specialized method for planning the coverage trajectory for the group of UAVs was developed to perform aerial monitoring of territories for marking out the zones for installing seismic modules. The proposed solution makes it possible to successfully generate high-precision three-dimensional maps of the study areas, which are one of the key input data in solving the problem of marking the zones for seismic sensors. The advantages of the developed method are its low computational complexity, as well as the possibility of application in the presence of dynamic obstacles. This solution minimizes the total execution time of the monitoring mission by decomposing the global covering trajectory and distributing the UAV between the received terrain.

This study shows that the developed method for planning the coverage trajectory by a group of UAVs makes it possible to effectively solve the problem of forming high-precision three-dimensional maps of the certain area. Based on the results of the experiments, using the developed solution, it was possible to restore a number of maps of simulated areas with an average error in the ADNN metric of 13.01 cm. In the future, the proposed solution can be modified by introducing new algorithms for the decomposition of the global coverage trajectory, as well as methods for smoothing the covering trajectories.

Acknowledgements. This research is supported by RSF project No. 22-69-00231, https://rscf.ru/project/22-69-00231/.

References

1. Shahzad, A.Q., Lisa, M.: UAV-based photogrammetry and seismic zonation approach for earthquakes hazard analysis of pakistan. In: Ouaissa, M., Khan, I.U., Ouaissa, M., Boulouard, Z., Hussain Shah, S.B. (eds.) Computational Intelligence for Unmanned Aerial Vehicles Communication Networks. Studies in Computational Intelligence, vol. 1033, Springer, Cham (2022). https://doi.org/10.1007/978-3-030-97113-7_12
2. Shahzad, A.Q., Lisa, M., Khan, M.A., Khan, I.: UAV-based rescue system and seismic zonation for hazard analysis and disaster management. In: Ouaissa, M., Khan, I.U., Ouaissa, M., Boulouard, Z., Hussain Shah, S.B. (eds.) Computational Intelligence for Unmanned Aerial Vehicles Communication Networks. Studies in Computational Intelligence, vol. 1033. Springer, Cham (2022). https://doi.org/10.1007/978-3-030-97113-7_14
3. Bonali, F.L., Corti, N., Russo, E., Marchese, F., Fallati, L., Pasquaré Mariotto, F., Tibaldi, A.: Commercial-UAV-based structure from motion for geological and geohazard studies. In: Bonali, F.L., Pasquaré Mariotto, F., Tsereteli, N. (eds) Building Knowledge for Geohazard Assessment and Management in the Caucasus and other Orogenic Regions. NATO Science for Peace and Security Series C: Environmental Security. Springer, Dordrecht (2021). https://doi.org/10.1007/978-94-024-2046-3_22
4. Croce, V., Diamantidis, D., Sýkora, M.: Seismic damage evaluation and decisions on interventions supported by UAV-based surveys. In: Vayas, I., Mazzolani, F.M. (eds.) Protection of Historical Constructions. PROHITECH 2021. Lecture Notes in Civil Engineering, vol. 209. Springer, Cham (2022). https://doi.org/10.1007/978-3-030-90788-4_20
5. Ragab, A.R., Isaac, M.S.A., Luna, M.A., Flores Peña, P.: WILD HOPPER prototype for forest firefighting. Int. J. Online & Biomed. Eng. **17**(9), 148–168 (2021)
6. Chung, S.J., Paranjape, A.A., Dames, P., Shen, S., Kumar, V.: A survey on aerial swarm robotics. IEEE Trans. Rob. **34**(4), 837–855
7. Zhou, Y., Rao, B., Wang, W.: UAV swarm intelligence: Recent advances and future trends. IEEE Access **8**, 183856–183878 (2020)
8. Madridano, A., Al-Kaff, A., Martín, D.: Trajectory planning for multi-robot systems: Methods and applications Expert Syst. Appl. **173**, 114660 (2021)
9. Galceran, E., Carreras, M.: A survey on coverage path planning for robotics. Robot. Auton. Syst. **61**, 1258–1276 (2013)
10. Darintsev, O., Migranov, A.: Analytical review of approaches to the distribution of tasks for mobile robot teams based on soft computing technologies. Inform. Autom. 21(4), 729–757 (2022). https://doi.org/10.15622/ia.21.4.4
11. Otto, A., Agatz, N., Campbell, J., Golden, B., Pesch, E.: Optimization approaches for civil applications of unmanned aerial vehicles (UAVs) or aerial drones: a survey. Networks **72**, 411–458 (2018)
12. Cabreira, T.M., Brisolara, L.B., Paulo R.F.J.: Survey on coverage path planning with unmanned aerial vehicles. Drones **3**(1), 4 (2019)
13. Valente, J., Sanz, D., Del Cerro, J., Barrientos, A. de Frutos, M.Á.: Near-optimal coverage trajectories for image mosaicing using a mini quad-rotor over irregular-shaped fields. Precision Agric. **14**(1), 115–132 (2013)
14. Torres, M., Pelta, D.A., Verdegay, J.L. Torres, J.C.: Coverage path planning with unmanned aerial vehicles for 3D terrain reconstruction. Expert Syst. Appl. **55**, 441–451 (2016)

15. Pham, T.H., Bestaoui Y., Mammar S.: Aerial robot coverage path planning approach with concave obstacles in precision agriculture. In: Workshop on Research, Education and Development of Unmanned Aerial Systems (RED-UAS), pp. 43–48. IEEE (2017)

16. Muñoz, J., López, B., Quevedo, F., Monje, C.A., Garrido, S. Moreno, L.E.: Multi UAV coverage path planning in urban environments. Sensors 21(21), 7365 (2021)

17. Albani, D., Nardi, D., Trianni, V.: Field coverage and weed mapping by UAV swarms. In: Proceedings of the 2017 IEEE/RSJ International Conference on Intelligent Robots and Systems (IROS), pp. 4319–4325. Vancouver, BC, Canada (2017)

18. Choi, Y., Choi, Y., Briceno, S., Mavris, D.N.: Energy-constrained multi-UAV coverage path planning for an aerial imagery mission using column generation. J. Intell. Rob. Syst. 97(1), 125–139 (2020)

19. Liu, C., Zhang, S., Akbar, A.: Ground feature oriented path planning for unmanned aerial vehicle mapping. IEEE J. Sel. Top. Appl. Earth Obs. Remote. Sens. 12(4), 1175–1187 (2019)

20. Avellar, G.S., Pereira, G.A., Pimenta, L.C., Iscold, P.: Multi-UAV routing for area coverage and remote sensing with minimum time. Sensors 15, 27783–27803 (2015)

21. Huang, W.H.: Optimal line-sweep-based decompositions for coverage algorithms. In: Proceedings of the 2001 ICRA, IEEE International Conference on Robotics and Automation (Cat. No. 01CH37164), vol. 1, pp. 27–32. Seoul, Korea (2001)

22. Gao, J., Zheng, Y., Ni, K., Mei, Q., Hao, B., Zheng, L.: Fast path planning for firefighting UAV based on A-Star algorithm. In: Journal of Physics. Conference Series, vol. 2029(1), p. 012103, IOP Publishing (2021). DOI:https://doi.org/10.1088/1742-6596/2029/1/012103

23. Xiao S., Tan X., Wang J.: A simulated annealing algorithm and grid map-based UAV coverage path planning method for 3D reconstruction. Electronics 10 (7), 853 (2021)

24. Nam, L., Huang, L., Li, X., Xu, J.: An approach for coverage path planning for UAVs. In: Proceedings of the 2016 IEEE 14th International Workshop on Advanced Motion Control (AMC), pp. 411–416. Auckland, New Zealand (2016)

25. Wang, C., Liu, P., Zhang, T., Sun, J.: The adaptive vortex search algorithm of optimal path planning for forest fire rescue UAV. In: 2018 IEEE 3rd Advanced Information Technology, Electronic and Automation Control Conference (IAEAC), pp. 400–403. IEEE (2018)

26. Luna, M.A., Ale Isaac, M.S., Ragab, A.R., Campoy, P., Flores Peña, P. Molina, M.: Fast multi-UAV path planning for optimal area coverage in aerial sensing applications. Sensors 22(6), 2297 (2022)

27. Intel RealSense, https://www.intelrealsense.com, last accessed 2022/08/24

28. Pomerleau, F., Colas, F. Siegwart, R.: A review of point cloud registration algorithms for mobile robotics. Foundations and Trends® in Robotics 4(1), 1–104 (2015)

29. Santos, J.M., Portugal, D. Rocha, R.P.: October. An evaluation of 2D SLAM techniques available in robot operating system. In: 2013 IEEE international symposium on safety, security, and rescue robotics (SSRR), pp. 1–6. (2013)

30. Sevostyanova, N., Lebedev, I., Lebedeva, V., Vatamaniuk, I.: An innovative approach to automated photo-activation of crop acreage using UAVs to stimulate crop growth Inform. Autom. 20(6), 1395–1417 (2021). https://doi.org/10.15622/ia.20.6.8

Simulation Program Model of Mobile Robots Groups for Multi-Robotic Complex

Sergey Kapustyan, Eduard Melnik[iD], and Marina Orda-Zhigulina[(⊠)][iD]

Southern Scientific Center, Russian Academy of Sciences, 41, St. Chehova, 344006
Rostov-on-Don, Russia
jigulina@mail.ru

Abstract. This paper describes a model of a multi-robotic complex which is based on a previously developed method of robustly stable motion control of a group of mobile robots (MR) with a leader in solving monitoring problems by multi-robotic systems (MRS) in the presence of an indefinite, limited time delay in the communication channels of the MR-leader with group of MRs arising from the exchange of information through a distributed data registry. MR complex is a group of robots of various types and numbers. Any robot could carry various types of smart sensors. The effectiveness of the proposed model is achieved by a control system, the multidimensional digital control device with sufficiently high order. Algorithms for calculating the values of control actions are obtained using decomposing control and the method of analytical synthesis of systems with control by output and actions. It was achieved the property of robustness to deviations of uncertain delays in the communication channels of each MR by using the property of the previously proposed polynomial control equations. There were testing the performance and effectiveness of the proposed approach by the help of the simulation software model for the functioning of MR groups as MatLab numerical experiments.

Keywords: Decentralized decision support system · Blockchain · Robotics

1 Introduction

Resource reconfiguration [1] and distributed ledger technology [2] the both could be used to improve the efficiency of processing and transferring information, the reliability and "openness" of monitoring systems for various fields of application. At the same time, the distributed registry allows to synchronize the exchange of data between the nodes of the computer network. Previously, the authors developed the structure of a distributed decentralized system for monitoring and predicting hazardous natural processes [3] with a subsystem for collecting and processing data, a decision support subsystem, a distributed data storage model, and mobile tools for collecting data about environmental parameters. The integration of the system components was carried out on the basis of the developed set of methods for intelligent data processing, as well as the methodology previously proposed by the authors [4–6] of building highly reliable reconfigurable systems for processing information, providing access, storage and transmission of data based on a distributed registry, the method of information integration and the robust method and so on [7–10]. The interaction between mobile robots was organized using a multi-agent dispatcher. The dispatcher manages the group members which are connected to separate copies of the distributed registry. Integrating the mobile robotic complex into the developed structure of the monitoring and diagnostic system is shown in Fig. 1.

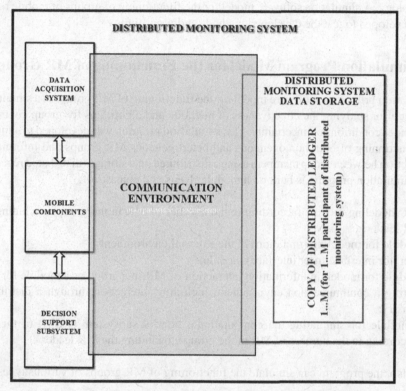

Fig. 1. The structure of a distributed monitoring system with a multi-robotic complex.

An analysis of the literature showed, the models of group interaction of robots in environmental monitoring are well developed theoretically [11]. At the same time there are less articles with real experimental results or numerical simulation results.

The authors have previously developed a "complex method" [3] for creating monitoring and diagnostic systems for various fields of application. Within the framework of this approach, a mobile robotic complex was used as mobile means. The mobile means contain a group of mobile robots (UAV robotic unmanned aerial vehicles) as terminal devices (sensors) for collecting information. Also, the UAVs have separate sensors or analyzers on board and realize photo and video shooting.

The problem of controlling a group of UAVs was solved for various delays and uncertainties between control signals

The monitoring system consists of a multi-robotic complex, a sub-system for collecting and storing information, a decision support sub-system, a distributed data storage and various software components that form a communication environment. Methods and algorithms for group control of robots within a group were developed [12–21] as part of the integration of a mobile robotic complex into a monitoring and diagnostic system. These developed methods eliminate the uncertainty in the transmission time of data for controlling robots to their on-board control devices through distributed ledger technology. A simulation software model for the functioning of groups of mobile robots was developed to test the developed methods and algorithms.

2   Simulation Program Model for the Functioning of MR Groups

Simulation program or software model for the functioning of MR groups is a simulation software for studying the effectiveness of methods and algorithms for group control of MR under conditions of uncertainty. This simulation program was developed to simulate the functioning of both homogeneous and heterogeneous MR groups and information interaction between group members using a distributed data storage (distributed registry). The simulation program is built on a modular basis and consists of:

– MR modeling module (according to the number of MR in the group), including the MR leader;
– module for modeling (imitation) of the external environment;
– operator interface (user interface) module;
– module for modeling information interaction of MR in a group or a module for simulating a communication environment, including interaction through a distributed registry;
– a module for simulating the computational control subsystem (CCM) of the MR (according to the number of MR in the group), including the MR leader.

Also, the program can simulate the functioning of MR groups of various types and sizes.

The operator interface provides the ability to:

– formation by the operator of various target tasks for MR groups;
– selection of the MR leader;
– setting the characteristics of the MR and the environment;
– visualization of the process of group functioning of MR;
– display of simulation results.

The structure of the software and hardware for simulation modeling of the MR group is generally shown in Fig. 2.

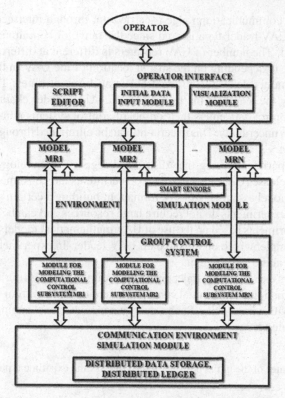

Fig. 2. The Structure of the simulation program for multi-robotic complex.

Also, the program model allows you to simulate the following types of uncertain-ty:

- uncertainty of the mathematical model of the control object, in this case, the MP group (or, for simplicity, the uncertainty of the control object);
- the uncertainty of the environment for the functioning of the MR group (or the model of the environment);
- uncertainty of the goal (or target task);
- uncertainty of data delay in information exchange channels, taking into ac-count restrictions on the maximum allowable delay time.

In addition, this model imitates the collective, flock and swarm types of self-organizing behavior of the MR group.

The simulation program can be implemented both on a single computer and in a local area network with a "client-server" architecture. The automated workstation of the operator is a server in this case.

Signals from the MR leader are received from the UAV, as well as the UAV from the leader with some time delay due to the random distribution of the group in space. Communication is carried out via a direct channel leader-UAV-leader if the UAV is within the range of the communication means. Communication with UAVs that are outside the direct communication range is carried out through intermediate UAVs that act as repeaters. UAV-leader type is used since the range of communication means of all types is limited. The number of UAV repeaters is different at different times and for different UAVs. It is depending on the spatial location of the UAV in these cases. This leads to an uncertainty delay for different UAVs at different times. The delay values are determined by the length of the leader-UAV-... -UAV-leader chain. Therefore, the necessary UAV control data enters their on-board control systems non-simultaneously, and this introduces uncertainty. This uncertainty can be eliminated through the distributed ledger technology.

Numerical experiments using the "distributed registry" technology for a group of 11 UAVs with a release (UAV 1). Also, these experiments are consumed in the MatLab environment on model examples of UAV formation, building a certain set, for example, a "wedge". Such experiments do not require large resources and can be used on a single computer. In experiments based on the use of UAV mathematical models and SGU group control systems implemented on the onboard UAV leader. In experiments, it was found that all UAVs are at the same height.

Figure 3 shows the movement trajectories of a group of 11 UAVs during the formation of a "wedge" formation for the initial coordinates and deviations from the given course given in Table 1 with a fixed delay. Such a delay occurs when exchanging control signals through a distributed ledger.

Table 1. Coordinates of the initial position of the UAV for the experiment presented in Fig. 3.

UAV	1	2	3	4	5	6	7	8	9	10	11
X	34	69	8	34	86	41	114	92	110	84	46
Y	10	18	69	43	102	115	24	73	72	89	30
ξ	0	0	0	0	0	0	0	0	0	0	0

ξ is the initial angle of deviation of each UAV from a given course ψ. The movement trajectories of a group of 11 UAVs are shown in Fig. 4 when forming a "wedge" formation for the initial coordinates and deviations from the given course given in Table 2 at fixed delays.

Figure 4 shows that the initial position of UAV 1 and UAV 11 differs significantly from the target values. Therefore, the UAV1 and UAV11 could not take the UAV's target positions in time. The difference from the previous experiment lies in the presence of initial angles of deviation from the given course ranging from minus 25 degrees to plus 25 degrees and other UAV initial coordinates. In this case, the UAVs reached the given target position, despite the existing delay in the exchange of information. This is due to the fact that the current deviation from the target position was insignificant.

Experiments have shown that the efficiency of solving the problems of group control of MR (UAV) strongly depends on the communication capabilities of the means of communication between the members of the group. The task of managing a group of UAVs was assigned to the computational control subsystem of the UAV leader, who was

Table 2. Coordinates of the initial position of the UAV for the experiment presented in Fig. 4.

UAV	1	2	3	4	5	6	7	8	9	10	11
X	75	10	93	52	37	61	95	45	64	113	66
Y	93	111	58	53	61	98	77	97	42	105	75
ξ	−14	4	−16	−1	−13	−14	−14	−10	17	−3	−15

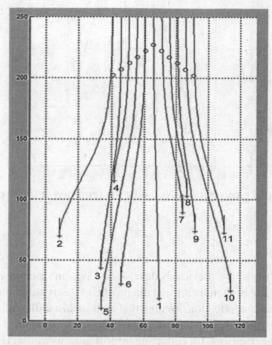

Fig. 3. Trajectories of a group of 11 UAVs during the formation of the "wedge" for the initial data in Table 1.

a member of the same group in the experiments. At the same time, the computational control subsystem of the leader forms the control of each UAV of the group through a distributed registry and takes into account the UAV response signals received via communication channels. UAV 1 and UAV 11 could not take the target positions at the specified time with this value of the initial data according to the results of the experiment. Therefore, it is necessary to look for new approaches to reduce the delay of information signals between the leader UAV and the group UAV through a distributed ledger.

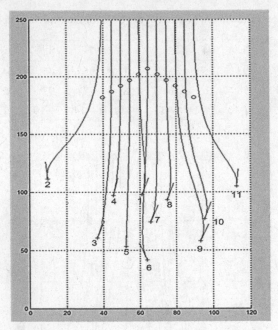

Fig. 4. Trajectories of a group of 11 UAVs during the formation of the "wedge" for the initial data in Table 2.

3 Conclusion

The authors of this work have previously developed a system structure and an "integrated method" for designing of monitoring and diagnostic systems based on the mobile components use for various applications. Within this approach, a multi-robot complex which is a group of mobile robots (unmanned aerial vehicles UAVs) was used as mobile components, as edge devices (sensors) for collecting information, as well as UAVs with separate sensors or analyzers on board. Methods and algorithms for controlling the robots group behavior have been developed for such a mobile robotic complex. To test the developed methods and algorithms, a simulation software model of the MR groups functioning was created. The method of the movement robustly stable control for a mobile robot's group with a leader was used as a base. This method takes in account specificity of solving of monitoring tasks with multi robot complexes in the presence of an indefinite, limited time delay in the communication channels of the MR leader with other MR in the group in case of data exchange, including through a distributed ledger. The mentioned method operability and effectiveness have confirmed using a simulation program and computing experiments in MatLab.

Also, the experimental studies results made it possible to conclude that further research is needed. Possible direction of this research may be the development of multi-robot complex management methods for monitoring and diagnostic tasks solving, in particular to minimize delays in communication channels in the organization of MR information interaction, including by minimizing the length of the data transmission chain MR-MR-...-MR-the leader and through the use of distributed ledger technology.

Acknowledgements. The study was carried out with the financial support of GZ No. 122020100270-3.

References

1. Kalyaev, I.A., Mel'nik, E.V.: Detsentralizovannye sistemy komp'yuternogo upravleniya: monografiya (Decentralized computer control: monograph). YuNTs RAN, Rostov-on-Don (2011)

2. Hedera hashgraph consensus and scalability: https://medium.com/@saratechnologiesinc/hedera-hashgraph-consensus-and-scalability-2315133a3e33

3. Orda-Zhigulina, M.V., Melnik, E.V., Ivanov, D.Y., Rodina, A.A., Orda-Zhigulina, D.V.: Combined method of monitoring and predicting of hazardous phenomena. In: Computer Science On-line Conference, pp. 55–61. Springer, Cham (2019)

4. Melnik, E.V., Orda-Zhigulina, M.V., Orda-Zhigulina, D.V.: Distributed library model based on distributed ledger technology for monitoring and diagnostics system. In: Computer Science On-line Conference, pp. 501–509. Springer, Cham (2021)

5. Melnik, E., Safronenkova, I., Kapustyan, S.: The efficiency improvement of robots group operation by means of workload relocation. In: International Conference on Interactive Collaborative Robotics, pp. 126–137. Springer, Cham (2021)

6. Gorelova, G., Melnik, E., Safronenkova, I.: The problem statement of cognitive modeling in social robotic systems. In: International Conference on Interactive Collaborative Robotics, pp. 62–75. Springer, Cham (2021)

7. Kapustyan, S.G., Orda-Zhigulina, D.V., Orda-Zhigulina, M.V., Prakapovich, R.A., Sychev, U.A.: Model of multi-robotic complex at the base of distributed registry for monitoring and diagnostics system. In: Computer Science On-line Conference, pp. 659–669. Springer, Cham (2021)

8. Gaiduk, A.R., Kapustyan, S.G.: Conceptual aspects of group application of unmanned aerial vehicles. J. Inf. Measur. Control Syst. **10**(7), 8–16 (2012)

9. Gaiduk, A.R., Kapustyan, S.G., Plaksienko, E.A., Kolokolova, K.V.: Multiagent control by parallel structure mechanisms based on the decoupled approach. Sci. Bull. Novosibir. State Tech. Univ. **1**(70), 51–66 (2018). (In Russ.)

10. Gaiduk, A.R., Martjanov, O.V., Medvedev, M.Y., Pshikhopov, V.K., Hamdan, N., Farhood, A.: Neural network based control system for robots group operating in 2-d uncertain environment. Mekhatr. Avtomat. Upr. **21**(8), 470–479 (2020). (In Russ.)

11. Boguslavskiy, A.A., Borovin, G.K., Kartashev, V.A., Pavlovsky, V.E., Sokolov, S.M.: Models and algorithms for intelligent control systems. M: IPM im. MV Keldysh (2019). (In Russ.)

12. Utkin, L.V., Zaborovsky, V.S., Popov, S.G.: Siamese neural network for intelligent information security control in multi-robot systems. Autom. Control. Comput. Sci. **51**(8), 881–887 (2017). https://doi.org/10.3103/S0146411617080235

13. Darintsev, O., Migranov, A.: Analytical review of approaches to the distribution of tasks for mobile robot teams based on soft computing technologies. Infor. Automat. **21**(4), 729–757 (2022). https://doi.org/10.15622/ia.21.4.4

14. Galin, R., Shiroky, A., Magid, E., Meshcheryakov, R., Mamchenko, M.: Effective functioning of a mixed heterogeneous team in a collaborative robotic system. Informat. Automat. **20**(6), 1224–1253 (2021). https://doi.org/10.15622/ia.20.6.2

15. De Moraes, R.S., de Freitas, E.P.: Distributed control for groups of unmanned aerial vehicles performing surveillance missions and providing relay communication network services. J. Intell. Robot. Syst. **92**(3), 645–656 (2018)

16. Gerla, M., Yi, Y.: Team communications among autonomous sensor swarms. ACM SIGMOD Rec. **33**(1), 20–25 (2004)
17. Zhu, Y., Su, H., Krstic, M.: Adaptive backstepping control of uncertain linear systems under unknown actuator delay. Automatica **54**, 256–265 (2015)
18. Nakayama, A., Ruelas, D., Savage, J., Bribiesca, E.: Teleoperated service robot with an immersive mixed reality interface. Informat. Automat. **20**(6), 1187–1223 (2021). https://doi. org/10.15622/ia.20.6.1
19. Endo, T., Maeda, R., Matsuno, F.: Stability analysis of swarm heterogeneous robots with limited field of view. Informat. Automat. **19**(5), 942–966 (2020). https://doi.org/10.15622/ia. 2020.19.5.2
20. Stojanović, S.B., Debeljković, D.L., Antić, D.S.: Finite-time stability analysis of discrete time-delay systems using discrete convolution of delayed states. Fact. Univ. Ser: Automat. Control Robot. **14**(3), 147–158 (2015)
21. Xue, L., Zhang, T., Zhang, W., Xie, X.J.: Global adaptive stabilization and tracking control for high-order stochastic nonlinear systems with time-varying delays. IEEE Trans. Autom. Control **63**(9), 2928–2943 (2018)

Algorithm for Replacing the Battery of a Robotic Tool Using Servicing Mobile Robots on Inhomogeneous Surfaces

Polina Kozyr⬤, Yuliya Vasunina⁽✉⁾, and Anton Saveliev⬤

St. Petersburg Federal Research Center of the Russian Academy of Sciences, 39, 14th Line, 199178 St. Petersburg, Russia
yuliya.vasunina@gmail.com

Abstract. The paper proposes an algorithm for replacing the battery of a robotic tool (RT) by a group of servicing mobile robots (SMR), which includes: positioning the SMR under the battery compartment of the RT; removal of the discharged and installation of a charged battery. For the positioning of the SMR, data from the LiDAR are used, on the basis of which the RT wheels are clustered and the set of necessary offsets for positioning is determined. Then positioning is carried out according to ArUco markers, images of which the system receives using cameras. After that, according to the data from the MEMS sensor, the platform is leveled in a horizontal plane, when positioning on an inhomogeneous surface. The proposed algorithm was implemented using ROS (Robotic Operating System) and tested in the Gazebo simulator. As a result of the experiments, mobile robots successfully removed and installed a battery, the average battery replacement time based on the developed algorithm on a homogeneous surface was 4 min 8 s, on a non-uniform surface 6 min 4 s. The advantage of the developed solution is the completely autonomous replacement of the battery, which reduces the idle time of the RT.

Keywords: Battery Replacement · Positioning · LiDAR · ArUco Markers · Mobile Robots

1 Introduction

Currently, there are more and more autonomous robotic systems (RS) that help people in production, in medicine, in the field of space exploration, military and agricultural fields, as well as in the household and entertainment sectors. For long-term and efficient performance of the necessary functions by a robot without human intervention, it is necessary to fully automate both the work process itself and the processes associated with servicing the RT. Since the use of the RT is characterized by a relationship between its operating time and the power limitations of the battery and involves constant recharging of the battery to continue operation, the development of systems for autonomous change of the RT battery is an urgent task. Ensuring accurate positioning of these systems relative to the RT is essential for battery replacement. In addition, it is important that the autonomous battery change system be able to move itself to the RT and dock with it.

© The Author(s), under exclusive license to Springer Nature Switzerland AG 2022
A. Ronzhin et al. (Eds.): ICR 2022, LNCS 13719, pp. 269–283, 2022.
https://doi.org/10.1007/978-3-031-23609-9_24

2 Current State of Research

To date, there are solutions that are aimed at overcoming the problem of inaccurate positioning of the robot with the charging station and ensuring efficient recharging of the RT. In particular, article [1] presents a positioning system for a mobile robot with a wireless charger based on displacement-sensitive coils. With the help of camera data and computer vision, the robot is positioned relative to the charger and is located above it. Sensing coils are fixed symmetrically around the wireless receiver and measure the magnetic flux density around the receiver. The robot successfully approaches and positions itself within ± 5mm of the center of the wireless charger in the experiments performed.

In [2], the search for the location of the charging station by the robot is carried out by turning it around its axis and detecting the ArUco marker fixed on the charging station. The accuracy of docking the robot with the charging station by the presented method was within 50 mm.

In similar research [3], the authors of the work presented a method for moving a cleaning robot to a charging station for recharging, the principle of which is based on the use of infrared (IR) LEDs and a camera. The charging station is equipped with IR LEDs that illuminate the area where the robot can wirelessly recharge. The docking process is determined by the number of infrared spots at the charging station, registered by the robotic system, using a rotating camera mounted on the robot. According to the results of the experiments, the average time of positioning the robot relative to the charging station by this method was 31 s.

The article [4] presents a charging method with automatic docking for a mobile robot based on infrared and ultrasonic sensors. Two ultrasonic sensors mounted on the robot are used to make the latter move along the wall. Two infrared receivers on the robot are needed to detect the charging station, which has two infrared emitters. The positioning error of the robot by the presented method was 20 mm.

In the study [5], the search for a charging station also occurs using rangefinders. The mobile robot uses the laser rangefinder mounted on it to find the charging station and calculates the trajectory of movement to it. The charging station has two holes for connecting to the mobile robot charger and a guide rod that specifies the insertion direction of the mobile robot contacts into the charging holes. The authors performed 100 robot positioning, docking and recharging experiments, as a result, the entire process of recharging a mobile robot was successful in 99% of cases. In [6], the positioning process of robots is based on three stages. First, based on computer vision, a preliminary adjustment of the position of the robot relative to the charging station is carried out. Then the precise positioning of the robotic system takes place using four Hall sensors, which measure the distance to the corresponding magnets on the target module and calculate the trajectory for the movement of the RT. The positioning time based on this method was 21 s.

As can be seen from the above review [4–6], in RT recharging systems, the task of positioning objects relative to each other is fundamental. In study [7], the preliminary positioning of two robots relative to each other is based on the data of a wireless vision sensor. The precise positioning is carried out using Hall sensors. After positioning the two robots are docked using a hook-type connection. The whole process of docking two robots took 2 min, 70% of the experiments were successful.

The authors of [8] presented a docking system for two mobile robots based on the use of IR receivers and IR emitters. Positioning is determined by the search for the IR signal of the emitter located on one robot, the IR receiver of another robot. In [9], the mobile robot was also positioned relative to the charging station using IR sensors. The experiments showed that the docking was successful in 90% of the experiments.

In [10], the determination of the position of the charging station is implemented based on the use of technical vision and AprilTag fiducial markers. The positioning process is divided into two parts, in one of which the robot moves using the ORB-SLAM algorithm, in the other one positioning occurs based on the marker position data obtained after processing the camera image. In 97.33% of the experiments, the positioning and docking of the mobile robot with the charging station were successful.

The authors of similar article [11] used a stereo camera to determine the position and orientation of the final positioning point of a mobile robot relative to a pallet with fiducial markers. As a result of the experiments, the positioning offset was 0.057 m, the deviation in angle was 0.043 radians. The presented system is not completely autonomous, since the robot approached the target under the control of the operator, after which the robot was automatically docked.

In [4], IR sensors are used for preliminary positioning of a mobile robot relative to the charging station. Precise positioning is realized on the basis of ultrasonic sensors. The authors of [12] use algorithms for processing sound vibrations and technical vision methods to find the direction of movement of the robot. As a result of experiments, using this method, the robot always found and followed a short path to the target. The study [13] presents an algorithm for searching and moving a mobile robot to a charging station based on IR sensor data and technical vision. The essence of the proposed algorithm is that during a mobile robot positioning, the center of the QR code must coincide with the center of the image. The positioning time based on this algorithm varies from 4 min to 40 s, depending on the complexity of the trajectory of movement to the charging station.

Wireless charging technologies [14, 15] allow batteries to be recharged, however, this process takes a long time. In order for the robots to perform their functions without wasting time for recharging, a system can be used that can provide replacement of the battery. The article [16] presents an automatic battery replacement system for a palm-sized wheeled mobile robot. The mobile robot is equipped with a built-in camera and a removable battery compartment on the front. The battery change station is a device consisting of a loading and unloading mechanism, a movable device, a locking device and a carcase. The developed system was tested, the results of the experiments showed that it takes an average of 84.2 s to complete the battery replacement operations.

The authors of the article [17] also presented in their work a battery replacement system for a mobile robot. The worker robot constantly monitors the battery charge and its location. If the battery charge falls below a certain threshold, the server sends a command to the helper robot to change a battery of the worker robot. The process of docking two robots is based on the analysis of the emission of five infrared LEDs of the mobile robot by a computer vision algorithm, which aligns the axes between the two robots. When docking has occurred, the slot in which the discharged battery is located releases the lock, unfastens it, and the battery enters the battery exchange mechanism. At the same time, using the battery exchange mechanism, a new battery is installed in the second slot of the working robot. According to the results of the experiments, the positioning error of the robots relative to each other was 12.5 mm. Docking of the robots was achieved in all experiments.

In the review of works presented above, the battery was recharged by positioning the robot relative to the wireless charging station, as well as by moving the target RT to the base to remove the battery. Since the use of the wireless charging method is characterized by a long idle time of the RT, in this study it was decided to remove the battery and replace it with a new one. In order to refuse to move the RT to the battery change station and minimize the downtime of the RT, the replacement of the battery at the target RT according to the developed algorithm is carried out using two servicing mobile robots (SMRs). This work is devoted to the development of an algorithm for autonomous recharging of the RT, using SMRs, which does not require human intervention. Further, the paper presents the algorithm for replacing the battery, the design of the battery module on the target RT, the design of small SMRs, as well as the processes of positioning the SMR relative to the battery compartment of the target RT, removing the old battery and installing a new battery.

3   Results Suggested Algorithm for Automatic Battery Replacement

In the framework of this work, an algorithm for automatic replacement of the RT battery using two SMRs was developed. One small robot removes the discharged battery from the RT, further in the work it will be called SMR-1. The second robot installs a charged battery in the RT and will be called SMR-2 in the future.

3.1   Description of Robots

The proposed conceptual model (Fig. 1a) of the service platform has a wheel-pedipulator type of propellers. This type of propellers allows to adjust the height of the platform body by changing the angle of inclination of the pedipulators and provides linear movement due to wheel drives.

The SMR body (Fig. 1a) allows you to place: a slot for a removable battery (1), a webcam (2), with changeable orientation horizontally for detecting ArUco markers and vertically for monitoring the environment, as well as a LiDAR (3) for detecting obstacles during the movement of the robot, as well as for its positioning relative to the RT. To check the success of the removal and subsequent installation of the battery a capacitive matrix of pressure sensors (4) is installed in the groove. The platform is equipped with drive wheels with separate control on the drive to the wheel (5), as well as drives that control the rotation of the paws installed in the body (6).

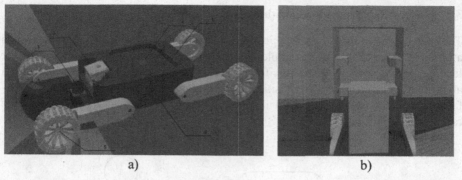

a)   b)

Fig. 1. (a) View of the SMR, where 1 is Battery groove, 2 is Webcam, 3 is LiDAR, 4 is Pressure sensor, 5 is Drive wheels with separate wheel drive control, 6 is Platform body; (b) Location of the RT battery compartment.

For easy battery replacement, the RT battery compartment is U-shaped and is located at the rear of the RT (Fig. 1b). This location of the compartment allows you to optimize the algorithms for installing and removing the battery due to the exit and arrival of the SMR in a raised position. Energy transfer between the battery and the target RT in the battery compartment (Fig. 2a) is carried out using contact pairs.

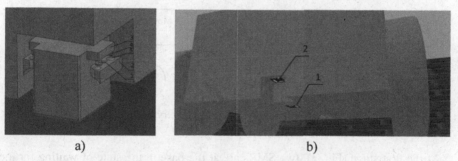

a)   b)

Fig. 2. (a) Battery compartment structure, where 1 is contact pads, 2 is RT battery compartment fasteners, 3 is battery container, 4 is centering pins, 5 is centering holes; (b) Location of ArUco markers.

The contact pads (1) are located on the fasteners (2) of the battery compartment, and the contacts themselves are located on the battery container (3). To prevent displacements in the horizontal plane, the battery container is equipped with centering pins (4) for installation in the centering grooves (5) of the mating part of the battery compartment. Fixation in the frontal plane occurs due to the own weight of the battery.

ArUco markers are used for positioning the mobile robot relative to the battery compartment. The location of the ArUco markers is shown in Fig. 2b. ArUco marker number 1 is located next to the battery compartment and is used in the task of extracting a discharged battery, ArUco marker number 2 is located on the inner surface of the battery compartment and is used to install a charged battery.

3.2 Battery Replacement Algorithm

The need for autonomous battery replacement using SMR arises both in work areas with a uniform, even surface, for example, in warehouses, industrial enterprises and other facilities, and in areas with a non-uniform surface, for example, in fields. The developed algorithm is universal both for positioning on inhomogeneous and homogeneous surfaces. The scheme of the developed algorithm for replacing the battery with two mobile robots is shown in Figs. 3–5.

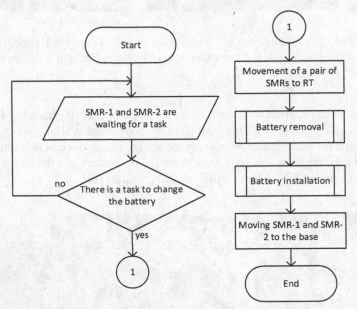

Fig. 3. Algorithm for replacing the battery using SMR.

At the first stage (Fig. 3), two SMRs are at the base in the state of waiting for the task. A charged battery is located in the SMR-2 slot, for subsequent installation on the RT. When a message comes from the RT about the need to replace the battery, mobile robots go into the state of moving along the global trajectory. The construction of the trajectory from the base to the RT and the movement according to it is based on the data of the LiDARs installed on each robot, using the LRLHD-A global trajectory planning algorithm [18].

Upon reaching the end point of the global trajectory, SMR-1 stops immediately before the target RT and enters the positioning state (Fig. 4). For the primary positioning of the SMR-1 relative to the RT, the position of the RT was corrected based on the clustering of data from the LiDAR. Then he rotates the camera so that the camera provides a vertical upward view, while the SMR-2 is in the standby mode.

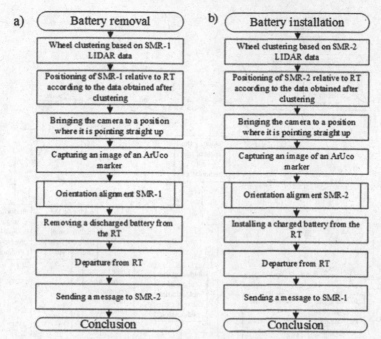

Fig. 4. Stages of the battery replacement algorithm using SMR: (a) removing a discharged battery, (b) installing a charged battery.

Upon reaching the end point of the global trajectory, SMR-1 stops immediately before the target RT and enters the positioning state (Fig. 4). For the primary positioning of the SMR-1 relative to the RT, the position of the RT was corrected based on the clustering of data from the LiDAR. Then he rotates the camera so that the camera provides a vertical upward view, while the SMR-2 is in the standby mode.

After turning the SMR-1 camera, the first ArUco marker, located next to the RT battery compartment, should fall into its field of view (Fig. 5). When it is detected, SMR-1 using the OpenCV library determines the angles of deviation of the camera plane from the marker plane. In addition, SMR-1 receives data from the MEMS sensor about the roll (α) and pitch (β) angles. If there are deviations, SMR-1 corrects the orientation of the platform body according to the algorithm shown in Fig. 5a. Depending on the value of the deviation angle, SMR-1 adjusts the position of the body by changing the angle of inclination of the pedipulators. In the process of adjusting the orientation of the SMR-1, its height increases by reducing the angle of inclination of the pedipulators, however, to drive under the serviced robot, it is necessary that the height of the SMR-1 body does not exceed 80 mm. If this value is exceeded, the replacement of the battery with a given accuracy cannot be completed, and SMR and RT will need to choose a more even surface. Deviations within 3 degrees mean that the platform is in a suitable RT orientation and can continue positioning relative to the battery compartment according to the ArUco marker. When the SMR-1 reaches the set position relative to the RT, it enters the battery removal state. The robot raises the body to the maximum possible upper position. With

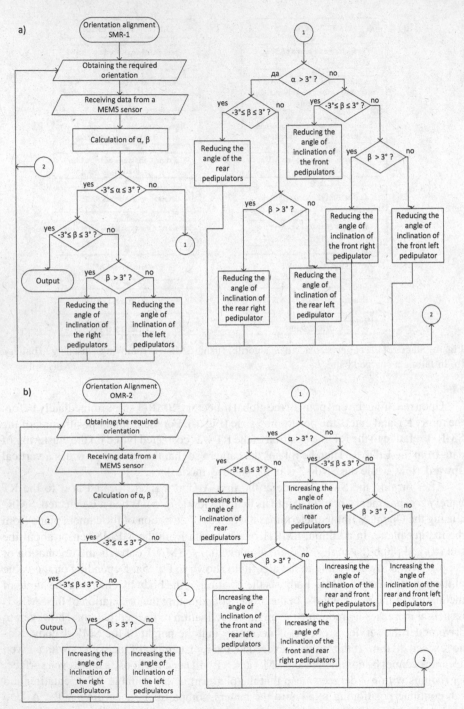

Fig. 5. (a) SMR-1 orientation alignment algorithm when removing a discharged battery from the RT (b) SMR-2 orientation alignment algorithm when installing a charged battery in the RT.

correct positioning, the center of the groove for the battery is located strictly in the center of the RT battery compartment, and, accordingly, in the center of the battery.

As a result of lifting, the battery enters the groove of the mobile robot and rises from the mating fasteners of the battery compartment, after which the robot receives feedback from the pressure sensor. Then SMR-1 moves with the battery in the opposite direction until the second ArUco marker is detected. After detecting marker 2, SMR-1 returns the body of the platform to its original position for subsequent transportation of the battery to the charging station.

Having received a message about the completion of the battery removal procedure, the SMR-2 is positioned with the battery compartment of the RT similarly to the positioning of the SMR-1, except that SMR-2 corrects the orientation of the platform body according to the algorithm shown in Fig. 5b. In the process of correcting the orientation of the SMR-2, its height is reduced by increasing the angle of inclination of the pedipulators. The design features of the developed battery replacement system impose restrictions on the position of the body before driving under the serviced robot, i.e., the height before driving should not be less than 120 mm. After completion of the rise, SMR-2 starts moving forward until marker 1 is in the center of the frame. After alignment, the marker should be in the center of the frame, this will mean that the battery is located exactly in the center battery compartment and can be installed. The SMR-2 case is lowered to its original position, as a result, the battery falls into the centering grooves. In case of successful installation of the battery, the feedback from the pressure sensors will show the absence of objects in the groove, then SMR-2, together with SMR-1, return to the base.

4 Materials and Methods

The positioning of SMR relative to the battery compartment was carried out according to the data obtained from the LiDAR and images of ArUco markers. Clustering of RT wheels based on LiDAR data was carried out using the DBSCAN algorithm [19]. Then, from all the points assigned to two separate wheel clusters, two reference points were selected for each cluster. Figure 6a shows an example of wheel clustering results.

The reference point of the left cluster was considered to be the point with the largest value along the X axis and the smallest value along the Y axis. The reference point of the right cluster was considered the point with the smallest value along the X axis and the smallest value along the Y axis. Based on the coordinates of these points the center between the two RT wheels along the X axis, the offset of the center point relative to the LiDAR origin along the X axis, angle between the LiDAR orientation vector and the vector between the LiDAR origin point and the center point between the two wheels are calculated. To be centered between the wheels of the RT along the X axis the SMR performs a turn at the calculated angle so that the orientation of the RT coincided with the orientation of the SMR and moves to the side by the calculated offset.

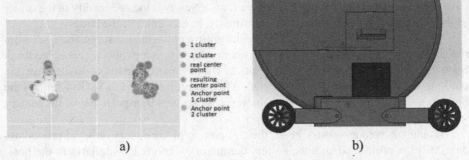

Fig. 6. (a) An example of wheel clustering results; (b) Positioning of the mobile robot relative to the RT battery compartment, where A is the distance between the center of ArUco marker 1 (Cm1) and the center of the battery compartment (Cbc), B is the distance between the center of the camera (Cc) and the center of the slot (Cs) on the body of SMR. A and B are equal according to the requirements for the design of the SMR and the battery compartment of the target RT.

After the completion of the procedure for positioning the SMR based on data obtained by LiDAR, the camera was rotated upwards using a servo drive. With this position of the camera, when an ArUco marker is detected on the frame, there is no heterogeneity in height between the camera and the ArUco marker. If the marker was not found after the camera turned, then the robot moved forward at a speed of 0.5 m/s until the marker appeared in the camera's field of view.

The RT battery compartment and the SMRs groove are arranged in such a way that the distance between the center of the marker detected by ArUco and the center of the battery compartment is equal to the distance between the center of the camera and the center of the slot on the body of the small robot, on which the charged battery is installed evenly (Fig. 8b). The main condition for accurate positioning is the coincidence of the center and orientation of the ArUco marker with the center and orientation of the frame. From Fig. 8b it can be seen that the SMR and the battery compartment are designed in such a way that when the positioning condition for removing the discharged battery is met, the center of the groove and the center of the battery compartment will be on the same vertical line. Therefore, when the SMR-1 case is smoothly raised, the discharged battery will be located in the center of the groove. With a similar positioning relative to ArUco marker located in the battery compartment, the center of the battery compartment will be exactly above the center of the camera and the charged battery located on the SMR-2 body, when mounted on the RT, will enter exactly into the battery compartment while SMR-2 is moving forward.

The search for the coordinate of the ArUco marker center, determination of its angular and center coordinates was performed using computer vision algorithms provided by the OpenCV. For positioning on heterogeneous terrain using OpenCV methods and according to the gyroscope data, the angle of inclination of the platform body relative to the horizontal plane was determined. Based on the calculated angle, the angle of rotation of the pedipulators was corrected to align the platform body.

Next, the position of the robot was corrected so that the orientation of the camera frame coincided with the orientation of the marker. To do this, the SMR rotated to the right or to the left until the coordinates of marker corners 1 and 2, 3 and 4, respectively, had the same values along the Y axis.

After adjusting the orientation, the SMR was positioned in such a way that the center of the ArUco marker was in the center of the camera frame along the Y and X axes. If the coordinate of the ArUco marker center along the Y axis is greater than the value of half the height of the frame, then the robot slowly moves forward until this y coordinate is reached. Otherwise - the robot moves in the opposite direction. When adjusting the position of the robot along the X axis, similar actions were performed, but in this case, the robot moved to the right and left.

After making adjustments to the orientation and centering of the robot relative to the battery module, the positioning algorithm was completed, and the robot entered the battery removal state.

5 Experiments

The software for performing positioning, removing the discharged battery and installing a new battery is developed using ROS (Robotic Operating System).

To evaluate the operation of the algorithm presented in this paper, ten experiments were carried out on a homogeneous and inhomogeneous surface in the Gazebo simulator, during which a replacing the RT battery was carried out from the moment the robots moved to the target RT [20]. A camera with a resolution of 2592×1920 pixels was used. The size of the first and second ArUco markers was 60×60 mm. In carrying out the experiment on an inhomogeneous surface, the RT was located on a plane at an inclination of 15 degrees. Surface drops for SMR under RT do not exceed 6 mm.

For assessing the positioning accuracy of a mobile robot relative to the battery compartment according to the data obtained from the LiDAR and ArUco markers, the average deviation modulus (1) for 10 experiments related to each experiment is used:

$$\overline{\Delta y} = \frac{1}{m} \sum_{i=1}^{m} |\hat{y}_i - y_i|, \tag{1}$$

where m is the number of experiments performed, $\hat{y}_i$ is the expected result, y_i is the result obtained using the algorithm presented in this article.

Table 1 presents the results of the DBSCAN algorithm in the problem of wheel clustering and the search for reference points.

Table 1. The results of the DBSCAN algorithm in the problem of wheel clustering and the search for reference points.

Features of the location of SMR and RT wheels	$\overline{\Delta y}$
Clustering when SMRs is displaced relative to the central axis of the RT less than 120 mm	20 mm

(*continued*)

Table 1. (*continued*)

Features of the location of SMR and RT wheels	$\overline{\Delta y}$
Clustering when SMRs is displaced relative to the central axis of the RT more than 120 mm	57 mm
Clustering with deployed RT wheels less than 15°	17 mm
Clustering with RT wheels deployed more than 15°	65 mm

Table 2 presents the results of determining the displacement of the position and orientation of the robot relative to the center of the RT according to the data from the LiDAR.

Table 2. Results of experiments to assess the accuracy of determining the displacement of the position and orientation of the robot relative to the center of the RT.

Experiment Type		$\overline{\Delta y}$
Determination of the angle at which the robot needs to turn around	Initial angle < 15°	0.8°
	Initial angle > 15°	3.7°
Determining the size of the robot offset		13 mm

It can be seen from the table that at an initial angle between the orientation of the SMR and the RT after moving along the global trajectory to the RT, equal to less than 15°, the average deflection modulus is 0.8°, and at more than 15°–3.7°. The average modulus of deviation in determining the size of the offset of the robot was 13 mm. The obtained data on the positioning of a mobile robot with a target RT are presented in Table 3.

According to the results presented in Table 1, the average modulus of deviation of the positioning of the mobile robot relative to the battery compartment is within the allowable accuracy interval.

Table 3. Results of experiments to assess the positioning accuracy of a mobile robot relative to the battery compartment of the target RT.

Positioning type	$\overline{\Delta y}_x$, mm	$\overline{\Delta y}_y$, mm	Orientation deviation, degrees
Positioning by the first ArUco marker in the problem of extracting a discharged battery on a homogeneous surface	4.2	3.9	3

(*continued*)

Table 3. (*continued*)

Positioning type	$\overline{\Delta y_x}$, mm	$\overline{\Delta y_y}$, mm	Orientation deviation, degrees
Positioning by the second ArUco marker in the task of inserting a new battery on a homogeneous surface	4.9	4.5	4
Positioning by the first ArUco marker in the problem of extracting a discharged battery on an inhomogeneous surface	5.2	4.2	4
Positioning by the second ArUco marker in the task of inserting a new battery on an inhomogeneous surface	5.1	5.1	6

For the first marker, the average deflection modulus on a homogeneous surface was 4.2 mm along the X axis, 3.9 mm along the Y axis, on a inhomogeneous surface – 5.2 mm along the X axis, and 4.2 mm along the Y axis, respectively. For the second marker - 4.9mm, 4.5mm on a homogeneous surface and 5.1mm, 5.1mm on an inhomogeneous surface along the X and Y axes, respectively. The deviation of the orientation of the robot slot from the battery module on a homogeneous surface was less than 4 degrees, and on a non-uniform one - less than 6 degrees. According to the results of experiments carried out at Gazebo, during which a complete battery replacement cycle was implemented ten times, the robots successfully performed their target function. The average time to replace the battery on a homogeneous surface was 4 min 8 s, on a non-uniform surface 6 min 1 s. The difference in positioning time lies in the need to adjust the rotation angles of the pedipulator to align the orientation of the platform body. These results indicate that the developed system is able to replace the battery in a short time and reduce the idle time of the target RT both on homogeneous and inhomogeneous surfaces.

6 Conclusion

The algorithm for replacing the battery of the target RT with two servicing mobile robots presented in this study consists of the stages of positioning the servicing robot relative to the battery module of the target RT based on data from the LiDAR and the image of one of the two ArUco markers, the step of removing the battery and the step of installing a new battery. This algorithm is simple to implement, and allows you to replace the battery in a short time. The advantage of the proposed solution is that the target RT does not require time spent on moving to the base due to the use of SMR, the battery is replaced both when the RT and SMR are located both on a homogeneous flat surface and on an inhomogeneous one. This reduces the idle time of the target RT, since it will be able to perform its main tasks before the SMR approaches it and immediately after the battery is changed.

The developed algorithm can be used both for specific robots presented in this paper and in other robotic systems with the introduction of a similar battery compartment mechanism and the implementation of mobile robots with appropriate dimensions.

Acknowledgement. This research is supported by RSF project No. 20–79-10325. https://rscf.ru/project/20-79-10325/.

References

1. Yeung, E., Liu, Z., Hodas, N.O.: A koopman operator approach for computing and balancing gramians for discrete time nonlinear systems. In: 2018 Annual American Control Conference (ACC), pp. 337–344. IEEE (2018)
2. Romanov, A.M., Tararin, A A.: An automatic docking system for wheeled mobile robots. In: 2021 IEEE Conference of Russian Young Researchers in Electrical and Electronic Engineering (ElConRus), pp. 1040–1045. IEEE (2021)
3. Chang, C.L., Chang, C.Y., Tang, Z.Y., Chen, S.T.: High-efficiency automatic recharging mechanism for cleaning robot using multi-sensor. Sensors **18**(11), 3911 (2018)
4. Zhang, J., Cai, L., Chu, Y., Zhou, Q.: A sectional auto-docking charging control method for the mobile robot. In: 2019 IEEE International Conference on Mechatronics and Automation (ICMA), pp. 330–335. IEEE (2019)
5. Su, K.L., Liao, Y.L., Lin, S.P., Lin, S.F.: An interactive auto-recharging system for mobile robots. Int. J. Autom. Smart Technol. **4**(1), 43–53 (2014)
6. Zhu, Y., Jin, H., Zhang, X., Yin, J., Liu, P., Zhao, J.: A multi-sensory autonomous docking approach for a self-reconfigurable robot without mechanical guidance. Int. J. Adv. Robot. Syst. **11**(9), 146 (2014)
7. Liu, P., Zhu, Y., Cui, X., Wang, X., Yan, J., Zhao, J.: Multisensor-based autonomous docking for UBot modular reconfigurable robot. In 2012 IEEE International Conference on Mechatronics and Automation, pp. 772–776. IEEE (2012)
8. Won, P., Biglarbegian, M., Melek, W.: Development of an effective docking system for modular mobile self-reconfigurable robots using extended kalman filter and particle filter. Robotics **4**(1), 25–49 (2015)
9. Song, G., Wang, H., Zhang, J., Meng, T.: Automatic docking system for recharging home surveillance robots. Trans. Consum. Electron. **57**(2), 428–435 (2011)
10. Guangrui, F., Geng, W.: Vision-based autonomous docking and re-charging system for mobile robot in warehouse environment. In: 2017 2nd International Conference on Robotics and Automation Engineering (ICRAE), pp. 79–83. IEEE (2017)
11. Wang, Y., Shan, M., Yue, Y., Wang, D.: Autonomous target docking of nonholonomic mobile robots using relative pose measurements. Trans. Indus. Electron. **68**(8), 7233–7243 (2020)
12. Luo, R. C., Huang, C. H., Huang, C. Y.: Search and track power charge docking station based on sound source for autonomous mobile robot applications. In: 2010 IEEE/RSJ International Conference on Intelligent Robots and Systems, pp. 1347–1352. IEEE (2010)
13. Quilez, R., Zeeman, A., Mitton, N., Vandaele, J.: Docking autonomous robots in passive docks with Infrared sensors and QR codes. In: International Conference on Testbeds and Research Infrastructures for the Development of Networks & Communities (TridentCOM) (2015)
14. Krestovnikov, K., Erashov, A.: Research of performance characteristics of WPT system associated with mutual arrangement of coils: Electromechanics and robotics. Smart Innov. Syst. Technol. **232**, 359–369 (2022)

15. Krestovnikov, K., Cherskikh, E., Saveliev, A.: Structure and circuit solution of a bidirectional wireless power transmission system in applied robotics. Radioengineering **30**(1), 142–149 (2021)

16. Wu, J., Qiao, G., Ge, J., Sun, H., Song, G.: Automatic battery swap system for home robots. Int. J. Adv. Rob. Syst. **9**(6), 255 (2012)

17. Saito, Y., Asai, K., Choi, Y., Iyota, T., Watanabe, K., Kubota, Y.: Development of a battery support system for the prolonged activity of mobile robots. Electron. Commun. Jpn. **94**(3), 60–71 (2011)

18. Zakharov, K., Saveliev, A., Sivchenko, O.: Energy-efficient path planning algorithm on three-dimensional large-scale terrain maps for mobile robots. In: International Conference on Interactive Collaborative Robotics, pp. 319–330. Springer (2020)

19. Ester, M., Kriegel, H.P., Sander, J., Xu, X.: A density-based algorithm for discovering clusters in large spatial databases with noise. KDD **96**(34), 226–231 (1996)

20. Erashov, A., Kamynin, K., Krestovnikov, K., Saveliev, A.: Method for estimating time of wireless transfer of energy resources between two robots. Informat. Autom. **20**(6), 1279–1306 (2021). https://doi.org/10.15622/ia.20.6.4

Software Library for KUKA Iiwa Robot to Improve the Efficiency of Human-Robot Interaction in Robotic Medical Applications

Olga Gerget[1] , Andrey Kravchenko[1] , Roman Meshcheryakov[2] ,
Tatiana Lysunets[1] , Rinat Galin[2(✉)] , Daniiar Volf[2] , and Mark Mamchenko[2]

[1] National Research Tomsk Polytechnic University, 30, Lenina Avenue, 634050 Tomsk, Russia
[2] V.A. Trapeznikov Institute of Control Sciences of Russian Academy of Sciences, 65 Profsoyuznaya Street, 117997 Moscow, Russia
rinat.r.galin@yandex.ru

Abstract. The article presents a client-server library for the interaction with the KUKA LBR iiwa collaborative robot via a remote personal computer (PC) in a medical-oriented collaborative robotic system (CRS). An intuitive high-level library implemented in the MathWorks MATLAB software framework includes a server for the KUKA iiwa controller, and a client-based application. The library has more than 30 functions for such operations as calculating forward and inverse kinematics, robot control in Cartesian space, path planning, graphical output, and feedback. The developed software runs on a remote computer connected to the controller of the robot via the TCP/IP protocol. The paper presents the requirements to the software related to the systems and strategies used to control the CRS, and the safety of collaborative human-robot interaction (HRI). The article also presents the description of the technical implementation of the library, its architecture, the scheme of "robot – remote PC" communication, software methods used for interaction with the robot, as well as data flow diagrams (DFDs) for the executable code. As an example of controlling the robot using the developed library, we show the results of a practical experiment: the calculation of the robot's inverse kinematics and the path coordinates on a given trajectory.

Keywords: Collaborative robot · Collaborative robotic system · Medical robot · KUKA iiwa · Sunrise.OS · MATLAB

1 Introduction

At present, robotization is one of the main directions of improving the quality and efficiency of medical care and services. The introduction of robots makes it possible to increase productivity in medicine by eliminating the need for routine physical work and reducing the risk of infection of medical workers by using a contactless approach to patient care. Robotic transportation of food and medical supplies to patients, 3D printing, robotic production of medicines, automated rehabilitation systems, therapeutic massage and patient care using robotic systems and complexes are actively introduced in medical

A. Ronzhin et al. (Eds.): ICR 2022, LNCS 13719, pp. 284–295, 2022.
https://doi.org/10.1007/978-3-031-23609-9_25

institutions [1–3]. It is necessary to distinguish the use of robots with manipulators, which can be used to assist surgery (or independently perform simple medical procedures), carry out diagnostics (e.g., robotic systems for blood collection and analysis, ultrasound, etc.) and perform therapeutic operations (e.g., robotic systems in radiotherapy). This type of robots can be used both autonomously and in CRSs, where robots and humans work together in a single working space to achieve a common goal [4–6].

An example of such robots is KUKA iiwa – a lightweight 7-axle manipulator. Each axis of this robot is equipped with a force torque sensor as well as absolute encoders. Data from the axes and a high refresh rate (up to several milliseconds) allow the robot to react swiftly to external influences, making it suitable for interacting with people without applying additional security measures. KUKA iiwa can be programmed for various tasks using the KUKA Sunrise.OS environment. It includes the KUKA Sunrise.OS operating system (OS), which can run programs written in Java, and the KUKA Sunrise Cabinet controller. Although Java is a common language, programming the robot and using its functionality require deep knowledge of the Sunrise OS and various library methods (system's API). In addition, "out of the box" application implies the use of proprietary program running on the controller to control the robot, and thus all feedback data are not available outside the Sunrise.OS [7]. Although remote control of the robot is possible via the Sunrise. FRI interface, processing of feedback data requires installation, configuration or writing of additional software, and this requires the knowledge of different programming languages (Java, C++, Python, etc.). In case of using robot's organic controller instead of remote control, data about the robot's state and actions are available only locally – during the execution of proprietary application. This can significantly complicate the development of specific software solutions with remote control features and deployment of telemedicine systems [8], adaptive robotic cells [9], and remote-control using devices with virtual/augmented reality features in medical institutions [10].

To solve this problem, an external PC for the robotic controller can be used to perform computationally costly operations, process data from sensors, and implement control algorithms. In particular, in paper [8] the authors used the ROS library [11], to control the KUKA iiwa robot for autonomous ultrasound, and in work [12] the authors presented KUKA-IIWA-API – an interface to control the robot via ROS. This interface provides PTP motion and data collection functions, but does not support real-time control. However, other software solutions can be used to simplify the simulation of the motion and functioning of the robot, the development of control algorithms, models and scenarios of HRI in the medicine. In particular, the MATLAB software framework can be used. The advantage of the MATLAB environment is its own high-level interpreted programming language, the standard ROS interface (ROS Toolbox), as well as the ability to simulate robot behavior scenarios, their real-time execution and modification. For example, paper [13] provides an application using the Simulink library to implement a dynamic walking controller for a two-legged human-sized robot. KUKA Control Toolbox (KCT) [14] and JOpen-ShowVar [15, 16] software are used to control KUKA robots with 6 degrees of freedom using the MATLAB/Java frameworks. However, KCT and JOpenShowVar only support the KRC [17] industrial controller, so they cannot be used to control KUKA iiwa robots (supplied with the newer Sunrise controller). Article [18] presents the KUKA Sunrise Toolbox (KST) library – a set of MATLAB tools and a server for Sunrise.OS to operate KUKA iiwa robots from an external PC. KST implements the TCP/IP protocol to communicate with the robot. It combines several functions, including network, basic motion planning, real-time control, robot's parameters setting and acquisition, general-purpose functions, and physical interaction. However, this library has a limited set of supported external automation and tools, and does not support complex trajectories (path as a set of different motion frames) planning.

Thus, implementing a separate MATLAB-based software "wrapper" with extended functionality to control KUKA iiwa robots (with Sunrise controllers) is a relevant task. In this regard, we developed own client-server library for path planning and motion control of KUKA LBR iiwa robots. The library has advanced trajectory planning mode features, including "mixing" of different types of motions into one sequence (set of motion frames), optimized "client-robot" communication, and flexible management of input-output ports (I/O). Functional extension is available due to its modular architecture. In addition, the safety requirements of HRI, as well as the modularity of the CRS control system architecture are considered. This library was developed as a part of the prototype of a robotic medical tool for the reposition of pelvic bones with unstable fractures.

The work is structured as follows. Section 2 presents a description of control systems and strategies in the CRS, the safety of human-robot collaboration, and a list of additional requirements for the library. Section 3 describes the technical implementation of the library, its architecture, the "robot – remote PC" communication scheme, as well as the program functions used for interaction with the robot. Section 4 describes the results of the practical use of the library, shows the calculation of inverse kinematics of the robot and its coordinates of the motion on a given trajectory, as well as DFDs of the executable code.

2   Control Systems and Strategies in the CRS, Safety Requirements of HRI

2.1   CRS Control Systems and Strategies

Consider a detailed description of the control strategies and basic architectures of the control systems used in CRSs [19]:

1. Centralized control. Two classes are distinguished:

   - Unity of command (centralized control unit (CCU) which is responsible for the planning and management of CRS participants). The advantage of unity-of-command type of control systems is its simplicity of algorithmization and deployment. Disadvantages include long decision time due to solving the optimization problem for all members to achieve the common goal, as well as low survivability;
   - Hierarchical control (main CCU is included, but there is a hierarchy of control with subgroups and lower levels CCUs). Compared to the unity of command, the complexity of the tasks performed by individual CCU is significantly reduced, but the complexity of the control structure can result in severe delays or failures in command transfer.

2. Decentralized control. The following classes can be distinguished:

   – Collective control and management (the system has no CCUs, all members are equal and can make their own decisions with the best possible contribution to achieving the common goal by sharing information about their actions with each other). These types of control systems are significantly simplified, and the CRS can be managed almost in real-time mode due solving the problems of optimization by each member individually (rather than trying to optimize the actions of the whole CRS). However, this greatly complicates the algorithmization of the problem and requires a certain level of intelligence for all agents of the CRS (especially – cobots);
   – Swarm control (no CCUs in the system, all members are equal and can make their own decisions, ensuring the maximum possible contribution to achieving the common goal of the CRS, but there is no exchange of information between the members, and each of the participants adjusts its actions based on "indirect" data). The main feature of such control systems is the ability of scaling computing resources. This ensures quick operation of the group and allows the use of energy-efficient devices for receiving and transmitting data. As in previous type of control systems, the main drawback is ensuring a high level of intelligence of each participant, including robots.

3. Hybrid control. Hybrid management and control strategy allows strategic planning at the CCU level via centralized control, and tactical decision-making – at the sub-group level using decentralized control. Hybrid control systems are highly flexible and resistant to adverse factors, including failure of one or more control centers at different levels of control.

In general, a universal CRS control system can be derived from a modular architecture based on a distributed system and a hybrid control strategy. The modularity of such a system allows for the replacement of its individual parts without changing the rest of the elements, as well as both centralized and decentralized control strategies for the target system. Figure 1 shows the architecture of a universal modular hybrid control system for the CRS.

Collaborative systems require, inter alia, planning of coordinated action (based on the task analysis, its execution progress, and resources available), communication, logical interaction, and interoperability of the participants (both using common data formats, messages, commands, and instructions, and technical channels of their transmission). The CRS also implies the need of communication between human workers and robots (HRI), including the allocation and distribution of work among the participants. Ensuring data sharing and physical interaction among CRS members entails the need to generalize and formalize the collected heterogeneous sensor data, as well as create a common model of the external environment and working space. The availability of such models allows for efficient decision-making, including at the stage of the allocation and distribution of work (tasks) in mixed heterogeneous collaborative teams [20–22].

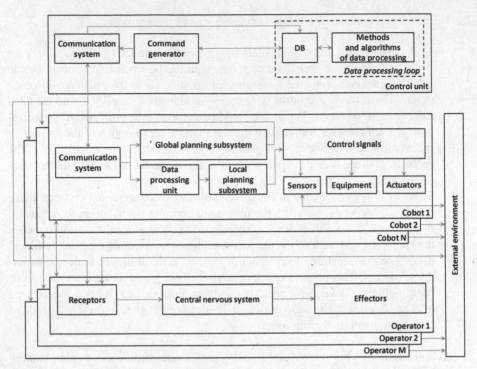

Fig. 1. A universal modular hybrid control system for the CRS.

2.2 Safety of Human-Robot Interaction

The concept of safety in the CRSs is considered in three ways [23]:

- Collision safety (between robots, people and obstacles) should be ensured and controlled. The main challenge is to limit the force/physical impact on human workers.
- Active safety for the timely detection of inevitable collisions (for the cobot) and the controlled termination of its operation. Proximity sensors, monitoring systems and force/torque sensors can be used for this purpose.
- Adaptive safety to interfere with the operation of the hardware and apply corrections to avoid collisions without stopping the operation of the robot.

To ensure safe collaboration with humans, cobots have a built-in set of additional safety functions [24, 25]:

- "Safe-rated monitored stop". The robot stops when the worker appears in the shared working space, and continues to work when the working space is free;
- "Hand guiding". The motion of the robot is controlled by the operator (the use of a hand-operated device to transmit motion commands);
- "Speed and separation monitoring" to ensure simultaneous actions of the operator and the cobot in the collaborative working space;

- "Power and force limiting". The force of collision of the cobot and the worker (either intentional or unintentional) is technically limited to a safe value.

Thus, based on the analysis of the existing types of control strategies in the CRS and their architectures, as well as the requirements for the safety of HRI, it is possible to set the following additional requirements to the developed library:

- Taking into account the control strategy used in the CRS, the composition, quantity and possible heterogeneity of its participants, the possibility of including or excluding the participant from the CRS and consequent adaptive adjustment of the CRS control system, as well as the specific features of the selected control scheme of collaboration;
- Execution of library-based low-level commands for the cobot should be safe to other agents located in the working space (primarily to the workers) as well as to objects of the external environment;
- The functionality of the library should support changing the cobot's workflow, when the CRS functioning is not adequate of inefficient;
- The developed library should have a high-level programmable interface for the workers to gain manual access to all the features of the cobots performing actions in a single working space;
- The application of the developed library should be primarily aimed at increasing productivity and reducing the probability of errors by taking into account the design features of the cobots used;
- The library should handle other data from the technical specification of the cobots and ensure efficient processing of the data from the robots' force/torque, as well as control the speed of their motion.

3 Technical Implementation of the Library

The library server is written in Java and uses the Sunrise.OS API 1.7 to implement the functions. The server is based on an asynchronous single-threaded TCP socket and supports multiple clients. The MATLAB client uses the built-in synchronous Java sockets, providing less than 1 ms communication latency. However, it is possible to connect to the server using the built-in MATLAB classes (tcpclient and tcpip) for backward compatibility and greater reliability. The structure of the developed library is shown in Fig. 2.

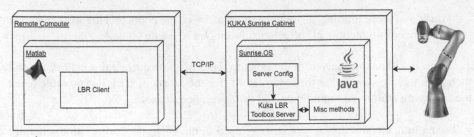

Fig. 2. The structure of the library.

The library has 35 methods for interacting with the robot. Most of the methods have a system of input arguments that allows flexible configuration of certain parameters of the robot and its actions. The library has an additional class for describing the motion of the robot and setting various parameters, such as type, speed, acceleration, and stop conditions. The methods are logically divided into 5 main categories:

1. Methods for obtaining information. This group includes feedback methods to obtain data about the position of the robot, its tool, kinematics data or the value of the force applied.
2. Methods of manipulating the robot to get or change the values of the parameters of the robot. They include the methods of working with tools (software-based connection to the tool, changing its frames, obtaining data about the current tool and tools available), and I/O ports.
3. Robot motion control methods. This group includes commands for basic position control (through basic motion operations such as PTP or linear (LIN) motion), as well as a method that requires a sequence of motion frames as input created by the operator using the motion description class.
4. Network control methods. This group includes monitoring communication with the robot – measuring the speed of the controller's response to commands, and a method for checking the link availability.
5. Auxiliary methods. They are not intended to interact with the robot during their work, but to simplify the programming of the robot for the user.

We also added own implementations of forward/inverse kinematics algorithms, as well as the support of the built-in Sunrise.OS inverse kinematics calculation function. The inverse kinematics algorithm is based on a proprietary implementation of the FABRIC algorithm [26]. The developed implementation is insensitive to kinematic singularities, compared to the built-in Sunrise.OS API.

Motion methods allow grouping different motions into one sequence, for example, the simultaneous use of PTP – LIN – PTP motion frames within one set. This allows forming complex trajectories and executing them within one robotic motion. This is possible due to the inheritance of various types of motions from a single parent class in the Sunrise.OS hierarchy, which allows placing the collected motion array into one motion frame set. Such motion sets can contain up to several hundreds of frames.

Compared to KST, the library allows obtaining some data from the robot's memory, such as the tools available in the database, their transformation matrices, data on saved points, objects, and templates saved in the system. It should be noted that the library is not linked to the I/O ports of the flange and can work with different input/output groups (after specifying them in the server configuration class).

The library runs on a remote system, interacting with the robot via the TCP/IP protocol using the X66 port on the robot controller. The system supports the entire line of KUKA LBR iiwa robots. No additional software packages are required for installing and executing. Since MATLAB is a cross-platform environment, the library can run on various OS: Windows, Linux, and macOS. It is possible to port the library to the free GNU Octave environment or implement clients using other languages and programming frameworks. The source code of the server, client, as well as examples of using the library are available on the GitHub [27].

4 Practical Use of the Library

As part of a practical experiment, the inverse kinematics calculation for the robot is considered and demonstrated. After calculating the coordinates, the robot moves along the resulting trajectory (circle) using a set of configurations.

Figure 3 shows the DFD of the program. When initialized, the library receives IP data to connect to the robot. The then client connects to the robot's remote server and loads input-output data as well as additional information. When loading the server, data on the tools and points stored in the system is also acquired. The next step is to calculate the points on the trajectory. Inverse kinematics algorithms and current tool data is used to calculate the robot configuration at the design point on the trajectory, and the user saves this data to an array within the MATLAB environment. The client then initiates the execution of the motion frame of robot configuration (SplineJP), which is passed to the method. Based on this data, the server generates a set of motion frames and sends it to the robot.

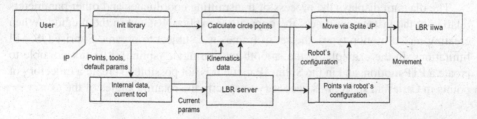

Fig. 3. Data flow diagram of the executable code (circle trajectory motion).

Forward and inverse kinematics can be used to pre-calculate the motion trajectory or to create new trajectory, which the robot will follow via smooth motion along a set of axle configurations. These techniques can be used for trajectory calculations, collision avoidance during motion planning, pre-calculation of robot configurations, and evaluation of the robot's motion area. The stored example of mixed motion implies connecting to a tool stored in robot's memory, moving through three 3 points stored in the controller: spline motion (PTP) – LIN – spline mode (PTP).

The DFD of the program is shown in Fig. 4. The start of the diagram is similar to the previous one. However, the user then requests the list of the saved tools from the system and virtually connects to one of them. This changes the current tool on the robot, the path calculation points, and feedback data, such as tool force and kinematics data. After that, a set of saved points is downloaded from the system to create basic motion frames and save them on the client. After the motion description classes are created, a motion execution function is called, an array of motion frames is passed to it as an input. The server forms a set of motion frames and sends it to the robot for execution.

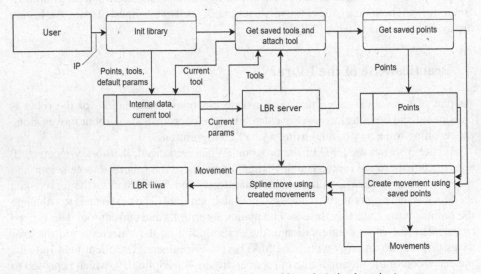

Fig. 4. Data flow diagram of the executable code (mixed motion).

The diagram displays the process of transmitting coordinates and other parameters relative to the instrument unless the opposite is explicitly stated in the method. When creating mixed motion types, the set of frames is a subject to organic Sunrise.OS API limitations. In the example, in the smooth motion mode (spline), it is not possible to create a PTP motion, and in the SplineJP mode it is not possible to create a trajectory of points in Cartesian space: it is necessary to specify the rotation angles of the axes.

5   Results

The results of the measurements of the operating time are shown in Table 1. The "Check Connection" method displays the total system delays for the communication in the system. This includes the time to encode data packages on the client side, send data to the controller, parse the packages, and generate the response on the controller side, send data from the controller to the client, and parse the response package. The communication time can be further reduced by increasing the priority of processing by the CPU on the client side.

The built-in FABRIC-based inverse kinematics algorithm on the client side runs faster than the inverse kinematics algorithm on the controller by an average of 37%. The running time of the FABRIC-based algorithm is also more predictable in comparison to the controller-based one.

Calling the built-in functions of iiwa controller generally depends on the speed of the iiwa API functions themselves (joint angels, end-effector (EEF) coordinates, force data), and the complexity of data obtaining process (in particular, the number of necessary calculations, and the amount of transmitted data – EEF transformation matrix). Despite this, the running time is low enough for real-time deployment and accurate robot control at low speeds.

Table 1. The measurements of the operating time by using the "Check Connection" method.

Function call	Average time, ms	Median time, ms	Std, ms
Check connection	0.5634	0.5258	0.1254
Inverse Kinematic, internal client method	3.0349	2.9673	0.2247
Inverse kinematics, iiwa call	4.8447	4.1202	1.2956
Joint angles	18.2796	18.2193	0.2707
EEF coordinates	24.7388	24.5935	0.3769
Force on flange	15.9356	15.8343	0.3341
EEF transformation matrix	39.5832	36.8830	5.8449

6 Conclusion

The work presents a client-server library for the interaction of the KUKA LBR iiwa collaborative robot and a remote PC (a server for the KUKA iiwa controller), as well as a MATLAB-based client. The library's toolset includes more than 30 functions covering such operations as calculating forward and inverse kinematics, controlling the robot in Cartesian space, path planning, graphical output, and feedback. The article presents the description of the technical implementation of the library, its architecture and the "robot – remote PC" communication scheme, as well as the used software methods for interaction with the robot and data flow diagrams of the executable code. The paper also gives specific requirements to the library related to the CRS control systems and strategies, and the safety of human-robot interaction. Developed as part of the prototype of a robotic medical tool for the reposition of pelvic bones with unstable fractures, the library allows performing a full range of tasks related to robot control, manipulation, and motion. The use of the library simplifies the code writing for the relevant robotic algorithms due to the use of the MATLAB environment with an understandable and accessible interface.

Built-in enhanced I/O groups and motion processing features allowed for the flexibility of the use of the developed library.

The results of the practical use the library for robot control included the calculation of inverse kinematics for the robot, and calculation of the coordinates of motion on a given trajectory, including in a mixed mode (PTP – LIN – PTP). A number of improvements in the library will be introduced soon. In particular, we plan to add a real-time control mode for the robot, as well as to expand the capabilities of fine-tuning the motion of the robot.

Acknowledgment. The study has been performed under the financial support by the Ministry of Science and Higher Education within the State Task "Research" (basic fundamental) project №FSWW-2020-0014, and by V.A. Trapeznikov Institute of Control Sciences of Russian Academy of Sciences (ICS RAS) according to the state project.

References

1. Wang, F.-Y.: Parallel healthcare: robotic medical and health process automation for secured and smart social healthcares. IEEE Trans. Comput. Soc. Syst. **7**(3), 581–586 (2020)
2. Fischer, K., Weigelin, H.M., Bodenhagen, L.: Increasing trust in human–robot medical interactions: effects of transparency and adaptability. Paladyn J. Behav. Robot. **9**(1), 95–109 (2018)
3. García, D.H., Esteban, P.G., Lee, H.R., Romeo, M., Senft, E., Billing, E.: Social robots in therapy and care. In: 2019 14th ACM/IEEE International Conference on Human-Robot Interaction (HRI), pp. 669–670. IEEE, Piscataway (2019)
4. Scimeca, L., Iida, F., Maiolino, P., Nanayakkara, T.: Human-robot medical interaction. In: Companion of the 2020 ACM/IEEE International Conference on Human-Robot Interaction (HRI '20), pp. 660–661. Association for Computing Machinery, New York (2020)
5. Mohan, M., Kuchenbecker, K.J.: A design tool for therapeutic social-physical human-robot interactions. In: 2019 14th ACM/IEEE International Conference on Human-Robot Interaction (HRI), pp. 727–729. Association for Computing Machinery, New York (2019)
6. Liang, J., et al.: Variable admittance control for human-robot collaboration in robot-assisted orthopedic surgery. In: 2019 IEEE International Conference on Robotics and Biomimetics (ROBIO), pp. 1544–1550. IEEE, Piscataway (2019)
7. KUKA Sunrise.OS. https://www.kuka.com/en-us/products/robotics-systems/software/system-software/sunriseos. Last Accessed 1 September 2022
8. Hennersperger, C., et al.: Towards MRI-based autonomous robotic US acquisitions: a first feasibility study. IEEE Trans. Med. Imaging **36**(2), 538–548 (2017)
9. Obal, P., Gierlak, P.: EGM toolbox – interface for controlling ABB robots in Simulink. Sensors. **21**(22), 7463, 1–17 (2021)
10. Ostanin, M., Yagfarov, R., Klimchik, A.: Interactive robots control using mixed reality. IFAC-PapersOnLine **52**(13), 695–700 (2019)
11. ROS: Home. https://www.ros.org. Last Accessed 1 September 2022
12. Mokaram, S., et al.: A ROS-integrated API for the KUKA LBR iiwa collaborative robot. IFAC-PapersOnLine **50**(1), 15859–15864 (2017)
13. Hubicki, C., et al.: Walking and running with passive compliance: lessons from engineering: a live demonstration of the ATRIAS biped. IEEE Robot. Autom. Mag. **25**(3), 23–39 (2018)
14. Chinello, F., Scheggi, S., Morbidi, F., Prattichizzo, D.: Kuka control toolbox. IEEE Robot. Autom. Mag. **18**(4), 69–79 (2011)

15. Sanfilippo, F., Hatledal, L.I., Zhang, H., Fago, M., Pettersen, K.Y.: JOpenShowVar: an open-source cross-platform communication interface to KUKA robots. In: 2014 IEEE International Conference on Information and Automation (ICIA), pp. 1154–1159. IEEE, Piscataway (2014)
16. Sanfilippo, F., Hatledal, L.I., Zhang, H., Fago, M., Pettersen, K.Y.: Controlling KUKA industrial robots: flexible communication interface JOpenShowVar. IEEE Robot. Autom. Mag. **22**, 96–109 (2015)
17. KUKA KR C4. https://www.kuka.com/en-us/products/robotics-systems/robot-controllers/kr-c4. Last Accessed 1 September 2022
18. Safeea, M., Neto, P.: KUKA sunrise toolbox: interfacing collaborative robots with MATLAB. IEEE Robot. Autom. Mag. **26**(1), 91–96 (2019)
19. Galin, R., Shiroky, A., Magid, E., Meshcheryakov, R., Mamchenko, M.: Effective functioning of a mixed heterogeneous team in a collaborative robotic system. Inform. Auto. **20**(6), 1224–1253 (2021)
20. Lemaignan, S., Warnier, M., Sisbot, E.A., Clodic, A., Alami, R.: Artificial cognition for social human–robot interaction: an implementation. Artif. Intell. **247**, 45–69 (2017)
21. Galin, R., Meshcheryakov, R.: Collaborative robots: development of robotic perception system, safety issues, and integration of AI to imitate human behavior. In: Ronzhin, A., Shishlakov, V. (eds.) Proceedings of 15th International Conference on Electromechanics and Robotics "Zavalishin's Readings". Smart Innovation, Systems and Technologies, vol. 187, pp. 175–185. Springer, Singapore (2021)
22. Galin, R.R., Meshcheryakov, R.V.: Human-robot interaction efficiency and human-robot collaboration. In: Kravets, A. (ed.) Robotics: Industry 4.0 Issues & New Intelligent Control Paradigms. Studies in Systems, Decision and Control, vol. 272, pp. 55–63. Springer, Cham (2020)
23. Michalos, G., Makris, S., Tsarouchi, P., Guasch, T., Kontovrakis, D., Chryssolouris, G.: Design considerations for safe human-robot collaborative workplaces. Procedia CIRP **37**, 248–253 (2015)
24. Galin, R., Mamchenko, M.: Human-robot collaboration in the society of the future: a survey on the challenges and the barriers. In: Singh, P.K., Veselov, G., Vyatkin, V., Pljonkin, A., Dodero, J.M., Kumar, Y. (eds.) Futuristic Trends in Network and Communication Technologies. FTNCT 2020. Communications in Computer and Information Science, vol. 1395, pp. 111–122. Springer, Singapore (2021)
25. Mihelj, M., et al.: Collaborative robots, 2nd edn. Springer, Cham (2019)
26. Kolpashchikov, D.Y., Laptev, N., Danilov, V.V., Skirnevskiy, I.P., Manakov, R.A., Gerget, O.M.: FABRIK-based inverse kinematics for multi-section continuum robots. In: Proceedings of the 2018 18th International Conference on Mechatronics, pp. 1–8. IEEE, Piscataway (2018)
27. GitHub – small23/Kuka_LBR_Toolbox. https://github.com/small23/Kuka_LBR_Toolbox. Last Accessed 1 September 2022

Author Index

Printed in the United States
by Baker & Taylor Publisher Services